Beginning JavaScript with DOM Scripting and Ajax

From Novice to Professional

Christian Heilmann

Apress®

Beginning JavaScript with DOM Scripting and Ajax: From Novice to Professional

Copyright © 2006 by Christian Heilmann

ISBN-13 (pbk): 978-1-59059-680-7

ISBN-10 (pbk): 1-59059-680-3

Printed and bound in the United States of America 9 8 7 6 5 4 3 2 1

Lead Editors: Charles Brown, Chris Mills
Technical Reviewer: Jon Stephens
Editorial Board: Steve Anglin, Ewan Buckingham, Gary Cornell, Jason Gilmore, Jonathan Gennick,
    Jonathan Hassell, James Huddleston, Chris Mills, Matthew Moodie, Dominic Shakeshaft, Jim Sumser,
    Keir Thomas, Matt Wade
Project Manager: Beth Christmas
Copy Edit Manager: Nicole LeClerc
Copy Editor: Ami Knox
Assistant Production Director: Kari Brooks-Copony
Production Editor: Katie Stence
Compositor: Pat Christenson
Proofreader: Lori Bring
Indexer: Broccoli Information Management
Artist: April Milne
Cover Designer: Kurt Krames
Manufacturing Director: Tom Debolski

Distributed to the book trade worldwide by Springer-Verlag New York, Inc., 233 Spring Street, 6th Floor, New York, NY 10013. Phone 1-800-SPRINGER, fax 201-348-4505, e-mail orders-ny@springer-sbm.com, or visit http://www.springeronline.com.

For information on translations, please contact Apress directly at 2560 Ninth Street, Suite 219, Berkeley, CA 94710. Phone 510-549-5930, fax 510-549-5939, e-mail info@apress.com, or visit http://www.apress.com.

The source code for this book is available to readers at http://www.beginningjavascript.com and http://www.apress.com.

To Ioanna, who can sleep and look like an angel while some geek next to her hacks on the keyboard of a laptop and constantly mutters "Why won't you work" under his breath.

Contents at a Glance

Foreword. xiii

About the Author xv

About the Technical Reviewer. xvii

Acknowledgments. xix

Introduction xxi

CHAPTER 1   Getting Started with JavaScript 1

CHAPTER 2   Data and Decisions 17

CHAPTER 3   From DHTML to DOM Scripting. 61

CHAPTER 4   HTML and JavaScript 85

CHAPTER 5   Presentation and Behavior (CSS and Event Handling). 123

CHAPTER 6   Common Uses of JavaScript: Images and Windows 183

CHAPTER 7   JavaScript and User Interaction: Navigation and Forms 241

CHAPTER 8   Back-End Interaction with Ajax 299

CHAPTER 9   Data Validation Techniques. 343

CHAPTER 10   Modern JavaScript Case Study: A Dynamic Gallery 387

CHAPTER 11   Using Third-Party JavaScript 415

APPENDIX   Debugging JavaScript. 451

INDEX 471

Contents

Foreword xiii

About the Author xv

About the Technical Reviewer xvii

Acknowledgments xix

Introduction xxi

CHAPTER 1   Getting Started with JavaScript 1

   The Why of JavaScript 3
   What Is JavaScript? 4
   Problems and Merits of JavaScript 5
   Why Use JavaScript If It Cannot Be Relied On? 6
   JavaScript in a Web Page and Essential Syntax 7
         JavaScript Syntax 8
         Code Execution 9
         An Aside About Functions 11
   Objects 12
   Simple JavaScript Example 13
   Summary 16

CHAPTER 2   Data and Decisions 17

   Data, Data Types, and Data Operators 18
         The String Data Type 18
         Operators 21
         JavaScript Variables 23
         Converting Different Types of Data 26
   The Composite Data Types: Array and Object 30
         Objects JavaScript Supplies You with: `String`, `Date`,
               and `Math` 30
   Arrays 39
         The `Array` Object's Methods and Properties 42

Making Decisions in JavaScript...................................... 45

The Logical and Comparison Operators 45

Conditional Statements 49

Testing Multiple Values: the `switch` Statement............... 52

Repeating Things: Loops 54

Summary 59

CHAPTER 3   From DHTML to DOM Scripting 61

JavaScript As "the Behavior Layer" 63

Object Detection vs. Browser Dependence 65

Progressive Enhancement...................................... 68

JavaScript and Accessibility....................................... 69

Good Coding Practices... 71

Naming Conventions.. 71

Code Layout... 72

Commenting... 74

Functions 76

Short Code via Ternary Operator 79

Sorting and Reuse of Functions 80

Variable and Function Scope................................... 80

Keeping Scripts Safe with the Object Literal 81

Summary 83

CHAPTER 4   HTML and JavaScript................................... 85

The Anatomy of an HTML Document............................... 85

Providing Feedback in Web Pages via JavaScript:
The Old School Ways 89

Using `window` Methods: `prompt()`, `alert()`,
and `confirm()`... 90

Accessing the Document via the DOM 96

Of Children, Parents, Siblings, and Values...................... 99

From the Parents to the Children 100

From the Children to the Parents 102

Among Siblings 103

Changing Attributes of Elements 107

Creating, Removing, and Replacing Elements. 109
    Avoiding NOSCRIPT 113
    Shortening Your Scripts via InnerHTML. 115
    DOM Summary: Your Cheat Sheet. 116
    DOMhelp: Our Own Helper Library. 118
Summary 122

CHAPTER 5 **Presentation and Behavior (CSS and Event Handling)** . . 123

Changing the Presentation Layer via JavaScript. 123
    Helping the CSS Designer 131
Changing the Document's Behavior via Event Handling 153
    Events in the W3C-Compliant World 156
    Fixing Events for the Non-W3C-Compliant World 165
    Never Stop Optimizing 172
    The Ugly Page Load Problem and Its Ugly Solutions. 173
    Reading and Filtering Keyboard Entries 174
    The Dangers of Event Handling 179
Summary 180

CHAPTER 6 **Common Uses of JavaScript: Images and Windows** 183

Images and JavaScript 183
    Basics of Image Scripting 184
    Preloading Images 186
    Rollover Effects 187
    Slide Shows 196
    Summary of Images and JavaScript 211
Windows and JavaScript. 212
    Window Properties 213
    Window Methods. 215
    Summary: Windows and JavaScript 238
Summary 239

■CHAPTER 7   **JavaScript and User Interaction: Navigation and Forms**...241

Navigation and JavaScript..241
   The Fear of the Page Reload.............................242
   Basics of Navigation and JavaScript 242
   Browser Navigation.....................................245
   In-Page Navigation 246
   Site Navigation..255
   Pagination...263
   Summary of Navigation with JavaScript..................272
Forms and JavaScript 272
   Basics of Forms with JavaScript 274
   Form Elements..275
   Interactive Forms: Hiding and Showing Dependent Elements....291
   Custom Form Elements 297
   Summary of Forms and JavaScript 297
Summary 297

■CHAPTER 8   **Back-End Interaction with Ajax** 299

Household Cleaning Liquid, Football Club, or Flash Gordon's
   Spacecraft: What Is Ajax? 300
Et Tu, Cache? 309
Putting the X Back into Ajax 309
   Replacing XML with JSON................................314
   Using Server-Side Scripts to Reach Third-Party Content....316
   XHR on Slow Connections 320
   A Larger Ajax Example: Connected Select Boxes 323
   Optional Dynamic Ajax Menus 331
Summary 340

■CHAPTER 9   **Data Validation Techniques**............................343

Pros and Cons of Client-Side JavaScript Validation 343
A Quick Reminder About Protecting Content with JavaScript.........344
The One-Size-Fits-All Validation Myth 345

Basic JavaScript Validation with String and Numeric Methods 346
  String Validation Methods 346
  Numeric Validation Methods 352
Regular Expressions 357
  Syntax and Attributes 357
  Wildcard Searches, Constraining Scope, and Alternatives 358
  Restricting the Number of Characters with Quantifiers 359
  Word Boundaries, Whitespace, and Other Shortcuts 360
  Methods Using Regular Expressions 361
  The Power of Parenthesis Grouping 361
  Regular Expression Resources 363
Summary of Validation Methods 363
Form Validation Techniques 364
  Designating Mandatory Fields 364
  The Hidden Field Method 364
  The Indicator Element Method 365
  The CSS Classes Method 366
  The Custom Attribute Method 366
  Failures of These Methods 367
  Sharing Validation Rules 367
Giving Users Validation Feedback 369
  Showing a List of Erroneous Fields 369
  Replacing the Main Form with a Clickable Error Message 374
  Highlighting Erroneous Fields Individually 376
  Instant Validation Feedback 379
Other Dynamic Validation Methods 381
Summary 385

CHAPTER 10   **Modern JavaScript Case Study: A Dynamic Gallery** 387

Basics of Thumbnail Galleries 387
What Is a Thumbnail Gallery and What Should It Do? 388
Static Thumbnail Galleries 388
Faking Dynamic Galleries with JavaScript 389
Displaying Captions 396
Dynamic Thumbnail Galleries 401
Creating an Image Badge from a Folder 406
Summary 414

■CHAPTER 11   **Using Third-Party JavaScript** 415

What the Web Offers You 415
Code Snippets, RSS Feeds, APIs, and Libraries 416
    RSS Feeds and REST APIs 417
    Examples of REST APIs 418
Using a Library: Short, Shorter, jQuery 419
    Dangers of jQuery and Other Libraries Using Their
        Own Syntax 426
Using an API: Adding a Map to Your Site with Google Maps 427
Full Service: The Yahoo Developer Network and User
    Interface Library 438
    Bouncy Headlines Using YUI 439
    Replacing Pop-Up Windows Using the YUI Connection
        Manager and Container Components 444
    Yahoo User Interface Library Summary 449
Summary 450

■APPENDIX   **Debugging JavaScript** 451

Common JavaScript Mistakes 451
    Misspellings and Case-Sensitivity Issues 451
    Trying to Access Undefined Variables 452
    Incorrect Number of Closing Braces and Parentheses 454
    Concatenation Gone Wrong 456
    Assigning Instead of Testing the Value of a Variable 458
Tracing Errors with `alert()` and "Console" Elements 458
Error Handling with `try` and `catch()` 459
Sequential Uncommenting 462
Error Reporting in Browsers 463
    Microsoft Internet Explorer 6 463
    Safari 464
    Opera 8.5 466
    Firefox 1.5.0.3 466
JSLint and JSUNIT 470
Summary 470

■INDEX 471

Foreword

There has never been a more exciting time to learn JavaScript. It may be a cliché, but it's certainly true. After years spent banished in a wilderness of browser wars and false promises, JavaScript has finally emerged as an essential part of any web developer's toolbox. No longer just a vehicle for ads and annoyances, it is now a valuable component of the next generation of web applications.

What has caused this sudden rush of interest? The first reason is purely practical: browser improvements have finally made it viable to write cross-browser JavaScript with some certainty that it will actually work. The second is more revolutionary: Ajax, an old technique with a new name that enables client-side code to communicate directly with a server without refreshing the whole page. This simple ability has thrown web application development wide open, enabling new, innovative interfaces and dramatically altering user expectations of how web interfaces can behave.

This adoption has been helped by the growing realization that JavaScript is not a toy language. Despite its numerous warts, beneath its deceptively simple exterior lie a host of powerful features not seen in many mainstream languages: closures, prototypal inheritance, and extensive support for the functional programming style. That such a flexible language is now installed on hundreds of millions of computers is a cause for celebration in itself.

Just because you can do something doesn't mean that you should. Not all browsers are born equal, and accessibility (both for people and for alternative devices) remains an essential aspect of developing for the Web. Understanding the issues and techniques around progressive enhancement is an important part of the JavaScript learning curve.

The set of challenges posed by JavaScript development is huge.

Browsers frequently deviate from what standard specifications there are, and pseudo-standards are common and frequently unavoidable.

Ambitious new applications are uncovering browser bugs that have laid dormant for years. The complexity of those applications is itself a problem, introducing new problems related to maintaining large code bases.

Thankfully, the global JavaScript community has risen to the challenge. A wealth of code and resources awaits the intrepid developer, but the value of this treasure trove can be unlocked only through a solid understanding of the underlying platform. This book will provide you with that knowledge.

As a long-standing teacher and leader in that community, Christian is the ideal guide to this intricate world. This book comprises accumulated wisdom obtainable only through years of experience.

Christian will teach you to apply JavaScript tastefully, responsibly, and elegantly in a way that will delight your users and impress your peers.

Simon Willison
Technology Development at Yahoo!

About the Author

■**CHRISTIAN HEILMANN** grew up in Germany and, after a year working with people with disabilities for the Red Cross, spent a year as a radio producer. From 1997 onwards, he worked for several agencies in Munich as a web developer. In 2000, he moved to the US to work for eToys and, after the dot-com crash, he moved to the UK where he led the web development department at Agilisys. In April 2006, he joined Yahoo! UK as a web developer. He publishes an almost daily blog at `http://wait-till-i.com` and runs an article repository at `http://icant.co.uk`. He is a member of the Web Standards Project's DOM Scripting Task Force.

About the Technical Reviewer

JON STEPHENS has contributed to numerous books on web and open source technologies as an author, reviewer, and editor. He's particularly keen on JavaScript, PHP, Linux, and MySQL. Jon coauthored *Professional JavaScript, Second Edition* (Wrox Press, 2001), *Beginning MySQL Database Design and Optimization: From Novice to Professional* (Apress, 2004), and *PHP 5 Recipes: A Problem-Solution Approach* (Apress, 2005). He was also the technical reviewer for Jeremy Keith's *DOM Scripting: Web Design with JavaScript and the Document Object Model* (friends of ED, 2005). Jon's day job (we use the term "day" loosely here) is with MySQL AB as a technical writer, where he's learned to appreciate the finer points of MySQL Cluster, DocBook XML, and very large fish caught in the Bay of Naples. His origins are lost in the depths of time and space, but he is rumored to have a 4-digit user ID on Slashdot.org and a daughter in Australia. (In recent years, we've posted Jon's checks to an address in Brisbane, and someone claiming to be him has cashed them.) Jon has also been sighted from time to time shoveling down really extremely dangerously spicy Thai food purchased from street vendors in Bangkok and Ayutthaya.

Acknowledgments

I'd like to acknowledge all who helped in getting this book done—Chris, Beth, Ami, Katie, and Charles at Apress, and Jon Stephens. I learned a lot, especially that writing a book is much more work than I thought.

I'd also like to thank those who helped me by solving problems and asking for more and more features—my fellow WaSP DOM Scripting Task Force Members, Stuart Colville, Matt Warden, Jens Grochtdreis, Ingo Chao, Volkan Ozcelik, and many others on the evolt list, CSS-discuss, and my blog comments.

Thanks to my former colleagues at Agilisys and my current colleagues at Yahoo for testing help and support, and to Good for Food, The Spence, Pizzadelique, and Belle Epoque for keeping me in shape by providing nourishment (and also to the neighbors of these places for not protecting their wireless access points).

And last but not least, I'd like to thank you, as buying this book shows that there are people who really want to learn JavaScript properly, instead of just copying and pasting in scripts. If this is a pirated PDF, just remember that I can trace all copies back to your computer, and I will know where you live.

Introduction

If you want to learn about JavaScript from scratch—what it is, what to use it for, and how to make it work with other technologies like CSS and HTML—you have picked up the right book. If you already have a considerable amount of experience with JavaScript, but want to bring your knowledge up to date, you have also picked up the right book—a lot has changed in JavaScript development in recent years.

When JavaScript first started being used for web development back in the mid-to-late 1990s (it was first supported in Netscape 2, back in 1996), it quickly became much maligned, for many reasons—browser support was mediocre at best, and at worst, you actually had different JavaScript functions being implemented in different ways by different browsers (Netscape 4 and Internet Explorer 4 were major culprits, at the height of the so-called browser wars). This led to developers having to write completely different versions of web sites or indulge in messy code forking, if they wanted to attempt to have cross-browser support.

And that was the consciencious ones—JavaScript's bad reputation was just as much the fault of the developers as the browser manufacturers. Developers back in those days tended to use JavaScript for all manner of flashy effects that looked cool, but caused all manner of problems in terms of usability and accessibility (the days of DHTML—another marketing buzzword back in the day, which referred to the application of JavaScript, CSS, and HTML to produce dynamic effects). Pages would break completely if JavaScript was unavailable for any reason or if the user was trying to use a screenreader. And a lot of web developers would copy and paste scripts into their web sites without understanding how they actually worked, causing more untold usability and code maintenance nightmares.

But as I said earlier, things have changed. Browser support is now at a manageable level, with the modern browsers largely using the same implementation of the Document Object Model and other constructs, and modern techniques are a lot more considerate of accessibility, etc. As you'll learn through the course of this book, modern techniques like DOM scripting are built around the premise of separating out not only the structure (in your markup) and the presentation (in your CSS), but also the behavior in your JavaScript files (not interspersed through your markup documents). JavaScript does not have to be evil—you can code your web sites so that the JavaScript enhancements you are using can add to the experience of users who can take advantage of them, but they don't break when JavaScript is not available. This is called *unobtrusive JavaScript*—JavaScript enhancements should be seen as a bonus for those who can use them, not an essential feature for the running of a site.

If you've used JavaScript before, then be prepared to take on a new mindset as you step forward through the book. If you are completely new to JavaScript, then breathe a sign of relief and consider yourself lucky that you never had to suffer the early days of JavaScript development that I just touched on!

What This Book Will Cover

JavaScript is probably simultaneously the most underrated *and* the most misused language in web development, but use it properly, and it can be a very valuable tool in your toolbox. In the following pages, we'll look at the basics of JavaScript and modern JavaScript techniques, including DOM scripting for dynamic behavior and styling, and event handling. We'll then look at essential applications of JavaScript, including data validation, image and window manipulation, and dynamic enhancements for forms and navigation menus.

Next, I turn your attention to probably the biggest JavaScript-related buzzword of the moment—Ajax. Ajax standards for "Asynchronous JavaScript and XML," which is a bit of a misnomer, as the technique doesn't necessarily have to involve XML, and is probably used with HTML more often. But don't concern yourself about that statement—it basically refers to creating dynamic functionality on web pages that works because small parts of the web page can be updated without having to refresh the whole page, for example, contact information in an online e-mail application (Gmail being the most obvious example that comes to mind). The most common way to do this right now is to use the XMLHttpRequest (XHR) object. It is very popular because it allows us to create web applications that have rich functionality and almost look and work like desktop applications. But Ajax does come with its own set of unique problems, which I'll touch on in this book.

Next follows a case study for you to work through, showing a full-blown modern JavaScript-enhanced web application.

Finally, Chapter 11 looks at another essential facet of modern JavaScript development—using third-party JavaScript solutions. When you're developing JavaScript applications, you don't need to code everything yourself from scratch every time. As well as creating reusable objects and functions of your own, which will be covered in the earlier chapters of the book, there are also countless third-party resources available on the Web for you to download and use in your own applications, from libraries of functions, to full-blown APIs (application programming interfaces) for you to hook into. Specifically, we look at jQuery, the Google Maps API, the Yahoo! APIs, and much more besides.

Community and Support

When you ask developers with different technology or design-oriented backgrounds what JavaScript is and what you should use it for, you will most probably get totally different answers. This book tries to teach you how to become a JavaScript developer who can work with each of these developers, and maybe get to change some views these people have by proving that you can use JavaScript to enhance a web site, build a web application, or even extend a piece of software without forcing the user to change his ways or hardware setup.

This is a book to work along with—all the code examples provided can be downloaded and tried at http://www.beginningjavascript.com; you will also find extra information, bug fixes, and other examples there (my publishers will also keep a copy of the errata and code download at http://www.apress.com).

But what happens when you get a problem? You have many options available to you. First, try getting ahold of me via my web site (`http://wait-till-i.com`) or mailing Apress about the issue (contact details available at `http://www.apress.com`).

Second, try visiting any of the JavaScript forums available on the Web. Some of the best are

- *evolt's thelist*: `http://lists.evolt.org/mailman/listinfo/thelist`

- *The Mozilla JavaScript forums*: `http://developer.mozilla.org/en/docs/JavaScript`

- *Webdeveloper.com JavaScript forum*: `http://www.webdeveloper.com/forum/forumdisplay.php?f=3`

- *The comp.lang.javascript FAQ*: `http://jibbering.com/faq/`

These forums are frequented by many knowledge seekers, such as yourself, but also many very experienced JavaScripters who are happy to help out the community with their problems to further the cause of modern JavaScript. Make sure you ask questions intelligently, and don't just paste in your code and ask, "What's wrong with this?" Also look over the other posts on the forums; you may find that your question has been asked by someone else, and answered already.

Last of all, read blogs! A lot of the most talented JavaScripters out there like to share their ideas, innovations, and experiments with the rest of the world through their blogs, myself included (OK, so I couldn't resist getting another plug in there!). This is a great way to pick up new ideas. I'd recommend reading the words of

- *Jeremy Keith*: `http://www.adactio.com`

- *Simon Willison*: `http://simon.incutio.com/`

- *The WaSP DOM scripting task force*: `http://www.webstandards.org/action/dstf/`

- *Stuart Langridge*: `http://kryogenix.org/days/`

- *Robert Nyman*: `http://robertnyman.com/`

- *Jon Snook*: `http://www.snook.ca/jonathan/`

Look at it like this—you're now part of a very vibrant community. As well as learning a lot of useful stuff, you'll meet a variety of interesting people, and have some fun along the way! Let's get on with the fun—keep reading . . .

CHAPTER 1

■ ■ ■

Getting Started with JavaScript

This book is about a scripting language called **JavaScript** and how to use it in a practical manner. After you read it, you'll be able to

- Understand JavaScript syntax and structures.

- Create scripts that are easy to understand and maintain.

- Write scripts that do not interfere with other JavaScripts.

- Write scripts that make web sites easier to use without blocking out non-JavaScript users.

- Write scripts that are independent of the browser or user agent trying to understand them—which means that in some years they will still be usable and won't rely on obsolete technology.

- Enhance a web site with JavaScript and allow developers without any scripting knowledge to change the look and feel.

- Enhance a web document with JavaScript and allow HTML developers to use your functionality by simply adding a CSS class to an element.

- Use progressive enhancement to make a web document nicer only when and if the user agent allows for it.

- Use Ajax to bridge the gap between back end and client side, thus creating sites that are easier to maintain and appear much slicker to the user.

- Use JavaScript as part of a web methodology that enables you to maintain it independently without interfering with the other development streams.

What you will not find here are

- Instructions on how to create effects that look flashy but do nothing of value for the visitor

- JavaScript applications that are browser specific

- JavaScripts that are only there to prove that they can be used and do not enhance the visitor's experience

- JavaScripts that promote unwanted content, such as pop-up windows or other flashy techniques like tickers or animation for animation's sake

It is my credo that JavaScript has a place in modern web development, but we cannot take it for granted that the visitor will be able to use or even experience all the effects and functionality we can achieve with JavaScript. JavaScript allows us to completely change the web page by adding and removing or showing and hiding elements. We can offer users richer interfaces like drag-and-drop applications or multilevel drop-down menus. However, some visitors cannot use a drag-and-drop interface because they can only use a keyboard or rely on voice recognition to use our sites. Other visitors might be dependent on *hearing* our sites rather than seeing them (via screen readers) and will not necessarily be notified of changes achieved via JavaScript. Last but not least, there are users who just cannot have JavaScript enabled, for example, in high-security environments like banks. Therefore, it is necessary to back up a lot of the things we do in JavaScript with solutions on the server side.

Sadly, JavaScript also has a history of being used as a way to force information onto the visitor that was not requested (pop-up windows are a good example). This practice is frowned on by me, as well as many professional web designers. It is my hope that you will not use the knowledge gained from this book to such an end.

■**Note** Web design has matured over the years—we stopped using FONT tags and deprecated visual attributes like bgcolor and started moving all the formatting and presentational attributes to a CSS file. The same cleaning process has to happen to JavaScript should it remain a part of web development. We separated content, structure, and presentation, and now it is time to separate the behavior of web sites from the other layers. Web development now is for business and for helping the user rather than for the sake of putting something out there and hoping it works in most environments.

It is high time we see JavaScript as a part of an overall development methodology, which means that we develop it not to interfere with other technologies like HTML or CSS, but to interact with them or complement them. To that end, we see the emergence of a new technology (or at least a new way of using existing technologies) called **Ajax**, which we will discuss in Chapter 8.

Web development has come quite a way since the 1990s, and there is not much sense in creating web sites that are static and fixed in their size. Any modern web design should allow for growth as needed. It should also be accessible to everyone (which does not mean that everybody gets the same appearance—a nice multicolumn layout, for example, might make sense on a high-resolution monitor but is hard to use on a mobile phone or a PDA)—and ready for internationalization. We cannot afford any longer to build something and think it'll last forever. Since the Web is about content and change, it'll become obsolete if we don't upgrade our web products constantly and allow other data sources to feed into it or get information from it.

Enough introductions—you got this book to learn about JavaScript, so let's start by talking quickly about JavaScript's history and assets before diving right into it.

In this chapter you'll learn

- What JavaScript is and what it can do for you

- The advantages and disadvantages of JavaScript

- How to add JavaScript to a web document and its essential syntax

- Object-oriented programming (OOP) in relation to JavaScript

- How to write and run a simple JavaScript program

Chances are that you have already come across JavaScript, and already have an idea of what it is and what it can do, so we'll move quite swiftly through some basics of the language and its capabilities first. If you know JavaScript well already, and you simply want to know more about the newer and more accessible features and concepts, you might skip to Chapter 3. I won't hold it against you—however, there might be some information you've forgotten, and a bit of a review doesn't hurt, either.

The Why of JavaScript

In the beginning of the Web, there was HTML and the Common Gateway Interface (CGI). HTML defines the parts of a text document and instructs the user agent (usually the web browser) how to show it—for example, text surrounded by the tags `<p></p>` becomes a paragraph. Within that paragraph you may have `<h1></h1>` tags that define the main page heading. Notice that for most opening tags, there is a corresponding closing tag that begins with `</`.

HTML has one disadvantage—it has a fixed state. If you want to change something, or use data the visitor entered, you need to make a round-trip to a server. Using a **dynamic technology** (such as ColdFusion, ASP, ASP.NET, PHP, or JSP) you send the information from forms, or from parameters, to a server, which then performs calculating/testing/database lookups, etc. The application server associated with these technologies then writes an HTML document to show the results, and the resulting HTML document is returned to the browser for viewing.

The problem with that is it means every time there is a change, the entire process must be repeated (and the page reloaded). This is cumbersome, slow, and not as impressive as the new media "Internet" promised us to be. It is true that at least the Western world has the benefit of fast Internet connections these days, but displaying a page still means a reload, which could be a slow process that frequently fails (ever get an `Error 404`?).

We need something slicker—something that allows web developers to give immediate feedback to the user and change HTML without reloading the page from the server. Just imagine a form that needs to be reloaded every time there's an error in one of its fields—isn't it handier when something flags the errors immediately, without needing to reload the page from the web server? This is one example of what JavaScript can do for you.

Some information, such as calculations and verifying the information on a form, may not need to come from the server. JavaScript is executed by the user agent (normally a browser) on the visitor's computer. We call this **client-side code**. This could result in fewer trips to the server and faster-running web sites.

What Is JavaScript?

JavaScript started life as **LiveScript**, but Netscape changed the name—possibly because of the excitement being generated by Java—to JavaScript. The name is confusing though, as there is no real connection between Java and JavaScript—although some of the syntax looks similar.

Java is to JavaScript what Car is to Carpet

———From a JavaScript discussion group on Usenet

Netscape created the JavaScript language in 1996 and included it in their Netscape Navigator (NN) 2.0 browser via an interpreter that read and executed the JavaScript added to .html pages. The language has steadily grown in popularity since then, and is now supported by the most popular browsers.

The good news is that this means JavaScript can be used in web pages for all major modern browsers. The not-quite-so-good news is that there are differences in the way the different browsers implement JavaScript, although the core JavaScript language is much the same. However, JavaScript can be turned off by the user—and many companies and other institutions require their users to do so for security reasons. We will discuss this further shortly, as well as throughout this book.

The great thing about JavaScript is that once you've learned how to use it for browser programming, you can move on to use it in other areas. Microsoft's server—IIS—uses JavaScript to program server-side web pages (ASP), PDF files now use JavaScript, and even Windows administration tasks can be automated with JavaScript code. A lot of applications such as Dreamweaver and Photoshop are scriptable with JavaScript. Operating system add-ons like the Apple Dashboard or Konfabulator on Linux and Windows even allow you to write small helper applications in JavaScript.

Lately a lot of large companies also offer application programming interfaces (APIs) that feature JavaScript objects and methods you can use in your own pages—Google Maps being one of them. You can offer a zoomable and scrollable map in your web site with just a few lines of code.

Even better is the fact that JavaScript is a lot easier to develop than higher programming languages or server-side scripting languages. It does not need any compilation like Java or C++, or to be run on a server or command line like Perl, PHP, or Ruby: all you need to write, execute, debug, and apply JavaScript is a text editor and a browser—both of which are supplied with any operating system. There are, of course, tools that make it a lot easier for you, examples being JavaScript debuggers like Mozilla Venkman, Microsoft Script Debugger, or kjscmd.

Problems and Merits of JavaScript

As I mentioned at the outset of this chapter, JavaScript has been an integral part of web development over the last few years, but it has also been used wrongly. As a result, it has gotten a bad reputation. The reason for this is gratuitous JavaScript effects, like moving page elements and pop-up windows, which might have been impressive the first time you saw them but soon turned out to be just a "nice to have" and in some cases even a "nice to not have any longer." A lot of this comes from the days of **DHTML** (more on this in Chapter 3).

The term **user agent** and the lack of understanding what a user agent is can also be a problem. Normally, the user agent is a browser like Microsoft Internet Explorer (MSIE), Netscape, Mozilla (Moz), Firefox (Fx), Opera, or Safari. However, browsers are not the only user agents on the Web. Others include

- Assistive technology that helps users to overcome the limitations of a disability—like text-to-speech software or Braille displays

- Text-only agents like Lynx

- Web-enabled applications

- Game consoles

- Mobile/cell phones

- PDAs

- Interactive TV set-top boxes

- Search engines and other indexing programs

- And many more

This large variety of user agents, of different technical finesse (and old user agents that don't get updated), is also a great danger for JavaScript.

Not all visitors to your web site will experience the JavaScript enhancements you applied to it. A lot of them will also have JavaScript turned off—for security reasons. JavaScript can be used for good and for evil. If the operating system—like unpatched Windows—allows you to, you can install viruses or Trojan Horses on a computer via JavaScript or read out user information and send it to another server.

■**Note** There is no way of knowing what the visitor uses or what his computer is capable of. Furthermore, you never know what the visitor's experience and ability is like. This is one of the beautiful aspects of the Web—everyone can participate. However, this can introduce a lot of unexpected consequences for the JavaScript programmer.

In many cases, you might want to have a server-side backup plan. It would test to see whether the user agent supports the functionality desired and, if it doesn't, the server takes over.

Independence of scripting languages is a legal requirement for web sites, defined in the Digital Discrimination Act for the UK, section 508 in the US law, and many more localized legal requirements throughout the world. This means that if the site you developed cannot be used without JavaScript, or your JavaScript enhancements are expecting a certain ability of the users or their user agent without a fallback, your client could be sued for discrimination.

However, JavaScript is not evil or useless, and it is a great tool to help your visitor to surf web sites that are a lot slicker and less time-consuming.

Why Use JavaScript If It Cannot Be Relied On?

As I just mentioned, just because it may not always be available doesn't mean that JavaScript shouldn't be used at all. It should simply not be the only means of user interaction.

The merits of using JavaScript are

- **Less server interaction**: You can validate user input before sending the page off to the server. This saves server traffic, which means saving money.

- **Immediate feedback to the visitors**: They don't have to wait for a page reload to see if they have forgotten to enter something

- **Automated fixing of minor errors**: For example, if you have a database system that expects a date in the format *dd-mm-yyyy* and the visitor enters it in the form *dd/mm/yyyy*, a clever JavaScript script could change this minor mistake prior to sending the form to the server. If that was the only mistake the visitor made, you can save her an error message— thus making it less frustrating to use the site.

- **Increased usability by allowing visitors to change and interact with the user interface without reloading the page**: For example, by collapsing and expanding sections of the page or offering extra options for visitors with JavaScript. A classic example of this would be select boxes that allow immediate filtering, such as only showing the available destinations for a certain airport, without making you reload the page and wait for the result.

- **Increased interactivity**: You can create interfaces that react when the user hovers over them with a mouse or activates them via the keyboard. This is partly possible with CSS and HTML as well, but JavaScript offers you a lot wider—and more widely supported— range of options.

- **Richer interfaces**: If your users allow for it, you can use JavaScript to include such items as drag-and-drop components and sliders—something that originally was only possible in thick client applications your users had to install, such as Java applets or browser plug-ins like Flash.

- **Lightweight environment**: Instead of downloading a large file like a Java applet or a Flash movie, scripts are small in file size and get cached (held in memory) once they have been loaded. JavaScript also uses the browser controls for functionality rather than its own user interfaces like Flash or Java applets do. This makes it easier for users, as they already know these controls and how to use them. Modern Flash and Macromedia Flex applications do have the option to stream media and—being vector based—are visually scalable, something JavaScript and HTML controls aren't. On the other hand, they require the plug-in to be installed.

JavaScript in a Web Page and Essential Syntax

Applying JavaScript to a web document is very easy; all you need to do is to use the script tag:

```
<script type="text/javascript">
  // Your code here
</script>
```

For older browsers, or if you want to use strict XHTML (the newest version of HTML) instead of transitional, you'll need to comment out the code to make sure the user agent does not display it inside the page or tries to render it as HTML markup. There are two different syntaxes for commenting out code. For HTML documents and transitional XHTML, you use the normal HTML comments:

```
<script type="text/javascript">
<!--
 // Your code here
-->
</script>
```

In strict XHTML, you will need to use the CDATA commenting syntax to comment out your code—however, it is best not to add any JavaScript inside strict XHTML documents, but keep it in its own document. More on this in Chapter 3.

```
<script type="text/javascript"><!--//--><![CDATA[//><!-
  // Your code here
//--><!]]></script>
```

Technically it is possible to include JavaScript anywhere in the HTML document, and browsers will interpret it. However, there are reasons in modern scripting why this is a bad idea. For now though, we will add JavaScript examples to the body of the document to allow you to see immediately what your first scripts are doing. This will help you get familiar with JavaScript a lot easier than the more modern and advanced techniques awaiting you in Chapter 3.

■**Note** There is also an "opposite" to the script tag—noscript—which allows you to add content that will only be displayed when JavaScript is not available. However, noscript is deprecated in XHTML and strict HTML, and there is no need for it—if you create JavaScript that is unobtrusive.

JavaScript Syntax

Before we go any further, we should discuss some JavaScript syntax essentials:

- // indicates that the rest of the current line is a comment and not code to be executed, so the interpreter doesn't try to run it. Comments are a handy way of putting notes in the code to remind us what the code is intended to do, or to help anyone else reading the code see what's going on.

- /* indicates the beginning of a comment that covers more than one line.

- */ indicates the end of a comment that covers more than one line. Multiline comments are also useful if you want to stop a certain section of code from being executed but don't want to delete it permanently. If you were having problems with a block of code, for example, and you weren't sure which lines were causing the problem, you could comment one portion of it at a time in order to isolate the problem.

- Curly braces ({ and }) are used to indicate a block of code. They ensure that all the lines inside the braces are treated as one block. You will see more of these when we discuss structures such as if or for, as well as functions.

- A semicolon or a newline defines the end of a statement, and a statement is a single command. Semicolons are in fact optional, but it's still a good idea to use them to make clear where statements end, because doing so makes your code easier to read and debug. (Although you can put many statements on one line, it's best to put them on separate lines in order to make the code easier to read.) You don't need to use semicolons after curly braces.

Let's put this syntax into a working block of code:

```
<!DOCTYPE HTML PUBLIC "-//W3C//DTD HTML 4.01//EN"
"http://www.w3.org/TR/html4/strict.dtd">
<html dir="ltr" lang="en">
<head>
<body>
<script type="text/JavaScript">
  // One-line comments are useful for reminding us what the code is doing

  /*
     This is a multiline comment. It's useful for longer comments and
     also to block out segments of code when you're testing
  */

  /*
     Script starts here. We're declaring a variable myName, and assigning to it the
     value of whatever the user puts in the prompt box (more on that in Chapter
     2), finishing the instruction with a semicolon because it is a statement
  */
```

```
    var myName = prompt ("Enter your name","");

    // If the name the user enters is Chris Heilmann
    if (myName == "Chris Heilmann")
    {
        // then a new window pops up saying hello
        alert("Hello Me");
    }

    // If the name entered isn't Chris Heilmann
    else
    {
        // say hello to someone else
        alert("hello someone else");
    }
</script>
</body>
</html>
```

Some of the code may not make sense yet, depending on your previous JavaScript experience. All that matters for now is that it's clear how comments are used, what a code block is, and why there are semicolons at the end of some of the statements. You can run this script if you like—just copy it into an HTML page, save the document with the file extension .html, and open it in your browser.

Although statements like if and else span more than one line and contain other statements, they are considered single statements and don't need a semicolon after them. The JavaScript interpreter knows that the lines linked with an if statement should be treated as one block because of the curly braces, {}. While not mandatory, it is a good idea to indent the code within the curly braces. This makes reading and debugging much easier. We'll be looking at variables and conditional statements (if and else) in the next chapter.

Code Execution

The browser reads the page from top to bottom, so the order in which code executes depends on the order of the script blocks. A **script block** is the code between the <script> and </script> tags. (Also note that it's not just the browser that can read our code; the user of a web site can view your code, too, so it's not a good idea to put anything secret or sensitive in there.) There are three script blocks in this next example:

```
<!DOCTYPE HTML PUBLIC "-//W3C//DTD HTML 4.01//EN"
"http://www.w3.org/TR/html4/strict.dtd">
<html dir="ltr" lang="en">
<head>
<script type="text/javascript">
alert( 'First script Block ');
alert( 'First script Block - Second Line ');
</script>
```

```
</head>
<body>
<h1>Test Page</h1>
<script type="text/JavaScript">
  alert( 'Second script Block' );
</script>
<p>Some more HTML</p>
<script type="text/JavaScript">
  alert( 'Third script Block' );
  function doSomething() {
    alert( 'Function in Third script Block' );
  }
</script>
</body>
</html>
```

If you try it out, you'll see that the alert() dialog in the first script block appears first displaying the message

---

```
First script Block
```

---

followed by the next alert() dialog in the second line displaying the message

---

```
First script Block - Second Line.
```

The interpreter continues down the page and comes to the second script block, where the alert() function displays this dialog:

```
Second script Block
```

---

and the third script block following it with an alert() statement that displays

---

```
Third script Block
```

Although there's another `alert` statement inside the function a few lines down, it doesn't execute and display the message. This is because it's inside a function definition (`function doSomething()`) and code inside a function executes only when the function is called.

An Aside About Functions

We'll be talking about functions in much more depth in Chapter 3, but I introduce them here because you can't get very far in JavaScript without an understanding of functions. A *function* is a named, reusable block of code, surrounded by curly braces, that you create to perform a task. JavaScript contains functions that are available for us to use and perform tasks like displaying a message to the user. Proper use of functions can save a programmer a lot of writing of repetitive code.

We can also create our own functions, which is what we did in the previous code block. Let's say we create some code that writes out a message to a page in a certain element. We'd probably want to use it again and again in different situations. While we could cut and paste code blocks wherever we wanted to use them, this approach can make the code excessively long; if you want the same piece of code three or four times within one page, it'll also get pretty hard to decipher and debug. Instead we can wrap the messaging code into a function and then pass in any information that the function needs in order to work using **parameters**. A function can also return a value to the code that called the function into action originally.

To call the function, you simply write its name followed by parentheses, (). (Note—you use the parentheses to pass the parameters. However, even when there are no parameters, you must still use the parentheses.) But you can't call the function, as you might expect, until the script has created it. We can call it in this script by adding it to the third script block like this:

```
<script type="text/JavaScript">
alert( 'Third script Block ');
function doSomething(){
  alert( 'Function in Third script Block ');
}
// Call the function doSomething
doSomething();
</script>
</body>
</html>
```

So far in this chapter you've looked at the pros and cons of the JavaScript language, seen some of the syntax rules, learned about some of the main components of the language (albeit briefly), and run a few JavaScript scripts. You've covered quite a lot of distance. Before we move on to a more detailed examination of the JavaScript language in the next chapter, let's talk about something key to successful JavaScript development: **objects**.

Objects

Objects are central to the way we use JavaScript. Objects in JavaScript are in many ways like objects in the world outside programming (it does exist, I just had a look). In the real world, an object is just a "thing" (many books about object-oriented programming compare objects to nouns): a car, a table, a chair, and the keyboard I'm typing on. Objects have

Properties (analogous to adjectives): The car is *red*.

Methods (like verbs in a sentence): The method for starting the car might be *turn ignition key*.

Events: Turning the ignition key results in the *car starting* event.

Object Oriented Programming (OOP) tries to make programming easier by modeling real-world objects. Let's say we were creating a car simulator. First, we would create a car object, giving it properties like *color* and *current speed*. Then we'd need to create methods: perhaps a *start* method to start the car, and a *break* method to slow the car, into which we'd need to pass information about how hard the brakes should be pressed so that we can determine the slowing effect. Finally, we would want some events, for example, a *gasoline low* event to remind us to fill up the car.

Object-oriented programming works with these concepts. This way of designing software is now very commonplace and influences many areas of programming—but most importantly to us, it's central to JavaScript and web browser programming.

Some of the objects we'll be using are part of the language specification: the String object, the Date object, and the Math object, for example. The same objects would be available to JavaScript in a PDF file and on a web server. These objects provide lots of useful functionality that could save us tons of programming time. The Date object, for example, allows you to obtain the current date and time from the client (such as a user's PC). It stores the date and provides lots of useful date-related functions, for example, converting the date/time from one time zone to another. These objects are usually referred to as **core objects**, as they are independent of the implementation. The browser also makes itself available for programming through objects that allow us to obtain information about the browser and to change the look and feel of the application. For example, the browser makes available the Document object, which represents a web page available to JavaScript. We can use this in JavaScript to add new HTML to the web page being viewed by the user of the web browser. If you were to use JavaScript with a different host, with a Windows server for example, then you'd find that the server hosting JavaScript exposes a very different set of host objects, their functionality being related to things you want to do on a web server.

You'll also see in Chapter 3 that JavaScript allows us to create our own objects. This is a powerful feature that allows us to model real-world problems using JavaScript. To create a new object, we need to specify the properties and methods it should have using a template called a **class**. A class is a bit like an architect's drawing in that it specifies what should go where and do what, but it doesn't actually create the object.

Note There is some debate as to whether JavaScript is an object-based language or an object-oriented language. The difference is that an object-based language uses objects for doing programming but doesn't allow the coder to use object-oriented programming in their code design. An object-oriented programming language not only uses objects, but also makes it easy to develop and design code in line with object-oriented design methodology. JavaScript allows us to create our own objects, but this is not accomplished in the same way as in class-based languages like Java or C#. However, we'll be concentrating not on debates about what is or isn't object oriented here, but on how objects are useful in practical terms in this book, and we'll look at some basic object-oriented coding where it helps make life easier for us.

As you progress through the book, you'll get a more in-depth look at objects: the objects central to the JavaScript language, the objects that the browser makes available for access and manipulation using JavaScript, and creating your own custom objects. For now, though, all you need to know is that objects in JavaScript are "entities" you can use to add functionality to web pages, and that they can have properties and methods. The Math object, for example, has among its properties one that represents the value of pi and among its methods one that generates a random number.

Simple JavaScript Example

We'll finish the chapter with a simple script that determines first the width of the visitor's screen and then applies a suitable style sheet (by adding an extra LINK element to the page). We'll do this using the Screen object, which is a representation of the user's screen. This object has an availWidth property that we'll retrieve and use to decide which style sheet to load.

Here's the code:

```
<!DOCTYPE HTML PUBLIC "-//W3C//DTD HTML 4.01//EN"
"http://www.w3.org/TR/html4/strict.dtd">
<html dir="ltr" lang="en">
  <head>
    <meta http-equiv="Content-Type" content="text/html; charset=iso-8859-1">
    <title>CSS Resolution Demo</title>
    <!-- Basic style with all settings -->
    <link rel="StyleSheet" href="basic.css" type="text/css" />
    <!--
    Extra style (applied via JavaScript) to override default settings
    according to the screen resolution
    -->
```

```
<script type="text/javascript">
  // Define a variable called cssName and a message
  // called resolutionInfo
  var cssName;
  var resolutionInfo;
  // If the width of the screen is less than 650 pixels
  if( screen.availWidth < 650 ) {
  // define the style Variable as the low-resolution style
    cssName = 'lowres.css';
    resolutionInfo = 'low resolution';
  // Or if the width of the screen is less than 1000 pixels
  } else {
    if( screen.availWidth > 1000 ) {
  // define the style Variable as the high-resolution style
      cssName = 'highres.css';
      resolutionInfo = 'high resolution';
  // Otherwise
    } else {
  // define the style Variable as the mid-resolution style
      cssName = 'lowres.css';
      resolutionInfo = 'medium resolution';
    }
  }
  document.write( '<link rel="StyleSheet" href="' +
  cssName + '" type="text/css" />' );
  </script>
  </head>
<body>
  <script type="text/javascript">
    document.write( '<p>Applied Style:' +
    resolutionInfo + '</p>' );
  </script>
</body>
</html>
```

Although we'll be looking at the details of if statements and loops in the next chapter, you can probably see how this is working already. The if statement on the first line asks whether the screen.availWidth is less than 650:

```
if ( screen.availWidth < 650 )
```

If the user's screen is 640×480, then the width is less than 650, so the code within the curly braces is executed and the low-resolution style and message get defined.

```
if ( screen.availWidth < 650 ) {
// define the style Variable as the low-resolution style
  cssName = 'lowres.css';
  resolutionInfo = 'low resolution';
}
```

The code carries on checking the screen size using the else statement. The final else only occurs if neither of the other evaluations have resulted in code being executed, so we assume that the screen is 800×600, and define the medium style and message accordingly:

```
else {
// define the style Variable as the mid-resolution style
  cssName = 'lowres.css';
  resolutionInfo = 'medium resolution';
}
```

It's also worth noting that we're measuring the screen size here, and the user may have a 800×600 screen, but that doesn't mean their browser window is maximized. We may be applying a style that may not be appropriate.

We're using another object, the document object, to write to the page (HTML document). The document object's write() method allows us to insert HTML into the page. Note that document.write() doesn't actually change the source HTML page, just the page the user sees on his computer.

Note In fact, you'll find document.write() very useful as you work through the first few chapters of the book. It's good for small examples that show how a script is working, for communicating with the user, and even for debugging an area of a program that you're not sure is doing what you think it should be doing. It also works on all browsers that support JavaScript. More modern browsers have better tools and methods for debugging, but more on that in Chapter 3.

We use document.write() to write out the appropriate link element with our defined style in the head:

```
document.write( '<link rel="StyleSheet" href="' +
cssName + '" type="text/css" />' );
```

And in the document's body, we write out the message explaining which resolution style was applied:

```
<script type="text/javascript">
  document.write( '<p>Applied Style: '+ resolutionInfo + '</p>' );
</script>
```

Later on, we'll be working with more complex examples that use JavaScript to test capabilities of the user's agent and interface. For now though, I hope this simple example gives you an inkling of the kind of flexibility you can add to your web pages using JavaScript.

Summary

In this chapter, we've taken a look at what JavaScript is, how it works, and what its advantages and disadvantages are. I noted that the biggest disadvantage is that we cannot rely on it as a given. However, I also mentioned that using JavaScript can make web sites a nicer and slicker experience.

You've run some JavaScript code, seen how to add comments to the code, and how to separate JavaScript statements using semicolons. You also saw that you can tell JavaScript to treat a group of lines of code as a single block using curly braces, following an `if` statement, for example. You learned that JavaScript execution generally runs from top to bottom, and from the first `script` block to the last, with the exception of functions that only execute when you tell them to.

We also looked at objects, which are central to writing JavaScript. Not only is JavaScript itself very much dependent on objects, but the browser also uses objects and methods to make itself and the document available for scripting. Finally, we looked at a simple example that reads out the user's screen resolution and applies a suitable style sheet.

In the next chapter, I'll cover the language fundamentals of JavaScript. You'll see how JavaScript stores and manipulates data, and uses it in calculations. We'll also look at creating "intelligent" JavaScript programs using decision-making statements that allow us to evaluate data, do calculations with it, and decide on an appropriate course of action. With that chapter under your belt, you'll have most of the fundamental knowledge needed to go on to more exciting and useful web programming.

CHAPTER 2

■ ■ ■

Data and Decisions

Data and decision making are fundamental to every "intelligent" program. We'll begin this chapter by looking at how JavaScript understands, or represents, data. This is important because JavaScript works with a number of **data types** and manipulates data according to its data type. You can generate unexpected results by mismatching data of different types. We'll look at some of the more common data type problems, and you'll see how to convert one type of data to another.

We'll also be working with **conditional statements** and **loops**: two of the most valuable tools for decision making. In order to make decisions in a computer language, we need to let the program know what should happen in response to certain conditions, which is where conditional statements come in. Loops, on the other hand, simply allow you to repeat an action until a specified circumstance is met. For example, you might want to loop through each input box in a form and check the information it contains is valid.

I'll be covering a lot of different facets of JavaScript in this chapter:

- Classifying and manipulating information in JavaScript: data types and data operators

- Variables

- Converting data types

- Introducing data objects: `String`, `Date`, and `Math` objects

- Arrays: storing ordered sets of data like the items in a shopping basket

- Decision making with conditional statements, loops, and data evaluation

---

Note The examples in this chapter are kept as simple as possible and therefore use `document.write()` as a feedback mechanism for you to see the results. You'll learn in later chapters about other methods for doing this that are more modern and versatile.

Data, Data Types, and Data Operators

Data is used to store information, and, in order to do that more effectively, JavaScript needs to have each piece of data assigned a **type**. This type stipulates what can or cannot be done with the data. For example, one of the JavaScript data types is **number**, which allows you to perform certain calculations on the data that it holds.

The three most basic data types that store data in JavaScript are

- **String**: A series of characters, for example, "some characters"

- **Number**: A number, including floating point numbers

- **Boolean**: Can contain a true or false value

These are sometimes referred to as **primitive** data types in that they store only single values. There are two slightly different primitive data types as well. These don't store information, but instead warn us about a particular situation:

- **Null**: Indicates that there is no data.

- **Undefined**: Indicates that something has not been defined and given a value. This is important when you're working with variables.

We'll be working extensively with these data types throughout the chapter.

The String Data Type

The JavaScript interpreter expects string data to be enclosed within single or double quotation marks (known as **delimiters**). This script, for example, will write some characters onto the page:

```
<html>
  <body>
    <script type="text/javascript">
      document.write( "some characters" );
    </script>
  </body>
</html>
```

The quotation marks won't be written out to the page because they are not part of the string; they simply tell JavaScript where the string starts and ends. We could just as easily have used single quotation marks:

```
<html>
  <body>
    <script type="text/javascript">
      document.write( 'some characters' );
    </script>
  </body>
</html>
```

Both methods are fine, just as long as you close the string the same way you opened it and don't try to delimit it like this:

```
document.write( 'some characters" );
document.write( "some characters' );
```

Of course, you might want to use a single or double quotation mark inside the string itself, in which case you need to use a distinct delimiter. If you used double quotation marks, the instructions will be interpreted as you intended:

```
document.write( "Paul's characters " );
```

But if you used single quotations marks, they won't be:

```
document.write( 'Paul's characters' );
```

This will give you a syntax error because the JavaScript interpreter thinks the string ends after the *l* in *Paul* and doesn't understand what is happening afterwards.

■**Note** JavaScript syntax, like English syntax, is a set of rules that makes the language "intelligible." Just as a syntax error in English can render a sentence meaningless, a syntax error in JavaScript can render the instruction meaningless.

You can avoid creating JavaScript syntax errors like this one by using single quotation marks to delimit any string containing double quotes and vice versa:

```
document.write( "Paul's numbers are 123" );
document.write( 'some "characters"' );
```

If, on the other hand, you wanted to use both single and double quotation marks in your string, you need to use something called an **escape sequence**. In fact, it's better coding practice to use escape sequences instead of the quotation marks we've been using so far, because they make your code easier to read.

Escape Sequences

Escape sequences are also useful for situations where you want to use characters that can't be typed using a keyboard (like the symbol for the Japanese yen, ¥, on a Western keyboard). Table 2-1 lists some of the most commonly used escape sequences.

Table 2-1. *Common Escape Sequences*

Escape Sequences	Character Represented
\b	Backspace.
\f	Form feed.
\n	Newline.
\r	Carriage return.
\t	Tab.
\'	Single quote.
\"	Double quote.
\\	Backslash.
\xNN	*NN* is a hexadecimal number that identifies a character in the Latin-1 character set (the Latin-1 character is the norm for English-speaking countries).
\uDDDD	*DDDD* is a hexadecimal number identifying a Unicode character.

Let's amend this string, which causes a syntax error:

```
document.write( 'Paul's characters' );
```

so that it uses the escape sequence (\') and is correctly interpreted:

```
document.write( 'Paul\'s characters' );
```

The escape sequence tells the JavaScript interpreter that the single quotation mark belongs to the string itself and isn't a delimiter.

ASCII is a character encoding method that uses values from 0 to 254. As an alternative, we could specify characters using the ASCII value in hexadecimal with the \xNN escape sequence. The letter *C* is 67 in decimal and 43 in hex, so we could write that to the page using the escape sequence like this:

```
document.write( "\x43" );
```

The \uDDDD escape sequence works in much the same way but uses the Unicode character encoding method, which has 65,535 characters. As the first few hundred ASCII and Unicode character sets are similar, you can write out the letter *C* using this escape sequence as follows:

```
document.write( '\u0043' );
```

ASCII and Unicode information can get quite detailed, so the best place to look for information is on the Web. For Unicode, try http://www.unicode.org.

Operators

JavaScript has a number of operators that you can use to manipulate the data in your programs; you'll probably recognize them from math. Table 2-2 presents some of the most commonly used operators.

Table 2-2. *JavaScript Operators*

Operator	What It Does
+	Adds two numbers together or concatenates two strings.
-	Subtracts the second number from the first.
*	Multiplies two numbers.
/	Divides the first number by the second.
%	Finds the modulus—the reminder of a division. For example, 98 % 10 = 8.
--	Decreases the number by 1: only useful with variables, which we'll see at work later.
++	Increases the number by 1: only useful with variables, which we'll see at work later.

Here they are in use:

```
<html>
  <body>
    <script type="text/javascript">
      document.write( 1 - 1 );
      document.write( "<br />" );
      document.write( 1 + 1 );
      document.write( "<br />" );
      document.write( 2 * 2 );
      document.write( "<br />" );
      document.write( 12 / 2 );
      document.write( "<br />" );
      document.write( 1 + 2 * 3 );
      document.write( "<br />" );
      document.write( 98 % 10 );
    </script>
  </body>
</html>
```

You should get this output:

```
0
2
4
6
7
8
```

JavaScript, just like math, gives some operators precedence. Multiplication takes a higher precedence than addition, so the calculation 1 + 2 * 3 is carried out like this:

2 * 3 = 6

6 + 1 = 7

All operators have an order of precedence. Multiplication, division, and modulus have equal precedence, so where they all appear in an equation the sum will be calculated from left to right. Try this calculation:

2 * 10 / 5%3

The result is 1, because the calculation simply reads from left to right:

2 * 10 = 20

20 / 5 = 4

4%3 = 1

Addition and subtraction also have equal precedence.

You can use parentheses to give part of a calculation higher precedence. For example, you could add 1 to 1 and then multiply by 5 like this:

(1 + 1) * 5

The result will then be 10, but without the parentheses it would have been 6. In fact, it's a good idea to use parentheses even when they're not essential because they help make the order of the execution clear.

If you use more than one set of parentheses, JavaScript will simply work from left to right or, if you have inner parentheses, from the inside out:

```
document.write( ( 1 + 1 ) * 5 * ( 2 + 3 ) );
```

This is how the calculations for the preceding are performed:

(1 + 1) = 2

(2 + 3) = 5

2 * 5 = 10

10 * 5 = 50

As we've seen, JavaScript's addition operator adds the values. What it actually does with the two values depends on the data type that you're using. For example, if you're working with two numbers that have been stored as the number data type, the + operator will add them together. However, if one of the data types you're working with is a string (as indicated by the delimiters), the two values will be concatenated. Try this:

```html
<html>
  <body>
    <script type="text/javascript">
      document.write( 'Java' + 'Script' );
      document.write( 1 + 1 );
      document.write( 1 + '1' );
    </script>
  </body>
</html>
```

Being able to use the addition operator with strings can be handy (and is called the **concatenation operator** in this case), but it can also generate unexpected results if one of the values you're working with happens to be of a different data type from the one you were expecting. We'll be looking at some examples like this, and resolving them, later on.

It's less of a problem if you're working with **literal** values as we have been doing so far. However, much of the data you'll be working with in your programs will be entered by the user, or generated by the script, so you won't know in advance exactly what values you're going to be working with. This is where **variables** come in. Variables are placeholders for data in your script, and they're central to JavaScript.

JavaScript Variables

JavaScript is probably the most forgiving language when it comes to variables. You don't need to define what a variable is before you can use it, and you can change the type of a variable any time in the script. However, to ease maintenance and keep up a stricter coding syntax, it is a good idea to declare variables explicitly at the beginning of your script or—in the case of local variables—your function.

We declare a variable by giving it a unique name and using the var keyword.

Variable names have to start with a letter of the alphabet or with an underscore, while the rest of the name can be made up only of numbers, letters, the dollar sign ($), and underscore characters. Do not use any other characters.

■Note Like most things in JavaScript, variable names are case sensitive: thisVariable and ThisVariable are different variables. Be very careful about naming your variables; you can run into all sorts of trouble if you don't name them consistently. To that end, most programmers use **camel notation**: the name of the variable begins with a lowercase letter while subsequent words are capitalized and run in without spaces. Thus the name thisVariable.

Always give your variables meaningful names. In the next example we'll build, we're going to write an exchange rate conversion program, so we'll use variable names like euroToDollarRate and dollarToPound. There are two advantages to naming variables descriptively: it's easier to remember what the code is doing if you come back to it at a later date, and it's easier for someone new to the code to see what's going on. Code readability and layout are very important to the development of web pages. It makes it quicker and easier to spot errors and debug them, and to amend the code as you want to.

■Note While it is not technically necessary, variable declarations should begin with the keyword var. Not using it could have implications, which you will see as we progress.

With all that said, let's start declaring variables. We can declare a variable without initializing it (giving it a value):

```
var myVariable;
```

Then it's ready and waiting for when we have a value. This is useful for variables that will hold user input.

We can also declare and initialize the variable at the same time:

```
var myVariable = "A String";
var anotherVariable = 123;
```

Or we can declare and initialize a variable by assigning it the return value of the prompt() function or the sum of a calculation:

```
var eurosToConvert = prompt( "How many Euros do you wish to➡
 convert", "" );
var dollars = eurosToConvert * euroToDollarRate;
```

The prompt() function is a JavaScript function that asks the user to enter a value and then returns it to the code. Here we're assigning the value entered to the variable eurosToConvert.

Initializing your variables is a very good idea, especially if you can give them a default value that's useful to the application. Even initializing a variable to an empty string can be a good idea, because you can check back on it without bringing up the error messages that would have popped up if it didn't have a value.

Let's look at how variables can improve both the readability of your code and its functionality. Here's a block of code without any variables:

```
<html>
  <body>
    <script type="text/javascript">
      document.write( 0.872 * prompt( "How many Euros do you➨
 wish to convert", "" ) );
    </script>
  </body>
</html>
```

It's not immediately obvious that this code is converting euros to dollars, because there's nothing to tell us that 0.872 is the exchange rate. The code works fine though; if you try it out with the number 10, you should get the following result:

```
8.72
```

We are using the prompt() method of the window object to get user feedback in this example (the window is optional in this instance, and to keep the code shorter you can omit it). This method has two parameters: one label displayed above an entry field and an initial value of the field. You'll learn more about prompt() and how to use it in Chapter 4. Supposing that we wanted to make the result a little more informative, like this:

```
10 Euros is 8.72 Dollars
```

Without variables, the only way to do it would be to ask users to enter the euros they want to convert twice, and that really wouldn't be user friendly. Using variables, though, we can store the data temporarily, and then call it up as many times as we need to:

```
<html>
  <body>
    <script type="text/javascript">
      // Declare a variable holding the conversion rate
      var euroToDollarRate = 0.872;
```

```
    // Declare a new variable and use it to store the
    // number of euros
    var eurosToConvert = prompt( "How many Euros do you wish➥
to convert", "" );
    // Declare a variable to hold the result of the euros
    // multiplied by the conversion
    var dollars = eurosToConvert * euroToDollarRate;
    // Write the result to the page
    document.write( eurosToConvert + " euros is " + dollars +➥
" dollars" );
    </script>
  </body>
</html>
```

We've used three variables: one to store the exchange rate from euros to dollars, another to store the number of euros that will be converted, and the final one to hold the result of the conversion into dollars. Then all we need to do is write out the result using both variables. Not only is this script more functional, it's also much easier to read.

Converting Different Types of Data

For the most part, the JavaScript interpreter can work out what data types we want to be used. In the following code, for example, the interpreter understands the numbers 1 and 2 to be of number data type and treats them accordingly:

```
<html>
  <body>
    <script type="text/javascript">
      var myCalc = 1 + 2;
      document.write( "The calculated number is " + myCalc );
    </script>
  </body>
</html>
```

This will be written to your page:

```
The calculated number is 3
```

However, if we rewrite the code to allow the user to enter his own number using the `prompt()` function, then we'll get a different calculation altogether:

```
<html>
  <body>
    <script type="text/javascript">
      var userEnteredNumber = prompt( "Please enter a number",➡
 "" );
      var myCalc = 1 + userEnteredNumber;
      var myResponse = "The number you entered + 1 = " + myCalc;
      document.write( myResponse );
    </script>
  </body>
</html>
```

If you enter 2 at the prompt, then you'll be told that

```
The number you entered + 1 =   12
```

Rather than add the two numbers together, the JavaScript interpreter has concatenated them. This is because the `prompt()` function actually returns the value entered by the user as a string data type, even though the string contains number characters. The concatenation happens in this line:

```
var myCalc = 1 + userEnteredNumber;
```

In effect, it's the same as if we'd written

```
var myCalc = 1 + "2";
```

If, however, we use the subtraction operator instead:

```
var myCalc = 1 - userEnteredNumber;
```

`userEnteredNumber` is subtracted from 1. The subtraction operator isn't applicable to string data, so JavaScript works out that we wanted the data to be treated as a number, converts the string to a number, and does the calculation. The same applies to the * and / operators. The `typeof()` operator returns the type of data that has been passed to it, so we can use that to see which data types the JavaScript interpreter is working with:

```
<html>
  <body>
    <script type="text/javascript">
      var userEnteredNumber = prompt( "Please enter a number",➡
 "" );
```

```
      document.write( typeof( userEnteredNumber ) );
    </script>
  </body>
</html>
```

This will write string into the page. The way to ensure that the interpreter is using the desired number data type is to **explicitly** declare that the data is a number. There are three functions you can use to do this:

- `Number()`: Tries to convert the value of the variable inside the parentheses into a number.

- `parseFloat()`: Tries to convert the value to a floating point. It parses the string character by character from left to right, until it encounters a character that can't be used in a number. It then stops at that point and evaluates this string as a number. If the first character can't be used in a number, the result is **NaN** (which stands for **Not a Number**).

- `parseInt()`: Converts the value to an integer by removing any fractional part without rounding the number up or down. Anything nonnumerical passed to the function will be discarded. If the first character is not +, -, or a digit, the result is NaN.

Let's see how these functions work in practice:

```
<html>
  <body>
    <script type="text/javascript">
      var userEnteredNumber = prompt( "Please enter a number",➥
"" );
      document.write( typeof( userEnteredNumber ) );
      document.write( "<br />" );
      document.write( parseFloat( userEnteredNumber ) );
      document.write( "<br />" );
      document.write( parseInt( userEnteredNumber ) );
      userEnteredNumber = Number( userEnteredNumber )
      document.write( "<br />" );
      document.write( userEnteredNumber );
      document.write( "<br />" );
      document.write( typeof( userEnteredNumber ) );
    </script>
  </body>
</html>
```

Try entering the value 23.50. You should get this output:

```
string
23.5
23
23.5
number
```

The data entered is read as a string in the first line. Then `parseFloat()` converts 23.50 from a string to a floating point number, and in the next line `parseInt()` strips out the fractional part (without rounding up or down). The variable is then converted to a number using the `Number()` function, stored in the `userEnteredNumber` variable itself (overwriting the string held there), and on the final line we see that `userEnteredNumber`'s data type is indeed number.

Try entering 23.50abc at the user prompt:

```
string
23.5
23
NaN
number
```

The results are similar, but this time `Number()` has returned NaN. The `parseFloat()` and `parseInt()` functions still return a number because they work from left to right converting as much of the string to a number as they can, and then stop when they hit a nonnumeric value. The `Number()` function will reject any string that contains nonnumerical characters (digits, a valid decimal place, and + and - signs are allowed but nothing else).

If you try entering abc, you'll just get

```
string
NaN
NaN
NaN
number
```

None of the functions can find a valid number, and so they all return NaN, which we can see is a number data type, but not a valid number. This is a good way of checking user input for validity, and we'll be using it to do exactly that later on.

So let's get back to the problem we started with: using `prompt()` to retrieve a number. All we need to do is tell the interpreter the data entered by the user should be converted to a number data type, using one of the functions discussed with the `prompt()` function:

```
<html>
  <body>
    <script type="text/javascript">
      var userEnteredNumber = Number( prompt( "Please enter➥
a number", "" ) );
      var myCalc = 1 + userEnteredNumber;
      var myResponse = "The number you entered + 1 = " +➥
myCalc;
      document.write( myResponse );
    </script>
  </body>
</html>
```

This will not throw any error, but it does not help the visitor much, as the meaning of NaN is not common knowledge. Later on we will deal with conditions, and you'll see how you could prevent an output that does not make much sense to the non-JavaScript-savvy user.

And that's all you need to know about primitive data types and variables for now. Primitive data types, as you have seen, simply hold a value. However, JavaScript can also deal with complex data, and it does this using **composite** data types.

The Composite Data Types: Array and Object

Composite data types are different from simple data types, as they can hold more than one value. There are two composite data types:

- **Object**: Contains a reference to any object, including the objects that the browser makes available

- **Array**: Contains one or more of any other data types

We'll look at the object data type first. As you might recall from the discussion in Chapter 1, objects model real-world entities. These objects can hold data and provide us with properties and methods.

Objects JavaScript Supplies You with: String, Date, and Math

These three objects do three different things:

- String **object**: Stores a string, and provides properties and methods for working with strings

- Date **object**: Stores a date, and provides methods for working with it

- Math **object**: Doesn't store data, but provides properties and methods for manipulating mathematical data

Let's start with the String object.

The String Object

Earlier we created string primitives by giving them some characters to hold, like this:

```
var myPrimitiveString = "ABC123";
```

A String **object** does things slightly differently, not only allowing us to store characters, but also providing a way to manipulate and change those characters. You can create String objects explicitly or implicitly.

Creating a String Object

Let's work with the implicit method first: we'll begin declaring a new variable and assign it a new string primitive to initialize it. Try that now using typeof() to make sure that the data in the variable myStringPrimitive is a string primitive:

```
<html>
  <body>
    <script type="text/javascript">
      var myStringPrimitive= "abc";
      document.write( typeof( myStringPrimitive ) );
    </script>
  </body>
</html>
```

We can still use the String object's methods on it though. JavaScript will simply convert the string primitive to a temporary String object, use the method on it, and then change the data type back to string. We can try that out using the length **property** of the String object:

```
<html>
  <body>
    <script type="text/javascript">
      var myStringPrimitive= "abc";
      document.write( typeof( myStringPrimitive ) );
      document.write( "<br>" );
      document.write( myStringPrimitive.length );
      document.write( "<br>" );
      document.write( typeof( myStringPrimitive ) );
    </script>
  </body>
</html>
```

This is what you should see in the browser window:

```
string
3
string
```

So `myStringPrimitive` is still holding a string primitive after the temporary conversion. We can also create `String` objects explicitly, using the `new` keyword together with the `String()` **constructor**:

```
<html>
  <body>
    <script type="text/javascript">
      var myStringObject = new String( "abc" );
      document.write( typeof( myStringObject ) );
      document.write( "<br />" );
      document.write( myStringObject.length );
      document.write( "<br />" );
      document.write( typeof( myStringObject ) );
    </script>
  </body>
</html>
```

Loading this page displays the following:

```
object
3
object
```

The only difference between this script and the previous one is in the first line where we create the new object and supply some characters for the `String` object to store:

```
var myStringObject = new String( "abc" );
```

The result of checking the `length` property is the same whether we create the `String` object implicitly or explicitly. The only real difference between creating `String` objects explicitly or implicitly is that creating them explicitly is marginally more efficient if you're going to be using the same `String` object again and again. Explicitly creating `String` objects also helps prevent the JavaScript interpreter getting confused between numbers and strings, as it can do.

Using the String Object's Methods

The `String` object has a lot of methods, so we'll limit our discussion to two of them here, the `indexOf()` and `substring()` methods.

JavaScript strings, as you've seen, are made up of characters. Each of these characters is given an index. The index is zero-based, so the first character's position has the index 0, the second 1, and so on. The method `indexOf()` finds and returns the position in the index at which a substring begins (and the `lastIndexOf()` method returns the position at which the substring ends). For example, if we want our user to enter an e-mail address, we could check that they'd included the @ symbol in their entry. (While this wouldn't ensure that the address is valid, it would at least go some way in that direction. We'll be working with much more complex data checking later on in the book.)

Let's do that next, using the prompt() method to obtain the user's e-mail address and then check the input for the @ symbol, returning the index of the symbol using indexOf():

```
<html>
    <body>
    <script type="text/javascript">
      var userEmail= prompt( "Please enter your email➡
 address ", "" );
      document.write( userEmail.indexOf( "@" ) );
    </script>
  </body>
</html>
```

If the @ is not found, -1 is written to the page. As long as the character is there in the string somewhere, its position in the index, in other words something greater than –1, will be returned.

The substring() method carves one string from another string, taking the indexes of the start and end position of the substring as parameters. We can return everything from the first index to the end of the string by leaving off the second parameter.

So to extract all the characters from the third character (at index 2) to the sixth character (index 5), we'd write

```
<html>
  <body>
    <script type="text/javascript">
      var myOldString = "Hello World";
      var myNewString = myOldString.substring( 2, 5 );
      document.write( myNewString );
    </script>
  </body>
</html>
```

You should see llo written out to the browser. Note that the substring() method copies the substring that it returns, and it doesn't alter the original string.

The substring() method really comes into its own when you're working with unknown values. Here's another example that uses both the indexOf() and substring() methods:

```
<html>
  <body>
    <script type="text/javascript">
      var characterName = "my name is Simpson,  Homer";
      var firstNameIndex = characterName.indexOf( "Simpson,➡
 " ) + 9;
      var firstName = characterName.substring( firstNameIndex );
      document.write( firstName );
    </script>
  </body>
</html>
```

We're extracting Homer from the string in the variable characterName, using indexOf() to find the start of the last name, and adding 9 to it to get the index of the start of the first name (as "Simpson, " is 9 characters long), and storing it in firstNameIndex. This is used by the substring() method to extract everything from the start of the first name—we haven't specified the final index, so the rest of the characters in the string will be returned.

Now let's look at the Date object. This allows us to store dates and provides some useful date/time-related functionality.

The Date Object

JavaScript doesn't have a primitive date data type, so we can only create Date objects explicitly. We create new Date objects the same way as we create String objects, using the new keyword together with the Date() constructor. This line creates a Date object containing the current date and time:

```
var todaysDate = new Date();
```

To create a Date object that stores a specific date or time, we simply put the date, or date and time, inside the parentheses:

```
var newMillennium = new Date( "1 Jan 2000 10:24:00" );
```

Different countries describe dates in a different order. For example, in the US dates are specified in *MM/DD/YY*, while in Europe they are *DD/MM/YY*, and in China they are *YY/MM/DD*. If you specify the month using the abbreviated name, then you can use any order:

```
var someDate = new Date( "10 Jan 2002" );
var someDate = new Date( "Jan 10 2002" );
var someDate = new Date( "2002 10 Jan" );
```

In fact, the Date object can take a number of parameters:

```
var someDate = new Date( aYear, aMonth, aDate,➥
anHour, aMinute, aSecond, aMillisecond )
```

To use these parameters, you first need to specify year and month, and then use the parameters you want—although you do have to run through them in order and can't select among them. For example, you can specify year, month, date, and hour:

```
var someDate = new Date( 2003, 9, 22, 17 );
```

You can't specify year, month, and then hours though:

```
var someDate = new Date( 2003, 9, , 17 );
```

■**Note** Although we usually think of month 9 as September, JavaScript starts counting months from 0 (January), and so September is represented as month 8.

Using the Date Object

The Date object has a lot of methods that you can use to get or set a date or time. You can use local time (the time on your computer in your time zone) or UTC (Coordinated Universal Time, once called Greenwich Mean Time). While this can be very useful, you need to be aware when you're working with Date that many people don't set their time zone correctly.

Let's look at an example that demonstrates some of the methods:

```
<html>
  <body>
    <script type="text/javascript">
      // Create a new date object
      var someDate = new Date( "31 Jan 2003 11:59" );
      // Retrieve the first four values using the
      // appropriate get methods
      document.write( "Minutes = " + someDate.getMinutes() + "<br>" );
      document.write( "Year = " + someDate.getFullYear() + "<br>" );
      document.write( "Month = " + someDate.getMonth() + "<br>" );
      document.write( "Date = " + someDate.getDate() + "<br>" );
      // Set the minutes to 34
      someDate.setMinutes( 34 );
      document.write( "Minutes = " + someDate.getMinutes() + "<br>" );
      // Reset the date
      someDate.setDate( 32 );
      document.write( "Date = " + someDate.getDate() + "<br>" );
      document.write( "Month = " + someDate.getMonth() + "<br>" );
    </script>
  </body>
</html>
```

Here's what you should get:

```
Minutes = 59
Year = 2003
Month = 0
Date = 31
Minutes = 34
Date = 1
Month = 1
```

This line of code might look a bit counterintuitive at first:

```
someDate.setDate( 32 );
```

JavaScript knows that there aren't 32 days in January, so instead of trying to set the date to the January 32, the interpreter counts 32 days beginning with January 1, which gives us February 1.

This can be a handy feature if you need to add days onto a date. Usually we'd have to take into account the number of days in the different months, and whether it's a leap year, if we wanted to add a number of days to a date, but it's much easier to use JavaScript's understanding of dates instead:

```
<html>
  <body>
    <script type="text/javascript">
      // Ask the user to enter a date string
      var originalDate = prompt( Enter a date (Day, Name of➡
      the Month, Year), "31 Dec 2003" );
      // Overwrite the originalDate variable with a new Date
      // object
      var originalDate = new Date( originalDate );
      // Ask the user to enter the number of days to be
      // added,  and convert to number
      var addDays = Number( prompt( "Enter number of days➡
to be added", "1" ) )
      // Set a new value for originalDate of originalDate
      // plus the days to be added
      originalDate.setDate( originalDate.getDate( ) + addDays )
      // Write out the date held by the originalDate
      // object using the toString( ) method
      document.write( originalDate.toString( ) )
    </script>
  </body>
</html>
```

If you enter 31 Dec 2003 when prompted, and 1 for the number of days to be added, then the answer you'll get is Thu Jan 1 00:00:00 UTC 2004.

■**Note** Notice that we're using the Number() method of the Math object on the third line of the script. The program will still run if we don't, but the result won't be the same. If you don't want to use the method, there is a trick to convert different data types: if you subtract 0 from a string that could be converted to a number using parseInt(), parseFloat(), or Number(), then you convert it to a number, and if you add an empty string, '', to a number, you convert it to a string, something you normally do with toString().

On the fourth line, we set the date to the current day of the month, the value returned by originalDate.getDate() plus the number of days to be added; then comes the calculation, and the final line outputs the date contained in the Date object as a string using the toString()

method. If you're using IE5.5+ or Gecko-based browsers (Mozilla, Netscape >6), `toDateString()` produces a nicely formatted string using the date alone. You can use the same methods for `get` and `set` if you're working with UTC time—all you need to do is add UTC to the method name. So `getHours()` becomes `getUTCHours()`, `setMonth()` becomes `setUTCMonth()`, and so on. You can also use the `getTimezoneOffset()` method to return the difference, in hours, between the computer's local time and UTC time. (You'll have to rely on users having set their time zones correctly, and be aware of the differences in daylight saving time between different countries.)

Note For crucial date manipulation, JavaScript might not be the correct technology, as you cannot trust the client computer to be properly set up. You could, however, populate the initial date of your JavaScript via a server-side language and go from there.

The Math Object

The `Math` object provides us with lots of mathematical functionality, like finding the square of a number or producing a random number. The `Math` object is different from the `Date` and `String` objects in two ways:

- You can't create a `Math` object explicitly, you just go ahead and use it.

- The `Math` object doesn't store data, unlike the `String` and `Date` object.

You call the methods of the `Math` object using the format:

```
Math.methodOfMathObject( aNumber ):
alert( "The value of pi is " + Math.PI );
```

We'll look at a few of the commonly used methods next (you can find a complete reference by running a search at `http://www.mozilla.org/docs/web-developer/`). We'll look at the methods for rounding numbers and generating random numbers here.

Rounding Numbers

You saw earlier that the `parseInt()` function will make a fractional number whole by removing everything after the decimal point (so 24.999 becomes 24). Pretty often you'll want more mathematically accurate calculations, if you're working with financial calculations, for example, and for these you can use one of the `Math` object's three rounding functions: `round()`, `ceil()`, and `floor()`. This is how they work:

- `round()`: Rounds a number up when the decimal is .5 or greater

- `ceil()` **(as in ceiling)**: Always rounds up, so 23.75 becomes 24, as does 23.25

- `floor()`: Always rounds down, so 23.75 becomes 23, as does 23.25

Here they are at work in a simple example:

```
<html>
  <body>
    <script type="text/javascript">
      var numberToRound = prompt( "Please enter a number", "" )
      document.write( "round( ) = " + Math.round( numberToRound ) );
      document.write( "<br>" );
      document.write( "floor( ) = " + Math.floor( numberToRound ) );
      document.write( "<br>" );
      document.write( "ceil( ) = " + Math.ceil( numberToRound ) );
    </script>
  </body>
</html>
```

Even though we used prompt() to obtain a value from the user, which as we saw earlier returns a string, the number returned is still treated as a number. This is because the rounding methods do the conversion for us just so long as the string contains something that can be converted to a number.

If we enter 23.75, we get the following result:

```
round() = 24
floor() = 23
ceil() = 24
```

If we enter -23.75, we get

```
round() = -24
floor() = -24
ceil() = -23
```

Generating a Random Number

You can generate a fractional random number that is 0 or greater but smaller than 1 using the Math object's random() method. Usually you'll need to multiply the number, and then use one of the rounding methods in order to make it useful.

For example, in order to mimic a die throw, we'd need to generate a random number between 1 and 6. We could create this by multiplying the random fraction by 5, to give a fractional number between 0 and 5, and then round the number up or down to a whole number using the round() method. (We couldn't just multiply by 6 and then round up every time using ceil(), because that would give us the occasional 0.) Then we'd have a whole number between

0 and 5, so by adding 1, we can get a number between 1 and 6. This approach won't give you a perfectly balanced die, but it's good enough for most purposes. Here's the code:

```html
<html>
  <body>
    <script type="text/javascript">
      var diceThrow = Math.round( Math.random( ) * 5 ) + 1;
      document.write( "You threw a " + diceThrow );
    </script>
  </body>
</html>
```

Arrays

JavaScript allows us to store and access related data using an **array**. An array is a bit like a row of boxes (**elements**), each box containing a single item of data. An array can work with any of the data types that JavaScript supports. So, for example, you could use an array to work with a list of items that the users will select from, or for a set of graph coordinates, or to reference a group of images.

Array objects, like String and Date objects, are created using the new keyword together with the constructor. We can initialize an Array object when we create it:

```
var preInitArray = new Array( "First item", "Second item",➡
  "Third Item" );
```

Or set it to hold a certain number of items:

```
var preDeterminedSizeArray = new Array( 3 );
```

Or just create an empty array:

```
var anArray = new Array();
```

You can add new items to an array by assigning values to the elements:

```
anArray[0] = "anItem"
anArray[1] = "anotherItem"
anArray[2] = "andAnother"
```

■**Tip** You do not have to use the array() constructor; instead it is perfectly valid to use a shortcut notation:

```
var myArray = [1, 2, 3];
var yourArray = ["red", "blue", "green"]
```

Once we've populated an array, we can access its elements through their indexes or positions (which, once again, are zero-based) using square brackets:

```
<html>
  <body>
    <script type="text/javascript">
      var preInitArray = new Array( "First Item",➥
"Second Item", "Third Item" );
      document.write( preInitArray[0] + "<br>" );
      document.write( preInitArray[1] + "<br>" );
      document.write( preInitArray[2] + "<br>" );
    </script>
  </body>
</html>
```

Using index numbers to store items is useful if you want to loop through the array—we'll be looking at loops next.

You can use keywords to access the array elements instead of a numerical index, like this:

```
<html>
  <body>
    <script type="text/javascript">
      // Creating an array object and setting index
      // position 0 to equal the string Fruit
      var anArray = new Array( );
      anArray[0] = "Fruit";
      // Setting the index using the keyword
      // 'CostOfApple' as the index.
      anArray["CostOfApple"] = 0.75;
      document.write( anArray[0] + "<br>" );
      document.write( anArray["CostOfApple"] );
    </script>
  </body>
</html>
```

Keywords are good for situations where you can give the data useful labels, or if you're storing entries that are only meaningful in context, like a list of graph coordinates. You can't, however, access entries using an index number if they have been set using keywords (as you can in some other languages, like PHP). We can also use variables for the index. We can rewrite the previous example using variables (one holding a string and the other a number), instead of literal values:

```
<html>
  <body>
    <script type="text/javascript">
      var anArray = new Array( );
      var itemIndex = 0;
      var itemKeyword = "CostOfApple";
```

```
        anArray[itemIndex] = "Fruit";
        anArray[itemKeyword] = 0.75;
        document.write( anArray[itemIndex] + "<br>" );
        document.write( anArray[itemKeyword] );
      </script>
    </body>
</html>
```

Let's put what we've discussed about arrays and the Math object into an example. We'll write a script that randomly selects a banner to display at the top of the page.

We'll use an Array object to hold some image source names, like this:

```
var bannerImages = new Array();
bannerImages[0] = "Banner1.jpg";
bannerImages[1] = "Banner2.jpg";
bannerImages[2] = "Banner3.jpg";
bannerImages[3] = "Banner4.jpg";
bannerImages[4] = "Banner5.jpg";
bannerImages[5] = "Banner6.jpg";
bannerImages[6] = "Banner7.jpg";
```

Then we need six images with corresponding names to sit in the same folder as the HTML page. You can use your own or download mine from http://www.beginningjavascript.com.

Next we'll initialize a new variable, randomImageIndex, and use it to generate a random number. We'll use the same method that we used to generate a random die throw earlier, but without adding 1 to the result because we need a random number from 0 to 6:

```
var randomImageIndex = Math.round( Math.random( ) * 6 );
```

Then we'll use document.write() to write the randomly selected image into the page. Here's the complete script:

```
<html>
  <body>
    <script type="text/javascript">
      var bannerImages = new Array( );
      bannerImages[0] = "Banner1.jpg";
      bannerImages[1] = "Banner2.jpg";
      bannerImages[2] = "Banner3.jpg";
      bannerImages[3] = "Banner4.jpg";
      bannerImages[4] = "Banner5.jpg";
      bannerImages[5] = "Banner6.jpg";
      bannerImages[6] = "Banner7.jpg";
      var randomImageIndex = Math.round( Math.random( ) * 6 );
      document.write( "<img alt=\"\" src=\"" + ➥
bannerImages[randomImageIndex] + "\">" );
    </script>
  </body>
</html>
```

And that's all there is to it. Having the banner change will make it more noticeable to visitors than if you displayed the same banner every time they came to the page—and, of course, it gives the impression that the site is being updated frequently.

The Array Object's Methods and Properties

One of the most commonly used properties of the Array object is the length property, which returns the index one count higher than the index of the last array item in the array. If, for example, you're working with an array with elements with indexes of 0, 1, 2, 3, the length will be 4—which is useful to know if you want to add another element.

The Array object provides a number of methods for manipulating arrays, including methods for cutting a number of items from an array, or joining two arrays together. We'll look at the methods for concatenating, slicing, and sorting next.

Cutting a Slice of an Array

The slice() method is to an Array object what the substring() method is to a String object. You simply tell the method which elements you want to be sliced. This would be useful, for example, if you wanted to slice information being passed using a URL.

The slice() method takes two parameters: the index of the first element of the slice, which will be included in the slice, and the index of the final element, which won't be. To access the second, third, and fourth values from an array holding five values in all, we use the indexes 1 and 4:

```
<html>
  <body>
    <script type="text/javascript">
      // Create and initialize the array
      var fullArray = new Array( "One", "Two", "Three",➥
"Four", "Five" );
      // Slice from element 1 to element 4 and store
      // in new variable sliceOfArray
      var sliceOfArray = fullArray.slice( 1, 4 );
      // Write out new ( zero-based ) array of 3 elements
      document.write( sliceOfArray[0] + "<br>" );
      document.write( sliceOfArray[1] + "<br>" );
      document.write( sliceOfArray[2] + "<br>" );
    </script>
  </body>
</html>
```

The new array stores the numbers in a new zero-based array, so slicing indexes 0, 1, and 2 gives us the following:

Two
Three
Four

The original array is unaffected, but you could overwrite the `Array` object in the variable by setting it to the result of the `slice()` method if you needed to:

```
fullArray = fullArray.slice( 1, 4 );
```

Joining Two Arrays

The `Array` object's `concat()` method allows us to concatenate arrays. We can add two or more arrays using this method, each new array starting where the previous one ends. Here we're joining three arrays: `arrayOne`, `arrayTwo`, and `arrayThree`:

```
<html>
  <body>
    <script type="text/javascript">
      var arrayOne = new Array( "One", "Two", "Three",➥
 "Four", "Five" );
      var arrayTwo = new Array( "ABC", "DEF", "GHI" );
      var arrayThree = new Array( "John", "Paul", "George",➥
 "Ringo" );
      var joinedArray = arrayOne.concat( arrayTwo, arrayThree );
      document.write( "joinedArray has " + joinedArray.length +➥
 " elements<br>" );
      document.write( joinedArray[0] + "<br>" )
      document.write( joinedArray[11] + "<br>" )
    </script>
  </body>
</html>
```

The new array, `joinedArray`, has 12 items. The items in this array are the same as they were in each of the previous arrays; they've simply been concatenated together. The original arrays remain untouched.

Converting an Array to a String and Back

Having data in an array is dead handy when you want to loop through it or select certain elements. However, when you need to send the data somewhere else, it might be a good idea to convert that data to a string. You could do that by looping through the array and adding each element value to a string. However, there is no need for that, as the `Array` object has a method called `join()` that does that for you. The method takes a string as a parameter. This string will be added in between each element.

```
<script type="text/javascript">
  var arrayThree = new Array( "John", "Paul", "George",➥
 "Ringo" );
  var lineUp=arrayThree.join( ',  ' );
  alert( lineUp );
</script>
```

The resulting string, lineUp, has the value "John, Paul, George, Ringo". The opposite of join() is split(), which is a method that converts a string to an array.

```
<script type="text/javascript">
  var lineUp="John, Paul, George, Ringo";
  var members=lineUp.split( ', ' );
  alert( members.length );
</script>
```

Sorting an Array

The sort() method allows us to sort the items in an array into alphabetical or numerical order:

```
<html>
  <body>
    <script type="text/javascript">
      var arrayToSort = new Array( "Cabbage", "Lemon",➥
"Apple", "Pear", "Banana" );
      var sortedArray = arrayToSort.sort( );
      document.write( sortedArray[0] + "<br>" );
      document.write( sortedArray[1] + "<br>" );
      document.write( sortedArray[2] + "<br>" );
      document.write( sortedArray[3] + "<br>" );
      document.write( sortedArray[4] + "<br>" );
    </script>
  </body>
</html>
```

The items are arranged like this:

```
Apple
Banana
Cabbage
Lemon
Pear
```

If, however, you lower the case of one of the letters—the *A* of *Apple*, for example—then you'll end up with a very different result. The sorting is strictly mathematical—by the number of the character in the ASCII set, not like a human being would sort the words.

If you wanted to change the order the sorted elements are displayed, you can use the reverse() method to display the last in the alphabet as the first element:

```
<script type="text/javascript">
  var arrayToSort = new Array( "Cabbage", "Lemon", ➥
"Apple", "Pear", "Banana" );
  var sortedArray = arrayToSort.sort( );
  var reverseArray = sortedArray.reverse( );
  document.write( reverseArray[0] + "<br />" );
  document.write( reverseArray[1] + "<br />" );
  document.write( reverseArray[2] + "<br />" );
  document.write( reverseArray[3] + "<br />" );
  document.write( reverseArray[4] + "<br />" );
</script>
```

The resulting list is now in reverse order:

Pear
Lemon
Cabbage
Banana
Apple

Making Decisions in JavaScript

Decision making is what gives programs their apparent intelligence. You can't write a good program without it, whether you're creating a game, checking a password, giving the user a set of choices based on previous decisions they have made, or something else.

Decisions are based on conditional statements, which are simply statements that evaluate to true or false. This is where the primitive Boolean data type comes in useful. Loops are the other essential tool of decision making, enabling you to loop through user input or an array, for example, and make decisions accordingly.

The Logical and Comparison Operators

There are two main groups of operators we'll look at:

- **Data comparison operators**: Compare operands and return Boolean values.

- **Logical operators**: Test for more than one condition.

We'll start with the comparison operators.

Comparing Data

Table 2-3 lists some of the more commonly used comparison operators.

Table 2-3. *Comparisons in JavaScript*

Operator	Description	Example
==	Checks whether the left and right operands are equal	123 == 234 returns false. 123 == 123 returns true.
!=	Checks whether the left operand is not equal to the right side	123 != 123 returns false. 123 != 234 returns true.
>	Checks whether the left operand is greater than the right	123 > 234 returns false. 234 > 123 returns true.
>=	Checks whether the left operand is greater than or equal to the right	123 >= 234 returns false. 123 >= 123 returns true.
<	Checks whether the left operand is less than the right	234 < 123 returns false. 123 < 234 returns true.
<=	Checks whether the left operand is less than, or equal to, the right	234 <= 123 returns false. 234 <= 234 returns true.

■Caution Beware the == equality operator: it's all too easy to create errors in a script by using the assignment operator, =, by mistake.

These operators all work with string type data as well as numerical data, and are case sensitive:

```
<html>
  <body>
    <script type="text/javascript">
      document.write( "Apple" == "Apple" )
      document.write( "<br />" );
      document.write( "Apple" < "Banana" )
      document.write( "<br />" );
      document.write( "apple" < "Banana" )
    </script>
  </body>
</html>
```

This is what you should get back:

```
true
true
false
```

When evaluating an expression comparing strings, the JavaScript interpreter compares the ASCII codes for each character in turn of both strings—the first character of each string, then the second character, and so on. Uppercase *A* is represented in ASCII by the number 65, *B* by 66, *C* by 67, and so on. To evaluate the expression "Apple" < "Banana", the JavaScript interpreter tests the comparison by substituting the ASCII code for the first character in each string: 65 < 66, so *A* sorts first, and the comparison is true. When testing the expression "apple" < "Banana", the JavaScript interpreter does the same thing; however, the lowercase letter *a* has the ASCII code 97, so the expression "a" < "B" reduces to 97 < 66, which is false. You can do alphabetical comparisons using <, <=, >, >= operators. If you need to ensure that all the letters are of the same case, you can use the String object's toUpperCase( ) and toLowerCase( ) methods. Comparison operators, just like the numerical operators, can be used with variables. If we wanted to compare apple and Banana alphabetically, we'd do this:

```
<html>
  <body>
    <script type="text/javascript">
      var string1 = "apple";
      var string2 = "Banana";
      string1 = string1.toLowerCase( );
      string2 = string2.toLowerCase( );
      document.write( string1 < string2 )
    </script>
  </body>
</html>
```

There is something else you need to be aware of when you're comparing String objects using the equality operator, though. Try this:

```
<html>
  <body>
    <script type="text/javascript">
      var string1 = new String( "Apple" );
      var string2 = new String( "Apple" );
      document.write( string1 == string2 )
    </script>
  </body>
</html>
```

You'll get `false` returned. In fact, what we've done here is compare two `String` *objects* rather than the *characters* of two string primitives and, as the returned `false` indicates, two `String` objects can't be the same object even if they do hold the same characters.

If you do need to compare the strings held by two objects, then you can use the `valueOf()` method to perform a comparison of the data values:

```
<html>
  <body>
    <script type="text/javascript">
      var string1 = new String( "Apple" );
      var string2 = new String( "Apple" );
      document.write( string1.valueOf() == string2.valueOf() );
    </script>
  </body>
</html>
```

Logical Operators

Sometimes you'll need to combine comparisons into one condition group. You might want to check that the information users have given makes sense, or restrict the selections they can make according to their earlier answers. You can do this using the logical operators shown in Table 2-4.

Table 2-4. *Logical Operators in JavaScript*

Symbol	Operator	Description	Example
&&	And	Both conditions must be true.	123 == 234 && 123 < 20 (false) 123 == 234 && 123 == 123 (false) 123 == 123 && 234 < 900 (true)
||	Or	Either or both of the conditions must be true.	123 == 234 || 123 < 20 (false) 123 == 234 || 123 == 123 (true) 123 == 123 || 234 < 900 (true)
!	Not	Reverses the logic.	!(123 == 234) (true) !(123 == 123) (false)

Once we've evaluated the data, we need to be able to make decisions according to the outcome. This is where conditional statements and loops come in useful. You'll find that the operators that we've looked at in this chapter are most often used in the context of a conditional statement or loop.

Conditional Statements

The if...else structure is used to test conditions and looks like this:

```
if ( condition ) {
// Execute code in here if condition is true
} else {
// Execute code in here if condition is false
}
// After if/else code execution resumes here
```

If the condition being tested is true, the code within the curly braces following the if will be executed, but won't if it isn't. You can also create a block of code to execute should the condition set out in the if *not* be met, by using a final else statement.

Let's improve on the currency exchange converter we built earlier on in the chapter and create a loop to deal with nonnumeric input from the user:

```
<html>
  <body>
    <script type="text/javascript">
      var euroToDollarRate = 0.872;
      // Try to convert the input into a number
      var eurosToConvert = Number( prompt( "How many Euros➡
 do you wish to convert", "" ) );
      // If the user hasn't entered a number,  then NaN
      // will be returned
      if ( isNaN( eurosToConvert ) ) {
        // Ask the user to enter a value in numerals
        document.write( "Please enter the number in numerals" );
        // If NaN is not returned,  then we can use the input
      } else {
        // and do the conversion as before
        var dollars = eurosToConvert * euroToDollarRate;
        document.write( eurosToConvert + " euros is " + ➡
dollars + " dollars" );
      }
    </script>
  </body>
</html>
```

The if statement is using the isNaN()function, which will return true if the value in variable eurosToConvert is not a number.

■**Note** Remember to keep error messages as polite and helpful as possible. Good error messages that inform users clearly what is expected of them make using applications much more painless.

We can create more complex conditions by using logical operators and nesting `if` statements:

```
<html>
  <body>
    <script type="text/javascript">
      // Ask the user for a number and try to convert the
      // input into a number
      var userNumber = Number( prompt( "Enter a number between➥
1 and 10", "" ) );
        // If the value of userNumber is NaN, ask the user
        // to try again
      if ( isNaN( userNumber ) ) {
        document.write( "Please ensure a valid number is ➥
entered" );
        // If the value is a number but over 10, ask the
        //user to try again
      } else {
        if ( userNumber > 10 || userNumber < 1 ) {
          document.write( "The number you entered is not➥
between 1 and 10" );
        // Otherwise the number is between 1 and 10 so
        // write to the page
        } else {
          document.write( "The number you entered was " + userNumber );
        }
      }
    </script>
  </body>
</html>
```

We know that the number is fine just so long as it is a numeric value and is under 10.

■**Note** Observe the layout of the code. We have indented the `if` and `else` statements and blocks so that it's easy to read and to see where code blocks start and stop. It's essential to make your code as legible as possible.

Try reading this code without the indenting or spacing:

```
<html>
<body>
<script type="text/javascript">
// Ask for a number using the prompt() function and try to make it a number
var userNumber = Number(prompt("Enter a number between 1 and 10",""));
// If the value of userNumber is NaN, ask the user to try again
if (isNaN(userNumber)){
document.write("Please ensure a valid number is entered");
}
// If the value is a number but over 10, ask the user to try again
else {
if (userNumber > 10 || userNumber < 1) {
document.write("The number you entered is not between 1 and 10");
}
// Otherwise the number is between 1 and 10, so write to the screen
else{
document.write("The number you entered was " + userNumber);
}
}
</script>
</body>
</html>
```

It's not impossible to read, but even in this short script, it's harder to decipher which code blocks belong to the if and else statements. In longer pieces of code, inconsistent indenting or illogical indenting makes code very difficult to read, which in turn leaves you with more bugs to fix and makes your job unnecessarily harder.

You can also use else if statements, where the else statement starts with another if statement, like this:

```
<html>
  <body>
    <script type="text/javascript">
      var userNumber = Number( prompt( "Enter a number between➡
1 and 10", "" ) );
      if ( isNaN( userNumber ) ){
        document.write( "Please ensure a valid number is➡
entered" );
      } else if ( userNumber > 10 || userNumber < 1 ) {
        document.write( "The number you entered is not➡
between 1 and 10" );
      } else {
```

```
        document.write( "The number you entered was " + ➡
userNumber );
    }
  </script>
 </body>
</html>
```

The code does the same thing as the earlier piece, but uses an else if statement instead of a nested if, and is two lines shorter.

Breaking Out of a Branch or Loop

One more thing before we move on: you can break a conditional statement or loop using the break statement. This simply terminates the block of code running and drops the processing through to the next statement. We'll be using this in the next example.

You can have as many if, else, and else ifs as you like, although they can make your code terribly complicated if you use too many. If there are a lot of possible conditions to check a value against in a piece of code, then the switch statement, which we'll look at next, can be helpful.

Testing Multiple Values: the switch Statement

The switch statement allows us to "switch" between sections of code based on the value of a variable or expression. This is the outline of a switch statement:

```
switch( expression ) {
  case someValue:
  // Code to execute if expression == someValue;
  break; // End execution
  case someOtherValue:
  // Code to execute if expression == someOtherValue;
  break; // End execution
  case yesAnotherValue:
  // Code to execute if expression == yetAnotherValue;
  break; // End execution
  default:
  // Code to execute if no values matched
}
```

JavaScript evaluates switch (expression), and then compares it to each case. As soon as a match is found, the code starts executing at that point and continues through all the case statements until a break is found. It's often useful to include a default case that will execute if none of the case statements match. This is a helpful tool for picking up on errors, where, for example, we expect a match to occur but a bug prevents that from happening.

The values of the cases can be of any data type, numbers or strings, for example. We can have just one or as many cases as we need. Let's look at a simple example:

```html
<html>
  <body>
    <script type="text/javascript">
      // Store user entered number between 1 and 4 in userNumber
      var userNumber = Number( prompt( "Enter a number between 1 and 4", "" ) );
      switch( userNumber ) {
        // If userNumber is 1,  write out and carry on
        // executing after case statement
        case 1:
          document.write( "Number 1" );
        break;
        case 2:
          document.write( "Number 2" );
        break;
        case 3:
          document.write( "Number 3" );
        break;
        case 4:
          document.write( "Number 4" );
        break;
        default:
          document.write( "Please enter a numeric value between➥
  1 and 4." );
        break;
      }
      // Code continues executing here
    </script>
  </body>
</html>
```

Try it out. You should just get the number that you've entered written out or the sentence "Please enter a numeric value between 1 and 4."

This example also illustrates the importance of the break statement. If we hadn't included break after each case, execution would have carried on within the block until the end of the switch. Try removing the breaks and then enter 2. Everything after the match will execute, giving you this output:

```
Number 2Number 3Number 4Please enter a numeric value between 1 and 4
```

You can use any valid expression inside the switch statement—a calculation, for example:

```
switch( userNumber * 100 + someOtherVariable )
```

You can also have one or more statements in between the case statements.

Repeating Things: Loops

In this section, we look at how we can repeat a block of code for as long as a set condition is true. For example, we might want to loop through each input element on an HTML form or through each item in an array.

Repeating a Set Number of Times: the for Loop

The for loop is designed to loop through a code block a number of times and looks like this:

```
for( initial-condition; loop-condition; alter-condition ) {
  //
  // Code to be repeatedly executed
  //
}
// After loop completes,  execution of code continues here
```

Like the conditional statement, the for keyword is followed by parentheses. This time, the parentheses contain three parts separated by a semicolon.

The first part initializes a variable that will serve as the counter to keep track of the number of loops made. The second part tests for a condition. The loop will keep running as long as this condition is true. The last part either increments or decrements the counter, created in the first part, after each loop (the fact that it is *after* is an important one in programming as you shall see).

For example, take a look at a loop that keeps running for as long as loopCounter is less than 10:

```
for( loopCounter = 1; loopCounter <= 10; loopCounter++ )
```

The loop keeps executing as long as the loop condition evaluates to true—for as long as loopCounter is less than or equal to 10. Once it hits 11, the looping stops and execution of the code continues at the next statement after the loop's closing parenthesis.

Let's look at an example that uses the for loop to run through an array. We'll use a for loop to run through an array called theBeatles using a variable called loopCounter to keep the loop running while the value of loopCounter is less than the length of the array:

```
<html>
  <body>
    <script type="text/javascript">
      var theBeatles = new Array( "John", "Paul", "George",➥
  "Ringo" );
```

```
      for ( var loopCounter = 0; loopCounter < ➡
theBeatles.length; loopCounter++ ) {
         document.write( theBeatles[loopCounter] + "<br>" );
      }
    </script>
  </body>
</html>
```

This example works because we are using a zero-based array in which the items have been added to the index in sequence. The loop wouldn't have run if we'd used keywords to store items in an array like this:

```
theBeatles["Drummer"] = "Ringo";
```

Earlier, when we discussed arrays, I stated that the Array object has a property that knows the length (how many elements). When looping through arrays, such as the previous example, we use the name of the array followed by a dot and length as the condition. This prevents the loop from counting beyond the length of the array, which would cause an "Out of Bounds" error.

JavaScript also supports the for..in loop (which has been around since NN2, although IE has supported it only since IE5). Instead of using a counter, the for...in loop runs though each item in the array using a variable to access the array. Let's create an array this way and see how it works:

```
<html>
  <body>
    <script type="text/javascript">
      // Initialize theBeatles array and store in a variable
      var theBeatles = new Array( );
      // Set the values using keys rather than numbers
      theBeatles["Drummer"] = "Ringo";
      theBeatles["SingerRhythmGuitar"] = "John";
      theBeatles["SingerBassGuitar"] = "Paul";
      theBeatles["SingerLeadGuitar"] = "George";
      var indexKey;
      // Write out each indexKey and the value for that
      // indexKey from the array
      for ( indexKey in theBeatles ) {
        document.write( "indexKey is " + indexKey + "<br>" );
        document.write( "item value is " + theBeatles[indexKey] + "<br><br>" );
      }
    </script>
  </body>
</html>
```

The results of the item key in indexKey at each iteration of the loop is written out alongside the value extracted from the array using that key in the same order as it occurs in the array:

```
indexKey is Drummer
item value is Ringo

indexKey is SingerRhythmGuitar
item value is John

indexKey is SingerBassGuitar
item value is Paul

indexKey is SingerLeadGuitar
item value is George
```

Repeating Actions According to a Decision: the `while` Loop

The loops we have been working with so far take the instruction to stop looping from inside the script itself. There are likely to be times when you'll want the user to determine when the loop should stop, or for the loop to stop when a certain user-led condition is met. The while and do...while loops are intended for just this sort of situation.

In its simplest form, a while loop looks like this:

```
while ( some condition true ) {
  // Loop code
}
```

The condition inside the curly braces can be anything you might use in an if statement. We could use some code like this to allow users to enter numbers and stop the entering process by typing the number 99.

```
<html>
  <body>
    <script type="text/javascript">
      var userNumbers = new Array( );
      var userInput = 0;
      var arrayIndex = 0;
      var message = '';
      var total = 0;
      // Loop for as long as the user doesn't input 99
      while ( userInput != 99 ) {
        userInput = prompt( "Enter a number,  or 99 to exit",➥
"99" );
        userNumbers[arrayIndex] = userInput;
        arrayIndex++;
      }
```

```
      message += 'You entered the following:\n';
      for ( var i = 0; i < arrayIndex-1; i++ ) {
        message += userNumbers[i] + '\n';
        total += Number( userNumbers[i] );
      }
      message += 'Total: ' + total + '\n';
      alert( message );
    </script>
  </body>
</html>
```

Here the while loop's condition is that userInput is not equal to 99, so the loop will continue so long as that condition is true. When the user enters 99 and the condition is tested, it will evaluate to false and the loop will end. Note the loop doesn't end as soon as the user enters 99, but only when the condition is tested again at the start of another iteration of the loop.

There is one small but significant difference between the while loop and the do...while: the while loop tests the condition before the code is executed, and only executes the code block if the condition is true, while the do...while loop executes the code block before testing the condition, only doing another iteration if the condition is true. In short, the do...while loop is useful when you know you want the loop code to execute at least once before the condition is tested. We could write our previous example with a do...while loop like this:

```
<html>
  <body>
    <script type="text/javascript">
      var userNumbers = new Array( );
      var message = '';
      var total = 0;
      // Declare the userInput but don't initialize it
      var userInput;
      var arrayIndex = 0;
      do {
        userInput = prompt( "Enter a number,  or 99 to exit",➥
  "99" );
        userNumbers[arrayIndex] = userInput;
        arrayIndex++;
      } while ( userInput != 99 )
      message+='You entered the following:\n';
      for ( var i = 0; i < arrayIndex-1; i++ ) {
        message += userNumbers[i] + '\n';
        total += Number( userNumbers[i] );
      }
      message += 'Total: ' + total + '\n';
      alert( message );
    </script>
  </body>
</html>
```

We don't need to initialize userInput because the code inside the loop sets a value for it before testing it for the first time.

Continuing the Loop

As you've already seen, the break statement is great for breaking out of any kind of loop once a certain event has occurred. The continue keyword works like break in that it stops the execution of the loop. However, instead of dropping out of the loop, continue causes execution to resume with the next iteration.

Let's first alter the previous example so that if the user enters something other than a number, the value is not recorded and the loop finishes, using break:

```
<html>
  <body>
    <script type="text/javascript">
      var userNumbers = new Array( );
      var userInput;
      var arrayIndex = 0;
      do {
        userInput = Number( prompt( "Enter a number, or 99➼
  to exit", "99" ) );
        // Check that user input is a valid number,
        // and if not,  break with error msg
        if ( isNaN( userInput ) ) {
          document.write( "Invalid data entered: please➼
  enter a number between 0 and 99 in numerals" );
          break;
        }
        // If break has been activated,  code will continue from here
        userNumbers[arrayIndex] = userInput;
        arrayIndex++;
      } while ( userInput != 99 )
      // Next statement after loop
    </script>
  </body>
</html>
```

Now let's change it again, so that we don't break out of the loop but instead just ignore the user's input and keep looping, using the continue statement:

```
<html>
  <body>
    <script type="text/javascript">
      var userNumbers = new Array( );
      var userInput;
      var arrayIndex = 0;
      do {
        userInput = prompt( "Enter a number, or 99 to exit",➼
  "99" );
```

```
        if ( isNaN( userInput ) ) {
            document.write( "Invalid data entered: please ➡
enter a number between 0 and 99 in numerals " );
            continue;
        }
        userNumbers[arrayIndex] = userInput;
        arrayIndex++;
    } while ( userInput != 99 )
    // Next statement after loop
    </script>
  </body>
</html>
```

The break statement has been replaced with continue, so no more code will be executed in the loop, and the condition inside the while statement will be evaluated again. If the condition is true, another iteration of the loop will occur; otherwise the loop ends.

Use the following rules of thumb in deciding which looping structure to use:

- Use a for loop if you want to repeat an action a set number of times.

- Use a while loop when you want an action to be repeated until a condition is met.

- Use a do...while loop if you want to guarantee that the action will be performed at least once.

Summary

We've covered a lot of ground in this chapter: in fact, we've discussed most of the essentials of the JavaScript language.

You've learned how JavaScript handles data and seen that there are a number of data types: string, number, Boolean, and object, as well as some special types of data like NaN, null, and undefined. You saw that JavaScript supplies a number of operators that perform operations on data, such as numerical calculations or joining strings together.

We then looked at how JavaScript allows us to store values using variables. Variables last for the lifetime of the page, or the lifetime of the function if they are inside a user-created function and declared locally via the var keyword. We also looked at how to convert one type of data to another.

Next we worked with three JavaScript built-in objects: the String, Date, and Math objects. You saw that these provide useful functionality for manipulating strings, dates, and numbers. I also showed you the Array object, which allows a number of items of data to be stored in a single variable.

We finished the chapter by looking at decision making, which provides the logic or intelligence of a programming language. We used if and switch statements to make decisions, using conditions to test the validity of data and acting upon the findings. Loops also use conditions and allow us to repeat a block of code for a certain number of times or while a condition is true.

■■■

CHAPTER 3

From DHTML to DOM Scripting

In this chapter, you'll learn what DHTML was, why it is regarded as a bad way to go nowadays, and what modern techniques and ideas should be used instead. You'll learn what functions are, and how to use them. You'll also hear about variable and function scope and some state-of-the-art best practices that'll teach your scripts how to play extremely well with others.

If you are interested in JavaScript and you have searched the Web for scripts, you surely have come upon the term **DHTML**. DHTML was one of the big buzz words of the IT and web development industry in the late 1990s and beginning of the millennium. You may have seen a lot of tutorials about achieving a certain visual effect on now outdated browsers rather than explaining why this effect makes sense and what the script does. And that is exactly what DHTML was about.

Note DHTML, or Dynamic HTML, was never a real technology or World Wide Web Consortium (W3C) standard, merely a term invented by marketing and advertising agencies.

DHTML is JavaScript interacting with Cascading Style Sheets (CSS) and web documents (written in HTML) to create seemingly dynamic pages. Parts of the page had to fly around and zoom out and in, every element on the page needed to react when the visitor passed over it with the mouse cursor, and we invented a new way of web navigation every week.

While all this was great fun and a technological challenge, it did not help visitors much. The "wow" effect lost its impact rather quickly, especially when their browsers were unable to support it and they ended up on a page that was a dead end for them.

As DHTML sounded like a great term, it did bring out a kind of elitism: JavaScript developers who were "in the know" did not bother much with keeping the code maintainable, as anybody who didn't understand the art of making things move was not worth changing their code for in any case. For freelance developers, it also meant a steady income, as every change had to be done by them.

When the big money stopped coming in, a lot of this code got thrown out on the Web for other developers to use, either as large JavaScript DHTML libraries or as small scripts on script collection sites. Nobody bothered to update the code, which means that it is unlikely that these resources are a viable option to use in a modern professional environment.

Common DHTML scripts have several issues:

- **JavaScript dependence and lack of graceful degradation**: Visitors with JavaScript turned off (either by choice or because of their company security settings) will not get the functionality, but elements that don't do anything when they activate them or even pages that cannot be navigated at all.

- **Browser and version dependence**: A common way to test whether the script can be executed was to read out the browser name in the navigator object. As a lot of these scripts were created when Netscape 4 and Internet Explorer 5 were state-of-the-art, they fail to support newer browsers—the reason being browser detection that doesn't take newer versions into account and just tests for versions 4 or 5.

- **Code forking**: As different browsers supported different DOMs, a lot of code needed to be duplicated and several browser quirks avoided. This also made it difficult to write modular code.

- **High maintenance**: As most of the look and feel of the script was kept in the script, any change meant you needed to know at least basic JavaScript. As JavaScript was developed for several different browsers, you needed to apply the change in all of the different scripts targeted to each browser.

- **Markup dependence**: Instead of generating or accessing HTML via the DOM, a lot of scripts wrote out content via the document.write directive and added to each document body instead of keeping everything in a separate—cached—document.

All of these stand in a stark contrast to the requirements we currently have to fulfill:

- Code should be cheap to maintain and possible to reuse in several projects.

- Legal requirements like the Digital Discrimination Act (DDA) in the UK and Section 508 in the US strongly advise against or in some cases even forbid web products to be dependent on scripting.

- More browsers, user agents (UAs) on devices such as mobile phones, or assistive technology helping disabled users to take part in the Web make it impossible to keep our scripts dependent on browser identification.

- Newer marketing strategies make it a requirement to change the look and feel of a web site or a web application quickly and without high cost—possibly even by a content management system.

There is a clear need to rethink the way we approach JavaScript as a web technology, if we still want to use and sell it to clients and keep up with the challenge of the changing market.

The first step is to make JavaScript less of a show-stopper by making it a "nice to have" item rather than a requirement. No more empty pages or links that don't do anything when JavaScript is not available. The term **unobtrusive JavaScript** was christened by Stuart Langridge at http://www.kryogenix.org, and if you enter it in Google, you'll end up on an older self-training course on the subject by me.

Unobtrusive JavaScript refers to a script that does not force itself on users or stand in their way. It tests whether it can be applied and does so if it is possible. Unobtrusive JavaScript is like a stagehand—doing what she is good at backstage for the good of the whole production rather than being a diva who takes the whole stage for herself and shouts at the orchestra and her colleagues every time something goes wrong or is not to her liking.

Later on, the term **DOM scripting** got introduced, and in the aftermath of the @media conference in London 2004, the WaSP DOM Scripting Task Force was formed. The task force consists of many coders, bloggers, and designers who want to see JavaScript used in a more mature and user-centered manner—you can check out what it has to say at `http://domscripting.webstandards.org`.

As JavaScript did not have a fixed place in common web development methodologies—instead being considered as either "something you can download from the web and change" or "something that will be generated by the editing tool if it is needed"—the term "behavior layer" came up in various web publications.

JavaScript As "the Behavior Layer"

Web development can be thought of as being made up of several different "layers," as shown in Figure 3-1.

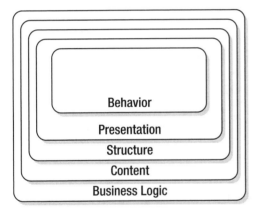

Figure 3-1. *The different layers of web development*

- **The behavior layer**: Is executed on the client and defines how different elements behave when the user interacts with them (JavaScript or ActionScript for Flash sites).

- **The presentation layer**: Is displayed on the client and is the look of the web page (CSS, imagery).

- **The structure layer**: Is converted or displayed by the user agent. This is the markup defining what a certain text or media is (XHTML).

- **The content layer**: Is stored on the server and consists of all the text, images, and multimedia content that are used on the site (XML, database, media assets).

- **The business logic layer (or back end)**: Runs on the server and determines what is done with incoming data and what gets returned to the user.

Notice that this simply defines what layers are available, not how they interact. For example, something needs to convert content to structure (such as XSLT), and something needs to connect the upper four layers with the business logic.

If you manage to keep all these layers separate, yet talking to each other, you will have succeeded in developing an accessible and easy-to-maintain web site. In the real development and business world, this is hardly the case. However, the more you make this your goal, the fewer annoying changes you'll have to face at a later stage. Cascading Style Sheets are powerful because they allow you to define the look and feel of numerous web documents in a single file that will be cached by the user agent. JavaScript can act in the same fashion by using the src attribute of the script tag and a separate .js file.

In earlier chapters of this book, we embedded JavaScript directly in HTML documents (and you may remember that this is tough to do for XHTML documents). This we will not do from this point on; instead, we'll create separate JavaScript files and link to them in the head of the document:

```
<!DOCTYPE HTML PUBLIC "-//W3C//DTD HTML 4.01//EN"
"http://www.w3.org/TR/html4/strict.dtd">
<html dir="ltr" lang="en">
<head>
    <meta http-equiv="Content-Type" content="text/html;➡
        charset=iso-8859-1">
    <title>Demo</title>
    <style type="text/css">@import 'styles.css';</style>
    <script type="text/javascript" src="scripts.js"></script>
    <script type="text/javascript" src="morescripts.js"></script>
  </head>
  <body>
  </body>
</html>
```

We should also try not to use any script blocks inside the document any longer, mainly because that would mix the structure and the behavior layers and can cause a user agent to stop showing the page should a JavaScript error occur. It is also a maintenance nightmare—adding all JavaScript to separate .js files means we can maintain the scripts for a whole site in one place rather than searching through all the documents.

■**Note** While Firefox, Safari, and Opera display .js files as text, Microsoft Internet Explorer tries to execute them. This means that you cannot double-click or point your browser to a JavaScript file to debug it in MSIE—something that is pretty annoying when debugging code. This instant code execution is a security problem, which is why Windows XP2 does flag up any JavaScript content in local files as a security issue as shown in Figure 3-2. Do not get fooled by this—it is your code, and, unless you are a malicious coder, it is not a security issue.

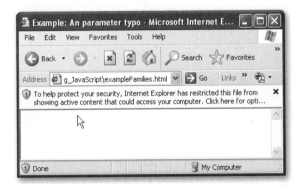

Figure 3-2. *Microsoft Internet Explorer on Windows XP2 shows a warning message when you try to execute JavaScript locally.*

This separation of JavaScript into its own file makes it simpler to develop a web site that still works when the script is not available; and if a change in the site's behavior is needed, it is easy to change only the script files.

This is one of the bad habits of DHTML squashed: HTML can exist without JavaScript, and you do not need to scan a lot of documents to find out where a bug occurred. The next bad habit of DHTML was browser dependence, which we'll now replace with object detection.

Object Detection vs. Browser Dependence

One way to determine which browser is in use is by testing the navigator object, which reveals the name and the version of the browser in its appName and appVersion attributes.

For example, the following script gets the browser name and version and writes it out to the document:

```
<script type=" text/javascript">
  document.write("You are running " + navigator.appName);
  document.write(" and its version is " + navigator.appVersion);
</script>
```

On my computer, inside Macromedia HomeSite's preview mode, this script reports the following (as HomeSite uses the MSIE engine for previewing HTML).

```
You are running Microsoft Internet Explorer
and its version is 4.0 (compatible; MSIE 6.0;
Windows NT 5.1; SV1; .NET CLR 1.1.4322)
```

If I run the same script in Firefox 1.07 on the same computer, I get

```
You are running Netscape and its version is 5.0 (Windows; en-GB)
```

A lot of older scripts use this information to determine whether a browser is capable of supporting their functionality.

```
<script type="text/javascript">
 if(browserName.indexOf('Internet Explorer')!=-1
  && browserVersion.indexOf('6')!=-1)
  {
    document.write('<p>This is MSIE 6!</p>');
  }
  else
  {
    document.write('<p>This isn\'t MSIE 6!</p>');
  }
</script>
```

This appears rather clever at first glance, but as the output of Firefox shows, it is not a bullet-proof method of finding out which browser is in use. Some browsers like Opera won't even reveal themselves to scripts, but appear as Microsoft Internet Explorer instead.

■**Tip** Opera is by default set up to tell scripts that it is MSIE. The reason for this is that Opera Software didn't want its browser to be blocked by web sites that were developed for MSIE only. Sadly enough, a lot of development went that route and Opera Software just didn't want to lose customers or answer a lot of angry e-mails why its "bad" browser doesn't work with web site XYZ. However, it also means that Opera doesn't show up in browser statistics of web sites and remains unimportant for those who just see the visitor numbers and what browser they use (a lot of statistics software uses the `navigator` object). If you are an Opera user and you want to turn off this preset, press F12 and choose "Identify as Opera" instead of "Identify as Internet Explorer."

Reading out the browser name and version—commonly known as **browser sniffing**—is not advisable, not only because of the inconsistencies we just encountered, but also because it makes your script dependent on a certain browser rather than supporting any user agent that is actually capable of supporting the script.

The solution to this problem is called **object detection**, and it basically means that we determine whether a user agent supports a certain object and make this our key differentiator. In really old scripts, like the first image rollovers, you might have seen something like this:

```
<script type="text/ javascript">
  // preloading images
  if(document.images)
```

```
  {
    // Images are supported
    var home=new Image();
    home.src='home.gif';
    var aboutus=new Image();
    aboutus.src='home.gif';
  }
</script>
```

The `if` condition checks whether the browser understands the `images` object, and only runs the code inside the condition if that is the case. For a long time, scripts like these were the standard way of dealing with images. In newer browsers, a lot of the JavaScript image effects can be achieved with CSS, effectively rendering scripts of this kind obsolete. However, Java-Script can manipulate images in ways CSS cannot, and we will come back to this in Chapter 6.

Every browser offers us the document it displays for manipulation, via something called the **Document Object Model**, or **DOM** for short. Older browsers supported their own DOMs, but there is a standard one, defined by the W3C, that is supported by most browsers these days. You might have encountered test scripts like this one in the past:

```
<script type="text/javascript">
  if(document.all)
  {
    // MSIE
  }
  else if (document.layers)
  {
    // Netscape Communicator
  }
  else if (document.getElementById)
  {
    // Mozilla, Opera 6, Safari
  }
</script>
```

The `document.all` DOM was invented by Microsoft and supported by MSIE 4 and 5, while Netscape 4 had its own DOM that supported `document.layers`. You can test for the W3C-recommended DOM via `document.getElementById`, and unless you have a genuine need to support MSIE versions previous to 5.5 or Netscape 4, it is the only one you really need to test for in this day and age.

One problem is that some in-between versions of Opera support the `getElementById` object, but fail to support the entire W3C DOM. To determine whether this is the case, test for support of the `createTextNode` as well:

```
<script type="text/javascript">
  if (document.getElementById && document.createTextNode)
  {
    // Mozilla, Opera 6, Safari
  }
</script>
```

If you embed this test in your scripts in this condition, you can be quite sure that only user agents that do support DOM scripting will execute what you've written. You can save yourself one code indentation by simply returning if neither of the two conditions is true.

```
<script type="text/javascript">
  if (!document.getElementById || !document.createTextNode){return;}
  // Other code
</script>
```

The same idea applies to any other methods to come in the future—as you are checking for a standard defined by the W3C, there is a big chance that user agents will support it—a much bigger chance than any other standard different vendors might come up with. You could also support different user agents on different levels, but this can lead to a lot of code duplication and less-optimized scripts.

Rather than catering to specific user agents, you test for the UA's capabilities before you apply your functionality—a process that is part of a bigger modern web design idea called **progressive enhancement**.

Progressive Enhancement

Progressive enhancement is the practice of providing functionality only to those who can see and use it by starting with a lowest common denominator and then testing whether successive improvements are supported. Users who don't have the capability to support those higher features will still be able to use the web site perfectly adequately. A comparable real-life process is to put on your clothes in the morning:

- You start with a naked body that is hopefully in full working condition—or at least in the same condition as it was yesterday, so that it is no shock to you (we discount PJs and/or underwear to keep this example easy).

- You may have a wonderful nude body, but it is insufficient in cold weather and might not appeal to other people around you—you'll need something to cover it with.

- If there are clothes available, you can check which fit the weather, your mood, the group of people you'll be seeing this day, and whether the different garments are in good order, clean, and are the right sizes.

- You put them on, and you can face the day. If you want to, you can start accessorizing, but please make sure to take other people into consideration when doing so (too much perfume might not be a good idea in a crowded train carriage).

In web development terms, this means the following:

- We start with a valid, semantically correct (X)HTML document with all the content—including relevant images with text alternatives as `alt` attributes—and a meaningful structure.

- We add a style sheet to improve this structure's appearance, legibility, and clarity—possibly we even add some simple rollover effects to liven it up a little.

- We add JavaScript:

  - The JavaScript starts when the document is loaded, by using the `window` object's `onload` event handler.

  - The JavaScript tests whether the current user agent supports the W3C DOM.

  - It then tests whether all the necessary elements are available and applies the desired functionality to them.

Before you can apply the idea of progressive enhancement in JavaScript, you'll need to learn how to access and interact with HTML and CSS from your scripts. I devote two chapters of this book to that task—Chapters 4 and 5. For the moment, however, it is enough to realize that the object detection we have practiced earlier helps us implement progressive enhancement—we make sure that only those browsers understanding the right objects will try to access them.

JavaScript and Accessibility

Web accessibility is the practice of making web sites usable by everybody, regardless of any disabilities they might have—for example, users with visual impairments may well use special software called **screen readers** to read out the web page content to them, and users with motor disabilities may well use a tool of some kind to manipulate the keyboard for navigating around the web, because they are unable to use the mouse. People with disabilities form a significant proportion of web users, so companies that choose not to allow them to use their web sites could well be missing out on a lot of business, and in some countries, legislation (such as Section 508 in the US) means that any sites that provide a public service have to be accessible, by law.

So where does JavaScript come into this? Outdated JavaScript techniques can be very bad for accessibility, because they can mess up the document flow, so, for example, screen readers cannot read them back to the user properly (especially when essential content is generated by JavaScript—there's a chance that the screen reader won't see it at all!) and thus force users to use the mouse to navigate their sites (for example, in the case of complicated DHTML whiz-bang navigation menus). The whole issue goes a lot deeper than this, but this is just to give you a feel for the area.

Tip If you want to read more about web accessibility, pick up a copy of *Web Accessibility: Web Standards and Regulatory Compliance*, by Jim Thatcher et al. (friends of ED, 2006).

JavaScript and accessibility is holy war material. Many a battle between disgruntled developers and accessibility gurus is fought on mailing lists, forums, and in chats, and the two sides all have their own—very good—arguments.

The developers who had to suffer bad browsers and illogical assumptions by marketing managers ("I saw it on my cousin's web site, surely you can also use it for our multinational portal") don't want to see years of research and trial and error go down the drain and not use JavaScript any longer.

The accessibility gurus point out that JavaScript can be turned off, that the accessibility guidelines by the W3C seem not to allow for it at all (a lot of confusion on that in the guidelines), and that a lot of scripts just assume that the visitors have and can use a mouse with the precision of a neurosurgeon.

Both are right, and both can have their cake: **there is no need to completely remove JavaScript from an accessible web site**.

What has to go is JavaScript that assumes too much. Accessible JavaScript has to ensure the following:

- The web document has to have the same content with and without JavaScript—no visitor should be blocked or forced to turn on JavaScript (as it is not always the visitor's decision whether he can turn it on).

- If there is content or HTML elements that only make sense when JavaScript is available, this content and those elements have to be created by JavaScript. Nothing is more frustrating than a link that does nothing or text explaining a slick functionality that is not available to you.

- All JavaScript functionality has to be independent of input device—for example, the user can be able to use a drag-and-drop interface, but should also be able to activate the element via clicking it or pressing a key.

- Elements that are not interactive elements in a page (practically anything but links and form elements) should not become interactive elements—unless you provide a fallback. Confusing? Imagine headlines that collapse and expand the piece of text that follows them. You can easily make them clickable in JavaScript, but that would mean that a visitor dependent on a keyboard will never be able to get to them. If you create a link inside the headlines while making them clickable, even that visitor will be able to activate the effect by "tabbing" to that link and hitting Enter.

- Scripts should not redirect the user automatically to other pages or submit forms without any user interaction. This is to avoid premature submission of forms—as some assistive technology will have problems with onchange event handlers. Furthermore, viruses and spyware send the user to other pages via JavaScript, and this is therefore blocked by some software these days.

That is all there is to make a web site with JavaScript accessible. That and, of course, all the assets of an accessible HTML document like allowing elements to resize with larger font settings, and providing enough contrast and colors that work for the color-blind as well as for people with normal vision.

Good Coding Practices

Now that I hopefully have gotten you into the mindset of forward-compatible and accessible scripting, let's go through some general best practices of JavaScript.

Naming Conventions

JavaScript is case dependent, which means that a variable or a function called moveOption is a different one than moveoption or Moveoption. Any name—no matter whether it is a function, an object, a variable, or an array, must only contain letters, numbers, the dollar sign, or the underscore character, and must not start with a number.

```
<script type="text/javascript">
  // Valid examples
  var dynamicFunctionalityId = 'dynamic';
  var parent_element2='mainnav';
  var _base=10;
  var error_Message='You forgot to enter some fields: ';

  // Invalid examples
  var dynamic ID='dynamic';  // Space not allowed!
  var 10base=10; // Starts with a number
  var while=10; // while is a JavaScript statement
</script>
```

The last example shows another issue: JavaScript has a lot of reserved words—basically all the JavaScript statements use reserved words like while, if, continue, var, or for. If you are unsure what you can use as a variable name, it might be a good idea to get a JavaScript reference. Good editors also highlight reserved words when you enter them to avoid the issue.

There is no length limitation on names in JavaScript; however, to avoid huge scripts that are hard to read and debug, it is a good idea to keep them as easy and descriptive as possible. Try to avoid generic names:

- function1

- variable2

- doSomething()

These do not mean much to somebody else (or yourself two months down the line) who tries to debug or understand the code. It is better to use descriptive names that tell exactly what the function does or what the variable is:

- `createTOC()`

- `calculateDifference()`

- `getCoordinates()`

- `setCoordinates()`

- `maximumWidth`

- `address_data_file`

As mentioned in previous chapters, you can use underscores or "camelCase" (that is, camel notation—lowercasing the first word and then capitalizing the first character of each word after that) to concatenate words; however, camelCase is more common (DOM itself uses it), and getting used to it will make it a lot easier for you to move on to more complex programming languages at a later stage. Another benefit of camelCase is that you can highlight a variable with a double-click in almost any editor, while you need to highlight an underscore-separated name with your mouse.

■**Caution** Beware the lowercase letter *l* and the number *1*! Most editors will use a font face like courier, and they both look the same in this case, which can cause a lot of confusion and make for hours of fun trying to find bugs.

Code Layout

First and foremost, code is there to be converted by the interpreter to make a computer do something—or at least this is a very common myth. The interpreter will swallow the code without a hiccup when the code is valid—however, the real challenge for producing really good code is that a human will be able to edit, debug, amend, or extend it without spending hours trying to figure out what you wanted to achieve. Logical, succinct variable and function names are the first step to make it easier for the maintainer—the next one is proper code layout.

■**Note** If you are really bored, go to any coder forum and drop an absolute like "spaces are better than tabs" or "every curly brace should get a new line." You are very likely to get hundreds of posts that point out the pros and cons of what you claimed. Code layout is a hotly discussed topic. The following examples work nicely for me and seem to be a quite common way of laying out code. It might be a good idea to check whether there are any contradictory standards to follow before joining a multideveloper team on a project and using the ones mentioned here.

Simply check the following code examples; you might not understand now what they do (they present a small function that opens every link that has a CSS class of smallpopup in a new window and adds a message that this is what will happen), but just consider which one would be easier to debug and change?

Without indentation:

```
function addPopUpLink(){
if(!document.getElementById||!document.createTextNode){return;}
var popupClass='smallpopup';
var popupMessage= '(opens in new window)';
var pop,t;
var as=document.getElementsByTagName('a');
for(var i=0;i<as.length;i++){
t=as[i].className;
if(t&&t.toString().indexOf(popupClass)!=-1){
as[i].appendChild(document.createTextNode(popupMessage));
as[i].onclick=function(){
pop=window.open(this.href,'popup','width=400,height=400');
returnfalse;
}}}}
window.onload=addPopUpLink;
```

With indentation:

```
function addPopUpLink(){
  if(!document.getElementById || !document.createTextNode){return;}
  var popupClass='smallpopup';
  var popupMessage= ' (opens in new window)';
  var pop,t;
  var as=document.getElementsByTagName('a');
  for(var i=0;i<as.length;i++){
    t=as[i].className;
    if(t && t.toString().indexOf(popupClass)!=-1){
      as[i].appendChild(popupMessage);
      as[i].onclick=function(){
        pop=window.open(this.href,'popup','width=400,height=400');
        return false;
      }
    }
  }
}
window.onload=addPopUpLink;
```

With indentation and curly braces on new lines:

```
function addPopUpLink()
{
  if(!document.getElementById || !document.createTextNode){return;}
  var popupClass='smallpopup';
  var popupMessage= ' (opens in new window)';
  var pop,t;
  var as=document.getElementsByTagName('a');
  for(var i=0;i<as.length;i++)
  {
    t=as[i].className;
    if(t && t.toString().indexOf(popupClass)!=-1)
    {
      as[i].appendChild(document.createTextNode(popupMessage));
      as[i].onclick=function()
      {
        pop=window.open(this.href,'popup','width=400,height=400');
        return false;
      }
    }
  }
}
window.onload=addPopUpLink;
```

I think it is rather obvious that indentation is a good idea; however, there is a big debate whether you should indent via tabs or spaces. Personally, I like tabs, mainly because they are easy to delete and less work to type in. Developers that work a lot on very basic (or pretty amazing, if you know all the cryptic keyboard shortcuts) editors like vi or emacs frown upon that, as the tabs might display as very large horizontal gaps. If that is the case, it is not much of a problem to replace all tabs with double spaces with a simple regular expression.

The question of whether the opening curly braces should get a new line or not is another you need to decide for yourself. The benefit of not using a new line is that it is easier to delete erroneous blocks, as they have one line less. The benefit of new lines is that the code does look less crammed. Personally, I keep the opening one on the same line in JavaScript and on a new line in PHP—as these seem to be the standard in those two developer communities.

Another question is line length. Most editors these days will have a line-wrap option that will make sure you don't have to scroll horizontally when you want to see the code. However, not all of them print out the code properly, and there may be a maintainer later on that has no fancy editor like that one. It is therefore a good idea to keep lines short—approximately 80 characters.

Commenting

Commenting is something that only humans benefit from—although in some higher programming languages, comments are indexed to generate documentation (one example is the PHP manual, which is at times a bit cryptic for nonprogrammers exactly because of this). While commenting is not a necessity for the code to work—if you use clear names and indent your code, it should be rather self-explanatory—it can speed up debugging immensely. The previous example might make more sense for you with explanatory comments:

```
/*
  addPopUpLink
  opens the linked document of all links with a certain
  class in a pop-up window and adds a message to the
  link text that there will be a new window
*/
function addPopUpLink(){
  // Check for DOM and leave if it is not supported
  if(!document.getElementById || !document.createTextNode){return;}
  // Assets of the link - the class to find out which link should
  // get the functionality and the message to add to the link text
  var popupClass='smallpopup';
  var popupMessage= ' (opens in new window)';
  // Temporary variables to use in a loop
  var pop,t;
  // Get all links in the document
  var as=document.getElementsByTagName('a');
  // Loop over all links
  for(var i=0;i<as.length;i++)
  {
    t=as[i].className;
    // Check if the link has a class and the class is the right one
    if(t && t.toString().indexOf(popupClass)!=-1)
    {
      // Add the message
      as[i].appendChild(document.createTextNode(popupMessage));
      // Assign a function when the user clicks the link
      as[i].onclick=function()
      {
        // Open a new window with
        pop=window.open(this.href,'popup','width=400,height=400');
        // Don't follow the link (otherwise the linked document
        // would be opened in the pop-up and the document).
        return false;
      }
    }
  }
}
window.onload=addPopUpLink;
```

A lot easier to grasp, isn't it? It is also overkill. An example like this can be used in training documentation or a self-training course, but it is a bit much in a final product—moderation is always the key when it comes to commenting. In most cases, it is enough to explain what something does and what can be changed.

```
/*
  addPopUpLink
  opens the linked document of all links with a certain
  class in a pop-up window and adds a message to the
  link text that there will be a new window
*/
function addPopUpLink()
{
  if(!document.getElementById || !document.createTextNode){return;}

  // Assets of the link - the class to find out which link should
  // get the functionality and the message to add to the link text
  var popupClass='smallpopup';
  var popupMessage=document.createTextNode(' (opens in new window)');

  var pop,t;
  var as=document.getElementsByTagName('a');
  for(var i=0;i<as.length;i++)
  {
    t=as[i].className;
    if(t && t.toString().indexOf(popupClass)!=-1)
    {
      as[i].appendChild(popupMessage);
      as[i].onclick=function()
      {
        pop=window.open(this.href,'popup','width=400,height=400');
        return false;
      }
    }
  }
}
window.onload=addPopUpLink;
```

These comments make it easy to grasp what the whole function does and to find the spot where you can change some of the settings. This makes quick changes easier—changes in functionality would need the maintainer to analyze your code more closely anyway.

Functions

Functions are reusable blocks of code and are an integral part of most programs today, including those written in JavaScript. Imagine you have to do a calculation or need a certain conditional check over and over again. You could copy and paste the same lines of code where necessary; however, it is much more efficient to use a function.

Functions can get values as parameters (sometimes called **arguments**) and can return values after they finished testing and changing what has been given to them.

You create a function by using the `function` keyword followed by the function name and the parameters separated by commas inside parentheses:

```
function createLink(linkTarget, LinkName)
{
  // Code
}
```

There is no limit as to how many parameters a function can have, but it is a good idea not to use too many, as it can become rather confusing. If you check some DHTML code, you can find functions with 20 parameters or more, and remembering their order when calling those in other functions will make you almost wish to simply write the whole thing from scratch. When you do that, it is a good idea to remember that too many parameters mean a lot more maintenance work and make debugging a lot harder than it should be.

Unlike PHP, JavaScript has no option to preset the parameters should they not be available. You can work around this issue with some `if` conditions that check whether the parameter is `null` (which means "nothing, not even 0" in interpreter speak):

```
function createLink(linkTarget, LinkName)
{
  if (linkTarget == null)
  {
    linkTarget = '#';
  }
  if (linkName == null)
  {
    linkName = 'dummy';
  }
}
```

Functions report back what they have done via the `return` keyword. If a function that's invoked by an event handler returns the Boolean value `false`, then the sequence of events that is normally triggered by the event gets stopped. This is very handy when you want to apply functions to links and stop the browser from navigating to the link's `href`. We also used this in the "Object Detection vs. Browser Dependence" section.

Any other value following the `return` statement will be sent back to the calling code. Let's change our `createLink` function to create a link and return it once the function has finished creating it.

```
function createLink(linkTarget,linkName)
{
  if (linkTarget == null) { linkTarget = '#'; }
  if (linkName == null) { linkName = 'dummy'; }

  var tempLink=document.createElement('a');
```

```
    tempLink.setAttribute('href',linkTarget);
    tempLink.appendChild(document.createTextNode(linkName));

    return tempLink;
}
```

Another function could take these generated links and append them to an element. If there is no element ID defined, it should append the link to the body of the document.

```
function appendLink(sourceLink,elementId)
{
  var element=false;
  if (elementId==null || !document.getElementById(elementId))
  {
    element=document.body;
  }
  if(!element) {
    element=document.getElementById(elementId);
  }
  element.appendChild(sourceLink);
}
```

Now, to use both these functions, we can have another one call them with appropriate parameters:

```
function linksInit()
{
  if (!document.getElementById || !document.createTextNode) { return; }
  var openLink=createLink('#','open');
  appendLink(openLink);
  var closeLink=createLink('closed.html','close');
  appendLink(closeLink,'main');
}
```

The function linksInit() checks whether DOM is available (as it is the only function calling the others, we don't need to check for it inside them again) and creates a link with a target of # and open as the link text.

It then invokes the appendLink() function and sends the newly generated link as a parameter. Notice it doesn't send a target element, which means elementId is null and appendLink() adds the link to the main body of the document.

The second time initLinks() invokes createLink(), it sends the target closed.html and close as the link text and applies the link to the HTML element with the ID main via the appendLink() function. If there is an element with the ID main, appendLink() adds the link to this one; if not, it uses the document body as a fallback option.

If this is confusing now, don't worry, you will see more examples later on. For now, it is just important to remember what functions are and what they should do:

- Functions are there to do one task over and over again—keep each task inside its own function; don't create monster functions that do several things at once.

- Functions can have as many parameters as you wish, and each parameter can be of any type—string, object, number, variable, or array.

- You cannot predefine parameters in the function definition itself, but you can check whether they were defined or not and set defaults with an `if` condition. You can do this very succinctly via the ternary operator, which you will get to know in the next section of this chapter.

- Functions should have a logical name describing what they do; try to keep the name close to the task topic, as a generic `init()`, for example, could be in any of the other included JavaScript files and overwrite their functions. Object literals can provide one way to avoid this problem, as you'll see later in this chapter.

Short Code via Ternary Operator

Looking at the `appendLink()` function shown earlier, you might get a hunch that a lot of `if` conditions or `switch` statements can result in very long and complex code. A trick to avoid some of the bloating involves using something called the **ternary operator**. The ternary operator has the following syntax:

```
var variable = condition ? trueValue:falseValue;
```

This is very handy for Boolean conditions or very short values. For example, you can replace this long `if` condition with one line of code:

```
// Normal syntax
var direction;
If(x<200)
{
  direction=1;
}
else
{
  direction=-1
}
// Ternary operator
var direction = x < 200 ? 1 : -1;
```

Other examples:

```
t.className = t.className == 'hide' ? '' : 'hide';
var el = document.getElementById('nav')
        ? document.getElementById('nav')
        : document.body;
```

You can also nest the ternary selector, but that gets rather unreadable:

```
y = x <20 ? (x > 10 ? 1 : 2) : 3;
// equals
if(x<20)
{
  if(x>10)
  {
    y=1;
  }
  else
  {
    y=2;
  }
}
else
{
 y=3
}
```

Sorting and Reuse of Functions

If you have a large number of JavaScript functions, it might be a good idea to keep them in separate .js files and apply them only where they are needed. Name the .js files according to what the functions included in them do, for example, formvalidation.js or dynamicmenu.js.

This has been done to a certain extent for you, as there are a lot of prepackaged JavaScript libraries (collections of functions and methods) that help create special functionality. We will look at some of them in Chapter 11 and create our own during the next few chapters.

Variable and Function Scope

Variables defined inside a function with a new var are only valid inside this function, not outside it. This might seem a drawback, but it actually means that your scripts will not interfere with others—which could be fatal when you use JavaScript libraries or your own collections.

Variables defined outside functions are called global variables and are dangerous. We should try to keep all our variables contained inside functions. This ensures that our script will play nicely with other scripts that may be applied to the page. Many scripts use generic variable names like navigation or currentSection. If these are defined as global variables, the scripts will override each other's settings. Try running the following function to see what omitting a var keyword can cause:

```
<script type="text/javascript">
  var demoVar=1 // Global variable
  alert('Before withVar demoVar is' +demoVar);
  function withVar()
  {
    var demoVar=3;
  }
  withVar();
  alert('After withVar demoVar is' +demoVar);
  function withoutVar()
  {
    demoVar=3;
  }
  withoutVar();
  alert('After withoutVar demoVar is' +demoVar);
</script>
```

While `withVar` keeps the variable untouched, `withoutVar` changes it:

```
Before withVar demoVar is 1
After withVar demoVar is 1
After withoutVar demoVar is 3
```

Keeping Scripts Safe with the Object Literal

Earlier we talked about keeping variables safe by defining them locally via the var keyword. The reason was to avoid other functions relying on variables with the same name and the two functions overwriting each other's values. The same applies to functions. As you can include several JavaScripts to the same HTML document in separate script elements your functionality might break as another included document has a function with the same name. You can avoid this issue with a naming convention, like `myscript_init()` and `myscript_validate()` for your functions. However, this is a bit cumbersome, and JavaScript offers a better way to deal with this in the form of objects.

You can define a new object and use your functions as methods of this object—this is how JavaScript objects like Date and Math work. For example:

```
<script type="text/javascript">
  myscript=new Object();
  myscript.init=function()
  {
    // Some code
  };
  myscript.validate=function()
  {
   // Some code
  };
</script>
```

Notice that if you try to call the functions init() and validate(), you get an error, as they don't exist any longer. Instead, you need to use myscript.init() and myscript.validate().

Wrapping all your functions in an object as methods is analogous to the programming classes used by some other languages such as C++ or Java. In such languages, you keep functions that apply to the same task inside the same class, thus making it easier to create large pieces of code without getting confused by hundreds of functions.

The syntax we used is still a bit cumbersome, as you have to repeat the object name over and over again. There is a shortcut notation called the **object literal** that makes it a lot easier.

The object literal has been around for a long time but has been pretty underused. It is becoming more and more fashionable nowadays, and you can pretty much presume that a script you find on the web using it is pretty good, modern JavaScript.

What the object literal does is use a shortcut notation to create the object and apply each of the functions as object methods instead of stand-alone functions. Let's see our three functions of the dynamic links example as a big object using the object literal:

```
var dynamicLinks={
  linksInit:function()
  {
    if (!document.getElementById || !document.createTextNode)➡
      { return; }
    var openLink=dynamicLinks.createLink('#','open');
    dynamicLinks.appendLink(openLink);
    var closeLink=dynamicLinks.createLink('closed.html','close');
    dynamicLinks.appendLink(closeLink,'main');
  },
  createLink:function(linkTarget,linkName)
  {
    if (linkTarget == null) { linkTarget = '#'; }
    if (linkName == null) { linkName = 'dummy'; }
    var tempLink=document.createElement('a');
    tempLink.setAttribute('href',linkTarget);
    tempLink.appendChild(document.createTextNode(linkName));
    return tempLink;
  },
  appendLink:function(sourceLink,elementId)
  {
    var element=false;
    if (elementId==null || !document.getElementById(elementId))
    {
      element=document.body;
    }
    if(!element){element=document.getElementById(elementId)}
    element.appendChild(sourceLink);
  }
}

window.onload=dynamicLinks.linksInit;
```

As you can see, all the functions are contained as methods inside the dynamicLinks object, which means that if we want to call them, we need to add the name of the object before the function name.

The syntax is a bit different; instead of placing the function keyword before the name of the function, we add it behind the name preceded by a colon. Additionally, each closing curly brace except for the very last one needs to be followed by a comma.

If you want to use variables that should be accessible by all methods inside the object, you can do that with syntax that is quite similar:

```
var myObject=
{
  objMainVar:'preset',
  objSecondaryVar:0,
  objArray:['one','two','three'],
  init:function(){},
  createLinks:function(){},
  appendLinks:function(){}
}
```

This might be a lot right now, but don't worry. This chapter is meant as a reference for you to come back to and remind you of a lot of good practices in one place. We will continue in the next chapter with more tangible examples, and rip open an HTML document to play with the different parts.

Summary

You have done it; you finished this chapter, and you should now be able to separate modern and old scripts when you see them on the Web. Older scripts are likely to

- Use a lot of document.write().

- Check for browsers and versions instead of objects.

- Write out a lot of HTML instead of accessing what is already in the document.

- Use proprietary DOM objects like document.all for MSIE and document.layers for Netscape Navigator.

- Appear anywhere inside the document (rather in the <head> or included via <script src="---.js">) and rely on javascript: links instead of assigning events.

You've learned about putting JavaScript into stand-alone .js documents instead of embedding it into HTML and thereby separating behavior from structure.

You then heard about using object detection instead of relying on browser names and what progressive enhancement means and how it applies to web development. Testing user agent capabilities instead of names and versions will ensure that your scripts also work for user agents you might not have at hand to test yourself. It also means that you don't have to worry every time there is a new version of a browser out—if it supports the standards, you'll be fine.

We talked about accessibility and what it means for JavaScript, and you got a peek at a lot of coding practices. The general things to remember are

- Test for the objects you want to use in your scripts.

- Make improvements in an existing site that already works well without client-side scripting instead of adding scripts first and adding nonscripting fallbacks later on.

- Keep your code self-contained and don't use any global variables that might interfere with other scripts.

- Code with the idea in mind that you will have to hand this code over to someone else to maintain. This person might be you in three months' time, and you should be able to immediately understand what is going on.

- Comment your code's functionality and use readable formatting to make it easy to find bugs or change the functions.

This is the lot—except for something called an event handler, which I've talked about but not actually defined. I'll do so in Chapter 5. But for now, sit back, get a cup of coffee or tea, and relax for a bit, until you're ready to proceed with learning how JavaScript interacts with HTML and CSS.

CHAPTER 4

■■■

HTML and JavaScript

In this chapter, you finally get your hands dirty in real JavaScript code. You'll learn how Java-Script interacts with the page structure—defined in HTML—and how to receive data and give back information to your visitors. I start with an explanation of what an HTML document is and how it is structured and explain several ways to create page content via JavaScript. You'll then hear about the JavaScript developer's Swiss Army knife—the Document Object Model (DOM)—and how to separate JavaScript and HTML to create now-seamless effects that developers used to create in an obtrusive manner with DHTML.

The Anatomy of an HTML Document

Documents displayed in user agents are normally HTML documents. Even if you use a server-side language like ASP.NET, PHP, ColdFusion, or Perl, the outcome is HTML if you want to use browsers to their full potential. Modern browsers like Mozilla or Safari do also support XML, SVG, and other formats, but for 99% of your day-to-day web work, you'll go the HTML or XHTML route.

An HTML document is a text document that starts with a DOCTYPE that tells the user agent what the document is and how it should be dealt with. It then uses an HTML element that encompasses all other elements and text content. The HTML element should have a lang attribute that defines the language in use (human language, not programming language) and a dir attribute that defines the reading order of the text (left to right [ltr] for [Indo]European/American languages or right to left [rtl] for Semitic ones). Inside the HTML element needs to be a HEAD element with a TITLE element. You can add an optional META element determining what encoding should be used to display the text—if you haven't set the encoding on the server. On the same level as the HEAD element, but after the closing <head> tag, is the BODY—the element that contains all the page content.

```
<!DOCTYPE HTML PUBLIC "-//W3C//DTD HTML 4.01//EN"➥
  "http://www.w3.org/TR/html4/strict.dtd">
<html dir="ltr" lang="en">
  <head>
    <meta http-equiv="Content-Type"➥
        content="text/html; charset=utf-8" />
    <title>Our HTML Page</title>
  </head>
```

```
    <body>
    </body>
</html>
```

A markup document like this consists of **tags** (words or letters enclosed in tag brackets, like
<p>) and text content. Documents should be well formed (meaning that every opening tag
like <p> must be matched by a closing tag like </p>) and validate against the DTD provided. You
can validate documents on the W3C web site (http://validator.w3.org/).

HTML elements are everything in the brackets, <>, with a starting tag like <h1> followed by
content and a closing tag of the same name—like </h1>. Each element can have content in
between the opening and the closing tag. Each element may have several **attributes**. The
Document Type Definition, or DTD, linked in the DOCTYPE determines the set of tags that are
permitted, how they may be nested, and which attributes each tag may have. The following
example is a P element with an attribute whose name is class. The attribute has the value
intro. The P contains the text "Lorem Ipsum".

```
<p class="intro">Lorem Ipsum</p>
```

A browser checks the DOCTYPE and compares the elements it encounters with the DTD. The
HTML4.01 DTD definition tells it that P is a paragraph and that the class attribute is valid for
this element. It also realizes that the class attribute should check the linked CSS style sheet, get
the definitions for a P with that class, and render it accordingly. Now, what happens if you use
an attribute that is not defined in the DTD—like myattribute?

```
<p class="intro" myattribute="left">Lorem Ipsum</p>
```

Nothing—although you technically made a mistake. Browsers are very forgiving and will
not stop rendering even if they encounter unknowns like these, but instead they make the
attribute available in the DOM tree. This makes them very user and developer friendly, but it
makes it hard to advocate proper HTML syntax and standards compliance. There are, however,
several reasons why we should strive for standards compliance—even in HTML generated via
JavaScript:

- It is easier to trace errors when we know the HTML is valid.

- It is easier to maintain documents that adhere to the rules—as you can use a validator to
  measure its quality.

- It is a lot more likely that user agents will render or convert your pages properly when
  you develop against an agreed standard.

- The final documents can be easily converted to other formats if they are valid HTML.

Now, if we add some more elements to our example HTML and open it in a browser, we get
a rendered output as shown in Figure 4-1:

```
<!DOCTYPE HTML PUBLIC "-//W3C//DTD HTML 4.01//EN"➥
    "http://www.w3.org/TR/html4/strict.dtd">
<html dir="ltr" lang="en">
    <head>
        <meta http-equiv="Content-Type"➥
            content="text/html; charset=utf-8" />
```

```
    <title>DOM Example</title>
  </head>
  <body>
    <h1>Heading</h1>
    <p>Paragraph</p>
    <h2>Subheading</h2>
    <ul id="eventsList">
      <li>List 1</li>
      <li>List 2</li>
      <li><a href="http://www.google.com">Linked List Item</a></li>
      <li>List 4</li>
    </ul>
    <p>Paragraph</p>
    <p>Paragraph</p>
  </body>
</html>
```

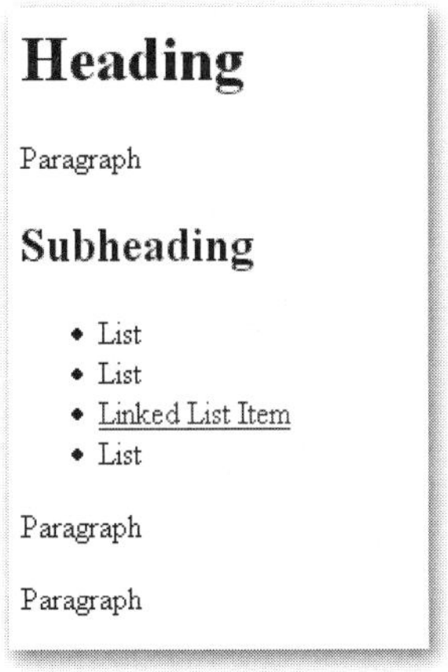

Figure 4-1. *An HTML document rendered by a browser*

A QUICK WORD ON XHTML

You might have glanced at the earlier code examples and got annoyed that I am using HTML 4.01 STRICT instead of the more modern XHTML. The reason is that more browsers support HTML 4.01 STRICT, and it is as clean as XHTML when it comes to syntax. Real XHTML documents should be sent as application/XML+XHTML and not as text/HTML on the server—a step not many developers dare to take, as it means the pages will not display in MSIE. Once the most common browsers do support real XHTML, it won't be hard to convert the documents. For now, 4.01 STRICT does the trick and makes browsers display our documents as the W3C planned them to be displayed—well, most of them do. Also be aware that I am using uppercase for HTML element names in the text, like `H1`, while all elements in the code examples are lowercase—as this is necessary for XHTML. XML and XHTML are case sensitive, whereas older and lesser strict HTML versions aren't.

The user agent "sees" the document a bit differently. The DOM models a document as a set of nodes, including element nodes, text nodes, and attribute nodes. Both elements and their text content are separate *nodes*. Attribute nodes are the *attributes* of the elements. The DOM includes other sorts of nodes for other parts of a markup document, but these three—element nodes, text nodes, and attribute nodes—are the important ones if you keep your JavaScript and HTML hat on. If you want to see the document through the eyes of the browser, you can use a tool like the DOM Inspector of Firefox, which shows the document as a tree structure, as depicted in Figure 4-2.

Figure 4-2. *The DOM representation of a document illustrated in the Mozilla DOM Inspector*

■**Tip** You can access the DOM Inspector via Tools ➤ DOM Inspector in the Firefox toolbar or by pressing Ctrl+Shift+I. It allows you to check each part of the document in detail, and even remove elements, which is very handy when printing out pages. You can read more about the DOM Inspector in the Appendix, which covers validation and debugging.

■Note Notice all the #text nodes between the elements? These are not text we added to the document, but the line breaks we added at the end of each line. Some browsers see those as text nodes while others don't—which can be very annoying when we try to access elements in the document via JavaScript later on.

Figure 4-3 shows another way we can visualize the document tree.

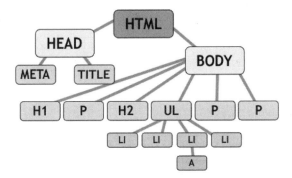

Figure 4-3. *The structure of an HTML document*

It is very important to recognize HTML for what it is: HTML is structured content and not a visual construct like an image with elements placed at different coordinates. When you have a proper, valid HTML document, the sky is the limit, and you can access and change it via JavaScript. An invalid HTML document might trip up your scripts, no matter how much testing you do. A classic mistake is using the same id attribute value twice in a single document, which negates the purpose of having a unique identifier (ID).

Providing Feedback in Web Pages via JavaScript: The Old School Ways

We already used one way—document.write()—of giving feedback to the user in an HTML document by writing out content. We also discussed the problems this method has, namely mixing the structure and the presentation layer and losing the maintenance benefits of keeping all JavaScript code in a separate file.

Using `window` Methods: `prompt()`, `alert()`, and `confirm()`

A different way of giving feedback and retrieving user-entered data is using methods the browser offers you via the `window` object, namely `prompt()`, `alert()`, and `confirm()`.

The most commonly used `window` method is `alert()`, an example of which appears in Figure 4-4. What it does is display a value in a dialog (and perhaps play a sound, if the user's hardware supports it). The user then has to activate (click with the mouse or hit Enter on the keyboard) the OK button to get rid of the message.

Figure 4-4. *A JavaScript alert (on Firefox on Windows XP)*

Alerts look different from browser to browser and operating system to operating system.

As a user feedback mechanism, `alert()` has the merit of being supported by most user agents, but it is also a very "in-your-face" and clumsy way of passing information to the user. An alert is a message that normally bears bad news or warns someone of danger ahead—which is not necessarily your intention.

Say, for example, you want to tell the visitor to enter something in a search field before submitting a form. You could use an alert for that:

```
<!DOCTYPE HTML PUBLIC "-//W3C//DTD HTML 4.01//EN"➥
  "http://www.w3.org/TR/html4/strict.dtd">
<html dir="ltr" lang="en">
  <head>
    <meta http-equiv="Content-Type"➥
        content="text/html; charset=utf-8" />
    <title>Search example</title>
    <script type="text/javascript">
      function checkSearch()
      {
        if(!document.getElementById ||➥
            !document.createTextNode){return;}
        if(!document.getElementById('search')){return;}
        var searchValue=document.getElementById('search').value;
        if(searchValue=='')
        {
          alert('Please enter a search term');
          return false;
        }
        else
        {
          return true;
```

```
        }
      }
    </script>
  </head>
  <body>
    <form action="sitesearch.php" method="post"➥
        onsubmit="return checkSearch();">
      <p>
        <label for="search">Search the site:</label>
        <input type="text" id="search" name="search" />
        <input type="submit" value="Search" />
      </p>
    </form>
  </body>
</html>
```

If a visitor tries to submit the form via the Submit button, he'll get the alert, and the browser will not send the form to the server after he activates the OK button. On Mozilla Firefox on Windows XP, the alert looks like what you see in Figure 4-5.

Figure 4-5. *Giving feedback on a form error via an alert*

Alerts do not return any information to the script—they simply give a message to the user and stop any further code execution until the OK button is activated.

This is different for prompt() and confirm(). The former allows visitors to enter something, and the latter asks users to confirm an action.

■**Tip** As a debugging measure, alert() is simply too handy not to use. All you do is add an alert(variableName) in your code where you want to know what the variable value is at that time. You'll get the information and stop the rest of the code from executing until the OK button is activated—which is great for tracing back where and how your script fails. Beware of using it in loops though—there is no way to stop the loop, and you might have to press Enter a hundred times before you get back to your editing. There are other debugging tools like Mozilla's, Opera's, and Safari's JavaScript consoles and Mozilla Venkman—more on these in the Appendix.

We could extend the earlier example to ask the visitor to confirm a search for the common term *JavaScript* (see also Figure 4-6):

```
function checkSearch()
{
  if(!document.getElementById ||➥
     !document.createTextNode){return;}
  if(!document.getElementById('search')){return;}
  var searchValue=document.getElementById('search').value;
  if(searchValue=='')
  {
   alert('Please enter a search term before sending the form');
   return false;
  }
  else if(searchValue=='JavaScript')
  {
    var really=confirm('"JavaScript" is a very common term.\n' +➥
    'Do you really want to search for this?');
    return really;
  }
  else
  {
    return true;
  }
}
```

Figure 4-6. *Example of asking for user confirmation via* confirm()

Notice that the confirm() is a method that returns a Boolean value (true or false) depending on the visitor activating OK or Cancel. Confirm dialogs are an easy way to stop visitors from taking really bad steps in web applications. While they are not the prettiest way of asking a user to confirm a choice, they are really stable and offer some functionality your own confirmation functions most probably will not have—for example, playing the alert sound.

Both alert() and confirm() send information to the user, but what about retrieving information? A simple way to retrieve user input is the prompt() method. This one takes two parameters, the first one being a string displayed above the entry field as a label and the second a preset value for the entry field. Buttons labeled OK and Cancel (or something similar) will be displayed next to the field and the label, as shown in Figure 4-7.

```
var user=prompt('Please choose a name','User12');
```

Figure 4-7. *Allowing the user to enter data in a prompt*

When the visitor activates the OK button, the value of the variable user will be either User12 (when she hasn't changed the preset) or whatever she entered. When she activates the Cancel button, the value will be null.

We can use this functionality to allow a visitor to change a value before sending a form to the server:

```
<!DOCTYPE HTML PUBLIC "-//W3C//DTD HTML 4.01//EN"➥
"http://www.w3.org/TR/html4/strict.dtd">
<html dir="ltr" lang="en">
  <head>
    <meta http-equiv="Content-Type"➥
        content="text/html; charset=utf-8" />
    <title>Date example</title>
    <script type="text/javascript">
      function checkDate()
      {
        if(!document.getElementById ||➥
          !document.createTextNode){return;}
        if(!document.getElementById('date')){return;}
        // Define a regular expression to check the date format
        var checkPattern=new➥
          RegExp("\\d{2}/\\d{2}/\\d{4}");
        // Get the value of the date entry field
        var dateValue=document.getElementById('date').value;
        // If there is no date entered, don't send the form
        if(dateValue=='')
```

```
      {
        alert('Please enter a date');
        return false
      }
      else
      {
        // Tell the user to change the date syntax either until
        // she presses Cancel or entered the right syntax
        while(!checkPattern.test(dateValue) && dateValue!=null)
        {
          dateValue=prompt('Your date was not in the right format. '➥
          + 'Please enter it as DD/MM/YYYY.', dateValue);
        }
        return dateValue!=null;
      }
    }
  </script>
</head>
<body>
  <h1>Events search</h1>
  <form action="eventssearch.php" method="post"➥
      onsubmit="return checkDate();">
    <p>
      <label for="date">Date in the format DD/MM/YYYY:</label><br />
      <input type="text" id="date" name="date" />
      <input type="submit" value="Check " />
      <br />(example 26/04/1975)
    </p>
  </form>
</body>
</html>
```

Don't worry if the Regular Expression and the test() method are confusing you now; these will be covered in Chapter 9. All that is important now is that we use a while loop with a prompt() inside it. The while loop displays the same prompt over and over again until either the visitor presses Cancel (which means dateValue becomes null) or enters a date in the right format (which satisfies the test condition of the regular expression checkPattern).

Summary

You can create pretty nifty JavaScripts using the prompt(), alert(), and confirm() methods, and they have some points in their favor:

- They are easy to grasp, as the methods use the functionality and look and feel of the browser and offer a richer interface than HTML (specifically, the alert sound, if and when present, can help a lot of users).

- They are dead easy to implement and only need JavaScript instead of the appropriate HTML elements—that is also why they are used in bookmarklets/favelets (small scripts you can call via a bookmark or a favorite that alter the current document—in essence browser extensions that are available in all JavaScript capable browsers; see http://www.bookmarklets.com).

- They appear outside and above the current document—which gives them utmost importance.

However, there are some points that speak against the use of these methods to retrieve data and give feedback:

- You cannot style the messages, and they obstruct the web page, which does give them more importance, but also makes them appear clumsy from a design point of view. As they are part of the user's operating system or browser UI, they are easy to recognize for the user, but they break design conventions and guidelines the product may have to adhere to.

- Feedback does not happen in the web site's look and feel—which renders the site less important and stops dead the user's journey through our usability enhancing design elements.

- They are dependent on JavaScript—feedback should also be available when JavaScript is turned off.

- Unless you use Mozilla or older Netscape browsers, there is no way of telling whether the alert() or the prompt() is from this site or a different one. This is a security problem, as you could make a prompt() appear on a third-party site and read and transfer user input to yours. This is one technique of the phenomenon called **phishing**, and it is a big security and privacy threat. As some security companies publish information on the subject, visitors might not trust your site if it uses these feedback and input mechanisms (http://secunia.com/advisories/15489/).

Accessing the Document via the DOM

In addition to the window methods you now know about, you can access a web document via the DOM. In a manner of speaking, we have done that already with the document.write() examples. The document object is what we want to alter and add to, and write() is one method to do that. However, document.write() adds a string to the document and not a set of nodes and attributes, and you cannot separate the JavaScript out into a separate file—document.write() only works where you put it in the HTML. What we need is a way to reach where we want to change or add content, and this is exactly what the DOM and its methods provide us with. Earlier on you found out that user agents read a document as a set of nodes and attributes, and the DOM gives us tools to grab these. We can reach elements of the document via two methods:

- document.getElementsByTagName('p')

- document.getElementById('id')

The getElementsByTagName('p') method returns a list of all the elements with the name p as objects (where p can be any HTML element) and getElementById('id') returns us the element with the ID as an object. If you are already familiar with CSS, you could compare these two methods with the CSS selectors for elements and for IDs—tag{} and #id{}.

Note Similarities with CSS end here, as there is no DOM equivalent of the class selector .class{}. However, as this might be a handy method to have, some developers have come up with their own solutions to that problem and created getElementsByClassName() functions.

If you go back to the HTML example we used earlier, you can write a small JavaScript that shows how to use these two methods:

```
<!DOCTYPE HTML PUBLIC "-//W3C//DTD HTML 4.01//EN"➥
  "http://www.w3.org/TR/html4/strict.dtd">
<html dir="ltr" lang="en">
  <head>
    <meta http-equiv="Content-Type"➥
        content="text/html; charset=utf-8" />
    <title>DOM Example</title>
    <script type="text/JavaScript"  src="exampleFindElements.js">
    </script>
  </head>
  <body>
    <h1>Heading</h1>
    <p>Paragraph</p>
    <h2>Subheading</h2>
    <ul id="eventsList">
      <li>List 1</li>
      <li>List 2</li>
```

```
      <li><a href="http://www.google.com">Linked List Item</a></li>
      <li>List 4</li>
    </ul>
    <p>Paragraph</p>
    <p>Paragraph</p>
  </body>
</html>
```

Our script could now read the number of list items and paragraphs in the document by calling the getElementsByTagName() method and assigning the return value to variables—one time with the tag name li and the other time with p.

```
var listElements=document.getElementsByTagName('li');
var paragraphs=document.getElementsByTagName('p');
var msg='This document contains '+listElements.length+' list items\n';
msg+='and '+paragraphs.length+' paragraphs.';
alert(msg);
```

As Figure 4-8 shows, if you open the HTML document in a browser, you will find that both values are zero!

Figure 4-8. *Unwanted result when trying to reach elements before the page was rendered*

There aren't any list elements because the document has not yet been rendered by the browser when we try to read its content. We need to delay that reading until the document has been fully loaded and rendered.

You can achieve this by calling a function when the window has finished loading. The document has finished loading when the onload event of the window object gets triggered. You'll hear more about events in the next chapter; for now, let's just use the onload event handler of the window object to trigger the function:

```
function findElements()
{
  var listElements = document.getElementsByTagName('li');
  var paragraphs = document.getElementsByTagName('p');
  var msg = 'This document contains ' + listElements.length +➥
    ' list items\n';
  msg += 'and ' + paragraphs.length + ' paragraphs.';
  alert(msg);
}
window.onload = findElements;
```

If you open the HTML document in a browser now, you'll see an alert like the one in Figure 4-9 with the right number of list elements and paragraphs.

Figure 4-9. *Output alert indicating the number of found elements*

You can access each of the elements of a certain name like you access an array—once again bearing in mind that the counter of an array starts at 0 and not at 1:

```
// Get the first paragraph
var firstpara = document.getElementsByTagName('p')[0];
// Get the second list item
var secondListItem = document.getElementsByTagName('p')[1];
```

You can combine several getElementsByTagName() method calls to read child elements directly. For example, to reach the first link item inside the third list item, you use

```
var➡ targetLink=document.getElementsByTagName('li')[2].getElementsByTagName➡
('a')[0];
```

This can get pretty messy though, and there are more clever ways to reach child elements—we'll get to these in a second. If you wanted to reach the last element, you can use the length property of the array:

```
var lastListElement = listElements[listElements.length - 1];
```

The length property also allows you to loop through elements and change all of them one after the other:

```
var linkItems = document.getElementsByTagName('li');
for(var i = 0; i < linkItems.length; i++)
{
  // Do something...
}
```

Element IDs need to be unique to the document; therefore the return value of getElementById() is a single object rather than an array of objects.

```
var events = document.getElementById('eventsList');
```

You can mix both methods to cut down on the number of elements to loop through. While the earlier for loop accesses all LI elements in the document, this one will only go through those that are inside the element with the ID eventsList (the name of the object with the ID replaces the document object):

```
var events = document.getElementById('eventsList');
var eventlinkItems = events.getElementsByTagName('li');
for(var i = 0; i < eventLinkItems.length; i++)
{
  // Do something...
}
```

With the help of getElementsByTagName() and getElementById(), you can reach every element of the document or specifically target one single element. As mentioned earlier, getElementById() is a method of document and getElementsByTagName() is a method of any element. Now it is time to look at ways how to navigate around the document once you reached the element.

Of Children, Parents, Siblings, and Values

You know already that you can reach elements inside other elements by concatenating getElementsByTagName methods. However, this is rather cumbersome, and it means that you need to know the HTML you are altering. Sometimes that is not possible, and you have to find a more generic way to travel through the HTML document. The DOM already planned for this, via **children**, **parents**, and **siblings**.

These relationships describe where the current element is in the tree and whether it contains other elements or not. Let's take a look at our simple HTML example once more, concentrating on the body of the document:

```
<body>
  <h1>Heading</h1>
  <p>Paragraph</p>
  <h2>Subheading</h2>
  <ul id="eventsList">
    <li>List 1</li>
    <li>List 2</li>
    <li><a href="http://www.google.com">Linked List Item</a></li>
    <li>List 4</li>
  </ul>
  <p>Paragraph</p>
  <p>Paragraph</p>
</body>
```

All the indented elements are children of the BODY. H1, H2, UL, and P are siblings, and the LI elements are children of the UL element—and siblings to another. The link is a child of the third LI element. All in all, they are one big happy family.

However, there are even more children. The text inside the paragraphs, headings, list elements, and links also consists of nodes, as you may recall from Figure 4-2 earlier, and while they are not elements, they still follow the same relationship rules.

Every node in the document has several valuable properties.

- The most important is nodeType, which describes what the node is—an element, an attribute, a comment, text, and several more types (12 in all). For our HTML examples, only the nodeType values 1 and 3 are important, where 1 is an element node and 3 is a text node.

- Another important property is nodeName, which is the name of the element or #text if it is a text node. Depending on the document type and the user agent, nodeName can be either upper- or lowercase, which is why it is a good idea to convert it to lowercase before testing for a certain name. You can use the toLowerCase() method of the string object for that: if(obj.nodeName.toLowerCase()=='li'){};. For element nodes, you can use the tagName property.

- nodeValue is the value of the node: null if it is an element, and the text content if it is a text node.

In the case of text nodes, nodeValue can be read and set, which allows you to alter the text content of the element. If, for example, you wanted to change the text of the first paragraph, you might think it is enough to set its nodeValue:

```
document.getElementsByTagName('p')[0].nodeValue='Hello World';
```

However, this doesn't work (although—strangely enough—it does not cause an error), as the first paragraph is an element node. If you wanted to change the text inside the paragraph, you need to access the text node inside it or, in other words, the first child node of the paragraph:

```
document.getElementsByTagName('p')[0].firstChild.nodeValue='Hello World';
```

From the Parents to the Children

The firstChild property is a shortcut. Every element can have any number of children, listed in a property called childNodes.

- childNodes is a list of all the first-level child nodes of the element—it does not cascade down into deeper levels.

- You can access a child element of the current element via the array counter or the item() method.

- The shortcut properties yourElement.firstChild and yourElement.lastChild are easier versions of yourElement.childNodes[0] and yourElement.childNodes [yourElement.childNodes.length-1] and make it quicker to reach them.

- You can check whether an element has any children by calling the method hasChildNodes(), which returns a Boolean value.

Returning to the earlier example, you can access the UL element and get information about its children as shown here:

HTML

```
<ul id="eventsList">
  <li>List 1</li>
  <li>List 2</li>
  <li><a href="http://www.google.com">Linked List Item</a></li>
  <li>List 4</li>
</ul>
```

JavaScript:

```
function myDOMinspector()
{
  var DOMstring='';
  if(!document.getElementById || !document.createTextNode){return;}
  var demoList=document.getElementById('eventsList');
  if (!demoList){return;}
  if(demoList.hasChildNodes())
  {
    var ch=demoList.childNodes;
    for(var i=0;i<ch.length;i++)
    {
      DOMstring+=ch[i].nodeName+'\n';
    }
    alert(DOMstring);
  }
}
```

We create an empty string called DOMstring and check for DOM support and whether the UL element with the right id attribute is defined. Then we test whether the element has child nodes and, if it does, store them in a variable named ch. We loop through the variable (which automatically becomes an array) and add the nodeName of each child node to DOMString, followed by a line break (\n). We then look at the outcome using the alert() method.

If you run this script in a browser, you will see one of the main differences between MSIE and more modern browsers. While MSIE only shows four LI elements, other browsers like Firefox also count the line breaks in between the elements as text nodes, as you see in Figure 4-10.

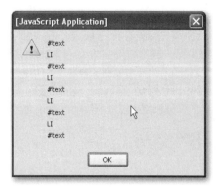

Figure 4-10. *Nodes found by our script, including text nodes that in reality are line breaks*

From the Children to the Parents

You can also navigate from child elements back to their parents, via the parentNode property. First let's make it easier for us to reach the link—by adding an ID to it:

```
<ul id="eventsList">
  <li>List</li>
  <li>List</li>
  <li>
    <a id="linkedItem" href="http://www.google.com">
      Linked List Item
    </a>
  </li>
  <li>List</li>
</ul>
```

Now we assign a variable to the link object and read the parent node's name:

```
var myLinkItem=document.getElementById('linkedItem');
alert(myLinkItem.parentNode.nodeName);
```

The result is LI, and if we add another parentNode to the object reference, we'll get UL, which is the link's grandparent element:

```
alert(myLinkItem.parentNode.parentNode.nodeName);
```

You can add as many of those as you want—that is, if there are parent elements left in the document tree and you haven't reached the top level yet. If you use parentNode in a loop, it is important that you also test the nodeName and end the loop when it reaches the BODY. Say for example you want to check whether an object is inside an element with a class called dynamic. You can do that with a while loop:

```
var myLinkItem = document.getElementById('linkedItem');
var parentElm = myLinkItem.parentNode;
while(parentElm.className != 'dynamic')
```

```
{
  parentElm = parentElm.parentNode;
}
```

However, this loop will end in an "object required" error when there is no element with the right class. If you tell the loop to stop at the body, you can avoid that error:

```
var myLinkItem = document.getElementById('linkedItem');
var parentElm = myLinkItem.parentNode;
while(!parentElm.className != 'dynamic' && parentElm != 'document.body')
{
  parentElm=parentElm.parentNode;
}
alert(parentElm);
```

Among Siblings

The family analogy continues with siblings, which are elements on the same level (they don't come in different genders like brothers or sisters though). You can reach a different child node on the same level via the previousSibling and nextSibling properties of a node. Going back to our list example:

```
<ul id="eventsList">
  <li>List Item 1</li>
  <li>List Item 2</li>
  <li>
    <a id="linkedItem" href="http://www.google.com/">
      Linked List Item
    </a>
  </li>
  <li>List Item 4</li>
</ul>
```

You can reach the link via getElementById() and the LI containing the link via parentNode. The properties previousSibling and nextSibling allow you to get List Item 2 and List Item 3 respectively:

```
var myLinkItem = document.getElementById('linkedItem');
var listItem = myLinkItem.parentNode;
var nextListItem = myLinkItem.nextSibling;
var prevListItem = myLinkItem.previousSibling;
```

▨**Note** This is a simplified example working only in MSIE; because of the difference of browser implementations, the next and previous siblings are not the LI elements on modern browsers, but text nodes with the line break as content.

If the current object is the last child of the parent element, nextSibling will be undefined and cause an error if you don't test for it properly. Unlike with childNodes, there are no short-cut properties for the first and last siblings, but you could write utility methods to find them; say, for example, you want to find the first and the last LI in our demo HTML:

```
window.onload=function()
{
  var myLinkItem=document.getElementById('linkedItem');
  var first=firstSibling(myLinkItem.parentNode);
  var last=lastSibling(myLinkItem.parentNode);
  alert(getTextContent(first));
  alert(getTextContent(last));
}
function lastSibling(node){
  var tempObj=node.parentNode.lastChild;
  while(tempObj.nodeType!=1 && tempObj.previousSibling!=null)
  {
    tempObj=tempObj.previousSibling;
  }
  return (tempObj.nodeType==1)?tempObj:false;
}
function firstSibling(node)
{
  var tempObj=node.parentNode.firstChild;
  while(tempObj.nodeType!=1 && tempObj.nextSibling!=null)
  {
    tempObj=tempObj.nextSibling;
  }
  return (tempObj.nodeType==1)?tempObj:false;
}
function getTextContent(node)
{
  return node.firstChild.nodeValue;
}
```

Notice that you need to check for nodeType, as the last or first child of the parentNode might be a text node and not an element.

Let's make our date checking script less obtrusive by using DOM methods to provide text feedback instead of sending an alert to the user. First, you need a container to show your error message:

```
<!DOCTYPE HTML PUBLIC "-//W3C//DTD HTML 4.01//EN"➥
  "http://www.w3.org/TR/html4/strict.dtd">
<html dir="ltr" lang="en">
  <head>
```

```
    <meta http-equiv="Content-Type"➥
          content="text/html; charset=utf-8" />
    <title>Date example</title>
    <style type="text/css">
      .error{color:#c00;font-weight:bold;}
    </style>
    <script type="text/javascript" src="checkdate.js"></script>
  </head>
  <body>
    <h1>Events search</h1>
    <form action="eventssearch.php" method="post"➥
          onsubmit="return checkDate();">
      <p>
        <label for="date">Date in the format DD/MM/YYYY:</label><br />
        <input type="text" id="date" name="date" />
        <input type="submit" value="Check " />
        <br />(example 26/04/1975) <span class="error">  </span>
      </p>
    </form>
  </body>
</html>
```

The checking script more or less stays the same as it was before—the difference is that we use the SPAN as a means of displaying the error:

```
function checkDate(){
  if(!document.getElementById || !document.createTextNode){return;}
  var dateField=document.getElementById('date');
  if(!dateField){return;}
  var errorContainer=dateField.parentNode.getElementsByTagName➥
    ('span')[0];
  if(!errorContainer){return;}
  var checkPattern=new RegExp("\\d{2}/\\d{2}/\\d{4}");
  var errorMessage='';
  errorContainer.firstChild.nodeValue=' ';
  var dateValue=dateField.value;
  if(dateValue=='')
  {
    errorMessage='Please provide a date.';
  }
  else if(!checkPattern.test(dateValue))
  {
    errorMessage='Please provide the date in the defined format.';
  }
```

```
    if(errorMessage!='')
    {
      errorContainer.firstChild.nodeValue=errorMessage;
      dateField.focus();
      return false;
    }
    else
    {
      return true;
    }
}
```

First, test whether DOM is supported and that all the needed elements are there:

```
if(!document.getElementById || !document.createTextNode){return;}
var dateField=document.getElementById('date');
if(!dateField){return;}
var errorContainer=dateField.parentNode.getElementsByTagName➥
  ('span')[0];
if(!errorContainer){return;}
```

Then define the test pattern and an empty error message. Set the text value of the error Span to a single space. This is necessary to avoid multiple error messages to display when the visitor sends the form a second time without rectifying the error.

```
var checkPattern=new RegExp("\\d{2}/\\d{2}/\\d{4}");
var errorMessage='';
errorContainer.firstChild.nodeValue=' ';
```

Next is the validation of the field. Read the value of the date field and check whether there is an entry. If there is no entry, the error message will be that the visitor should enter a date. If there is a date, but it is in the wrong format, the message will indicate so.

```
var dateValue=dateField.value;
  if(dateValue=='')
  {
    errorMessage='Please provide a date.';
  }
  else if(!checkPattern.test(dateValue))
  {
    errorMessage='Please provide the date in the defined format.';
  }
```

All that is left then is to check whether the initial empty error message was changed or not. If it wasn't changed, the script should return true to the form onsubmit="return checkDate();"— thus submitting the form and allowing the back end to take over the work. If the error message was changed, the script adds the error message to the text content (the nodeValue of the first child node) of the error SPAN, and sets the focus of the document back to the date entry field without submitting the form.

```
if(errorMessage!='')
{
  errorContainer.firstChild.nodeValue+=errorMessage;
  dateField.focus();
  return false;
}
else
{
  return true;
}
```

As Figure 4-11 shows, the end result is a lot more visually appealing than the alert message, and you can style it in any way you want to.

Figure 4-11. *Displaying a dynamic error message*

Now you know how to access and to change the text value of existing elements. But what if you want to change other attributes or you need HTML that is not necessarily provided for you?

Changing Attributes of Elements

Once you have reached the element you want to change, you can read and change its attributes in two ways: an older way—which is more widely supported by user agents—and the way of using newer DOM methods.

Older and newer user agents allow you to get and set element attributes as object properties:

```
var firstLink=document.getElementsByTagName('a')[0];
if(firstLink.href=='search.html')
{
  firstLink.href='http://www.google.com';
}
var mainImage=document.getElementById('nav').getElementsByTagName➥
  ('img')[0];
```

```
mainImage.src='dynamiclogo.gif';
mainImage.alt='Generico Corporation - We do generic stuff';
mainImage.title='Go back to Home';
```

All the attributes defined in the HTML specifications are available and can be accessed. Some are read-only for security reasons, but most can be set and read. You can also come up with your own attributes—JavaScript does not mind. Sometimes storing a value in an attribute of an element can save you a lot of testing and looping.

■**Caution** Beware of attributes that have the same name as JavaScript commands—for example, for. If you try to set element.for='something', it will result in an error. Browser vendors came up with workarounds for this; in the case of for—which is a valid attribute of the label element—the property name is htmlFor. Even more bizarre is the class attribute—something we will need a lot in the next chapter. This is a reserved word; you need to use className instead.

The DOM specifications provide two methods to read and set attributes—getAttribute() and setAttribute(). The getAttribute() method has one parameter—the attribute name; setAttribute() takes two parameters—the attribute name and the new value.

The earlier example using the newer methods looks like this:

```
var firstLink=document.getElementsByTagName('a')[0];
if(firstLink.getAttribute('href') =='search.html')
{
  firstLink.setAttribute('href') ='http://www.google.com';
}
var mainImage=document.getElementById('nav').getElementsByTagName➥
  ('img')[0];
mainImage.setAttribute('src') ='dynamiclogo.gif';
mainImage.getAttribute('alt') ='Generico Corporation - We do generic stuff';
mainImage.getAttribute('title') ='Go back to Home';
```

This may seem a bit superfluous and bloated, but the benefit is that it is a lot more consistent with other—higher—programming languages. It is also more likely to be supported by future user agents than the property way of assigning attributes to elements, and they work easily with arbitrary attribute names.

Creating, Removing, and Replacing Elements

DOM also provides methods for changing the structure of the document you can use in an HTML/JavaScript environment (there are more if you do XML conversion via JavaScript). You can not only change existing elements, but also create new ones and replace or remove old ones as well. These methods are as follows:

- `document.createElement('element')`: Creates a new element node with the tag name element.

- `document.createTextNode('string')`: Creates a new text node with the node value of string.

- `node.appendChild(newNode)`: Adds newNode as a new child node to node, following any existing children of node.

- `newNode=node.cloneNode(bool)`: Creates newNode as a copy (clone) of node. If bool is true, the clone includes clones of all the child nodes and attributes of the original.

- `node.insertBefore(newNode,oldNode)`: Inserts newNode as a new child node of node before oldNode.

- `node.removeChild(oldNode)`: Removes the child oldNode from node.

- `node.replaceChild(newNode, oldNode)`: Replaces the child node oldNode of node with newNode.

Note Notice that both `createElement()` and `createTextNode()` are methods of document; all the others are methods of any node.

All of these are indispensable when you want to create web products that are enhanced by JavaScript but don't rely exclusively on it. Unless you give all your user feedback via alert, confirm, and prompt pop-ups, you will have to rely on HTML elements to be provided to you—like the error message SPAN in the earlier example. However, as the HTML you need for your JavaScript to work only makes sense when JavaScript is enabled, it should not be available when there is no scripting support. An extra SPAN does not hurt anybody—however, form controls that offer the user great functionality (like date picker tools) but don't work are a problem.

Let's use these methods to counteract a problem that is quite common in web design: replacing Submit buttons with links. There are two ways to submit form data: a Submit button or an image button (actually, there are three—if you count hitting the Enter key).

Submit buttons are a thorn in the side of a lot of designers, as you cannot style them consistently across operating systems and browsers. Image buttons are a problem, as they require a lot of work on sites with localization, and they do not resize when a visitor has a larger font setting (unless you define their size in ems, which results in unsightly pixelation artifacts).

Links are much nicer, as you can style them with CSS, they resize, and they can be easily populated from a localized dataset. The problem with links though is that you need JavaScript to submit a form with them. That is why the lazy or too busy developer's answer to this dilemma is a link that simply submits the form using the `javascript:` protocol (a lot of code generators or frameworks will come up with the same):

```
<a href="javascript:document.forms[0].submit()">Submit</a>
```

A lot earlier in this book I established that this is just not an option—as without JavaScript this will be a dead link, and there won't be any way to submit the form. If you want to have the best of both worlds—a simple Submit button for non-JavaScript users and a link for the ones with scripting enabled—you'll need to do the following:

1. Loop through all INPUT elements of the document.

2. Test whether the type is submit.

3. If that is not the case, continue the loop, skipping the rest of it.

4. If it is the case, create a new link with a text node.

5. Set the node value of the text node to the value of the INPUT element.

6. Set the href of the link to the invalid javascript:document.forms[0].submit().

7. Replace the input element with the link.

■**Note** Setting the href attribute to the javascript: construct is not the cleanest way of doing this—in the next chapter, you'll learn about event handlers—a much better way to achieve this solution.

In code, this could be

```
<!DOCTYPE HTML PUBLIC "-//W3C//DTD HTML 4.01//EN"➥
  "http://www.w3.org/TR/html4/strict.dtd">
<html dir="ltr" lang="en">
  <head>
    <meta http-equiv="Content-Type"➥
          content="text/html; charset=utf-8">
    <title>Example: Submit buttons to links</title>
    <style type="text/css"></style>
    <script type="text/javascript" src="submitToLinks.js"></script>
  </head>
  <body>
    <form action="nogo.php" method="post">
      <label for="Name">Name:</label>
      <input type="text" id="Name" name="Name" />
      <input type="submit" value="send" />
    </form>
  </body>
</html>
function submitToLinks()
{
  if(!document.getElementById || !document.createTextNode){return;}
  var inputs,i,newLink,newText;
  inputs=document.getElementsByTagName('input');
  for (i=0;i<inputs.length;i++)
  {
    if(inputs[i].getAttribute('type').toLowerCase()!='submit')➥
      {continue;i++}
    newLink=document.createElement('a');
    newText=document.createTextNode(inputs[i].getAttribute('value'));
    newLink.appendChild(newText);
    newLink.setAttribute('href','javascript:document.forms[0]➥
      .submit()');
    inputs[i].parentNode.replaceChild(newLink,inputs[i]);
  }
}
window.onload=submitToLinks;
```

When JavaScript is available, the visitor gets a link to submit the form; otherwise, he gets a Submit button, as shown in Figure 4-12.

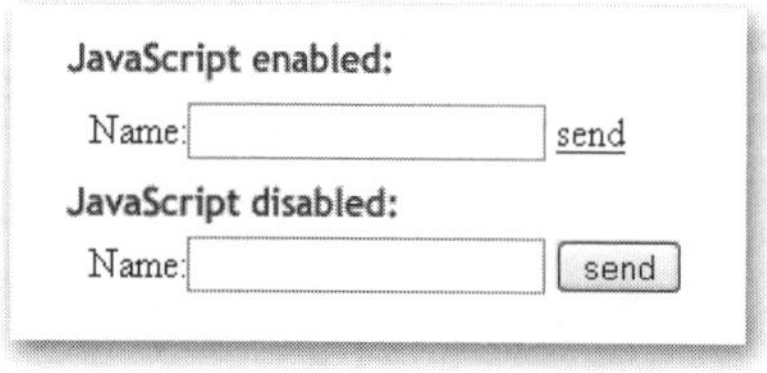

Figure 4-12. *Depending on JavaScript availability, the user gets a link or a button to send the form.*

However, the function has one major flaw: it will fail when there are more input elements following the Submit button. Change the HTML to have another input after the Submit button:

```html
<form action="nogo.php" method="post">
  <p>
    <label for="Name">Name:</label>
    <input type="text" id="Name" name="Name" />
    <input type="submit" value="check" />
    <input type="submit" value="send" />
  </p>
  <p>
    <label for="Email">email:</label>
    <input type="text" id="Email" name="Email" />
  </p>
</form>
```

You will see that the "send" Submit button does not get replaced with a link. This happens because you removed an input element, which changes the size of the array, and the loop gets out of sync with the elements it should reach. A fix for this problem is to decrease the loop counter every time you remove an item. However, you need to check whether the loop is already in the final iteration by comparing the loop counter with the length of the array (simply decreasing the counter would cause the script to fail, as it tries to access an element that is not there):

```javascript
function submitToLinks()
{
  if(!document.getElementById || !document.createTextNode){return;}
  var inputs,i,newLink,newText;
  inputs=document.getElementsByTagName('input');
  for (i=0;i<inputs.length;i++)
  {
    if(inputs[i].getAttribute('type').toLowerCase()!='submit')➥
      {continue;i++}
    newLink=document.createElement('a');
    newText=document.createTextNode(inputs[i].getAttribute('value'));
```

```
    newLink.appendChild(newText);
    newLink.setAttribute('href','javascript:document.forms[0]➡
      .submit()');
    inputs[i].parentNode.replaceChild(newLink,inputs[i]);
    if(i<inputs.length){i--};
  }
}
window.onload=submitToLinks;
```

This version of the script will not fail, and replaces both buttons with links.

Note There is one usability aspect of forms that this script will break: you can submit forms by hitting the Enter button when there is a Submit button in them. When we remove all Submit buttons, this will not be possible any longer. A workaround is to add a blank image button or hide the Submit buttons instead of removing them. We'll get back to that option in the next chapter. The other usability concern is whether you should change the look and feel of forms at all—as you lose the instant recognizability of form elements. Visitors are used to how forms look on their browser and operating system—if you change that, they'll have to look for the interactive elements and might expect other functionality. People trust forms with their personal data and money transactions—anything that might confuse them is easily perceived as a security issue.

Avoiding NOSCRIPT

The SCRIPT element has a counterpart in NOSCRIPT. This element was originally intended to provide visitors alternative content when JavaScript was not available. Semantic HTML discourages the use of script blocks inside the document (the body should only contain elements that contribute to the document's structure, and SCRIPT does not do that); NOSCRIPT became deprecated. However, you will find a lot of accessibility tutorials on the Web that advocate the use of NOSCRIPT as a safety measure. It is tempting to simply add a message inside a <noscript> tag to the page that explains that you'll need JavaScript to use the site to its full extent, and it seems to be a really easy approach to the problem. This is why a lot of developers frowned upon the W3C deprecating NOSCRIPT or simply sacrificed HTML validity for the cause. However, by using DOM methods, you can work around the issue.

In a perfect world, there wouldn't be any web site that needed JavaScript to work—only web sites that work faster and are sometimes easier to use when scripting is available. In the real world, however, you will sometimes have to use out-of-the-box products or frameworks that simply generate code that is dependent on scripting. When reengineering or replacing those with less obtrusive systems is not an option, you might want to tell visitors that they need scripting for the site to work.

With NOSCRIPT, this was done quite simply:

```
<script type="text/javascript">myGreatApplication();</script>
<noscript>
  Sorry but you need to have scripting enabled to use this site.
</noscript>
```

A message like that is not very helpful—the least you should do is to allow visitors who cannot have scripting enabled (for example, workers in banks and financial companies that turn off scripting as it poses a security threat) to contact you.

Modern scripting tackles this problem from the other side: we give some information and replace it when scripting is available. In the case of an application dependent on scripting, this can be

```
<p id="noscripting">
  We are sorry, but this application needs JavaScript
  to be enabled to work. Please <a href="contact.html">contact us</a>
  If you cannot enable scripting and we will try to help you in other
  ways.
</p>
```

You then write a script that simply removes it and even use this opportunity to test for DOM support at the same time.

```
<!DOCTYPE HTML PUBLIC "-//W3C//DTD HTML 4.01//EN"➥
  "http://www.w3.org/TR/html4/strict.dtd">
<html dir="ltr" lang="en">
  <head>
    <meta http-equiv="Content-Type" content="text/html; charset=utf-8">
    <title>Example: Replacing noscript</title>
    <script type="text/javascript">
      function noscript()
      {
        if(!document.getElementById || ➥
          !document.createTextNode){return;}
        // Add more tests as needed (cookies, objects...)
        var noJSmsg=document.getElementById('noscripting');
        if(!noJSmsg){return;}
        var headline='Browser test succeeded';
        replaceMessage='We tested if your browser is capable of ';
        replaceMessage+='supporting the application, and all checked➥
          out fine. ';
        replaceMessage+='Please proceed by activating the following➥
          link.';
        var linkMessage='Proceed to application.';
        var head=document.createElement('h1');
        head.appendChild(document.createTextNode(headline));
```

```
      noJSmsg.parentNode.insertBefore(head,noJSmsg);
      var infoPara=document.createElement('p');
      infoPara.appendChild(document.createTextNode(replaceMessage));
      noJSmsg.parentNode.insertBefore(infoPara,noJSmsg);
      var linkPara=document.createElement('p');
      var appLink=document.createElement('a');
      appLink.setAttribute('href','application.aspx');
      appLink.appendChild(document.createTextNode(linkMessage));
      linkPara.appendChild(appLink);
      noJSmsg.parentNode.replaceChild(linkPara,noJSmsg);
    }
    window.onload=noscript;
  </script>
 </head>
 <body>
  <p id="noscripting">
    We are sorry, but this application needs JavaScript to be
    enabled to work. Please <a href="contact.html">contact us</a>
    if you cannot enable scripting and we will try to help you in
    other ways
  </p>
 </body>
</html>
```

You can see that generating a lot of content via the DOM can be rather cumbersome, which is why for situations like these—where you really don't need every node you generate as a variable—a lot of developers use innerHTML instead.

Shortening Your Scripts via InnerHTML

Microsoft implemented the nonstandard property innerHTML quite early in the development of Internet Explorer. It is now supported by most browsers; there has even been talk of adding it to the DOM standard. What it allows you to do is to define a string containing HTML and assign it to an object. The user agent then does the rest for you—all the node generation and adding of the child nodes. The NOSCRIPT example using innerHTML is a lot shorter:

```
<!DOCTYPE HTML PUBLIC "-//W3C//DTD HTML 4.01//EN"➥
  "http://www.w3.org/TR/html4/strict.dtd">
<html dir="ltr" lang="en">
  <head>
    <meta http-equiv="Content-Type"➥
        content="text/html; charset=utf-8">
    <title>Example: Replacing noscript</title>
    <script type="text/javascript">
      function noscript()
      {
        if(!document.getElementById || ➥
          !document.createTextNode){return;}
```

```
      // Add more tests as needed (cookies, objects...)
      var noJSmsg=document.getElementById('noscripting');
      if(!noJSmsg){return;}
      var replaceMessage='<h1>Browser test succeeded<h1>';
      replaceMessage='<p>We tested if your browser is capable of ';
      replaceMessage+='supporting the application, and all checked➡
        out fine. ';
      replaceMessage+='Please proceed by activating the following➡
        link.</p>';
      replaceMessage+='<p><a href="application.aspx">➡
        Proceed to application</a></p>';
      noJSmsg.innerHTML=replaceMessage;
    }
  </script>
</head>
<body>
  <p id="noscripting">
    We are sorry, but this application needs JavaScript to be
    enabled to work. Please <a href="contact.html">contact us</a>
    if you cannot enable scripting and we will try to help you in
    other ways.
  </p>
</body>
</html>
```

It is also possible to read out the innerHTML property of an element, which can be extremely handy when debugging your code—as not all browsers have a "view generated source" feature. It is also very easy to replace whole parts of HTML with other HTML, which is something we do a lot when we display content retrieved via Ajax from the back end.

DOM Summary: Your Cheat Sheet

That was a lot to take in, and it might be good to have all the DOM features you need in one place to copy and have on hand, so here you go.

Reaching Elements in a Document

- document.getElementById('id'): Retrieves the element with the given id as an object

- document.getElementsByTagName('tagname'): Retrieves all elements with the tag name tagname and stores them in an array-like list

Reading Element Attributes, Node Values, and Other Node Data

- `node.getAttribute('attribute')`: Retrieves the value of the attribute with the name `attribute`

- `node.setAttribute('attribute', 'value')`: Sets the value of the attribute with the name `attribute` to `value`

- `node.nodeType`: Reads the type of the node (1 = element, 3 = text node)

- `node.nodeName`: Reads the name of the node (either element name or `#textNode`)

- `node.nodeValue`: Reads or sets the value of the node (the text content in the case of text nodes)

Navigating Between Nodes

- `node.previousSibling`: Retrieves the previous sibling node and stores it as an object.

- `node.nextSibling`: Retrieves the next sibling node and stores it as an object.

- `node.childNodes`: Retrieves all child nodes of the object and stores them in an list. There are shortcuts for the first and last child node, named `node.firstChild` and `node.lastChild`.

- `node.parentNode`: Retrieves the node containing `node`.

Creating New Nodes

- `document.createElement(element)`: Creates a new element node with the name `element`. You provide the element name as a string.

- `document.createTextNode(string)`: Creates a new text node with the node value of `string`.

- `newNode =node.cloneNode(bool)`: Creates `newNode` as a copy (clone) of `node`. If `bool` is true, the clone includes clones of all the child nodes of the original.

- `node.appendChild(newNode)`: Adds `newNode` as a new (last) child node to `node`.

- `node.insertBefore(newNode,oldNode)`: Inserts `newNode` as a new child node of `node` before `oldNode`.

- `node.removeChild(oldNode)`: Removes the child `oldNode` from `node`.

- `node.replaceChild(newNode, oldNode)`: Replaces the child node `oldNode` of `node` with `newNode`.

- `element.innerHTML`: Reads or writes the HTML content of the given `element` as a string—including all child nodes with their attributes and text content.

DOMhelp: Our Own Helper Library

The most annoying thing when working with the DOM is browser inconsistencies—especially when this means you have to test the nodeType every time you want to access a nextSibling, as the user agent might or might not read the line break as its own text node.

It is therefore a good idea to have a set of tool functions handy to work around these issues and allow you to concentrate on the logic of the main script instead. There are many JavaScript frameworks and libraries available on the Web—the biggest and most up to date is probably prototype (http://prototype.conio.net/).

Let's start our own helper method library right here and now to illustrate the issues you'd have to face without it otherwise.

■**Note** You'll find the DOMhelp.js file and a test HTML file in the code demo zip file accompanying this book—the version in the zip has more methods, which will be discussed in the next chapter, so don't get confused.

The library will consist of one object called DOMhelp with several utility methods. The following is the skeleton for the utility that we will flesh out over the course of this and the next chapter.

```
DOMhelp=
{
  // Find the last sibling of the current node
  lastSibling:function(node){},

  // Find the first sibling of the current node
  firstSibling:function(node){},

  // Retrieve the content of the first text node sibling of the current node
  getText:function(node){},

  // Set the content of the first text node sibling of the current node
  setText:function(node,txt){},

  // Find the next or previous sibling that is an element
  //  and not a text node or line break
  closestSibling:function(node,direction){},

  // Create a new link containing the given text
  createLink:function(to,txt){},

  // Create a new element containing the given text
  createTextElm:function(elm,txt){},
```

```
// Simulate a debugging console to avoid the need for alerts
initDebug:function(){},
setDebug:function(bug){},
stopDebug:function(){}
}
```

You've already encountered the last and first sibling functions earlier in this chapter; the only thing that was missing in those was a test for whether there really is a previous or next sibling to check before trying to assign it to the temporary object. Each of these two methods checks for the existence of the sibling in question, and returns false if it isn't available:

```
lastSibling:function(node)
{
  var tempObj=node.parentNode.lastChild;
  while(tempObj.nodeType!=1 && tempObj.previousSibling!=null)
  {
    tempObj=tempObj.previousSibling;
  }
  return (tempObj.nodeType==1)?tempObj:false;
},
firstSibling:function(node)
{
  var tempObj=node.parentNode.firstChild;
  while(tempObj.nodeType!=1 && tempObj.nextSibling!=null)
  {
    tempObj=tempObj.nextSibling;
  }
  return (tempObj.nodeType==1)?tempObj:false;
},
```

Next up is the getText method, which reads out the text value of the first text node of an element:

```
getText:function(node)
{
  if(!node.hasChildNodes()){return false;}
  var reg=/^\s+$/;
  var tempObj=node.firstChild;
  while(tempObj.nodeType!=3 && tempObj.nextSibling!=null ||➥
    reg.test(tempObj.nodeValue))
  {
    tempObj=tempObj.nextSibling;
  }
  return tempObj.nodeType==3?tempObj.nodeValue:false;
},
```

The first problem we might encounter is that the node has no children whatsoever, therefore we check for hasChildNodes. The other problems are embedded elements in the node and whitespace such as line breaks and tabs being read as nodes by browsers other than MSIE. Therefore, we test the first child node and jump to the next sibling until the nodeType is text (3), and the node does not consist solely of whitespace characters (this is what the regular expression checks). We also test whether there is a next sibling node to go to before we try to assign it to tempObj. If all works out fine, the method returns the nodeValue of the first text node; otherwise it returns false.

The same testing pattern works for setText, which replaces the first real text child of the node with new text and avoids any line breaks or tabs:

```
setText:function(node,txt)
{
  if(!node.hasChildNodes()){return false;}
  var reg=/^\s+$/;
  var tempObj=node.firstChild;
  while(tempObj.nodeType!=3 && tempObj.nextSibling!=null ||➥
    reg.test(tempObj.nodeValue))
  {
    tempObj=tempObj.nextSibling;
  }
  if(tempObj.nodeType==3){tempObj.nodeValue=txt}else{return false;}
},
```

The next two helper methods help us with the common tasks of creating a link with a target and text inside it and creating an element with text inside.

```
createLink:function(to,txt)
{
  var tempObj=document.createElement('a');
  tempObj.appendChild(document.createTextNode(txt));
  tempObj.setAttribute('href',to);
  return tempObj;
},
createTextElm:function(elm,txt)
{
  var tempObj=document.createElement(elm);
  tempObj.appendChild(document.createTextNode(txt));
  return tempObj;
},
```

They contain nothing you haven't already seen here earlier, but they are very handy to have in one place.

The fact that some browsers read line breaks as text nodes and others don't means that you cannot trust nextSibling or previousSibling to return the next element—for example, in an unordered list. The utility method closestSibling() works around that problem. It needs node and direction (1 for the next sibling, -1 for the previous sibling) as parameters.

```
closestSibling:function(node,direction)
{
  var tempObj;
  if(direction==-1 && node.previousSibling!=null)
  {
    tempObj=node.previousSibling;
    while(tempObj.nodeType!=1 && tempObj.previousSibling!=null)
    {
        tempObj=tempObj.previousSibling;
    }
  }
  else if(direction==1 && node.nextSibling!=null)
  {
    tempObj=node.nextSibling;
    while(tempObj.nodeType!=1 && tempObj.nextSibling!=null)
    {
      tempObj=tempObj.nextSibling;
    }
  }
  return tempObj.nodeType==1?tempObj:false;
},
```

The final set of methods is there to simulate a programmable JavaScript debug console. Using alert() as a means to display values is handy, but it can become a real pain when you want to watch changes inside a large loop—who wants to press Enter 200 times? Instead of using alert(), we add a new DIV to the document and output any data we want to check as new child nodes of that one. With a proper style sheet, we could float that DIV above the content. We start with an initialization method that checks whether the console already exists and removes it if that is the case. This is necessary to avoid several consoles existing simultaneously. We then create a new DIV element, give it an ID for styling, and add it to the document.

```
initDebug:function()
{
  if(DOMhelp.debug){DOMhelp.stopDebug();}
  DOMhelp.debug=document.createElement('div');
  DOMhelp.debug.setAttribute('id',DOMhelp.debugWindowId);
  document.body.insertBefore(DOMhelp.debug,document.body.firstChild);
},
```

The setDebug method takes a string called bug as a parameter. It tests whether the console already exists and calls the initialization method to create the console if necessary. It then adds the bug string followed by a line break to the HTML content of the console.

```
setDebug:function(bug)
{
  if(!DOMhelp.debug){DOMhelp.initDebug();}
  DOMhelp.debug.innerHTML+=bug+'\n';
},
```

The final method is the one that removes the console from the document if it exists. Notice that we both need to remove the element and set the object property to `null`; otherwise testing for `DOMhelp.debug` would be `true` even if there is no console to write to.

```
stopDebug:function()
{
  if(DOMhelp.debug)
  {
    DOMhelp.debug.parentNode.removeChild(DOMhelp.debug);
    DOMhelp.debug=null;
  }
}
```

We will extend this helper library over the course of the next chapters.

Summary

After reading this chapter, you should be fully equipped to tackle any HTML document, get the parts you need, and change or even create markup via the DOM.

You learned about the anatomy of an HTML document and how the DOM offers you what you see as a collection of element, attribute, and text nodes. You also saw the window methods `alert()`, `confirm()`, and `prompt()`; these are quick and widely supported—albeit insecure and clumsy—ways of retrieving data and giving feedback.

You then learned about the DOM, and how to reach elements, navigate between them, and how to create new content.

In the next chapter, you'll learn how to deal with presentation issues and to track how a visitor has interacted with the document in her browser, and to react accordingly via event handling.

■■■

CHAPTER 5

Presentation and Behavior (CSS and Event Handling)

In the last chapter, you took apart an HTML document to see what is under the hood. You fiddled with some of the cables, exchanged some parts, and got the engine in pristine condition. Now it is time to take a look at how to give the document a new lick of paint with CSS and kick-start it via events. If beauty is what you are after, you are in luck, as we start with the presentation layer.

Changing the Presentation Layer via JavaScript

Every element in the HTML document has as one of its properties a `style` attribute that is a collection of all its visual properties. You can read or write the attribute's value, and if you write a value into the attribute, you will immediately change the look and feel of the element.

■Note Notice that we use the DOMhelp library we created in the previous chapter throughout the whole chapter (and, indeed, in the rest of the book).

Try this script for starters:

exampleStyleChange.html

```
<!DOCTYPE HTML PUBLIC "-//W3C//DTD HTML 4.01//EN"
"http://www.w3.org/TR/html4/strict.dtd">
<html dir="ltr" lang="en">
<head>
  <meta http-equiv="Content-Type" content="text/html; charset=utf-8">
  <title>Example: Accessing the style collection</title>
  <style type="text/css">
  </style>
  <script type="text/javascript" src="DOMhelp.js"></script>
  <script type="text/javascript" src="styleChange.js"></script>
</head>
```

```
<body>
<h3>Contact Details</h3>
<address>
  Awesome Web Production Company<br />
  Going Nowhere Lane 0<br />
  Catch 22<br />
  N4 2XX<br />
  England<br />
</address>
</body>
</html>
```

styleChange.js

```
sc = {
  init:function(){
    sc.head = document.getElementsByTagName('h3')[0];
    if(!sc.head){return;}
    sc.ad = DOMhelp.closestSibling(sc.head,1);
    sc.ad.style.display='none';
    var t = DOMhelp.getText(sc.head);
    var collapseLink = DOMhelp.createLink('#',t);
    sc.head.replaceChild(collapseLink,sc.head.firstChild);
    DOMhelp.addEvent(collapseLink,'click',sc.peekaboo,false)
    collapseLink.onclick = function(){return;} // Safari fix
  },
  peekaboo:function(e){
    sc.ad.style.display=sc.ad.style.display=='none'? '':'none';
    DOMhelp.cancelClick(e);
  }
}
DOMhelp.addEvent(window,'load',sc.init,false);
```

■**Note** Patience is the key; the addEvent() and cancelClick() parts will be explained in the second part of this chapter. For now, focus on the bold parts of the script.

The script grabs the first H3 element in the document and gets the ADDRESS element via the closestSibling helper method of the DOMhelp library (the method makes sure that it retrieves the next element and not line breaks that are seen as text nodes). It then modifies the display property of its style collection to hide the address. It replaces the text inside the heading with a link pointing to the function peekaboo. The link is necessary to allow keyboard users to expand and collapse the address. While mouse users could easily click the heading, it is not accessible by tabbing through the document. The peekaboo() function reads the display value of the style collection of the address and replaces it with an empty string if display is set to none and with none when the display is set to something other than an empty string—effectively hiding and showing the address as shown in Figure 5-1.

Figure 5-1. *The two states of the address (collapsed and expanded)*

■**Note** You might have encountered scripts in the past that use element.style.display='block' as the opposite of none. This works for most elements, but simply setting the display value to nothing resets it to the initial display value—which does not necessarily have to be block; it could be inline or table-row. If you add an empty string, you leave it to the browser to set the appropriate value; otherwise you'd have to add a switch block or if conditions for different elements.

The style collection contains all the style settings of the current element that you can modify by using the property notation of the different CSS selectors. A rule of thumb for the property notation is that you remove the dash in the CSS selector and use camelCase for the whole selector. For example, `line-height` becomes `lineHeight` and `border-right` becomes `borderRight`. Here's a list of all available properties (notice that `float` becomes `cssFloat`!):

- `background`, `backgroundAttachment`, `backgroundColor`, `backgroundImage`, `backgroundPosition`, and `backgroundRepeat`

- `border`, `borderBottom`, `borderTop`, `borderLeft`, `borderRight`, and for each of them `style`, `width`, and `color`

- `color`, `direction`, `display`, `visibility`, `letterSpacing`, `lineHeight`, `textAlign`, `textDecoration`, `textIndent`, `textTransform`, `wordSpacing`, `letterSpacing`

- `margin`, `padding` (each for `top`, `left`, `bottom`, and `right`)

- `width`, `height`, `minWidth`, `maxWidth`, `minHeight`, `maxHeight`

- `captionSide`, `emptyCells`, `tableLayout`, `verticalAlign`

- `top`, `bottom`, `left`, `right`, `zIndex`, `cssFloat`, `position`, `overflow`, `clip`, `clear`

- `listStyle`, `listStyleImage`, `listStylePosition`, `listStyleType`

- `font`, `fontFamily`, `fontSize`, `fontStretch`, `fontStyle`, `fontVariant`, `fontWeight`

You can read and write all of these using `getAttribute()` and `setAttribute()`; however, if you write them, it might be quicker to simply set the `style` attribute to a string value using JavaScript object property syntax. For the browser, both of the following examples are the same, but the latter might be a bit quicker to render and keeps your JavaScript shorter.

```
var warning=document.createElement('div');

warning.style.borderColor='#c00';
warning.style.borderWidth='1px';
warning.style.borderStyle='solid';
warning.style.backgroundColor='#fcc';
warning.style.padding='5px';
warning.style.color='#c00';
warning.style.fontFamily='Arial';

// is the same as
warning.setAttribute( 'style' , 'font-family:arial;color:#c00;
padding:5px;border:1px solid #c00;background:#fcc');
```

While setting `style` attributes directly is frowned upon in modern web design (you are effectively mixing behavior and presentation and you make maintenance a lot harder), there are situations where you will have to set `style` attributes directly via JavaScript—for example:

- Fixing browser shortcomings when it comes to CSS support

- Dynamically changing the dimensions of elements to fix layout glitches

- Animating parts of the document

- Creating rich user interfaces with drag-and-drop functionality

---

■**Note** You will hear about the first two later on in this chapter; however, you won't find animation or drag-and-drop examples here, as these are very advanced JavaScript topics and need a lot of explanation that falls outside of the scope of this book. You will find examples you can use out-of-the-box in Chapter 11.

For simple styling tasks, you should avoid defining the look and feel in JavaScript in order to simplify maintenance of your script. In Chapter 3, we talked about the main feature of modern web development: separation of the development layers.

If you use a lot of style definitions in JavaScript, you mix the presentation and the behavior layers. If some months down the line the look and feel of your application has to change, you—or some third-party developer—will have to revisit your script code and change all the settings in it. This is neither necessary nor advisable, as you can separate the look and feel out into the CSS document.

You can achieve this separation by dynamically changing the `class` attribute of elements. That way you can apply or remove style settings defined in your site's style sheet. The CSS designer does not have to worry about your script code, and you don't have to know about all the problems browsers have when it comes to supporting CSS. All you need to communicate is the names of the classes.

For example, to apply a class called `dynamic` to an element with the ID `nav`, you change its `className` attribute:

```
var n=document.getElementById('nav');
n.className='dynamic';
```

■**Note** Logically, you should also be able to change the class via the `setAttribute()` method, but browser support for this is flaky (Internet Explorer does not allow `class` or `style` as the attribute), which is why for the moment it is a good plan to stick with `className`. The name of the property is `className` and not `class`, as `class` is a reserved word in JavaScript and results in an error when used as a property.

You can remove the class by setting its value to an empty string. Again, `removeAttribute()` does not work reliably across different browsers.

As you may be aware, HTML elements can have more than one CSS class assigned to them. A construct of the following kind is valid HTML—and sometimes a good idea:

```
<p class="intro special kids">Lorem Ipsum</p>
```

In JavaScript, you can achieve this by simply appending a value preceded by a space to the `className` value. However, there is a danger that browsers will not display your class settings correctly, especially when adding or removing results in leading or trailing spaces in the `className` value. The following two examples might not display correctly in some browsers (especially in MSIE 5 on Macs):

```
<p class="intro special kids ">Lorem Ipsum</p>
<p class=" intro special kids">Lorem Ipsum</p>
```

You can work around this problem with a helper method. Writing this helper method to dynamically add and remove classes should be easy: you append a class value preceded by a space if the `className` attribute is not empty and without the space if it is empty. You remove the class name from the original value just like you would remove a word from a string. However, as you need to cater to browser problems with orphan spaces, it gets a bit more complicated than this. The following tool method is included in DOMhelp and allows you to dynamically add and remove classes from an element. It also allows you to test whether a certain class is already added to it.

```
function cssjs(a,o,c1,c2){
  switch (a){
    case 'swap':
      if(!domtab.cssjs('check',o,c1)){
        o.className.replace(c2,c1)
      }else{
        o.className.replace(c1,c2);
      }
    break;
    case 'add':
      if(!domtab.cssjs('check',o,c1)){
        o.className+=o.className?' '+c1:c1;
      }
    break;
    case 'remove':
      var rep=o.className.match(' '+c1)?' '+c1:c1;
      o.className=o.className.replace(rep,'');
    break;
    case 'check':
      var found=false;
      var temparray=o.className.split(' ');
      for(var i=0;i<temparray.length;i++){
        if(temparray[i]==c1){found=true;}
      }
```

```
      return found;
    break;
  }
}
```

Don't worry too much about the inner workings of this method—it will get clearer to you once you master the match() and replace() methods, which will be covered in Chapter 8. For now, all you need to know is how to use it, and for that you use the method's four parameters:

- a is the action that has to be taken and has the following options:

  - swap replaces one class with another.

  - add adds a new class.

  - remove removes a class.

  - check tests whether the class is already applied or not.

- o is the object you want to add classes to or remove classes from.

- c1 and c2 are the class names—c2 is only needed when the action is swap.

Let's use the method to recode the earlier example—this time hiding and showing the address by dynamically applying and removing a class.

exampleClassChange.html

```html
<!DOCTYPE HTML PUBLIC "-//W3C//DTD HTML 4.01//EN"
"http://www.w3.org/TR/html4/strict.dtd">
<html dir="ltr" lang="en">
<head>
  <meta http-equiv="Content-Type" content="text/html; charset=utf-8">
  <title>Example: Dynamically changing classes</title>
  <style type="text/css">
    @import "dynamic.css";
  </style>
  <script type="text/javascript" src="DOMhelp.js"></script>
  <script type="text/javascript" src="classChange.js"></script>
</head>
<body>
<h3>Contact Details</h3>
<address>
  Awesome Web Production Company<br />
  Going Nowhere Lane O<br />
  Catch 22<br />
  N4 2XX<br />
  England<br />
</address>
</body>
</html>
```

The style sheet contains, among others, a class called hide that will hide any element it gets applied to. In this example, you use the off-left technique (http://css-discuss.incutio.com/?page=screenReaderVisibility) for that, which is possibly the most accessible way of hiding content. The problem with altering the visibility or display properties to hide elements is that screen readers helping blind users may not make content available to them, although it is visible in a browser.

classChange.css *(excerpt)*

```
.hide{
  position:absolute;
  top:0;
  left:-9999px;
  height:0;
  overflow:hidden;
}
```

You specify the name of the class as a parameter at the start of the script, which means that if someone needs to change the name at a later stage, he won't have to check the whole script.

If you develop a really complex site with lots of different classes to be added and removed, you could move them out into their own JavaScript include with their own object. For this example, such a move would be overkill—but we will come back to this option later.

Note Notice that DOMhelp already includes the cssjs() method, therefore you don't need to include it in this example.

---

classChange.js

```
sc={

  // CSS classes
  hidingClass:'hide', // Hide elements

  init:function(){
    sc.head=document.getElementsByTagName('h3')[0];
    if(!sc.head){return;}
    sc.ad=DOMhelp.closestSibling(sc.head,1);

    DOMhelp.cssjs('add',sc.ad,sc.hidingClass);

    var t=DOMhelp.getText(sc.head);
    var collapseLink=DOMhelp.createLink('#',t);
    sc.head.replaceChild(collapseLink,sc.head.firstChild);
```

```
      DOMhelp.addEvent(collapseLink,'click',sc.peekaboo,false)
      collapseLink.onclick=function(){return;} // Safari fix
    },
    peekaboo:function(e){

      if(DOMhelp.cssjs('check',sc.ad,sc.hidingClass)){
         DOMhelp.cssjs('remove',sc.ad,sc.hidingClass)
      } else {
         DOMhelp.cssjs('add',sc.ad,sc.hidingClass)
      }

      DOMhelp.cancelClick(e);
   }
}
DOMhelp.addEvent(window,'load',sc.init,false);
```

Helping the CSS Designer

DOM scripting and separating the CSS out into classes that get applied and removed dynamically allows you to make the life of web designers a lot easier. Using DOM and JavaScript allows you to reach much further into the document than CSS selectors allow you to. One common request is a way to reach a parent element in CSS for hover effects, for example. In CSS this is impossible; in JavaScript it is pretty easy to achieve via parentNode. With JavaScript and DOM, you can provide the designer with dynamic hooks for her style sheet by altering the HTML content to apply classes and IDs, generate content, or even add and remove whole style sheets by adding or removing STYLE and LINK elements.

Styling Dynamic Pages Made Easy

It is very important to make it as easy as possible for the designer to create different styles for the scripting enhanced version of a site and the nonscripting version. The nonscripting version can be much simpler, and the styles needed for it tend to be fewer (for example, in the HTML address example you only need link styles defined for inside the H3 when JavaScript is enabled, as the link is generated via JavaScript). A really easy option to give the designer a unique identifier when scripting is enabled is to apply a class to the body or to the main element of the layout.

dynamicStyling.js—*used in* exampleDynamicStyling.html

```
sc={

  // CSS classes
  hidingClass:'hide', // Hide elements
  DOMClass:'dynamic', // Indicate DOM support

  init:function(){
```

```
    // Check for DOM and apply a class to the body if it is supported
    if(!document.getElementById || !document.createElement){return;}
    DOMhelp.cssjs('add',document.body,sc.DOMClass);

    sc.head=document.getElementsByTagName('h3')[0];
    if(!sc.head){return;}
    sc.ad=DOMhelp.closestSibling(sc.head,1);
    DOMhelp.cssjs('add',sc.ad,sc.hidingClass);
    var t=DOMhelp.getText(sc.head);
    var collapseLink=DOMhelp.createLink('#',t);
    sc.head.replaceChild(collapseLink,sc.head.firstChild);
    DOMhelp.addEvent(collapseLink,'click',sc.peekaboo,false)
    collapseLink.onclick=function(){return;} // Safari fix
  },
  peekaboo:function(e){
    if(DOMhelp.cssjs('check',sc.ad,sc.hidingClass)){
      DOMhelp.cssjs('remove',sc.ad,sc.hidingClass)
    } else {
      DOMhelp.cssjs('add',sc.ad,sc.hidingClass)
    }
    DOMhelp.cancelClick(e);
  }
}
DOMhelp.addEvent(window,'load',sc.init,false);
```

That way the CSS designer can define in the style sheet which settings to apply when JavaScript is disabled and overwrite them with others when JavaScript is enabled by using the body with the class name in a descendant selector:

dynamicStyling.css

```
*{
  margin:0;
  padding:0;
}
body{
  font-family:Arial,Sans-Serif;
  font-size:small;
  padding:2em;
}
```

```css
/* JS disabled */
address{
  background:#ddd;
  border:1px solid #999;
  border-top:none;
  font-style:normal;
  padding:.5em;
  width:15em;
}
h3{
  border:1px solid #000;
  color:#fff;
  background:#369;
  padding:.2em .5em;
  width:15em;
  font-size:1em;
}

/* JS enabled */
body.dynamic address{
  background:#fff;
  border:none;
  font-style:normal;
  padding:.5em;
  border-top:1px solid #ccc;
}
body.dynamic h3{
  padding-bottom:.5em;
  background:#fff;
  border:none;
}
body.dynamic h3 a{
  color:#369;
}

/* dynamic classes */
.hide{
  position:absolute;
  top:0;
  left:-9999px;
  height:0;
}
```

The address example can now—depending on JavaScript and DOM being available or not—have two completely different looks (one of these having two states) as shown in Figure 5-2.

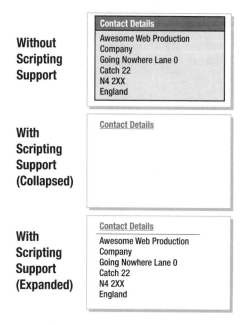

Figure 5-2. *The three states of the address (nondynamic version, collapsed, and expanded)*

This works nicely if your site is not overly complex and does not have many dynamic elements. For more complex sites, you could use a different style sheet for the non-JavaScript and the JavaScript versions and add the latter via JavaScript. This also has an added benefit: the low-level user does not have to load a style sheet that isn't of any use to him. You can add dynamic style sheets by creating a new LINK element in the head of the document. In this example, you start by including a low-level style sheet.

exampleStyleSheetChange.html

```
<!DOCTYPE HTML PUBLIC "-//W3C//DTD HTML 4.01//EN"
"http://www.w3.org/TR/html4/strict.dtd">
<html dir="ltr" lang="en">
<head>
  <meta http-equiv="Content-Type" content="text/html; charset=utf-8">
  <title>Example: Dynamically applying new Style Sheets </title>
  <style type="text/css">
     @import "lowlevel.css";
  </style>
  <script type="text/javascript" src="DOMhelp.js"></script>
  <script type="text/javascript" src="styleSheetChange.js"></script>
</head>
```

```
<body>
<h3>Contact Details</h3>
<address>
  Awesome Web Production Company<br />
  Going Nowhere Lane 0<br />
  Catch 22<br />
  N4 2XX<br />
  England<br />
</adress>
</body>
</html>
```

The script checks for DOM support and adds a new link element pointing to the high-level style sheet:

styleSheetChange.js

```
sc={
  // CSS classes

  hidingClass:'hide', // Hide elements
  highLevelStyleSheet:'highlevel.css', // Style sheet for dynamic site

  init:function(){

    // Check for DOM and apply a class to the body if it is supported
    if(!document.getElementById || !document.createElement){return;}

    var newStyle=document.createElement('link');
    newStyle.setAttribute('type','text/css');
    newStyle.setAttribute('rel','StyleSheet');
    newStyle.setAttribute('href',sc.highLevelStyleSheet);
    document.getElementsByTagName('head')[0].appendChild(newStyle);

    sc.head=document.getElementsByTagName('h3')[0];
    if(!sc.head){return;}
    sc.ad=DOMhelp.closestSibling(sc.head,1);
    DOMhelp.cssjs('add',sc.ad,sc.hidingClass);
    var t=DOMhelp.getText(sc.head);
    var collapseLink=DOMhelp.createLink('#',t);
    sc.head.replaceChild(collapseLink,sc.head.firstChild);
    DOMhelp.addEvent(collapseLink,'click',sc.peekaboo,false)
    collapseLink.onclick=function(){return;} // Safari fix
  },
```

```
  peekaboo:function(e){
    if(DOMhelp.cssjs('check',sc.ad,sc.hidingClass)){
       DOMhelp.cssjs('remove',sc.ad,sc.hidingClass)
    } else {
       DOMhelp.cssjs('add',sc.ad,sc.hidingClass)
    }
    DOMhelp.cancelClick(e);
  }
}
DOMhelp.addEvent(window,'load',sc.init,false);.
```

The head of the HTML example is the following after the script has executed (you can test this in Firefox by selecting the whole document via Ctrl+A or Cmd+A and then right-clicking anywhere and choosing View Selected Source).

exampleStyleSheetChange.html *after script execution (excerpt)*

```
<head>
  <meta http-equiv="Content-Type" content="text/html; charset=utf-8">
  <title>Example: Using dynamic classes</title>
  <style type="text/css">
     @import "lowlevel.css";
  </style>
  <script type="text/javascript" src="DOMhelp.js"></script>
  <script type="text/javascript" src="styleSheetChange.js"></script>
  <link href="highlevel.css" rel="StyleSheet" type="text/css">
</head>
```

You might have encountered the dynamic changing of styles earlier. As early as 2001, so-called style switchers became fashionable. These are small page widgets that allow the user to choose a page's look and feel by selecting a style from a given list. Modern browsers have this option built in—in Firefox, for example, you can choose View ➤ Page Style and get all the available styles to select from. For MSIE, JavaScript developers came up with a clever trick—if you set the disabled attribute of a link element, the browser would not apply it. So all you need to do is to loop through all the link elements of the document and disable all but the chosen one.

The demo exampleStyleSwitcher.html shows how this is done. In the HTML, you define a main style sheet and alternate style sheets for large print and high contrast.

exampleStyleSwitcher.html *(excerpt)*

```
<link href="demoStyles.css" title="Normal"
      rel="stylesheet" type="text/css">
<link href="largePrint.css" title="Large Print"
      rel="alternate stylesheet" type="text/css">
<link href="highContrast.css" title="High Contrast"
      rel="alternate stylesheet" type="text/css">
```

The script is not complex. You loop through all LINK elements in the document and for each one determine whether its attribute is either stylesheet or alternate stylesheet. You create a new list with links pointing to a function that disables all but the currently chosen style sheet and add this list to the document.

You start with two properties: one to store the ID of the "style menu" to allow for CSS styling, and one to store a label to show as the first list item preceding all the available styles.

styleSwitcher.js

```
switcher={
  menuID:'styleswitcher',
  chooseLabel:'Choose Style:',
```

An initialization method called init() creates a new HTML list and adds a list item with the label as text content. You set the ID of the list to the one defined in the property.

styleSwitcher.js *(continued)*

```
  init:function(){
    var tempLI,tempA,styleTitle;
    var stylemenu=document.createElement('ul');
    tempLI=document.createElement('li');
    tempLI.appendChild(document.createTextNode(switcher.chooseLabel));
    stylemenu.appendChild(tempLI);
    stylemenu.id=switcher.menuID;
```

You loop through all the LINK elements in the document. For each element, test for the value of its rel attribute. If the value is neither stylesheet nor alternate stylesheet, skip this LINK element. This is necessary to avoid other alternative content offered via the LINK tags—like an RSS feed—from being disabled.

styleSwitcher.js *(continued)*

```
    var links=document.getElementsByTagName('link');
    for(var i=0;i<links.length;i++){
      if(links[i].getAttribute('rel')!='stylesheet' &&
      links[i].getAttribute('rel')!='alternate stylesheet'){
        continue;
      }
```

Create a new list item with a link for each style and set the text value of the link to the value of the LINK element's title attribute. Set a dummy href attribute to make the link appear as a link; otherwise the user may not recognize the new link as an interactive element.

styleSwitcher.js *(continued)*

```
      tempLI=document.createElement('li');
      tempA=document.createElement('a');
      styleTitle=links[i].getAttribute('title');
```

```
tempA.appendChild(document.createTextNode(styleTitle));
tempA.setAttribute('href','#');
```

Apply an event handler to the link that triggers the setSwitch() method and sends the link itself as a parameter via the this keyword. You can then continue to add the new list items to the menu list and append the list to the document body when the loop is complete.

styleSwitcher.js *(continued)*

```
    tempA.onclick=function(){
      switcher.setSwitch(this);
    }
    tempLI.appendChild(tempA);
    stylemenu.appendChild(tempLI);
  }
  document.body.appendChild(stylemenu);
},
```

In the setSwitch() method, you'll retrieve the link that was activated as the parameter o. Loop through all LINK elements, and test each to see whether the title attribute is the same as the text content of the link (you can safely read the text via firstChild.nodeValue without testing for the node type, as you generated the links). If the title is different, set the disabled property of the LINK to true; and if it is the same, set disable to false and the rel attribute to stylesheet instead of alternate stylesheet. Then stop the link from being followed by returning false.

styleSwitcher.js *(continued)*

```
  setSwitch:function(o){
    var links=document.getElementsByTagName('link');
    for(var i=0;i<links.length;i++){
      if(links[i].getAttribute('rel')!='stylesheet' &&
      links[i].getAttribute('rel')!='alternate stylesheet'){
        continue;
      }
      var title=o.firstChild.nodeValue;
      if(links[i].getAttribute('title')!=title){
        links[i].disabled=true;
      } else {
        links[i].setAttribute('rel','stylesheet');
        links[i].disabled=false;
      }
    }
    return false;
  }
}
```

You can test the functionality by opening exampleStyleSwitcher.html in a browser that has JavaScript and CSS enabled.

Paul Sowden pioneered this trick in 2001 at Alistapart.com with his article "Alternative Style: Working With Alternate Style Sheets" (`http://www.alistapart.com/articles/alternate/`). As Netscape 4 (remember this was 2001) did not support this method properly, Daniel Ludwin came up with "A Backward Compatible Style Switcher" in 2002 (`http://www.alistapart.com/articles/n4switch/`), which used `document.write` instead (a bit of a step backwards in terms of coding style).

Following comments about the inaccessibility of JavaScript style switchers, Chris Clark moved the trick server side with his "Build a PHP Switch" article (`http://www.alistapart.com/articles/phpswitch/`) in 2002. This method is more stable, but it means you have to reload the page to apply a new style.

A lot of variants of the same idea came up in between, and in 2005, Dustin Diaz took up the idea and mixed the stability of the PHP switcher with the slickness of a JavaScript enhanced interface in his "Unobtrusive Degradable Ajax Style Sheet Switcher" (`http://24ways.org/advent/introducing-udasss`), which uses Ajax to bridge the gap.

Style switchers can be a useful feature, especially when you offer styles that might help users overcome problems like poor eyesight such as larger fonts or a higher contrast between foreground and background. On the other hand, they can be quite pointless eye candy if you use them exclusively for the sake of offering different styles.

This evolution of the style switcher idea shows that JavaScript solutions are never set in stone, but need testing in "the real world" and feedback from users and other developers to be really applicable in a production environment or a live site. If you surf the web these days, you'll see many "experimental" scripts promising a lot but on closer inspection turning out to be slow, unstable, or just a neat trick that could be done a lot better with another technology. Just because we can do anything in JavaScript doesn't mean we should.

Easing the Maintenance

Keeping the whole look and feel out of your scripts and inside the style sheet (and thereby keeping it the responsibility of the CSS designer) is just half the battle. During maintenance of a project, the CSS class names might have to change—for example, to support a certain back end or Content Management System (CMS). One example would be Adobe's Contribute (a lightweight CMS that allows for WYSIWYG editing of web sites), which—in a standard configuration—needs classes that should not show up in the editor's style picker to start with `mmhide_`. Therefore, it is important to make it easy for the designer to change the names of your dynamically applied classes. The most basic trick is to keep the class names in their own variables or parameters. You've done that in the earlier examples already. You could have applied the class names directly:

```
sc={
  init:function(){
    // Check for DOM and apply a class to the body if it is supported
    if(!document.getElementById || !document.createElement){return;}
    DOMhelp.cssjs('add',document.body, 'dynamic');
    sc.head=document.getElementsByTagName('h3')[0];
    if(!sc.head){return;}
    sc.ad=DOMhelp.closestSibling(sc.head,1);
    DOMhelp.cssjs('add',sc.ad, 'hide');
    var t=DOMhelp.getText(sc.head);
```

```
      var collapseLink=DOMhelp.createLink('#',t);
      sc.head.replaceChild(collapseLink,sc.head.firstChild);
      DOMhelp.addEvent(collapseLink,'click',sc.peekaboo,false)
      collapseLink.onclick=function(){return;} // Safari fix
    },
  peekaboo:function(e){
      if(DOMhelp.cssjs('check',sc.ad,sc.hidingClass)){
        DOMhelp.cssjs('remove',sc.ad,sc.hidingClass)
      } else {
        DOMhelp.cssjs('add',sc.ad,sc.hidingClass)
      }
      DOMhelp.cancelClick(e);
  }
}
DOMhelp.addEvent(window,'load',sc.init,false);
```

Instead, you moved them out of the methods as properties of the main object and commented them to allow those who don't know JavaScript to change the class names without endangering the quality or functionality of your methods:

```
sc={

  // CSS classes
  hidingClass:'hide',        // Hide elements
  DOMClass:'dynamic',  // Indicate DOM support

  init:function(){
      if(!document.getElementById || !document.createElement){return;}
      DOMhelp.cssjs('add',document.body,sc.DOMClass);
      sc.head=document.getElementsByTagName('h3')[0];
      if(!sc.head){return;}
      sc.ad=DOMhelp.closestSibling(sc.head,1);
      DOMhelp.cssjs('add',sc.ad,sc.hidingClass);
      var t=DOMhelp.getText(sc.head);
      var collapseLink=DOMhelp.createLink('#',t);
      sc.head.replaceChild(collapseLink,sc.head.firstChild);
      DOMhelp.addEvent(collapseLink,'click',sc.peekaboo,false);
      collapseLink.onclick=function(){return;} // Safari fix
    },
  peekaboo:function(e){
      // More code snipped
  }
}
DOMhelp.addEvent(window,'load',sc.init,false);
```

For smaller scripts and projects that don't have many different JavaScript includes, this is enough—if accompanied by some documentation on the matter. If you have a lot of dynamic classes scattered over several documents, or you are rather paranoid about noncoders changing your code, you could use a separate JavaScript include file containing an object called CSS with all the classes as parameters. Give it an obvious file name like cssClassNames.js, and document its existence in the project documentation.

cssClassNames.js

```
css={
  // Hide elements
  hide:'hide',

  // Indicator for support of dynamic scripting
  // will be added to the body element
  supported:'dynamic'
}
```

You can apply it to the document just like any other of the scripts in use:

exampleDynamicStylingCSSObject.html

```
<head>
  <meta http-equiv="Content-Type" content="text/html; charset=utf-8">
  <title>Example: Importing class names from a CSS names object</title>
  <style type="text/css">
    @import "dynamicStyling.css";
  </style>
  <script type="text/javascript" src="DOMhelp.js"></script>
  <script type="text/javascript" src="cssClassNames.js"></script>
  <script type="text/javascript" src="dynamicStylingCSSObject.js"></script>
</head>
```

The practical upshot of this method is that you don't have to come up with parameter names for the different CSS class names (which normally contain "class" and are therefore confusing for programmers). Instead, use the following:

dynamicStylingCSSObject.js

```
sc={
  init:function(){
    if(!document.getElementById || !document.createElement){return;}

  DOMhelp.cssjs('add',document.body,css.supported);

    sc.head=document.getElementsByTagName('h3')[0];
    if(!sc.head){return;}
    sc.ad=DOMhelp.closestSibling(sc.head,1);

  DOMhelp.cssjs('add',sc.ad,css.hide);
```

```
      var t=DOMhelp.getText(sc.head);
      var collapseLink=DOMhelp.createLink('#',t);
      sc.head.replaceChild(collapseLink,sc.head.firstChild);
      DOMhelp.addEvent(collapseLink,'click',sc.peekaboo,false);
      collapseLink.onclick=function(){return;} // Safari fix
    },
    peekaboo:function(e){
      // More code snipped
    }
  }
  DOMhelp.addEvent(window,'load',sc.init,false);
```

In this example, the cssClassNames.js file uses object literal notation. You could go even further and get rid of the comments if you use JSON (http://www.json.org/), which is a format for transferring data from one program or system to another. You will hear more about JSON and its merits in Chapter 7. For now, it is enough to notice that JSON allows you to make the file with the class names a lot more readable for humans:

cssClassNameJSON.js

```
css={
  'hide elements' : 'hide',
  'dynamic scripting enabled' : 'dynamic'
}
```

Instead of the attribute notation used earlier, you'll now have to read the data as if it were an associative array:

dynamicStylingJSON.js

```
sc={
  init:function(){
    if(!document.getElementById || !document.createElement){return;}

  DOMhelp.cssjs('add',document.body,
                css['dynamic scripting enabled']);

    sc.head=document.getElementsByTagName('h3')[0];
    if(!sc.head){return;}
    sc.ad=DOMhelp.closestSibling(sc.head,1);

    DOMhelp.cssjs('add',sc.ad,css['hide elements']);
```

```
    var t=DOMhelp.getText(sc.head);
    var collapseLink=DOMhelp.createLink('#',t);
    sc.head.replaceChild(collapseLink,sc.head.firstChild);
    DOMhelp.addEvent(collapseLink,'click',sc.peekaboo,false);
    collapseLink.onclick=function(){return;} // Safari fix
  },
  peekaboo:function(e){
    // More code snipped
  }
}
DOMhelp.addEvent(window,'load',sc.init,false);
```

It is really up to you whether you want to go that far to separate presentation from behavior, but depending on the complexity of the project and the knowledge of the maintenance staff, it might just prevent a lot of avoidable errors.

Overcoming CSS Support Problems

In the last years, CSS has become more and more important for web development. Complex nested table layouts, on the decline, are being replaced by lightweight CSS layouts. Furthermore, CSS solutions for effects that were traditionally handled by JavaScript, like image rollovers and foldout menus, became fashionable and gave the design community a new hope for being able to create slick, interactive interfaces without having to understand JavaScript.

The problem that many CSS developers had to face sooner or later was lack of support by legacy browsers or hard-to-understand issues with newer browsers. As CSS is not a programming language that allows for looping, conditions, or testing of objects before you try to apply them, you need to rely both on CSS and JavaScript to support some effects. A lot is possible in CSS2 and CSS3 using pseudo-classes, generated content, and CSS hacks to exclude certain browsers, but you just cannot rely on them being supported—especially with CSS-problematic browsers like MSIE 6 still going strong, if not being the market lead. CSS hacks also tend to have the same problem browser sniffing has: when a new browser comes out, you'll have to check whether it still obeys the rules the hack demands. Right now, the beta versions of MSIE 7 require a lot of CSS developers to unhack their previous code.

A lot of very interesting CSS-only concepts counteract these issues by relying on a JavaScript fallback to support browsers like MSIE 6.

Multiple Columns with the Same Height

One of the most annoying things about CSS layouts for designers who only dealt with table layouts before is that, if you use CSS float techniques for columns, they don't have the same height, as shown in Figure 5-3.

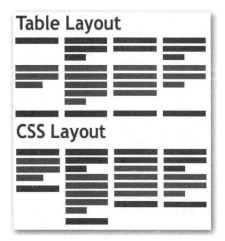

Figure 5-3. *The multiple-column height problem*

Let's start with a list of news items, each containing a heading, a "teaser" paragraph, and a "more" link.

exampleColumnHeightIssue.html *(with dummy content)*

```
<ul id="news">
  <li>
    <h3><a href="news.php?item=1">News Title 1</a></h3>
    <p>Description 1</p>
    <p class="more"><a href="news.php?item=1">more link 1</a></p>
  </li>
  <li>
    <h3><a href="news.php?item=2">News Title 2</a></h3>
    <p>Description 2</p>
    <p class="more"><a href="news.php?item=2">more link 2</a></p>
  </li>
  <li>
    <h3><a href="news.php?item=3">News Title 3</a></h3>
    <p>Description 3</p>
    <p class="more"><a href="news.php?item=1">more link 3</a></p>
  </li>
  <li>
    <h3><a href="news.php?item=1">News Title 1</a></h3>
    <p>Description 4</p>
    <p class="more"><a href="news.php?item=4">more link 4</a></p>
  </li>
</ul>
```

If you now apply a style sheet that floats the list items and the main list to the left and set some more text and layout styles, you get a multicolumn layout. The CSS to achieve this is pretty basic:

columnHeightIssue.css

```css
#news{
  width:800px;
  float:left;
}
#news li{
  width:190px;
  margin:0 4px;
  float:left;
  background:#eee;
}
#news h3{
  background:#fff;
  padding-bottom:5px;
  border-bottom:2px solid #369;
}
#news li p{
  padding:5px;
}
```

As you can see in the example, each column has a different height, and neither the paragraphs nor the "more" links are in the same position. This makes the design look uneven and can confuse the reader. There might be a CSS way to fix this issue (I am always impressed what kind of hacks and workarounds people find), but let's use JavaScript to work around this problem.

The following script—called in the HEAD of the document, will fix the problem:

fixColumnHeight.js—*used in* exampleFixedColumnHeightIssue.html

```javascript
fixcolumns={

  highest:0,
  moreClass:'more',

  init:function(){
    if(!document.getElementById || !document.createTextNode){return;}
    fixcolumns.n=document.getElementById('news');
    if(!fixcolumns.n){return;}
    fixcolumns.fix('h3');
    fixcolumns.fix('p');
    fixcolumns.fix('li');
  },
```

```
  fix:function(elm){
    fixcolumns.getHighest(elm);
    fixcolumns.fixElements(elm);
  },
  getHighest:function(elm){
    fixcolumns.highest=0;
    var temp=fixcolumns.n.getElementsByTagName(elm);
    for(var i=0;i<temp.length;i++){
      if(!temp[i].offsetHeight){continue;}
      if(temp[i].offsetHeight>fixcolumns.highest){
        fixcolumns.highest=temp[i].offsetHeight;
      }
    }
  },
  fixElements:function(elm){
    var temp=fixcolumns.n.getElementsByTagName(elm);
    for(var i=0;i<temp.length;i++){
      if(!DOMhelp.cssjs('check',temp[i],fixcolumns.moreClass)){
        temp[i].style.height=parseInt(fixcolumns.highest)+'px';
      }
    }
  }
}
DOMhelp.addEvent(window, 'load', fixcolumns.init, false);
```

First, define a parameter to store the height of the highest element and the class used for the "more" links. (The latter is very important, and will be explained soon.) Inside the init() method, test for DOM support and if the necessary element with the ID news is available. Store the element in the property n for reuse in other methods. Then call the fix() method for each element contained in the list—the headings, the paragraphs, and finally the list items. It is important to change the list items last, as their maximum heights might have changed when those of the other elements were fixed.

fixColumnHeight.js *(excerpt)*

```
fixcolumns={

  highest:0,
  moreClass:'more',

  init:function(){
    if(!document.getElementById || !document.createTextNode){return;}
    fixcolumns.n=document.getElementById('news');
    if(!fixcolumns.n){return;}
    fixcolumns.fix('h3');
    fixcolumns.fix('p');
    fixcolumns.fix('li');
  },
```

The `fix()` method invokes two additional methods, one to find out the maximum height to apply to each of the items and another to apply this height.

`fixColumnHeight.js` *(excerpt)*

```
fix:function(elm){
  fixcolumns.getHighest(elm);
  fixcolumns.fixElements(elm);
},
```

The `getHighest()` method first sets the parameter `highest` to 0 and then loops through all the elements inside the list that match the element name that was sent as the `elm` parameter. It then retrieves the element's height by reading the `offsetHeight` attribute. This attribute stores the height of the element after it has been rendered by the browser. The method then checks whether the height of the element is larger than the property `highest` and sets the property to the new value if that is the case. That way you find out which element is the highest.

`fixColumnHeight.js` *(excerpt)*

```
getHighest:function(elm){
  fixcolumns.highest=0;
  var temp=fixcolumns.n.getElementsByTagName(elm);
  for(var i=0;i<temp.length;i++){
    if(!temp[i].offsetHeight){continue;}
    if(temp[i].offsetHeight>fixcolumns.highest){
      fixcolumns.highest=temp[i].offsetHeight;
    }
  }
},
```

Caution It is important that you reset the `highest` parameter to 0 here, as `getHighest()` needs to find the highest of the elements that were sent as a parameter, not of all the elements you fix. If by some freak accident an H3 is higher than the highest paragraph, you'll get gaps between the paragraphs and the "more" links.

The `fixElements()` method then applies the maximum height to all the elements with the given name. Notice that you need to test for the class determining the "more" links, as otherwise the links would get the same height as the highest content paragraph.

```
fixElements:function(elm){
  var temp=fixcolumns.n.getElementsByTagName(elm);
  for(var i=0;i<temp.length;i++){
    if(!DOMhelp.cssjs('check',temp[i],fixcolumns.moreClass)){
      temp[i].style.height = fixcolumns.highest +'px';
    }
  }
}
```

Note Notice that you need to turn the highest parameter into a number and add a "px" suffix before you apply it to the height of the element. This is always the case; you cannot simply assign a number without a unit when it comes to CSS dimensions of elements.

Lacking Support for :hover

The CSS specifications allow you to use the :hover pseudo-class on any element of the document, and many browsers support this. This allows the designer to highlight larger parts of the document or even simulate dynamic foldout navigation menus that were hitherto only possible with JavaScript. While it is worthy of discussion whether something that is not interactive without CSS or JavaScript should get a different state when the mouse hovers over it, it is a feature designers can use a lot—highlighting a current section of a document might make it easier to read after all.

To see an example, take the list of news items once more and apply a different style sheet. If you want to highlight a full list item in CSS-2–compliant browsers, all you need to do is define a hover state on the list item:

listItemRolloverCSS.css *(excerpt) used with* exampleListItemRollover.html

```
#news{
  font-size:.8em;
  background:#eee;
  width:21em;
  padding:.5em 0;
}
#news li{
  width:20em;
  padding:.5em;
  margin:0;
}
#news li:hover{
  background:#fff;
}
```

On Firefox 1.5, the effect appears as shown in Figure 5-4.

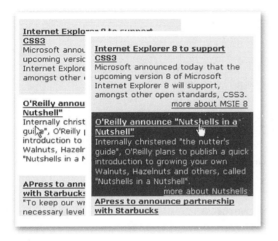

Figure 5-4. *A rollover effect in CSS using the* `:hover` *pseudo-selector*

In MSIE 6, you will not get this effect, as it does not support `:hover` for list items. However, it supports JavaScript; which means that you can use the `cssjs` method to add a class dynamically when the user hovers over the list items:

`listItemRollover.css` *(excerpt)*

```
#news{
  font-size:.8em;
  background:#eee;
  width:21em;
  padding:.5em 0;
}
#news li{
  width:20em;
  padding:.5em;
  margin:0;
}
#news li:hover{
  background:#fff;
}
#news li.over{
  background:#fff;
}
```

You add the class via the `onmouseover` and `onmouseout` event handlers and by using the `this` keyword—which we will examine closer later in this chapter.

listItemRollover.js *(excerpt)*

```
newshl={
  overClass:'over',
  init:function(){
  alert('d');
    if(!document.getElementById || !document.createTextNode){return;}
    var newsList=document.getElementById('news');
    if(!newsList){return;}
    var newsItems=newsList.getElementsByTagName('li');
    for(var i=0;i<newsItems.length;i++){
      newsItems[i].onmouseover=function(){
        DOMhelp.cssjs('add',this,newshl.overClass);
      }
      newsItems[i].onmouseout=function(){
        DOMhelp.cssjs('remove',this,newshl.overClass);
      }
    }
  }
}
DOMhelp.addEvent(window,'load',newshl.init,false);
```

If you check this example in MSIE 6, you will get the same effect as you get in more modern browsers.

You can use the pseudo-class selectors of CSS for dynamic effects (:hover, :active, and :focus), but they only apply their settings to elements contained in the current element (CSS gurus using Opera 8 or Safari can do a bit more by using these together with sibling selectors, but this is CSS sorcery beyond the scope of this book).

With JavaScript, you have the whole DOM family (including parentNode, nextSibling, firstChild, and so on) at your disposal.

If you for example wanted to have a different rollover state when the user hovers over the links, you can extend the script easily to do so. First you need a new class for the active state:

listItemDoubleRollover.css *as used in* listItemDoubleRollover.html

```
#news{
  font-size:.8em;
  background:#eee;
  width:21em;
  padding:.5em 0;
}
#news li{
  width:20em;
  padding:.5em;
  margin:0;
}
#news li:hover{
  background:#fff;
```

```
}
#news li.over{
  background:#fff;
}
#news li.active{
  background:#ffc;
}
```

Then you need to apply the events to the links inside the list items and change the class of their parent node's parent node (as the link in this example is either in a heading or in a paragraph):

listItemDoubleRollover.js

```
newshl={
  // CSS classes
  overClass:'over', // Hover state of list item
  activeClass:'active', // Hover state on a link

  init:function(){
    if(!document.getElementById || !document.createTextNode){return;}
    var newsList=document.getElementById('news');
    if(!newsList){return;}
    var newsItems=newsList.getElementsByTagName('li');
    for(var i=0;i<newsItems.length;i++){
      newsItems[i].onmouseover=function(){
        DOMhelp.cssjs('add',this,newshl.overClass);
      }
      newsItems[i].onmouseout=function(){
        DOMhelp.cssjs('remove',this,newshl.overClass);
      }
    }
    var newsItemLinks=newsList.getElementsByTagName('a');
    for(i=0;i<newsItemLinks.length;i++){
      newsItemLinks[i].onmouseover=function(){
        var p=this.parentNode.parentNode;
        DOMhelp.cssjs('add',p,newshl.activeClass);
      }
      newsItemLinks[i].onmouseout=function(){
        var p=this.parentNode.parentNode;
        DOMhelp.cssjs('remove',p,newshl.activeClass);
      }
    }
  }
}
DOMhelp.addEvent(window, 'load', newshl.init, false);
```

The result is two different states for the news item, as shown in Figure 5-5, depending on the user hovering over the text or over the links.

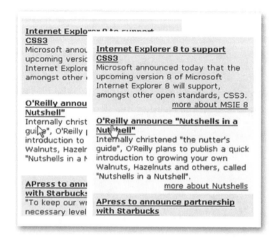

Figure 5-5. *Different rollover states for a single element*

Using JavaScript, you can also make the whole news item clickable, and this is where more events come into play.

If You Have a Hammer, Everything Looks Like a Nail

These few examples should have given you the insight that JavaScript and the DOM is very powerful when it comes to making the browser behave and allow for effects you'd like to achieve but cannot because the CSS support is not good enough.

The question, however, is whether it is worth the effort and where to draw the line. There are a lot of scripts out on the Web that teach MSIE 6 "manners" when it comes to CSS support, but these might also cause a lot of other issues—from slowing down the page up to opening security holes.

A lot of times you can get the impression that you are using JavaScript to force the browser to do things in CSS that were meant to be done in JavaScript in the first place. One example of this is multilevel drop-down menus. CSS-2–compliant browsers allow for hover effects on anything, and you can hide and show nested list elements when you move your mouse over the parent elements. However, the overall support for this is just not large enough, and even though some CSS designers like Stu Nicholls (http://www.cssplay.com) manage to keyboard-enable effects for browsers like Opera, Safari, and Mozilla via the :active and :focus pseudo-selectors, you'd still have to use a script that allows MSIE 6 to do the same.

JavaScript has one big advantage over CSS: communication with the document works in both directions. While CSS only styles or deals with what is already given, JavaScript can read values, test for support, check whether elements are available and what they are, and even create elements on the fly if they are needed. CSS can only read the document, much like you can only read a newspaper, but JavaScript can also alter it.

This capability of JavaScript is used by a lot of CSS tricks. Many effects are possible only with extraneous markup—nested elements, clearing elements, extra images to allow for flexible rounded corners, and so on. Therefore, developers started generating these via Java-Script rather than expecting them in the HTML. This makes the source document appear a lot cleaner, but for the end user the final DOM tree—including all generated content—is what he has to deal with. Bloated HTML does not get better by generating the bloat via JavaScript. Maybe it is sometimes better to look at simplifying an interface or making it more flexible from the start than trying to make it behave like tables via lots of CSS and JavaScript sorcery.

One final note related to presentation is that a clever DOM script can sometimes help where you didn't expect it. An example is Flash movies. For years Flash was advertised as the JavaScript killer, and recently Bobby van der Sluis has released a script called Unobtrusive Flash Object (`http://www.bobbyvandersluis.com/ufo/`), or UFO, that makes the life of Flash developers a lot easier.

The problem with Flash is that the way some browsers need the Flash movie to be embedded in the document is not standards compliant. XHTML requires an `<object>` tag to add multimedia content such as this; to accommodate for older browsers, a lot of developers also use an additional `<embed>` tag to add the Flash movie, which is not part of the HTML standard. Drew McLellan came up with a Flash-only solution for this as early as 2002, and confusingly called it Flash Satay (`http://www.alistapart.com/articles/flashsatay/`), but this fix is not always applicable (and I venture to guess that a lot more people would have learned about it had Drew called it "Embedding Flash the XHTML way").

Bobby's solution uses Unobtrusive JavaScript to replace alternative content with the real Flash movie when and if it is possible. This also makes it safer if Microsoft is going to go ahead with turning off its automatic execution of Flash content.

Microsoft plans to allow Flash content to start only once the user has clicked the main movie instead of starting it automatically. This change in MSIE's behavior is based on a copyright lawsuit between Microsoft and Eolas Technologies and the University of California. The code for Microsoft's own solutions to the problem is of rather dubious quality (`http://msdn.microsoft.com/library/default.asp?url=/workshop/author/dhtml/overview/activating_activex.asp`) as it uses `document.write()`, and UFO is a clean and clever way around this issue.

Changing the Document's Behavior via Event Handling

Event handling is probably the best thing JavaScript offers a user-interface-focused developer. It is also one of the most confusing JavaScript topics, not because it is complex, but because of different browsers implementing event handling in different ways. I will now explain to you what an event is; show an old, tried, and true approach to dealing with events; and then explain a newer approach that the W3C recommends. Finally, you'll learn how to tweak the W3C-compliant approach to allow browsers that don't support it to understand your scripts.

Events can be many things, for example:

- The initial loading and rendering of the document

- The loading of an image

- The user clicking a button

- The user pressing a key

- The user moving the mouse over a certain element

Note Picture an event handler like a motion detector or the contacts of a door bell—if someone moves closer to the door, the lights are turned on; and if that someone presses the button of the door bell, the circuit is closed and the ringing mechanism is triggered to play a sound. In the same way, you can detect when a user hovers the mouse over a link to trigger one function and to trigger another one when the user clicks this link.

You can apply event handlers to make your scripts aware of what is happening in several ways. The most obtrusive way is to use inline event calls in the HTML:

```
<a href="moreinfo.html" onclick="return infoWindow(this.href)">more information</a>
```

A cleaner way was already described in earlier chapters: you identify the element via a class or an ID and then set the event handler in your script instead. The easiest and most widely supported way is to apply the event handler directly to the object as a property:

```
HTML:
<a href="moreinfo.html" id="info">more information</a>

JavaScript:
var triggerLink=document.getElementById('info');
triggerlink.onclick=infoWindow;
```

Note Notice that there is no need to test for the element with the ID info, as the function can only have been called by it.

Triggering events in this way has several issues:

- You don't send the element to the function; instead you need to find the element again.

- You can only assign one function at a time

- You hijack the event of this element for your script exclusively—methods of other scripts trying to use this element for other events will not work any longer.

Unless you've defined `triggerLink` as a global variable or object property, the function `infoWindow()` will need to find the trigger element before it can be used.

```
function infoWindow(){
  var url=document.getElementById('info').getAttribute('href');
  // Other code
}
```

This and the problem of multiple functions connected to one event can be solved by applying an anonymous function calling your real function(s), which also allows you to send the current object via the `this` keyword:

```
var triggerLink=document.getElementById('info');
triggerlink.onclick=function(){
  showInfoWindow(this.href);
  highLight(this);
  setCurrent(this);
}
function showInfoWindow(url){
  // Other code
}
```

The third problem remains. Your script, provided it is the last one included in the document, will override the event triggers of other scripts, which means it won't easily work together with other scripts. Therefore you need a way to assign event handlers without overriding other scripts. This is especially important when you want to call different functions when the document is loaded.

Simon Willison (`http://simon.incutio.com/`) found a solution for that using this method for event handling:

```
function addLoadEvent(func) {
  var oldonload = window.onload;
  if (typeof window.onload != 'function') {
    window.onload = func;
  } else {
    window.onload = function() {
      oldonload();
      func();
    }
  }
}
```

If you use this tool function to add your function to the page, you will not override the other functions that should be invoked by the page's load event. It was and is a big step in the right direction.

The preceding methods work—to my knowledge—for all browsers that support JavaScript out there. In particular, if you have to support MSIE 5 on a Mac, this is as far as you can go. Newer browsers support an improved event model that clearly distinguishes between different aspects of event handling.

Events in the W3C-Compliant World

Note The examples in this section need to be executed in a DOM-2–compliant browser. I recommend Mozilla Firefox version 1.5. MSIE 6 is not DOM-2 compliant, and the examples will not work in it. This part of the chapter explains how events were defined and meant to work by the W3C. Afterward, we'll extend these methods to work with MSIE and other noncompliant browsers.

The W3C DOM-2 and the upcoming DOM-3 specifications approach the event handling issue a bit differently. First of all, they define different parts of the event's occurrence up to the use of the retrieved data in detail:

- The **event** is what happens, for example, click.

- The **event handler**, for example onclick, is in DOM-1 the location where the event gets recorded.

- In DOM-2, this is slightly different—you deal with **event target** and **event listener**:

  - The **event target** is where the event occurred, in most cases an HTML element.

  - The **event listener** is a function that deals with that event.

- DOM-3 also brings the concept of **event capturing**, which has no real browser support yet. If you really want to understand these, check the W3C specifications (http://www.w3.org/TR/DOM-Level-3-Events/events.html); I won't cover event capturing here, as it is not part of usable JavaScript yet.

Applying Events

You apply an event via the addEventListener() method. This function takes three parameters: the event as a string and without the "on" prefix, the name of the event listener function (without parentheses), and a Boolean value called useCapture, which defines whether event capturing should be used or not. For now, it is safe to set useCapture to false.

If you wanted to apply the function infoWindow() to the link via addEventListener(), you'd use the following:

```
var triggerLink=document.getElementById('info');
triggerLink.addEventListener( 'click', infoWindow, false);
```

If you wanted to add a hover effect by calling the function `highlight()` when the mouse is over the link and the function `unhighlight()` when the mouse leaves the link, you can add a couple more lines:

```
var triggerLink=document.getElementById('info');
triggerLink.addEventListener( 'click', infoWindow, false);
triggerLink.addEventListener( 'mouseout', highlight, false);
triggerLink.addEventListener( 'mouseover', unhighlight, false);
```

Checking Which Event Was Triggered Where and How

It may seem that in terms of ease of developing, you are back to square one: you once again have to find the element to read the `href` from inside `infoWindow()`. This is true; however, by using `addEventListener`, you prompt standards-compliant browsers to give you the **event object**, which you can read out via a parameter called e.

You might have seen this e before and wondered what it was and whether you should trust an e without knowing where it came from. It is very confusing at first to simply use a parameter without sending it when you apply the event, but once you learn about the event object, you'll never go back to using `onevent` properties. The event object has many attributes you can use in the event listener function:

- `target`: The element that fired the event.

- `type`: The event that was fired (for example, `click`).

- `button`: The mouse button that was pressed: 0 for left, 1 for middle, and 2 for right.

- `keyCode`/`data`/`charCode`: The character code of the key that was pressed. The W3C specifications use `data`; however, it is not widely supported. Most browsers use `charCode` instead, and `keyCode` is MSIE's implementation. The good news is that all modern browsers understand `keyCode`, which means you can use that for now until `data` is more widely supported in user agents.

- `shiftKey`/`ctrlKey`/`altKey`: A Boolean—true if the Shift, Ctrl, or Alt key (respectively) was pressed.

The full list of what is available is dependent on the event you are listening to. You can find the whole list of attributes in the DOM-2 specification: `http://www.w3.org/TR/DOM-Level-2-Events/events.html#Events-Registration-interfaces`.

Using the Event object, you can easily use one function to deal with several events:

```
var triggerLink=document.getElementById('info');
triggerLink.addEventListener( 'click', infoWindow, false);
triggerLink.addEventListener( 'mouseout', infoWindow, false);
triggerLink.addEventListener( 'mouseover', infoWindow, false);
```

You can use the same function for all three events and check the event type:

```
function infoWindow(e){
  switch(e.type){
    case 'click':
      // Code to deal with the user clicking the link
    break;
    case 'mouseover':
      // Code to deal with the user hovering over the link
    break;
    case 'mouseout':
      // Code to deal with the user leaving the link
    break;
}
```

You could also check the element the event occurred at by checking its nodeName. Notice that you once again have to use toLowerCase() to avoid cross-browser problems:

```
function infoWindow(e){
  targetElement=e.target.nodeName.toLowerCase();
  switch(targetElement){
    case 'input':
      // Code to deal with input elements
    break;
    case 'a':
      // Code to deal with links
    break;
    case 'h1':
      // Code to deal with the main heading
    break;
  }
}
```

Stopping Event Propagation

Assigning events and intercepting them with event listeners also means that you need to take care of two problems: one is that a lot of events have default actions—click for example might make the browser follow a link or submit a form, whereas keyup might add a character to a form field.

The other one is called **event bubbling**, and it basically means that when an event occurs at an element, it also occurs at all the parent elements of the initial element.

Event Bubbling

Let's go back to the HTML markup for the news list:

exampleEventBubble.html

```
<ul id="news">
  <li>
    <h3><a href="news.php?item=1">News Title 1</a></h3>
    <p>Description 1</p>
    <p class="more"><a href="news.php?item=1">more link 1</a></p>
  </li>
 <!-- and so on -->
</ul>
```

If you now assign a mouseover event to the links in the list, hovering over them will also trigger any event listener that might be on the paragraphs, the list items, the list, and all the other elements above that in the node tree right up to the document body. As an example, you'll see how to attach event listeners to each of them that point to appropriate functions:

eventBubble.js

```
bubbleTest={
  init:function(){
    if(!document.getElementById || !document.createTextNode){return;}
    bubbleTest.n=document.getElementById('news');
    if(!bubbleTest.n){return;}

    bubbleTest.addMyListeners('click',bubbleTest.liTest,'li');
    bubbleTest.addMyListeners('click',bubbleTest.aTest,'a');
    bubbleTest.addMyListeners('click',bubbleTest.pTest,'p');

  },
  addMyListeners:function(eventName,functionName,elements){
    var temp=bubbleTest.n.getElementsByTagName(elements);
    for(var i=0;i<temp.length;i++){
      temp[i].addEventListener(eventName,functionName,false);
    }
  },
  liTest:function(e){
    alert('li was clicked');
  },
  pTest:function(e){
    alert('p was clicked');
  },
```

```
  aTest:function (e){
    alert('a was clicked');
  }
}
window.addEventListener('load',bubbleTest.init,false);
```

Now all the list items will trigger the `liTest()` method when they are clicked, all the paragraphs will trigger the `pTest()` method, and all the links will trigger the `aTest()` method.

However, if you click the paragraph, you will get two alerts:

```
p was clicked
li was clicked
```

You can prevent this by using the `e.stopPropagation()` method, which will ensure that only the event listener applied to the links will get the event. If you change the `pTest()` method to the following:

`stopPropagation.js`—*used in* `exampleStopPropagation.html`

```
pTest:function(e){
  alert('p was clicked');
  e.stopPropagation();
},
```

the output will be

```
p was clicked
```

Event bubbling is not really that problematic, as you are not often likely to assign different listeners to embedded elements instead of to their parents. However, if you want to learn more about event bubbling and the order of what happens when an event occurs, Peter-Paul Koch has written an excellent explanation, available at `http://www.quirksmode.org/js/events_order.html`.

Preventing Default Actions

The other problem you might have is that events on certain elements have default actions. Links, for example, load another document. You might not want that to happen, and you have to stop the default action after you've executed your event listener function.

In the DOM-1 event handler model, you did this by returning a `false` value in the function that was called:

```
element.onclick=function(){
  // Do other code
  return false;
}
```

If you click any of the links in the earlier example, they load the linked document. You can override this by using the DOM-2 `preventDefault()` method. Let's test it by adding it to the aTest method:

preventDefault.js—*used in* examplePreventDefault.html

```
aTest:function (e){
  alert('a was clicked');
  e.stopPropagation();
  e.preventDefault();
}
```

Clicking the links now just causes the alert to show up:

---

a was clicked

The links, on the other hand, are not being followed, and you'll stay on the same page to do something different with the link data.

For example, you could initially show only the headlines and expand the content when they are clicked. First, you need some more classes in the style sheet to allow for these changes.

listItemCollapse.css *(excerpt)*

```
.hide{
  display:none;
}
li.current{
    background:#ccf;
}
li.current h3{
    background:#69c;
}
```

The script for collapsing the elements is not complex, but uses all the event handling elements we talked about:

```
newsItemCollapse.js

newshl={
  // CSS classes
  overClass:'over', // Rollover effect
  hideClass:'hide', // Hide things
  currentClass:'current', // Open item

  init:function(){
  var ps,i,hl;
  if(!document.getElementById || !document.createTextNode){return;}
    var newsList=document.getElementById('news');
    if(!newsList){return;}
    var newsItems=newsList.getElementsByTagName('li');
    for(i=0;i<newsItems.length;i++){
      hl=newsItems[i].getElementsByTagName('a')[0];
      hl.addEventListener('click',newshl.toggleNews,false);
      hl.addEventListener('mouseover',newshl.hover,false);
      hl.addEventListener('mouseout',newshl.hover,false);
    }
    var ps=newsList.getElementsByTagName('p');
    for(i=0;i<ps.length;i++){
      DOMhelp.cssjs('add',ps[i],newshl.hideClass);
    }
  },
  toggleNews:function(e){
    var section=e.target.parentNode.parentNode;
    var first=section.getElementsByTagName('p')[0];
    var action=DOMhelp.cssjs('check',first,newshl.hideClass)?'remove':'add';
    var sectionAction=action=='remove'?'add':'remove';
    var ps=section.getElementsByTagName('p');
    for(var i=0;i<ps.length;i++){
      DOMhelp.cssjs(action,ps[i],newshl.hideClass);
    }
    DOMhelp.cssjs(sectionAction,section,newshl.currentClass);
    e.preventDefault();
    e.stopPropagation();
  },
```

```
  hover:function(e){
    var hl=e.target.parentNode.parentNode;
    var action=e.type=='mouseout'?'remove':'add';
    DOMhelp.cssjs(action,hl,newshl.overClass);
  }
}
window.addEventListener ('load',newshl.init,false);
```

The results are clickable news headings that show associated news excerpts when you click them. The "more" links stay unaffected and will send the visitor to the full news article when clicked (see Figure 5-6).

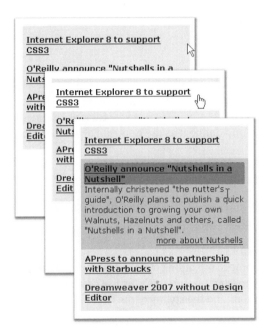

Figure 5-6. *Expanding new items by clicking the headings*

Let's go through the whole script step by step. After defining the CSS class properties and checking for the necessary elements, you start looping through the list items, grab the first link (which is the one inside the heading), and assign event listeners for click, mouseover, and mouseout. The click event should fire the newshl.toggleNews() method, while both mouseout and mouseover should trigger newshl.hover().

newsItemCollapse.js *(excerpt)*

```
  for(i=0;i<newsItems.length;i++){
    hl=newsItems[i].getElementsByTagName('a')[0];
    hl.addEventListener('click',newshl.toggleNews,false);
    hl.addEventListener('mouseover',newshl.hover,false);
    hl.addEventListener('mouseout',newshl.hover,false);
  }
```

You hide all paragraphs inside the list item by applying the hiding class to them:

newsItemCollapse.js *(excerpt)*

```
var ps=newsList.getElementsByTagName('p');
for(i=0;i<ps.length;i++){
  DOMhelp.cssjs('add',ps[i],newshl.hideClass);
}
```

The toggleNews() method grabs the current section by reading out the target of the event object. The target is the link, which means that if you want to reach the list item, you need to go up to the next parent node twice.

newsItemCollapse.js *(excerpt)*

```
toggleNews:function(e){
  var section=e.target.parentNode.parentNode;
```

You read the first paragraph of the list item and check whether it already has the hiding class assigned to it. If that is the case, define the variable action as remove; otherwise define it as add. Set another variable called sectionAction and define it as the opposite of action with the same options.

newsItemCollapse.js *(excerpt)*

```
var first=section.getElementsByTagName('p')[0];
var action=DOMhelp.cssjs('check',first,newshl.hideClass)?'remove':'add';
var sectionAction=action=='remove'?'add':'remove';
```

Loop through all the paragraphs and either remove the hiding class or add it, depending on the action. Do the same for the section and the current class, but this time use sectionAction. This effectively toggles the visibility of the paragraphs and the styling of the heading.

newsItemCollapse.js *(excerpt)*

```
var ps=section.getElementsByTagName('p');
for(var i=0;i<ps.length;i++){
  DOMhelp.cssjs(action,ps[i],newshl.hideClass);
}
DOMhelp.cssjs(sectionAction,section,newshl.currentClass);
```

Stop the link that was initially clicked from being followed by calling preventDefault() and disallow event bubbling by calling stopPropagation().

newsItemCollapse.js *(excerpt)*

```
    e.preventDefault();
    e.stopPropagation();
  },
```

The hover method grabs the list item via parentNode and checks the type of the event that was used to call the method. If the event was mouseout, it defines the action as remove, otherwise as add. It then applies or removes the class from the list item.

newsItemCollapse.js *(excerpt)*

```
  hover:function(e){
    var hl=e.target.parentNode.parentNode;
    var action=e.type=='mouseout'?'remove':'add';
    DOMhelp.cssjs(action,hl,newshl.overClass);
  }
```

And finally, add an event listener to the window object that fires off newshl.init() when the window has finished loading.

newsItemCollapse.js *(excerpt)*

```
}
window.addEventListener ('load',newshl.init,false);
```

Now you know how to make something change once clicked in DOM-2–compliant browsers. It is time to think about the other browsers out there, and make sure those get support, too.

Fixing Events for the Non-W3C-Compliant World

Now that you know the theory of event handling (and in part have support in a lot of new browsers and hopefully those to come), it is time to look at the offenders violating the agreed standard and learn how to deal with them.

■**Note** The helper methods here are already contained inside DOMhelp.js, and you can find them there if you want to use them without DOMhelp.

One of them is MSIE 6, which is actually understandable considering its age and the role it has to play—both browser and operating system file manager. MSIE has its own event model, and equivalents for the standard methods are named differently and sometimes behave differently.

Instead of addEventListener(), MSIE has attachEvent(); instead of passing an event object to each listener, MSIE keeps one global event object in window.event.

A developer named Scott Andrew came up with a portable function called addEvent() that works around the differences when it comes to adding events:

```
function addEvent(elm, evType, fn, useCapture) {
// Cross-browser event handling for IE5+, NS6+ and Mozilla/Gecko
// By Scott Andrew                    .
  if (elm.addEventListener) {
    elm.addEventListener(evType, fn, useCapture);
    return true;
  } else if (elm.attachEvent) {
    var r = elm.attachEvent('on' + evType, fn);
    return r;
  } else {
    elm['on' + evType] = fn;
  }
}
```

The function uses one more parameter than addEventListener(), which is the element itself. It tests whether addEventListener() is supported and simply returns true when it is able to attach the event in the W3C-compliant way.

Otherwise, it checks whether attachEvent() is supported (effectively meaning MSIE is used) and tries to attach the event that way. Notice that attachEvent() does need the "on" prefix for the event. For browsers that support neither addEventListener() nor attachEvent(), like MSIE on Mac, the function points the DOM-1 property to the function. This effectively overwrites any other events attached to this element in MSIE on Mac, but at least it works.

Note There is an ongoing discussion about how addEvent() can be improved—for example, to support retaining the option to send the current element as a parameter via this—and many clever solutions have been developed so far. As each has different drawbacks, I won't go into details here, but if you are interested, check the comments at the addEvent() recoding contest page at quirksmode.org (http://www.quirksmode.org/blog/archives/2005/10/_and_the_winner_1.html).

As MSIE uses a global event, you cannot rely on the event object being sent to your listeners, but you need to write a different function to get the element that was activated. Matters get confused even further as the properties of window.event are slightly different from the ones of the W3C event object:

- In Internet Explorer, target is replaced by srcElement.

- button returns different values. In the W3C model, 0 is the left button, 1 is the middle, and 2 is the right; however, MSIE returns 1 for the left button, 2 for the right, and 4 for the middle. It also returns 3 when the left and right buttons are pressed together, and 7 for all three buttons together.

To accommodate these changes, you can use this function:

```
function getTarget(e){
  var target;
  if(window.event){
    target = window.event.srcElement;
  } else if (e){
    target = e.target;
  } else {
    target = null ;
  }
  return target;
}
```

Or more briefly, using the ternary operator:

```
getTarget:function(e){
  var target = window.event ? window.event.srcElement :
      e ? e.target : null;
  if (!target){return false;}
  return target;
}
```

Safari has a nasty bug (or feature—one is never sure): if you click a link, it does not send the link, but the text node contained in the link, as the target. A workaround is to check whether the element's node name is really a link:

```
getTarget:function(e){
  var target = window.event ? window.event.srcElement : e ? e.target : null;
  if (!target){return false;}
  if (target.nodeName.toLowerCase() != 'a'){target = target.parentNode;}
  return target;
}
```

Preventing default actions and event bubbling also needs to accommodate the different browser implementations.

- stopPropagation() is not a method in MSIE, but a property of the window event called cancelBubble.

- preventDefault() is not a method either, but a property called returnValue.

This means that you have to write your own stopBubble() and stopDefault() methods:

```
stopBubble:function(e){
    if(window.event && window.event.cancelBubble){
      window.event.cancelBubble = true;
    }
    if (e && e.stopPropagation){
      e.stopPropagation();
    }
}
```

Note Safari supports stopPropagation() but does nothing with it. This means it will not stop the event from bubbling, and there is no quick way around that. Hopefully this will be fixed in future versions.

```
stopDefault:function(e){
  if(window.event && window.event.returnValue){
    window.event.cancelBubble = true;
  }
  if (e && e.preventDefault){
    e.preventDefault();
  }
}
```

As you normally want to stop both of these things from happening, it might make sense to collect them into one function:

```
cancelClick:function(e){
  if (window.event && window.event.cancelBubble
      && window.event.returnValue){
    window.event.cancelBubble = true;
    window.event.returnValue = false;
    return;
  }
  if (e && e.stopPropagation && e.preventDefault){
    e.stopPropagation();
    e.preventDefault();
  }
}
```

Using these helper methods should allow you to handle events unobtrusively and across browsers, with one exception:

Safari understands the preventDefault() method but doesn't implement what it should do. Therefore, if you add a handler to a link and call cancelClick() in the listener method, the link will still be followed.

The way around this for Safari is to add another dummy function via the old onevent syntax that stops the link from being followed. You'll see this fix in action now. Let's take the collapsing headline example again and replace the DOM-2–compliant methods and properties with the cross-browser helpers:

xBrowserListItemCollapse.js *used in* exampleXBrowserListItemCollapse.html

```
newshl = {
  // CSS classes
  overClass:'over', // Rollover effect
  hideClass:'hide', // Hide things
  currentClass:'current', // Open item

  init:function(){
  var ps,i,hl;
  if(!document.getElementById || !document.createTextNode){return;}
    var newsList = document.getElementById('news');
    if(!newsList){return;}
    var newsItems = newsList.getElementsByTagName('li');
    for(i = 0;i<newsItems.length;i++){
      hl = newsItems[i].getElementsByTagName('a')[0];
      DOMhelp.addEvent(hl,'click',newshl.toggleNews,false);
      hl.onclick = DOMhelp.safariClickFix;
```

```
      DOMhelp.addEvent(hl,'mouseover',newshl.hover,false);
      DOMhelp.addEvent(hl,'mouseout',newshl.hover,false);
    }
    var ps = newsList.getElementsByTagName('p');
    for(i = 0;i<ps.length;i++){
      DOMhelp.cssjs('add',ps[i],newshl.hideClass);
    }
  },
  toggleNews:function(e){
    var section = DOMhelp.getTarget(e).parentNode.parentNode;
    var first = section.getElementsByTagName('p')[0];
    var action = DOMhelp.cssjs('check',first,newshl.hideClass)?'remove':'add';
    var sectionAction = action == 'remove'?'add':'remove';
    var ps = section.getElementsByTagName('p');
    for(var i = 0;i<ps.length;i++){
      DOMhelp.cssjs(action,ps[i],newshl.hideClass);
    }
    DOMhelp.cssjs(sectionAction,section,newshl.currentClass);
    DOMhelp.cancelClick(e);
  },
  hover:function(e){
    var hl = DOMhelp.getTarget(e).parentNode.parentNode;
    var action = e.type == 'mouseout'?'remove':'add';
    DOMhelp.cssjs(action,hl,newshl.overClass);
  }
}
DOMhelp.addEvent(window,'load',newshl.init,false);
```

■Note `hl.onclick = DOMhelp.safariClickFix;` could be a simple `hl.onclick = function(){return false;};` however, it will be easier to search and replace this fix once the Safari development team has sorted the problem out.

The clickable headlines now work across all modern browsers; however, it seems that you could streamline the script a bit. Right now the examples loop a lot, which is not really necessary. Instead of hiding all paragraphs inside the list items individually, it is a lot easier to simply add a class to the list item and let the CSS engine hide all the paragraphs:

listItemCollapseShorter.css *(excerpt)—used in* exampleListItemCollapseShorter.html

```css
#news li.hide p{
  display:none;
}
#news li.current p{
  display:block;
}
```

This way you can get rid of the inner loop through all the paragraphs in the init() method and replace it with one line of code that applies the hide class to the list item itself as follows:

listItemCollapseShorter.js *(excerpt)—used in* exampleListItemCollapseShorter.html

```js
newshl={
  // CSS classes
  overClass:'over', // Rollover effect
  hideClass:'hide', // Hide things
  currentClass:'current', // Open item

  init:function(){
    var hl;
    if(!document.getElementById || !document.createTextNode){return;}
    var newsList=document.getElementById('news');
    if(!newsList){return;}
    var newsItems=newsList.getElementsByTagName('li');
    for(var i=0;i<newsItems.length;i++){
      hl=newsItems[i].getElementsByTagName('a')[0];
      DOMhelp.addEvent(hl,'click',newshl.toggleNews,false);
      DOMhelp.addEvent(hl,'mouseover',newshl.hover,false);
      DOMhelp.addEvent(hl,'mouseout',newshl.hover,false);
      hl.onclick = DOMhelp.safariClickFix;
      DOMhelp.cssjs('add',newsItems[i],newshl.hideClass);
    }
  },
```

The next change is in the `toggleNews()` method. There you replace the loop with a simple `if` condition that checks whether the current class is applied to the list item and replaces `hide` with `current` if that is the case and `current` with `hide` if it isn't. This shows or hides all the paragraphs inside the list item.

`listItemCollapseShorter.js` *(excerpt)—used in* `exampleListItemCollapseShorter.html`

```
toggleNews:function(e){
  var section=DOMhelp.getTarget(e).parentNode.parentNode;
  if(DOMhelp.cssjs('check',section,newshl.currentClass)){
    DOMhelp.cssjs('swap',section,newshl.currentClass,
                  newshl.hideClass);
  }else{
    DOMhelp.cssjs('swap',section,newshl.hideClass,
                  newshl.currentClass);
  }
  DOMhelp.cancelClick(e);
},
```

The rest stays the same:

`listItemCollapseShorter.js` *(excerpt)—used in* `exampleListItemCollapseShorter.html`

```
hover:function(e){
  var hl = DOMhelp.getTarget(e).parentNode.parentNode;
  var action = e.type == 'mouseout'?'remove':'add';
  DOMhelp.cssjs(action,hl,newshl.overClass);
  }
}
DOMhelp.addEvent(window,'load',newshl.init,false);
```

Never Stop Optimizing

Analyzing your own code to determine what can be optimized in this way should never cease, even though it is very tempting in the heat of the moment to merrily code away and create something too complex for its own good.

Taking a step back, analyzing the problem you want to solve, and reevaluating what's already in place is sometimes a lot more beneficial than just plowing on. In this case, the optimization is in leaving the hiding of the elements to the cascade in CSS, rather than looping through the child elements and hiding them individually.

When you take another look at code you have created, the following ideas are always good to keep in the back of your head:

- Any idea that avoids nested loops is a good one.

- Properties of the main object are a good place to store information that is of interest for several methods—for example, which element is active in site navigation.

- If you find yourself repeating bits of code over and over again, create a new method that fulfills this task—if you have to change the code in the future, you'll only have to change it in one place.

- Don't traverse the node tree too much. If a lot of elements need to know about some other element, find it once and store it in a property. This will shorten the code a lot, as something like `contentSection` is a lot shorter than `elm.parentNode.parentNode.nextSibling`.

- A long list of if and else statements might be much easier handled as a switch/case block.

- If something is likely to change in the future, like the Safari `stopPropagation()` hack, then it is a good idea to put it in its own method. The next time you see the code and you spot this seemingly useless method, you'll remember what was going on.

- Don't rely on HTML too much. It is always the first thing to change (especially when there is a CMS involved).

The Ugly Page Load Problem and Its Ugly Solutions

When developers started to use CSS extensively, they soon encountered some annoying browser bugs. One of them was the **flash of unstyled content**, otherwise known as FOUC. (`http://www.bluerobot.com/web/css/fouc.asp`). This effect shows the page without a style sheet for a brief moment before applying it.

We now face the same problem with JavaScript-enhanced pages. If you load the example of the collapsed news items, you'll see all the news expanded for a brief moment. This brief moment is the time needed for the document and all its dependencies like images and third-party content to finish loading.

This has been annoying scripting enthusiasts with a designer's eye for a long time; the `onload` event fired when the page and all contained media like images was loaded, and that was it—until a lot of clever DOM scripters put their heads together and had a go at it.

Dean Edwards (a name to remember when it comes to highly technical but ingenious solutions) came up with a script that allows you to execute code before the page has finished loading all the content elements, thus allowing for a smoother looking interface without things jumping around. You can test his solution at `http://dean.edwards.name/weblog/2005/09/busted/`.

The problem with this solution is that it relies heavily on browser-specific code and does not work on Safari or Opera. This might change in the future, so be sure to visit Dean's site from time to time.

A different solution that is supported by all JavaScript-capable browsers, but is a bit dirty in terms of separation of structure, presentation, and behavior, is to write out the necessary CSS to hide the elements via document.write() in the document's HEAD. If you wanted to apply this to the headline example, all you'd need to do is add the styles for the paragraphs inside the list item in the HTML document's head.

exampleListItemCollapseNoFlash.html *(excerpt)*

```
<head>
  <meta http-equiv="Content-Type" content="text/html; charset=utf-8">
  <title>Example: Collapsing List Items without Flashing</title>
  <style type="text/css">
    @import 'listItemCollapseNoFlash.css';
  </style>
  <script type="text/javascript" src="DOMhelp.js"></script>
  <script type="text/javascript" src="listItemCollapseNoFlash.js"></script>
  <script type="text/javascript">
    document.write('<'+'style type="text/css">');
    document.write('#news li p{display:none;}');
    document.write('<'+'/style>');
  </script>
</head>
```

■**Note** The concatenation of the style tags is necessary to avoid validation programs complaining about invalid HTML.

Both versions are feasible but seem dirty, and so far, I don't see any really clean solution for this problem.

Reading and Filtering Keyboard Entries

Probably the most common event for the web you'll use is click, as it has the benefit of being supported by every element and can be triggered by both keyboard and mouse if the element in question can be reached via keyboard.

However, there is nothing stopping you from checking keyboard entries in JavaScript with the keyup or keypress handler. The former is the W3C standard; the latter is not in the standards and occurs after keydown and keyup, but it is well supported in browsers.

As an example of how you could read out and use keyboard entries, let's write a script that checks whether the entered data in a form field is purely numbers. You've tested and converted entries to numbers in Chapter 2 already, but this time you want to check the entry while it occurs rather than after the user submits the form. If the user enters a nonnumerical character, the script should disable the Submit button and show an error message.

You start with a simple HTML form that has one entry field:

exampleKeyChecking.html

```
<!DOCTYPE HTML PUBLIC "-//W3C//DTD HTML 4.01//EN"
"http://www.w3.org/TR/html4/strict.dtd">
<html dir="ltr" lang="en">
<head>
  <meta http-equiv="Content-Type" content="text/html; charset=utf-8">
  <title>Example: Checking keyboard entry</title>
  <style type="text/css">
    @import 'keyChecking.css';
  </style>
  <script type="text/javascript" src="DOMhelp.js"></script>
  <script type="text/javascript" src="keyChecking.js"></script>
</head>
<body>
<p class="ex">Keychecking example, try to enter anything but
numbers in the form field below.</p>
<h1>Get Chris Heilmann's book cheaper!</h1>
<form action="nothere.php" method="post">
<p>
  <label for="Voucher">Voucher Number</label>
  <input type="text" name="Voucher" id="Voucher" />
  <input type="submit" value="redeem" />
</p>
</form>
</body>
</html>
```

And after applying the following script, the browser will check what the user enters and both show an error message and disable the Submit button when the entry is not a number, as shown in Figure 5-7.

Figure 5-7. *Testing an entry while it is being typed in*

keyChecking.js

```
voucherCheck={
  errorMessage:'A voucher can contain only numbers.',
  error:false,
  errorClass:'error',
  init:function(){
    if (!document.getElementById || !document.createTextNode) { return; }
    var voucher=document.getElementById('Voucher');
    if(!voucher){return;}
    voucherCheck.v=voucher;
    DOMhelp.addEvent(voucher, 'keyup', voucherCheck.checkKey, false);
  },
  checkKey:function(e){
    if(window.event){
      var key = window.event.keyCode;
    } else if(e){
      var key=e.keyCode;
    }
    var v=document.getElementById('Voucher');
    if(voucherCheck.error){
      v.parentNode.removeChild(v.parentNode.lastChild);
      voucherCheck.error=false;
      DOMhelp.closestSibling(v,1).disabled='';
    }
```

```
   if(key<48 || key>57){
     v.value=v.value.substring(0,v.value.length-1);
     voucherCheck.error=document.createElement('span');
     DOMhelp.cssjs('add', voucherCheck.error, voucherCheck.errorClass);
    var message = document.createTextNode(voucherCheck.errorMessage)
     voucherCheck.error.appendChild(msg);
     v.parentNode.appendChild(voucherCheck.error);
     DOMhelp.closestSibling(v,1).disabled='disabled';
   }
  }
}
DOMhelp.addEvent(window, 'load', voucherCheck.init, false);
```

First, you'll start by defining some properties, like an error message, a Boolean indicating whether there is an error already displayed, and a class to get applied to the error message. You test for the necessary element and attach a keyup event pointing to the checkKey() method.

keyChecking.js *(excerpt)*

```
voucherCheck={
  errorMessage:'A voucher can only contain numbers.',
  error:false,
  errorClass:'error',
  init:function(){
    if (!document.getElementById || !document.createTextNode) { return; }
    var voucher=document.getElementById('Voucher');
    if(!voucher){return;}
    voucherCheck.v=voucher;
    DOMhelp.addEvent(voucher, 'keyup', voucherCheck.checkKey, false);
  },
```

The checkKey method determines whether window.event or the event object is in use and reads out the keyCode in the appropriate manner.

keyChecking.js *(excerpt)*

```
checkKey:function(e){
    if(window.event){
      var key = window.event.keyCode;
    } else if(e){
      var key=e.keyCode;
    }
```

It then retrieves the element (in this case via getElementById(), although you could as easily use DOMhelp.getTarget(e), but why make it more complex than needed?) and checks whether the error property is true. If it is true, there is already a visible error message and the Submit button is disabled. In this case, you need to remove the error message, set the error property to false, and enable the Submit button (which is the next sibling of the input element—use closestSibling() here to ensure it is the button and not a line break).

keyChecking.js *(excerpt)*

```
var v=document.getElementById('Voucher');
if(voucherCheck.error){
  v.parentNode.removeChild(v.parentNode.lastChild);
  voucherCheck.error=false;
  DOMhelp.closestSibling(v,1).disabled='';
}
```

You determine that the key that was pressed is not any of the digits from 0 to 9—that is, that its ASCII code is not between 48 and 57 inclusive.

■**Tip** You can get the values of each key in any ASCII table, for example, at http://www.whatasciicode.com/.

If the key is not a number key, delete the last key entered from the field value and create a new error message. Create a new span element, add the class, add the error message, append it as a new child to the parent of the text entry box, and disable the form button. The last thing missing is to start voucherCheck.init() when the page has finished loading.

keyChecking.js *(excerpt)*

```
if(key<48 || key>57){
  v.value=v.value.substring(0,v.value.length-1);
  voucherCheck.error=document.createElement('span');
  DOMhelp.cssjs('add',
                voucherCheck.error,
                voucherCheck.errorClass);
  var message = document.createTextNode(voucherCheck.errorMessage)
  voucherCheck.error.appendChild(msg);
  v.parentNode.appendChild(voucherCheck.error);
  DOMhelp.closestSibling(v,1).disabled='disabled';
  }
 }
}
DOMhelp.addEvent(window, 'load', voucherCheck.init, false);
```

■**Note** Normally, it'd be enough to check whether the field contents is a number on every keyup event, but this demonstrates the power you have with keyboard events.

If you want to read keyboard combinations with Shift, Ctrl, or Alt, you need to check for the shiftKey, ctrlKey, or altKey event properties in your event listener method, for example:

```
if(e.shiftKey && key==48){alert('shift and 0');}
if(e.ctrlKey && key==48){alert('ctrl and 0');}
if(e.altKey && key==48){alert('alt and 0');}
```

The Dangers of Event Handling

With these functions, you can listen and react to any event initiated by the user. You can make navigations that react to rollovers rather than clicks of the links, you can add keyboard shortcuts only available to your page, and you can make things react on movements of the mouse.

It is very tempting to use event handling to the fullest and come up with whole new concepts of navigation, user journey flow, and how forms interact with the user. The question is whether that is a good or a bad thing.

With your own ideas of what is good and usable in mind, you might sometimes consider a drag-and-drop interface the best there is, but what about users who cannot move a mouse? You can make anything in the document an interactive element by attaching events; however, not all user agents will allow the visitor to reach the element without a mouse. A clickable headline is not available to keyboard users, but a headline with an embedded link is as the user can tab to the link, but cannot tab to the headline.

Basic accessibility guidelines and legal requirements make a very strong point that you have to remain input device independent if you want to create your own rich interfaces with DOM scripting and HTML.

There is nothing wrong with a drag-and-drop interface, as long as you also allow for keyboard access to it. As you should not rely on JavaScript being available, you'll need real links on the draggable elements anyway, which could be enhanced with a click event or even keyboard access.

Keyboard event handling is another can of worms. While most browsers support keypress (which is not mentioned in the W3C specs—they favor keyup), you can never know if the keyboard shortcut you want to assign to an element isn't necessary for another piece of software on the user's machine.

Keyboard access is universally part of the operating system, and visitors who need certain key combinations to use it will not take kindly to your hindering them in their work by hijacking those combinations for your purposes. Clever web applications therefore make their keyboard shortcuts optional or even customizable by the user.

The same problem occurs in HTML when you use the accesskey attribute. This attribute tells the browser to activate the element when the key defined in the attribute's value is pressed (together with the Alt key on MSIE and Mozilla —via other combinations on other browsers). In effect, this is adding an event and assigning an event listener that sets the focus of the element or follows the default action of that element. Until recently, it was common practice and deemed safe to use numerical keys for these attributes—which works, until you have a user who has special characters in her name and needs to use Alt and the ASCII number of the character to enter it.

All of this said, research is under way in the area of rich HTML and JavaScript interfaces, and you can take a look at and use the rich controls developed by IBM and Mozilla at `http://www.mozilla.org/access/dhtml/`.

Summary

You've made it to the end of this chapter, and I hope it was not too much information at once.

In the first half, we talked about the interaction of CSS and JavaScript, covering the following:

- How to change presentation in JavaScript via the style collection

- How to help CSS designers by keeping the look and feel of your script in CSS classes

- How to provide the CSS designers with hooks to style the document differently depending on scripting being enabled or disabled

- An introduction to different third-party style switchers and the idea that published JavaScript scripts are not necessarily set in stone but can be improved and refined over time

- How to ease the maintenance of CSS and JavaScript working together by introducing objects only containing CSS name information

- Fixing a CSS issue with JavaScript—in this chapter's example, multicolumn displays not having the same height

- Helping the CSS designer by applying cross-browser hover effects

- The dangers of using JavaScript to create lots of HTML elements to support CSS effects instead of implementing these effects via JavaScript from the start

We then moved on to what makes web sites click—literally at times—in other words, event handling. We talked about

- How to apply event handling in old browsers via the DOM-1 `onevent` properties (like `onclick`, `onmouseover`, and so on)

- What the W3C has to say about events in the DOM-2 specifications and how to use what they recommend

- How to make noncompliant browsers do the same

- How to avoid display glitches when the page is not fully loaded

- How to deal with keyboard entries

- The dangers of event handling

This is it—you should now have all the tools you need to go out there and "wow" the masses with stable, easy-to-maintain, slick JavaScript. In the next chapter, we will go through some of the most common uses of JavaScript and have a go at developing up-to-date solutions for them to replace old scripts you may already use.

CHAPTER 6

■ ■ ■

Common Uses of JavaScript: Images and Windows

If you read the last few chapters, you should be well equipped now with your knowledge of JavaScript and its interaction with CSS and HTML. Now you will learn about some of the most common uses of JavaScript on the Web these days, and we'll go through some examples. In these examples, you'll see how to ensure that they work independently of other scripts on the page, and I'll explain what problems might occur. We'll also touch on what functionality is tempting to use but might not be the safest of options.

Note This chapter consists of a lot of code examples, and you will be asked to open some of them in a browser to test the functionality for yourself, so if you haven't been to http://www.beginningjavascript.com yet to download the code examples for this book, it might be a good time to do so now.

Most of the full code examples here use DOM-2 event handling. This makes them a bit more complex than their DOM-1 equivalents, but it also makes them work a lot better with other scripts, and they are much more likely to work in future browsers. Just bear with me, and I promise that by repeatedly using these methods, you will get the hang of them quite quickly.

The examples are also developed with maintenance and flexibility in mind. This means that everything that might be changed at a later stage by non-JavaScript-savvy people is stored in properties and that you can easily have several parts of the same document use the scripts' functionality. This also adds to the complexity of some of the scripts, but it is a real-life deliverable most clients ask for.

Images and JavaScript

Dynamic changing of images was most likely the first "wow" effect JavaScript was used for. When CSS was not supported by browsers yet (and—to be fair—was still in the process of being defined), JavaScript was the only way to change an image when the user moved the mouse over it or clicked it. In recent years, more and more of the image effects traditionally achieved via JavaScript have been replaced by pure CSS solutions that make maintenance a lot easier. We'll discuss these later; for now, let's take a look at the basics of what JavaScript can do to images.

Basics of Image Scripting

In JavaScript you can reach and amend images in two ways: the DOM-2 way via
getElementsByTagName() and getElementById(), or an older way, which involves the
images collection that is stored in a property of the document object. As an example, let's
take an HTML document with a list of photos:

```
<ul class="slides">
  <li><img src="pictures/thumbs/cat2.jpg" alt="Lazy Cat" /></li>
  <li><img src="pictures/thumbs/dog10.jpg" alt="Dog using the shade" /></li>
  <li><img src="pictures/thumbs/dog12.jpg" alt="Squinting Dog" /></li>
  <li><img src="pictures/thumbs/dog63.jpg" alt="Dog cooling off in the sand" /></li>
  <li><img src="pictures/thumbs/dog7.jpg"  alt="Very flat dog" /></li>
  <li><img src="pictures/thumbs/donkeycloseup.jpg" alt="Curious Donkey" /></li>
  <li><img src="pictures/thumbs/donkeyeating.jpg" alt="Hay-eating Donkey" /></li>
  <li><img src="pictures/thumbs/kittenflat.jpg" alt="Ginger and White Cat" /></li>
</ul>
```

You can retrieve all these photos in JavaScript to do something to them in both ways:

```
// Old DOM
var photosOldDOM=document.images;
// New DOM
var photos=document.getElementsByTagName('img');
```

Both methods result in an array containing all the images as objects. As with any object,
you can read and manipulate their properties. Say, for example, you want to know the alternative text of the third image. All you need to do is to read out the alt property of the object:

```
// Old DOM alt property
var photosOldDOM=document.images;
alert(photosOldDOM[2].alt);
// W3C DOM-2 alt attribute
var photos=document.getElementsByTagName('img');
alert(photos[2].getAttribute('alt'));
```

Images have several properties, some of which are obvious, but others you may not have heard about:

- border: The value of the border attribute in the HTML

- name: The name attribute of the img tag

- complete: A property that is true if the image has finished loading (read-only—you cannot change this attribute)

- height: The height of the image (in pixels—returned as an integer)

- width: The width of the image (in pixels—returned as an integer)

- hspace: The horizontal space around the image

- vspace: The vertical space around the image

- lowsrc: The image preview as defined in the attribute of the same name

- src: The URL of the image

You can use these properties to access and change images dynamically. If you open the example document exampleImageProperties.html in a browser, you can read and write the properties of the demonstration image as Figure 6-1 shows.

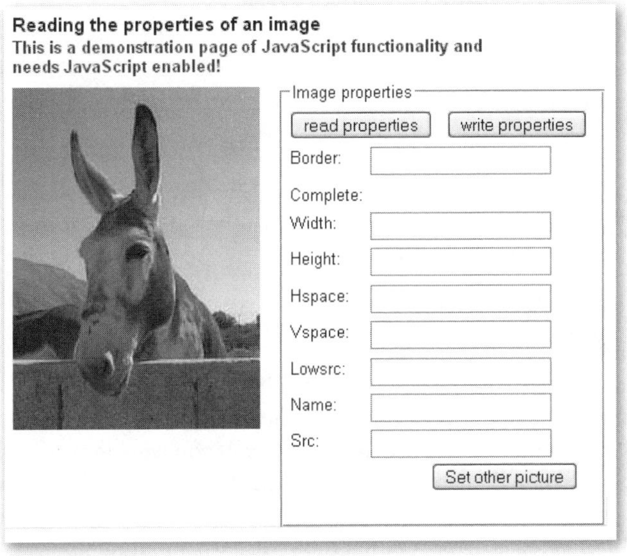

Figure 6-1. *Reading and writing the properties of an image*

> **Note** Notice that if the dimensions of the image have been defined via the HTML `width` and `height` attributes, and you change its source, you don't automatically change its dimensions. For an example, activate the Set other picture button in the demo. This can result in unsightly distortion of the other image, as browsers don't resize images in a sophisticated way.

Preloading Images

If you use images dynamically in the page for rollover or slide show effects, you'll want to have the images already loaded into the browser's memory cache to give the visitor a smooth experience. You can do this in several ways. One is to create a new image object for each image you want to preload when you initialize the page:

```
kitten = new Image();
kitten.src = 'pictures/kittenflat.jpg';
```

You'll see an example of this soon in the "Rollover Effects" section. Some development tools offer scripts that loop through all the images necessary like Macromedia's simple preloader:

```
function simplePreload() {
  var args = simplePreload.arguments;
  document.imageArray = new Array( args.length );
  for(var i = 0; i < args.length; i++ ) {
    document.imageArray[i] = new Image;
    document.imageArray[i].src = args[i];
  }
}
```

If you call this function with the images you want to preload, it'll create a new array with all the images in it, loading them one after the other, for example:

```
simplePreload( 'pictures/cat2.jpg', 'pictures/dog10.jpg' );
```

A different, scripting-independent, way of preloading images is putting them as 1×1-pixel images in the HTML inside a container element that you hide via CSS. This mixes structure and behavior and has the same issue as any image preloading technique has: You force the visitor to download a lot of images he might not want to see immediately. If you were to use preloaders, it might be a good option to keep them optional and let the user decide if he wants to preload all the images.

We'll keep image preloading brief here, as there is much more to learn about images.

Rollover Effects

Rollover or hover effects were the absolute craze when JavaScript first got supported widely in the most common user agents. Many scripts were written, and a lot of small tools came out that allowed "instant rollover generation without any need to code."

The idea of a rollover effect is pretty easy: you hover with your mouse over an image and the image changes, indicating that this is a clickable image and not just eye candy. Figure 6-2 shows a rollover effect.

Figure 6-2. *A rollover effect means the element changes its look when the mouse hovers over it.*

Rollovers Using Several Images

You can create a rollover effect by changing the `src` property of the image when the mouse hovers over it. Old-school rollover effects were tied to the name attribute of the `<img>` tag and used the `images` collection. A construct like this was not uncommon in web pages in the 1990s:

`exampleSimpleRollover.html` *(excerpts)*

    HTML:

```
<a href="contact.html"
   onmouseover="rollover('contact','but_contact_on.gif')"
   onmouseout="rollover('contact','but_contact.gif')">
   <img src="but_contact.gif" name="contact"
      width="103" height="28" alt="Contact Us" border="0" />
</a>
```

    JavaScript:

```
function rollover( img, url ) {
  document.images[img].src=url;
}
```

The problem with rollovers was (and still is) that the second image might not be loaded yet, which is counterproductive. The fact that this is an interactive element is not immediately obvious—only when the second image is shown—so this would confuse rather than aid the user in this case. This is why the classic rollover functions like the one that came bundled with

Macromedia Dreamweaver use the image object preloading technique explained earlier in conjunction with the name attribute:

examplePreloadingRollover.html *(excerpts)*

```
<a href="contact.html"
   onmouseover="rollover('contact',1)"
   onmouseout="rollover('contact',0)">
    <img src="but_contact.gif" name="contact"
      width="103" height="28" alt="Contact Us" border="0" />
</a>
```

JavaScript:

```
contactoff = new Image();
contactoff.src = 'but_contact.gif';
contacton = new Image();
contacton.src = 'but_contact_on.gif';
function rollover( img, state ) {
  var imgState = state == 1 ? eval(img + 'on.src') :➥
  eval(img + 'off.src');
  document.images[img].src = imgState;
}
```

The script creates two new image objects with the names contacton and contactoff. The rollover script checks the name of the image and the state of the rollover and uses eval() to retrieve the correct object and read its src property.

It then sets the src property of the image to the src property retrieved from the object. You can imagine the amount of code when you want to have 20 rollover images in a page, so you can see it was necessary to come up with a more advanced and generic way of creating rollovers.

Daniel Nolan came up with a very clever solution in 2003 as described at http://www.dnolan.com/code/js/rollover/. His solution uses the file name of the image and assumes a suffix of "_o" for the rollover state. All you need to add to the image you want to have a rollover effect for is a class called imgover.

You can replicate the same functionality easily using DOM-2 handlers. First you need an HTML document that has images with the correct class assigned to them:

exampleAutomatedRollover.html *(excerpt)*

```
<ul>
  <li>
    <a href="option1.html">
      <img src="but_1.gif" class="roll" alt="option one" />Option 1
    </a>
  </li>
```

```
<li>
  <a href="option2.html">
    <img src="but_2.gif" class="roll" alt="option two" /> Option 2
  </a>
</li>
[... code snipped ...]
</ul>
```

Then you plan your script. The main object of the script will be called `ro` for rollover. As you want to make things as easy as possible for future maintainers, you keep all the bits and bobs that might change in properties of the main object.

In this script, this is the class that defines which image should get a rollover state and the suffix of the mouseover image. In this case, you'll use "roll" and "_on", respectively. You will need two methods, one to initialize the effect and one to do the rollover. Furthermore, you will need an array to store the preloaded images. All of this together makes up the skeleton of the rollover script:

`automatedRollover.js` *(skeleton)*

```
ro = {
  rollClass : 'roll',
  overSrcAddOn : '_on',
  preLoads : [],
  init : function(){},
  roll : function( e ){}
}
DOMhelp.addEvent( window, 'load', ro.init, false );
```

Let's start fleshing out the skeleton. First up are the properties and the `init` method. In it you predefine a variable called `oversrc` and store all the images of the document in an array called `imgs`. You loop through the images and skip those that don't have the right CSS class attached to them.

`automatedRollover.js` *(excerpt)*

```
ro = {
  rollClass : 'roll',
  overSrcAddOn : '_on',
  preLoads : [],
  init : function() {
    var oversrc;
    var imgs = document.images;
    for( var i = 0; i < imgs.length; i++ ) {
      if( !DOMhelp.cssjs( 'check', imgs[i], ro.rollClass ) ) {
        continue;
      }
```

If the image has the right CSS class attached to it, you read its source attribute, replace the full stop in it by the suffix defined in the overSrcAddOn property followed by a full stop, and store the result in the oversrc variable.

automatedRollover.js *(continued)*

```
oversrc = imgs[i].src.toString().replace( '.',➡
ro.overSrcAddOn + '.');
```

Note For example, the first image in the document has the src but_1.gif. The value of oversrc with the suffix property defined here would be but_1_on.gif.

You then create a new image object and store it as a new item of the preLoads array. Set the src attribute of the new image to oversrc. Use addEvent() from the DOMhelp library to add an event handler for both mouseover and mouseout that points to the roll method.

automatedRollover.js *(continued)*

```
    ro.preLoads[i] = new Image();
    ro.preLoads[i].src = oversrc;
    DOMhelp.addEvent( imgs[i], 'mouseover', ro.roll, false );
    DOMhelp.addEvent( imgs[i], 'mouseout', ro.roll, false );
  }
},
```

The roll method retrieves the image the event occurred on via getTarget(e) and stores its src property in a variable called s. You then test which of the events occurred by reading out the event type. If the event type was mouseover, you replace the full stop in the file name with the add-on followed by a full stop, and vice versa if the event was mouseout. You add an event handler to the window that calls ro.init() when the window has finished loading.

automatedRollover.js *(continued)*

```
  roll : function( e ) {
    var t = DOMhelp.getTarget( e );
    var s = t.src;
    if( e.type == 'mouseover' ) {
      t.src = s.replace( '.', ro.overSrcAddOn + '.' );
    }
    if( e.type == 'mouseout' ) {
      t.src = s.replace( ro.overSrcAddOn + '.', '.' );
    }
  }
}
DOMhelp.addEvent( window, 'load', ro.init, false );
```

The outcome of the demo page as shown in Figure 6-3 features rollovers with highlight images that are already loaded into the browser's cache when the user hovers over the original ones.

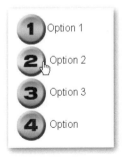

Figure 6-3. *The preloaded and automated rollovers*

As much as you can try to use clever scripting to preload images, it might not always work. The user's browser cache settings or special settings in her connection might make it impossible to sneakily preload something in the back without really adding the image to the document. Therefore, it might be a safer option to use a single image for the rollover effect.

Rollover Effects Using a Single Image

When CSS designers started exploring the :hover pseudo-selector to do a bit more than just changing the underline of a link, CSS-only rollovers were born. These basically mean that you assign different background images to the link and the hover state of the link.

The same problems occurred—images had to get loaded before they were displayed, which made the rollover effect flicker or not happen at all. The solution was to take one single image for both states and use the background-position property to change the location of the image as shown in Figure 6-4.

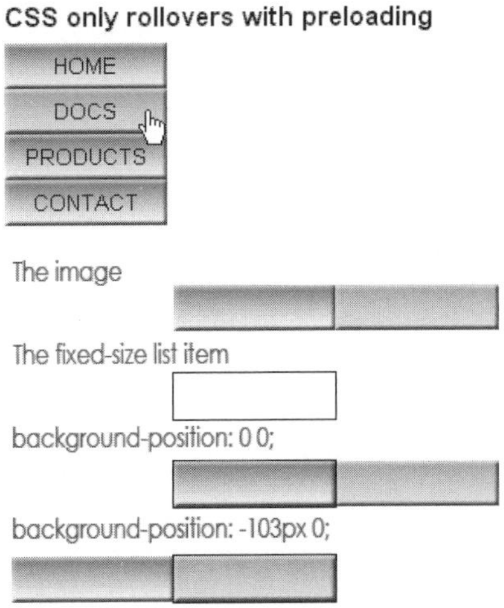

CSS only rollovers with preloading

HOME
DOCS
PRODUCTS
CONTACT

The image

The fixed-size list item

background-position: 0 0;

background-position: -103px 0;

Figure 6-4. *Rollover effects with background position and CSS*

You can see the effect by opening exampleCSSonlyRollover.html in a browser. The CSS in question constrains the link to a certain size and achieves the rollover effect by shifting the background image in the hover state to the left via a negative background-position value that is half the width of the image:

exampleCSSonlyRollover.html *(excerpt)*

```
#nav a{
  width:103px;
  padding-top:6px;
  height:22px;
  background:url(doublebutton.gif) top left no-repeat #ccc;
}
#nav a:hover{
  background-position:-103px 0;
}
```

You can do the same in JavaScript; however, let's be more creative and do something CSS cannot do.

Rollover Effects on Parent Elements

Let's take an HTML list and turn it into a snazzy navigation bar by adding a nice background image, and then make the links change the background image when you hover over them. The first thing you need is a background image with all the states of the background as shown in Figure 6-5.

Figure 6-5. *The navigation background with all states (resized)*

The HTML for the navigation bar is a list of links. As basic web usability strongly suggests never linking the current page, the current link is replaced with a <strong> tag.

exampleParentRollover.html *(excerpt)*

```
<ul id="nav">
  <li><a href="index.html">Home</a></li>
  <li><a href="documentation.html">Documentation</a></li>
  <li><strong>Products</strong></li>
  <li><a href="contact.html">Contact Us</a></li>
</ul>
```

However, as this navigation could be the first level in a multilevel navigation menu, it might also be that the highlight is not a STRONG element but a class on the list item instead:

```
<ul id="nav">
  <li><a href="index.html">Home</a></li>
  <li><a href="documentation.html">Documentation</a></li>
  <li class="current"><a href="products.html">Products</a></li>
  <li><a href="contact.html">Contact Us</a></li>
</ul>
```

Both scenarios have to be taken into account. Explaining the CSS in the demo page is not the purpose of this book; it suffices to say that you fix the dimensions of the list with the ID nav, float it to the left, and float all list elements in it.

Instead, let's go straight into planning the script. You'll need to define several properties for the main object (which is called pr for parent rollover): the ID of the navigation list, the height of the navigation (which is also the height of each of the images and necessary for the background position), and the optional class that might have been used to highlight the current section instead of a <strong> tag.

parentRollover.js *(excerpt)*

```
pr = {
  navId : 'nav',
  navHeight : 50,
  currentLink : 'current',
```

You start with an initialization method that checks for DOM support, and whether the necessary list with the right ID is available.

parentRollover.js *(continued)*

```
init : function() {
  if( !document.getElementById || !document.createTextNode ) {
    return;
  }
  pr.nav = document.getElementById( pr.navId );
  if( !pr.nav ){ return; }
```

The next task is to loop through all the list items contained in this list and check if there is either a STRONG element inside the item or the item has the "current" class. If either is true, the script should store the counter for the loop in the current property of the main object. This property will be used in the rollover method to reset the background to the original state.

parentRollover.js *(continued)*

```
var lis = document.getElementsByTagName( 'li' );

for(var i = 0; i < lis.length; i++)
{
```

```
    if( lis[i].getElementsByTagName( 'strong' ).length > 0 ||
        DOMhelp.cssjs('check', lis[i], pr.currentLink) ) {
      pr.current = i;
    }
```

Each of the list items gets a new property called index, which contains its counter value in the whole list array. Using this property is a trick that prevents you from having to loop through all the list items and compare them with the target in the event listener method.

You assign two event handlers pointing to the roll() method: one when the mouse is over the list item, and another when the mouse leaves the list item.

parentRollover.js *(continued)*

```
    lis[i].index = i;
    DOMhelp.addEvent( lis[i], 'mouseover', pr.roll, false );
    DOMhelp.addEvent( lis[i], 'mouseout', pr.roll, false );
    }
  },
```

The rollover method starts by predefining a variable called pos that later on becomes the offset value needed to show the correct image. It then calls getTarget() to determine which element was rolled over and compares the node name of the target with LI. This is a safety measure because —although you assigned the event handler to the LI—browsers may actually send the link instead as the event target. The reason might be that a link is an interactive page element, whereas an LI isn't, and the browser's rendering engine considers a link more important. You won't know, but you should be aware of the fact that some user agents will see the link instead of the list element as the event target.

parentRollover.js *(continued)*

```
  roll : function( e ) {
    var pos;
    var t = DOMhelp.getTarget(e);
    while(t.nodeName.toLowerCase() != 'li'
          && t.nodeName.toLowerCase() != 'body') {
      t = t.parentNode;
    }
```

Then, you define the position needed to show the right background image. This position is either the index value of the list item or the stored current property multiplied with the height of each image.

Which of the two gets applied depends on whether the user hovers his mouse over the list item or not—something you can find out by comparing the event type with mouseover. Set the style of the navigation's background position accordingly, and then call the init() method when the page has finished loading.

parentRollover.js *(excerpt)*

```
    pos = e.type == 'mouseover' ? t.index : pr.current;
    pos = pos * pr.navHeight;
    pr.nav.style.backgroundPosition = '0 -' + pos + 'px';
  }
}
DOMhelp.addEvent( window, 'load', pr.init, false );
```

When you open exampleParentRollover.html in a browser, you can see that rolling over the different links of the navigation shows the different background images as demonstrated in Figure 6-6.

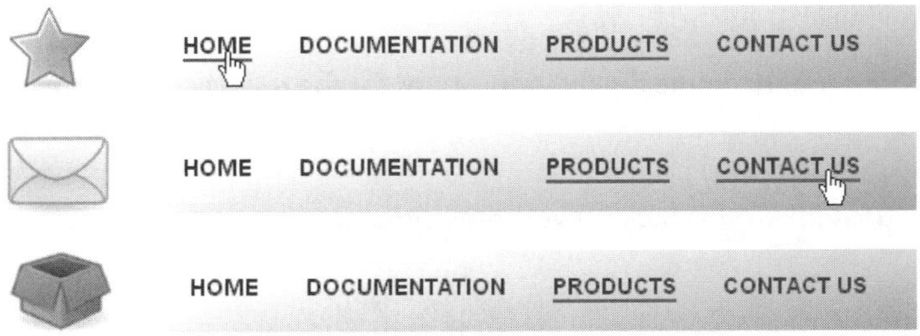

Figure 6-6. *The navigation in different rollover states*

This is a programmatic solution for the problem of rollovers affecting parent elements. However, it has one problem: if the order of the menu items were to change, the maintainer would also have to change the image accordingly. This is not a very flexible solution, which is why you might be better off using dynamically assigned classes to the navigation list to position the background image.

The necessary changes to the script affect the properties and the roll() method; the initialization stays the same. In addition to the currentLink and the navId property, you also need a class name to add to the navigation list. This new property can be called dynamicLink.

In the roll() method, you check once again whether the event triggering the method was mouseover, and add or remove a new dynamic class accordingly. This dynamically assigned and named class consists of the `dynamicLink` property value and the current index plus one (as it is easier for humans to have a first class called `item1` class instead of `item0`):

`parentCSSrollover.js` *as used in* `parentCSSrollover.html` *(abbreviated)*

```
pr = {
  navId : 'nav',
  currentLink : 'current',
  dynamicLink : 'item',
  init : function() {
   // [... same as in parentRollover.js ...]
  },
  Roll : function( e ) {
    // [... same as in parentRollover.js ...]
    var action = e.type == 'mouseover' ? 'add' : 'remove';
    DOMhelp.cssjs( action, pr.nav, pr.dynamicLink + ( t.index + 1 ) );
  }
}
DOMhelp.addEvent( window, 'load', pr.init, false );
```

This way you allow the CSS designer to define the different states for the rollover navigation as classes in the CSS:

`parentCSSrollover.css` *as used in* `parentCSSrollover.html` *(excerpt)*

```
#nav.item1{
  background-position:0 0;
}
#nav.item2{
  background-position:0 -50px;
}
#nav.item3{
  background-position:0 -100px;
}
#nav.item4{
  background-position:0 -150px;
}
```

This also provides the CSS designer with one more hook to design the navigation: the dynamic class can be used to define the current rollover or highlight state of the link itself differently from item to item.

Slide Shows

Slide shows are small images embedded in the page with previous and next buttons or sometimes even automatic changing of images after a certain time. They are used to illustrate text or offer different views of a product.

We can distinguish between two kinds of slide shows: embedded ones that have all the images in the same document and dynamic ones that load the images when they are needed.

Embedded Slide Shows

Probably the easiest way to add a slide show to a page is to add all the images as a list. You can then use JavaScript to turn this list into a slide show by hiding and showing the different list items with the embedded images. The demo document examplePhotoListInlineSlideShow.html does exactly that, as Figure 6-7 shows.

Figure 6-7. *An embedded slide show with JavaScript*

The underlying HTML is an unordered list with all the images as list items. Notice that this also allows you to set a proper alternative text for each of the images.

examplePhotoListInlineSlideShow.html *(excerpt)*

```
<ul class="slides">
  <li>
    <img src="pictures/thumbs/cat2.jpg" alt="Lazy Cat" />
  </li>
  <li>
    <img src="pictures/thumbs/dog10.jpg" alt="Dog using the shade" />
  </li>
  <li>
    <img src="pictures/thumbs/dog12.jpg" alt="Squinting Dog" />
  </li>
  <li>
    <img src="pictures/thumbs/dog63.jpg" alt="Dog cooling off in the sand" />
  </li>
  <li>
    <img src="pictures/thumbs/dog7.jpg"  alt="Very flat dog" />
  </li>
  <li>
    <img src="pictures/thumbs/donkeyeating.jpg" alt="Hay-eating Donkey" />
  </li>
  <li>
    <img src="pictures/thumbs/kittenflat.jpg" alt="Ginger and White Cat" />
  </li>
</ul>
```

All future maintainers have to do to change the order of the images or add or delete images is to change the HTML; there is no need to change the JavaScript at all. Provided that you supply an appropriate style sheet, visitors without JavaScript will get all the images displayed as shown in Figure 6-8. Users without style sheets will get a list with image thumbnails.

Figure 6-8. *The embedded slide show without JavaScript*

One effect of embedding all images in the document is that they will all be loaded when the visitor loads the page. This could be a good or a bad thing, depending on the visitor's connection speed. Later on we'll look at an example that loads the larger images only when the user clicks smaller ones.

Let's look at the script that turns this list into a slide show. You will use the DOMhelp library you developed in previous chapters to work around browser issues and shorten the code slightly.

As always, the first thing to do is to plan your script. In this case, you should give the CSS designer and HTML developer several classes as hooks to trigger functionality or define look and feel:

- A class to indicate that the list should be turned into a slide show

- A class to define the look and feel of the dynamic slide show list

- A class to show elements that were previously hidden

- A class to define the look of the image counter (e.g., image 1 of 3)

- A class to hide elements that should not be there at a certain state of play

You should also allow the maintainer to change the look and content of the forward and backward links and the text content of the image counter.

As for methods, all you need (apart from the helper methods contained in DOMhelp) is a global initialization method, a method to initialize each slide show, and one to show a slide. All of this together makes up the skeleton of your script:

photoListInlineSlides.js *(skeleton)*

```
inlineSlides = {

  // CSS classes
  slideClass : 'slides',
  dynamicSlideClass : 'dynslides',
  showClass : 'show',
  slideCounterClass : 'slidecounter',
  hideLinkClass : 'hide',

  // Labels
  // Forward and backward links, you can use any HTML here
  forwardsLabel : '<img src="control_fastforward_blue.png"➥
  alt="next" />',
  backwardsLabel : '<img src="control_rewind_blue.png"➥
  alt="previous" />',
  // Counter text, # will be replaced by the current image count
  // and % by the number of all pictures
  counterLabel : '# of %',

  init : function() {},
  initSlideShow : function( o ) {},
  showSlide : function( e ) {}
}
DOMhelp.addEvent( window, 'load', inlineSlides.init, false );
```

Note Notice that you offer an HTML-based option in the labels for the forward and backward links. This allows for much more flexible styling of the slide show, as the maintainer can add his own HTML (like images). Furthermore, if you want to allow the maintainer to change dynamic text like the counter, it might be beneficial to use placeholders like # and % and explain what they will be replaced with.

Let's go through the methods in the script step by step. First up is the global initialization method `init()`:

1. Test for DOM support.

2. If the test is successful, loop through all the UL elements of the document.

3. For each UL, check whether it has the class defining it as a slide show (which is stored in the `slideClass` property), and skip the rest of the steps performed by this function if it doesn't have the class (use `continue` to do this).

4. If the current UL is to become a slide show, you replace the class defining it as a slide show with the class defining the dynamic slide show; add a new property called `currentSlide` to the list and call the method `initSlideShow` with the list as a parameter.

`photoListInlineSlides.js` *(excerpt)*

```
init : function() {
  if( !document.getElementById  || !document.createTextNode ) {
    return;
  }
  var uls = document.getElementsByTagName( 'ul' );
  for( var i = 0; i < uls.length; i++ ) {
    if( !DOMhelp.cssjs( 'check', uls[i],➥
    inlineSlides.slideClass ) ) {
      continue;
    }
    DOMhelp.cssjs( 'swap', uls[i],inlineSlides.slideClass,➥
    inlineSlides.dynamicSlideClass );
    uls[i].currentSlide = 0;
    inlineSlides.initSlideShow( uls[i] );
  }
},
```

You can spare yourself a lot of looping and checking with these tricks. First of all, replacing the class only when JavaScript is available with another class allows you to hide all the list items in the CSS instead of looping through them in the `initSlideShow()` method:

`photoListInlineSlides.css` *(excerpt)*

```
.dynslides li{
  display:none;
  margin:0;
  padding:5px;
}
```

Other dynamically assigned CSS classes you have to define to make the slide show work are a `hide` class to remove the backward link when the first image is shown or the forward link when the last image is shown and a `show` class to overrule the hiding you achieved with the `.dynslides li` selector. All the other CSS selectors and properties inside the demo are of a purely cosmetic nature.

photoListInlineSlides.css *(excerpt)*

```css
.dynslides .hide{
  visibility:hidden;
}
.dynslides li.show{
  display:block;
}
```

By storing the current visible image in a property of the list, you don't need to loop through all the images and hide them before you show the current one. Instead, all you need to do is to determine which one will have to be shown, read the property of the parent list element, and hide the previous image stored in this property.

You then reset the property to the new image, and the next time an image gets shown, the cycle starts anew. You could have stored the current image in a property of the main object, but storing it in a property of the list means you allow for several slide shows on the same page.

The `initSlideShow()` method gets each slide show list as a parameter called o. First, define the variables you'll use with the `var` keyword to make sure they don't overwrite global variables with the same name. Then create a new paragraph element to host the forward and backward links and the image counter and insert it immediately after the list (using `o.nextSibling`).

photoListInlineSlides.js *(continued)*

```js
  initSlideShow : function( o ) {
    var p, temp, count;
    p = document.createElement( 'p' );
    DOMhelp.cssjs( 'add', p, inlineSlides.slideCounterClass );
    o.parentNode.insertBefore( p, o.nextSibling );
```

Next, create the backward link by means of DOMhelp's `createLink` method and add the proper label using `innerHTML`. Add an event handler to call the `showSlide` method, hide the link by applying the appropriate CSS class, and add the link to the newly created paragraph. You'll store the link in a property of the list called `rew` to make it easier to reach it later on.

photoListInlineSlides.js *(continued)*

```js
    o.rew = DOMhelp.createLink( '#', ' ' );
    o.rew.innerHTML = inlineSlides.backwardsLabel;
    DOMhelp.addEvent( o.rew, 'click', inlineSlides.showSlide, false );
    DOMhelp.cssjs( 'add', o.rew,inlineSlides.hideLinkClass );
    p.appendChild( o.rew );
```

A new SPAN element that acts as the image counter is next. Get the counterLabel property of the main object and replace the # character with the current list's currentSlide property value and add 1 to it (because humans start counting at 1 and not at 0 like computers do). Replace the % character with the number of LI elements in the list, and add the resulting string as a new text node to the SPAN before adding it as a new child node to the paragraph.

photoListInlineSlides.js *(continued)*

```
o.count = document.createElement( 'span' );
temp = inlineSlides.counterLabel.➥
replace( /#/, o.currentSlide + 1 );
temp = temp.replace( /%/, o.getElementsByTagName( 'li' ).length );
o.count.appendChild( document.createTextNode( temp ) );
p.appendChild( o.count );
```

■Note Notice that you store the counter SPAN in a property of the list, called count. This is pure laziness, as it saves you having to reach it via getElementsByTagName('span')[0] later on. It also makes the script less likely to be broken by maintainers who might add other spans inside the list items at a later stage.

Adding the forward link works analogously to adding the backward link, except that the forwardsLabel property is used as the content and a new property called fwd as the shortcut.

photoListInlineSlides.js *(continued)*

```
o.fwd = DOMhelp.createLink( '#', ' ' );
o.fwd.innerHTML = inlineSlides.forwardsLabel;
DOMhelp.addEvent( o.fwd, 'click', inlineSlides.showSlide, false );
p.appendChild( o.fwd );
```

The method concludes with taking the list item that corresponds to the currentSlide property and adding the show class to it. You could have just used o.firstChild instead, but a future maintainer might want to initially show a different photo than the first one.

photoListInlineSlides.js *(continued)*

```
temp = o.getElementsByTagName( 'li' )[o.currentSlide];
DOMhelp.cssjs( 'add', temp, inlineSlides.showClass );
},
```

The showSlide() method defines a variable called action and gets the event target via getTarget(e). Since you don't know if the maintainer used an image in the link labels, you need to find the link by testing whether the nodeName of the target's parentNode is A. This also counteracts the Safari bug of sending the text contained in a link as the target instead of the link itself. The method then grabs the list the event was triggered in by reading the closestSibling() of the target's parentNode.

photoListInlineSlides.js *(continued)*

```
showSlide : function( e ) {
  var action;
  var t = DOMhelp.getTarget( e );
  while( t.nodeName.toLowerCase() != 'a'
      && t.nodeName.toLowerCase() != 'body' ) {
    t=t.parentNode;
  }
  var parentList = DOMhelp.closestSibling( t.parentNode, -1 );
```

Summary The visitor clicks the content of the link to go one image forward or backward. The event target could be an image (as it is in this example) or text—or anything else the maintainer of this script put in the forwardsLabel and backwardsLabel properties. Therefore—and because Safari sends the text contained in a link as the target rather than the link itself—you need to check for the name of the node and compare it with A. Then, you take the parent node of this A—which is the paragraph that was newly created—and get its previous sibling, which is the UL that contains the images.

Next, you need to find the currentSlide property from the list in question and the total number of images by checking the length property of the list item array. Hide the previously shown image by removing the show class.

photoListInlineSlides.js *(continued)*

```
var count = parentList.currentSlide;
var photoCount = parentList.getElementsByTagName( 'li' ).➥
length - 1;
var photo = parentList.getElementsByTagName( 'li' )[count];
DOMhelp.cssjs( 'remove', photo, inlineSlides.showClass );
```

Determine whether the link that was activated was the forward link by comparing the target with the fwd property of the list, and then increment or decrement the counter accordingly.

If the counter is larger than 0, remove the hide class from the backward link; otherwise, add this class, effectively hiding or showing the link. The same logic applies for the forward link, although the comparison criteria this time is the counter being less than the total number of list items. This prevents the backward link from showing on the first slide and the forward link from showing on the last slide.

photoListInlineSlides.js *(continued)*

```
count = ( t == parentList.fwd ) ? count+1 : count-1;
action = ( count > 0 ) ? 'remove' : 'add' ;
DOMhelp.cssjs( action, parentList.rew,➥
inlineSlides.hideLinkClass );
action = ( count < photoCount ) ? 'remove' : 'add';
DOMhelp.cssjs( action, parentList.fwd,➥
inlineSlides.hideLinkClass);
```

That took care of the links; now you need to increment the counter display. Since the counter is stored as a property of the list, it is easy to read the first child node of that property—that is, the text inside the SPAN. You can then use the replace() method of the String object to replace the first numerical entry (here via a regular expression) with the new image number, which is count+1—again, because humans do count from 1 and not from 0. Next, reset the currentSlide property, grab the new photo (remember you changed count), and show the current photo by adding the show class. All that is left to do is start the init() method when the window has loaded.

photoListInlineSlides.js *(excerpt)*

```
photo = parentList.getElementsByTagName( 'li' )[count];
var counterText = parentList.count.firstChild
counterText.nodeValue = counterText.nodeValue.➥
replace( /\d/, count + 1 );
parentList.currentSlide = count;
photo = parentList.getElementsByTagName( 'li' )[count];
DOMhelp.cssjs( 'add', photo, inlineSlides.showClass );
DOMhelp.cancelClick( e );
  }
}
DOMhelp.addEvent( window, 'load', inlineSlides.init, false );
```

However, you are not quite finished yet. If you try out the slide show in Safari, you will realize that the forward and backward links do get hidden, but they are still clickable and cause errors when you try to reach images that are not there.

■**Caution** This is a common mistake in dynamic web development—hiding things visibly does not necessarily make them disappear for all users. Think of people who are blind, or users of textual browsers (such as Lynx). And then there are browser bugs and oddities to consider, too.

Preventing this issue is rather easy though: all you need to amend is the `showSlide()` method so as not to do anything when the target that was clicked has the `hide` CSS class assigned to it. And when fixing that you might as well add the Safari fix to cancel the default action of the newly generated links. The demo `examplePhotoListInlineSlideShowSafariFix.html` incorporates these changes:

photoListInlineSlidesSafariFix.js

```
inlineSlides = {

  // CSS classes
  slideClass : 'slides',
  dynamicSlideClass : 'dynslides',
  showClass : 'show',
  slideCounterClass : 'slidecounter',
  hideLinkClass : 'hide',
  // Labels
  // Forward and backward links, you can use any HTML here
  forwardsLabel : '<img src="control_fastforward_blue.png"➥
alt="next" />',
  backwardsLabel : '<img src="control_rewind_blue.png"➥
alt="previous" />',
  // Counter text, # will be replaced by the current image count
  // and % by the number of all pictures
  counterLabel : '# of %',

  init : function() {
    if( !document.getElementById || !document.createTextNode ) {
      return;
    }
    var uls = document.getElementsByTagName( 'ul' );
    for( var i = 0; i < uls.length; i++ ) {
      if( !DOMhelp.cssjs( 'check', uls[i],➥
      inlineSlides.slideClass ) ) {
       continue;
      }
      DOMhelp.cssjs( 'swap', uls[i], inlineSlides.slideClass,➥
      inlineSlides.dynamicSlideClass );
      uls[i].currentSlide = 0;
      inlineSlides.initSlideShow( uls[i] );
    }
  },
```

```
initSlideShow : function( o ) {
  var p, temp, count;
  p = document.createElement( 'p' );
  DOMhelp.cssjs( 'add', p, inlineSlides.slideCounterClass );
  o.parentNode.insertBefore( p, o.nextSibling );
  o.rew = DOMhelp.createLink( '#', ' ' );
  o.rew.innerHTML = inlineSlides.backwardsLabel;
  DOMhelp.addEvent( o.rew, 'click', inlineSlides.showSlide, false );
  DOMhelp.cssjs( 'add', o.rew, inlineSlides.hideLinkClass );
  p.appendChild( o.rew );
  o.count = document.createElement( 'span' );
  temp = inlineSlides.counterLabel._
  replace( /#/, o.currentSlide + 1 );
  temp = temp.replace( /%/, o.getElementsByTagName( 'li' ).length );
  o.count.appendChild( document.createTextNode( temp ) );
  p.appendChild( o.count );
  o.fwd=DOMhelp.createLink( '#', ' ' );
  o.fwd.innerHTML = inlineSlides.forwardsLabel;
  DOMhelp.addEvent( o.fwd, 'click', inlineSlides.showSlide, false );
  p.appendChild( o.fwd );
  temp = o.getElementsByTagName( 'li' )[o.currentSlide];
  DOMhelp.cssjs( 'add', temp,inlineSlides.showClass );
  o.fwd.onclick = DOMhelp.safariClickFix;
  o.rew.onclick = DOMhelp.safariClickFix;
},
showSlide : function( e ) {
  var action;
  var t = DOMhelp.getTarget( e );
  while( t.nodeName.toLowerCase() != 'a'
      && t.nodeName.toLowerCase() != 'body' ) {
    t = t.parentNode;
  }
  if( DOMhelp.cssjs( 'check', t,_
  inlineSlides.hideLinkClass ) ){
    return;
  }
  var parentList = DOMhelp.closestSibling( t.parentNode, -1 );
  var count = parentList.currentSlide;
  var photoCount = parentList.getElementsByTagName( 'li' ).length-1;
  var photo = parentList.getElementsByTagName( 'li' )[count];
  DOMhelp.cssjs( 'remove', photo, inlineSlides.showClass );
  count = ( t == parentList.fwd ) ? count + 1 : count - 1;
  action = ( count > 0 ) ? 'remove' : 'add' ;
  DOMhelp.cssjs( action, parentList.rew,➡
  inlineSlides.hideLinkClass );
  action = ( count < photoCount ) ? 'remove' : 'add';
```

```
    DOMhelp.cssjs( action, parentList.fwd,➥
    inlineSlides.hideLinkClass );
    photo = parentList.getElementsByTagName( 'li' )[count];
    var counterText = parentList.count.firstChild
    counterText.nodeValue = counterText.nodeValue.➥
    replace( /\d/, count + 1 );
    parentList.currentSlide = count;
    DOMhelp.cssjs( 'add', photo, inlineSlides.showClass );
    DOMhelp.cancelClick( e );
  }
}
DOMhelp.addEvent( window, 'load', inlineSlides.init, false );
```

Turning embedded image lists into slide shows is an effect that degrades nicely on non-JavaScript user agents, although it is not really image manipulation or even dynamic. The real power of JavaScript is to avoid page reloads and show larger images in the same document instead of just showing them in the browser. Let's take a look at some examples.

Dynamic Slide Shows

Let's take another HTML list and turn it into an example of a dynamic slide show. Start with the HTML, this time a list containing thumbnail images linked to larger images:

exampleMiniSlides.html

```
<ul class="minislides">
<li>
  <a href="pictures/thumbs/cat2.jpg">
    <img src="pictures/minithumbs/cat2.jpg" alt="Lazy Cat" />
  </a>
</li>
<li>
  <a href="pictures/thumbs/dog63.jpg">
    <img src="pictures/minithumbs/dog63.jpg"_
    alt="Dog cooling off in the sand" /></a>
  </li>
  <li>
    <a href="pictures/thumbs/dog7.jpg">
      <img src="pictures/minithumbs/dog7.jpg"  alt="Very flat dog" />
    </a>
  </li>
  <li>
    <a href="pictures/thumbs/kittenflat.jpg">
      <img src="pictures/minithumbs/kittenflat.jpg" alt="Ginger and White Cat" />
    </a>
  </li>
</ul>
```

If you open the example in a browser with JavaScript enabled, you get a list of small thumbnails and a larger image. Clicking the thumbnails will replace the larger image with the one the thumbnail points to, as shown in Figure 6-9.

Figure 6-9. *A slide show with small preview images (thumbnails)*

Visitors without JavaScript will only get a row of images linking to larger images, as shown in Figure 6-10.

Figure 6-10. *The slide show with small preview images without JavaScript*

Again, let's plan the skeleton of the script: you define a class to recognize which lists are to become slide shows, a class to give to the list item that contains the large photo, and an alternative text to add to the large photo.

The methods are the same as the last time: one global initialization method, one to initialize each slide show, and one to show the current photo.

miniSlides.js *(skeleton)*

```
minislides = {
  // CSS classes
  triggerClass : 'minislides',
  largeImgClass : 'photo',
  // Text added to the title attribute of the big picture
  alternativeText : ' large view',

  init : function(){  },
  initShow : function( o ){ },
  showPic : function( e ){  }
}
DOMhelp.addEvent( window, 'load', minislides.init, false );
```

The CSS for the slide show is pretty simple:

miniSlides.css *(excerpt)*

```css
.minislides, .minislides * {
  margin:0;
  padding:0;
  list-style:none;
  border:none;
}
.minislides{
  clear:both;
  margin:10px 0;
  background:#333;
}
.minislides,.minislides li{
  float:left;
}
.minislides li img{
  display:block;
}
.minislides li{
  padding:1px;
}
.minislides li.photo{
  clear:both;
  padding-top:0;
}
```

First, you do a global reset on anything inside the list with the right class and the list itself. A global reset means setting all margins and paddings to 0 and the borders and list styles to none. This prevents having to deal with cross-browser differences and also makes the CSS document a lot shorter, as you don't need to reset these values for every element.

Then float the lists and all the list items to the left to make them appear inline rather than one under the other. You need to float the main list to make sure it contains the others.

Set the images to display as block elements to avoid gaps around them and add padding on each list item of one pixel to show the background color.

The "photo" list item needs a float clearing to appear below the others. Set its top padding to 0 to avoid a double line between the smaller images and the big image.

The init() method functions analogously to the one in the last slide show. You test for DOM support, loop through all the lists in the document, and skip those that don't have the right class. The ones that have the right class get sent to the initShow() method as a parameter.

miniSlides.js *(excerpt)*

```
init : function() {
  if( !document.getElementById || !document.createTextNode ) {
    return;
  }
  var lists = document.getElementsByTagName( 'ul' );
  for( var i = 0; i < lists.length; i++ ) {
    if( !DOMhelp.cssjs( 'check', lists[i],➡
    minislides.triggerClass ) ) {
      continue;
    }
    minislides.initShow( lists[i] );
  }
},
```

The `initShow()` method starts by creating a new list item, a new image, and assigning the large image class to the new list item. It adds the image as a child of the list item and the new list item as a child of the main list. Together with the CSS defined earlier, this displays the new image below the others.

miniSlides.js *(excerpt)*

```
initShow : function( o ) {
  var newli = document.createElement( 'li' );
  var newimg = document.createElement( 'img' );
  newli.appendChild( newimg );
  DOMhelp.cssjs( 'add', newli, minislides.largeImgClass );
  o.appendChild( newli );
```

Then you grab the first image in the list and read its alternative text stored in the `alt` attribute. Add this text as the alternative text to the new image, add the text stored in the `alternativeText` property to it, and store the resulting string as a `title` attribute of the new image.

miniSlides.js *(excerpt)*

```
var firstPic = o.getElementsByTagName( 'img' )[0];
var alt = firstPic.getAttribute( 'alt' );
newimg.setAttribute( 'alt', alt );
newimg.setAttribute( 'title', alt + minislides.alternativeText );
```

Next, retrieve all the links in the list and apply an event pointing to `showPic` when the user clicks each link. Store the new image as a property called `photo` in the list object and set the `src` attribute of the newly created image to the target location of the first link.

miniSlides.js *(excerpt)*

```
  var links = o.getElementsByTagName( 'a' );
  for(i = 0; i < links.length; i++){
    DOMhelp.addEvent( links[i], 'click', minislides.showPic,➥
    false );
    links[i].onclick = function() { return false; } // Safari
  }
  o.photo = newimg;
  newimg.setAttribute( 'src', o.getElementsByTagName('a')[0].href );
},
```

Showing the pictures the links point to when they were clicked is a piece of cake. In the showPic() method, retrieve the event target via getTarget() and get the old picture by reading out the list's photo property.

This time you know the element the visitor will click is an image, which is why you don't need to loop and test the name of the element. Instead, you go up three parent nodes (A, LI, and UL) and read the previously stored image. Then you set the alternative text, the title, and the image src and stop the link's default behavior via cancelClick(). Add a handler that fires the init() method when the window has finished loading to complete your mini slide show.

miniSlides.js *(excerpt)*

```
  showPic : function( e ) {
    var t = DOMhelp.getTarget( e );
    var oldimg = t.parentNode.parentNode.parentNode.photo;
    oldimg.setAttribute( 'alt', t.getAttribute( 'alt' ) );
    oldimg.setAttribute( 'title', t.getAttribute('alt') +➥
    minislides.alternativeText );
    oldimg.setAttribute( 'src', t.parentNode.getAttribute( 'href' ) );
    DOMhelp.cancelClick( e );
  }
}
DOMhelp.addEvent( window, 'load', minislides.init, false );
```

Summary of Images and JavaScript

This concludes this introduction to images and JavaScript. Hopefully, you are not too overwhelmed by what is possible and how to approach scripting in this fashion and are interested in playing with the examples to see what else is possible. Keep these slide shows and how they work in mind though—at the end of this chapter we will come back to the document embedded slide show and make it play automatically. In Chapter 10, you will see how to develop a larger JavaScript-enabled gallery.

Things to Remember About Images and JavaScript

- You can do a lot of preloading with the image objects, but it is not a bulletproof approach. Browser cache settings, broken image links, and proxy servers might mess with your preload script. A lot of DHTML scripts use image preloader progress bars before showing the main page. If these scripts fail, all the user gets is a stuck or constantly changing progress bar, which is frustrating.

- While you can access the properties of each image directly, it might not be the best approach—leave the visuals to the CSS and your scripts will not be changed by others who might not know what is going on.

- CSS has come a long way since the days of DHTML, and these days it might be a better approach to help the CSS designer by providing hooks rather than achieving a visual effect purely by scripting—an example being the parent rollover you saw earlier.

Windows and JavaScript

Spawning new browser windows and altering the current window are very common uses for JavaScript. These are also very annoying and unsafe, as you can never be sure if the visitor of your web page can deal with resized windows or will be notified by her user agent when there is a new window. Think of screen reader users listening to your site or text browser users.

Windows have been used for unsolicited advertising (pop-up windows) and executing code in hidden windows for data retrieval purposes (phishing) in the past, which is why browser vendors and third-party software providers have come up with a lot of software and browser settings to stop this kind of abuse. Mozilla Firefox users can choose whether they want pop-up windows and what properties of the window can be changed by JavaScript as shown in Figure 6-11.

Figure 6-11. *The advanced JavaScript settings in Mozilla Firefox*

Other browsers like MSIE 7 or Opera 8 disallow hiding the location bar in new windows and can impose size and position constraints on new windows.

> **Note** This is a point of agreement between different browser makers wanting to stop security vulnerabilities. Opening a new window without a visible location bar can allow a malicious attacker to open a pop-up on a third-party site via Cross-Site Scripting (XSS), make it appear as if the window belonged to the site, and ask users to enter information. More about XSS can be found on Wikipedia: `http://en.wikipedia.org/wiki/XSS`.

This is all great news for web surfers, as they can stop unwanted advertising and are less likely to be fooled into giving away their data to the wrong people. It is not such great news for you, as it means that when you want to use windows extensively in JavaScript, you have to test a lot of different scenarios.

Such considerations aside, you can still do a lot with windows and JavaScript. Every JavaScript-capable browser provides you with an object called `window`, whose properties are listed in the next section, as well as some examples on how to use them.

Window Properties

> **Note** The following list does not show all the `window` properties available, only those that are supported across numerous browsers (Mozilla/Firefox, Opera 7 and higher, MSIE 5.5 and higher, and Safari). If a given property is not supported by a certain browser, I will note that where the property is discussed.

- `closed`: Boolean if the window was closed or not (read-only)

- `defaultStatus`: The default status message in the status bar (not supported by Safari)

- `innerHeight`: The height of the document part of the window

- `innerWidth`: The width of the document part of the window

- `outerHeight`: The height of the whole window

- `outerWidth`: The width of the whole window

- `pageXOffset`: Current horizontal start position of the document inside the window (read-only)

- `pageYOffset`: Current vertical start position of the document inside the window (read-only)

- `status`: The text content of the status bar

- `name`: The name of the window

- `toolbar`: Property that returns an object with a visible property of `true` when the window has a toolbar (read-only)

For example, if you want to obtain the inner size of a window, you could use some of these properties:

exampleWindowProperties.html *(excerpt)*

```
function winProps() {
  var winWidth = window.outerWidth;
  var winHeight = window.outerHeight;
  var docWidth = window.innerWidth;
  var docHeight = window.innerHeight;
  var message = 'This window is ';
  message += winWidth + ' pixels wide and ';
  message += winHeight + ' pixels high.\n';
  message += 'The inner dimensions are:';
  message += docWidth + ' * ' + docHeight + ' pixels';
  alert( message );
}
```

Some possible output from this function is shown in Figure 6-12.

Figure 6-12. *Reading out window properties*

There are other properties that are not supported by MSIE and Opera. These are scrollbars, locationbar, statusbar, menubar, and personalbar. Each of them stores an object with a read-only visible property having a value of true or false. In order to test whether the user has a menu bar open, you check the object and the property:

```
if ( window.menubar && window.menubar.visible == true ){
  // Code
}
```

Window Methods

The window object also has a number of methods, some of which have been discussed in earlier chapters. The most common ones apart from those that provide user feedback are for opening new windows and timed execution of functions.

User Feedback Methods

The user feedback methods listed here are covered in detail in Chapter 4.

- `alert('message')`: Displays an alert

- `confirm('message')`: Displays a dialog to confirm an action

- `prompt('message','preset')`: Displays a dialog to enter a value

Opening New Windows

Opening and closing of windows is technically quite easy; however, with browsers suppressing different properties and methods or badly written pop-up blocking software even blocking "good" pop-ups, doing so can become a nightmare and needs proper testing. The specifics of opening new windows are pretty easy. You have four methods at your disposal:

- `open('url','name','properties')`: Opens a new window called "name", loads the URL in it, and sets the window properties

- `close()`: Closes the window (If the window is not a pop-up window, this will cause a security alert.)

- `blur()`: Moves the focus of browser away from the window

- `focus()`: Moves the focus of browser to the window

The properties string of the open method has a very unique syntax: it lists all the properties of the window as strings—each consisting of a name and a value joined with an equal sign—which are separated by commas:

```
myWindow = window.open( 'demo.html', 'my', 'p1=v1,p2=v2,p3=v3' );
```

Not all of the properties listed here are supported in all browsers, but they can be used in most of them:

- `height`: Defines the height of the window in pixels.

- `width`: Defines the width of the window in pixels.

- `left`: Defines the horizontal position of the window on the screen in pixels.

- `top`: Defines the vertical position of the window on the screen in pixels.

- `location`: Defines whether the window has a location bar or not (yes or no)—remember this will be a fixed yes state in future browsers.

- `menubar`: Defines whether the window has a menu bar or not (yes or no)—this is not supported by Opera and Safari (being a Mac tool, Safari has no menu bar on the window but on top of the screen).

- `resizable`: Defines whether the user is allowed to resize the window in case it is too small or too big. Opera does not allow this property, so Opera users can resize any window.

- `scrollbars`: Defines whether the window has scrollbars or not (yes or no). Opera does not allow suppressing scrollbars.

- `status`: Defines whether the window has a status bar or not (yes or no). Opera does not allow turning off the status bar.

- `toolbar`: Defines whether the window has a toolbar or not (yes or no)—turning the toolbar off is not supported by Opera.

Note   Other Mozilla/Firefox-only properties are `hotkeys` (which turns the keyboard shortcuts on and off in a given window), `innerHeight` and `innerWidth` (which define the display size as opposed to window size), and `dependent` (which determines whether the window should be closed when the window that opened it is closed). The latter is also supported by Konqueror on Linux.

To open a window that is 200 pixels wide and high and 100 pixels from the top-left corner of the screen, and then load into it the document `grid.html`, you have to set the appropriate properties as shown here:

```
var windowprops = "width=200,height=200,top=100,left=100";
```

You can try to open the window when the page loads:

exampleWindowPopUp.html *(excerpt)*

```
function popup() {
  var windowprops = "width=200,height=200,top=100,left=100";
  var myWin =  window.open( "grid.html", "mynewwin" ,windowprops );
}
window.onload = popup;
```

Notice that the outcome is slightly different from browser to browser. MSIE 6 shows the window without any toolbars, MSIE 7 shows the location bar, and Firefox and Opera warn you that the page is trying to open a new window and asks you whether you want to allow it to do so.

This is handled slightly differently when the window is opened via a link:

exampleLinkWindowPopUp.html

```
<a href="#" onclick="popup();return false">
  Open grid
</a>
```

Neither Opera nor Firefox complain about the pop-up window now. However, if JavaScript is disabled, then there won't be a new window, and the link doesn't do anything. Therefore, you might want to link to the document in the href and send the URL as a parameter instead.

exampleParameterLinkWindowPopUp.html *(excerpts)*

```
function popup( url ) {
  var windowprops = "width=200,height=200,top=100,left=100";
  var myWin =  window.open( url, "mynewwin", windowprops );
}

<a href="grid.html" onclick="popup(this.href);return false">
  Open grid
</a>
```

Notice the name parameter of window.open() method. This one is seemingly pretty pointless for JavaScript, as it does not do anything (there is no windows collection that you could use to reach the window via windows.mynewwin, for example). However, it is used in the HTML target attribute to make links open their linked documents in the pop-up window instead of the main window.

In this example, you define the name of the window as "mynewwin", and you target a link to open `http://www.yahoo.co.uk/` in there:

`exampleParameterLinkWindowPopUp.html` *(excerpts)*

```
function popup( url ) {
  var windowprops = "width=200,height=200,top=100,left=100";
  var myWin = window.open( url, "mynewwin", windowprops );
}
<a href="http://www.yahoo.co.uk/" target="mynewwin">Open Yahoo</a>
```

Unless you use nontransitional XHTML or strict HTML (where `target` is deprecated), you can also use the `target` attribute with a value of _blank to open a new window regardless of the availability of JavaScript. It is good practice then to tell the visitor that the link is going to open in a new window inside the link to avoid confusion or accessibility issues:

```
<a href="grid.html" onclick="popup(this.href);return false" target="blank">
  Open grid  (opens in a new window)
</a>
```

However, as you might want to use strict HTML and XHTML, and you have a lot more control over the pop-up when using JavaScript, it might be a better solution to not rely on `target` but turn links into pop-up links only if and when scripting is available. For that you need something to hook into and identify the link as a pop-up link. You could for example use a class called popup.

`exampleAutomaticPopupLinks.html` *(excerpt)*

```
<p><a href="grid.html" class="popup">Open grid</a></p>
<p><a href="http://www.yahoo.co.uk/" class="popup">Open Yahoo</a></p>
```

Planning the script doesn't entail much: you need the class to trigger the pop-up, the textual add-on, and the window parameters as properties, an `init()` method to identify the links and add the changes, and an `openPopup()` method to trigger the pop-ups.

`automaticPopupLinks.js` *(skeleton)*

```
poplinks = {
  triggerClass : 'popup',
  popupLabel : ' (opens in a new window)',
  windowProps : 'width=200,height=200,top=100,left=100',
  init : function(){ },
  openPopup : function( e ){ },
}
```

The two methods are pretty basic. The `init()` method checks for DOM support and loops through all the links in the document. If the current link has the CSS trigger class, it adds the label to the link by creating a new text node from the label and adding it as a new child to the link. It adds an event when the link is clicked pointing to the `openPopup()` method and applies the Safari fix to stop the link from being followed in that browser.

automaticPopupLinks.js *(excerpt)*

```
init : function() {
  if( !document.getElementById || !document.createTextNode ) {
   return;
  }
  var label;
  var allLinks = document.getElementsByTagName( 'a' );
  for( var i = 0; i < allLinks.length; i++ ) {
    if( !DOMhelp.cssjs( 'check', allLinks[i],➥
    poplinks.triggerClass ) ) {
      continue;
    }
    label = document.createTextNode( poplinks.popupLabel );
    allLinks[i].appendChild( label );
    DOMhelp.addEvent( allLinks[i], 'click',➥
    poplinks.openPopup, false );
    allLinks[i].onclick = DOMhelp.safariClickFix;
  }
},
```

The openPopup() method retrieves the event target, makes sure that it was a link, and opens a new window by calling window.open() with the event target's href attribute as the URL, a blank name, and the window properties stored in windowProps. It finishes by calling the cancelClick() method to stop the link from being followed.

automaticPopupLinks.js *(excerpt)*

```
openPopup : function( e ) {
  var t = DOMhelp.getTarget( e );
  if( t.nodeName.toLowerCase() != 'a' ) {
    t = t.parentNode;
  }
  var win = window.open( t.getAttribute('href'), '',➥
  poplinks.windowProps );
  DOMhelp.cancelClick( e );
}
```

There is more to this topic, especially when it comes to usability and accessibility concerns, and making sure that pop-up windows are used only when they really are opened and not blocked by some software or otherwise fail to open; however, going deeper into the matter is not within the scope of the current discussion. It suffices to say that it is not easy to rely on pop-ups of any kind in today's environment.

Window Interaction

Windows can interact with other windows using a number of their properties and methods. First of all there is focus() and blur(): the former brings the pop-up window to the front, the latter pushes it to the back of the current window.

You can use the `close()` method to get rid of windows, and you can reach the window that opened the pop-up window via the `window.opener` property. Suppose that you've opened two new windows from a main document:

```
w1 = window.open( 'document1.html', 'win1' );
w2 = window.open( 'document2.html', 'win2' );
```

You can hide the first window behind the other by calling its `blur()` method:

```
w1.blur();
```

Note   In online advertising, the trick of opening an unsolicited window and hiding it immediately via `blur()` is called a **pop-under** and is considered by advertisers to be less annoying than pop-up windows, as they don't cover the current page. If you've ever found several windows you don't remember opening when you shut down the browser, this is likely what has happened.

You can close the window by calling its `close()` method:

```
w1.close();
```

If you want to reach the initial window from any of the documents in the pop-ups, you can do this via

```
var parentWin = window.opener;
```

If you want to reach the second window from the first window, you'll also need to go through the `window.opener`, as the second window was opened from this one:

```
var parentWin = window.opener;
var otherWin = parentWin.w2;
```

Notice that you need to use the variable name the window was assigned to, and not the window name.

You can use any of the window methods of any of the windows this way. Say for example you want to close `w2` from within `document1.html`; you do this by calling

```
var parentWin = window.opener;
var otherWin = parentWin.w2.close();
```

You can also call functions of the main window. If the main window has a JavaScript function that is called `demo()`, you could reach it from `document1.html` via

```
var parentWin = window.opener;
parentWin.demo();
```

Caution If you try to close the initial window with `window.opener.close()`, some browsers will give a security alert asking the user if he wants to allow that. This is another security feature to prevent site owners with malicious intentions spoofing a different web site. A lot of design agencies used to close the original browser in favor of a window with a predefined size—this is not possible any longer without the aforementioned security alert, and it might be a good idea to avoid this kind of behavior unless you want to scare or annoy your visitors.

Changing the Position and the Dimensions of a Window

Each of the methods in the following list has x and y parameters. x is the horizontal position and y the vertical position in pixels from the top left of the screen. The `moveBy()`, `resizeBy()`, and `scrollBy()` methods allow for negative values, which would move the window or the content to the left and up or make the window smaller by the stated amount of pixels.

- `moveBy(x,y)`: Moves the window by x and y pixels

- `moveTo(x,y)`: Moves the window to the coordinates x and y

- `resizeBy(x,y)`: Resizes the window by x and y

- `resizeTo(x,y)`: Resizes the window to x and y

- `scrollBy(x,y)`: Scrolls the window's content by x and y

- `scrollTo(x,y)`: Scrolls the window's content to x and y

If you check the example document `exampleWindowPosition.html`, you can test out the different methods as shown in Figure 6-13. Note that this example appears in Firefox. In Opera 8 or MSIE 7, the small window will have a location bar.

Figure 6-13. *Changing the window position and dimension*

Animation with Window Intervals and Timeouts

You can use the `setInterval()` and `setTimeout()` window methods to allow for timed execution of code. `setTimeout` means you wait a certain time before executing the code (once only); `setInterval()` executes the code every time the given time period has passed.

- `name = setInterval( 'someCode', x )`: Executes the JavaScript code passed to it as `someCode` every x milliseconds

- `clearInterval( name )`: Cancels the execution of the interval called `name` (keeps the code from being executed again)

- `name=setTimeout( 'someCode', x )`: Executes the JavaScript code `someCode` once, after waiting x milliseconds

- `clearTimeout( name )`: Stops the timeout called `name` if the code hasn't yet been run

---

■Note The parameter `someCode` in `setInterval()` and `setTimeout()` is a string and can be any valid JavaScript code. Usually, it's most convenient simply to call a function you've already defined elsewhere.

Classic examples for the use of these methods are news tickers, clocks, and animation. However, you can also use them to make your site less obtrusive and more user beneficial. One example of this is a warning message that vanishes after a certain amount of time. The demo `exampleTimeout.html` shows how you can use `setTimeout()` to display a very obvious warning message for a short period or allow the user to get rid of it immediately. The HTML has a paragraph warning the user that the document is out of date:

`exampleTimeout.html` *(excerpt)*

```
<p id="warning">This document is outdated
 and kept only for archive purposes.</p>
```

A basic style sheet colors this warning red and shows it in bold for non-JavaScript users. For users that have JavaScript enabled, add a dynamic class that makes the warning a lot more obvious.

`timeout.css`

```
#warning{
  font-weight:bold;
  color:#c00;
}
```

```css
.warning{
  width:300px;
  padding:2em;
  background:#fcc;
  border:1px solid #c00;
  font-size:2em;
}
```

The difference between the two is shown in Figure 6-14.

**This document is outdated and only
kept for archive purposes.**

**This document is outdated
and only kept for archive
purposes.**

remove warning

Figure 6-14. *Warning message without and with JavaScript*

The user can click the "remove warning" link to get rid of the warning or wait, and it will vanish automatically after 10 seconds.

The script is pretty easy; you check whether DOM is supported and whether the warning message with the right ID exists. Then you add the dynamic `warning` class to the message and create a new link with an event handler pointing to the `removeWarning()` method. You append this link as a new child node to the warning message and define a timeout that automatically triggers `removeWarning()` when 10 seconds are over.

`timeout.js` *(excerpt)*

```javascript
warn = {
  init : function() {
    if( !document.getElementById || !document.createTextNode ) {
      return;
    }
    warn.w = document.getElementById( 'warning' );
    if( !warn.w ){ return; }
    DOMhelp.cssjs( 'add', warn.w, 'warning' );
    var temp = DOMhelp.createLink( '#', 'remove warning' );
    DOMhelp.addEvent( temp, 'click', warn.removeWarning, false );
    temp.onclick = DOMhelp.safariClickFix;
    warn.w.appendChild( temp );
    warn.timer = window.setTimeout( 'warn.removeWarning()', 10000 );
  },
```

All the `removeWarning()` method needs to do is remove the warning message from the document, clear the timeout, and stop the default action of the link.

`timeout.js` *(continued)*

```
  removeWarning : function( e ){
    warn.w.parentNode.removeChild( warn.w );
    window.clearTimeout( warn.timer );
    DOMhelp.cancelClick( e );
  }
}
DOMhelp.addEvent( window, 'load', warn.init, false )
```

One web application that pioneered this kind of effect is Basecamp (`http://www.basecamphq.com/`), which highlights the recent changes to the document in yellow when the page loads and gradually fades out the highlight. You can see the effect rationale at 37signals (`http://www.37signals.com/svn/archives/000558.php`) and a demo JavaScript at YourTotalSite (`http://www.yourtotalsite.com/archives/javascript/yellowfade_technique_for/`).

Timeouts are tempting to use on web sites because they give the impression of a very dynamic site and allow you to transition smoothly from one state to the other.

■Tip There are several JavaScript effect libraries available that offer you premade scripts to achieve tansition and animation effects. While most of them are very outdated, there are some exceptions, like script.aculo.us (`http://script.aculo.us/`) and FACE (`http://kurafire.net/projects/face`).

However, it might be a good idea to reconsider using a lot of animation and transitions in your web site. Remember that the code is executed on the user's computer, and depending on how old or how busy it is with other tasks, the transitions and animations may look very clumsy and become a nuisance rather than a richer site experience.

Animations can also be an accessibility issue if the functionality of the site is dependent on them, as they might make it impossible for some groups of disabled visitors to use the site (cognitive disabilities, epilepsy). The Section 508 accessibility law (`http://www.section508.gov/`) states quite clearly that for software development you need to provide an option to turn off animation:

> *(h) When animation is displayed, the information shall be displayable in at least one non-animated presentation mode at the option of the user.*

—`http://www.section508.gov/index.cfm?FuseAction=Content&ID=12#Software`

However, for web sites this is not formulated as clearly. The W3C accessibility guidelines, on the other hand, state explicitly in a level-two priority that you should avoid any movement in web pages.

Until user agents allow users to freeze moving content, avoid movement in pages.

—http://www.w3.org/TR/WCAG10-TECHS/#tech-avoid-movement

Let's try an example that allows the user to start and stop an animation. Take the embedded slide show developed earlier in the chapter and instead of giving it forward and backward links, you'll add a link to start and stop an automated slide show using a setInterval().

The HTML and the CSS will stay the same, but the JavaScript has to change a lot.

If you open exampleAutoSlideShow.html in a browser, you'll get a slide show with a Play button that starts the show when you click it. You could easily start the animation when the page loads, but it is a good idea to leave the choice to the user. This is especially the case when you need to comply with accessibility guidelines, as unsolicited animation can cause problems for users suffering from disabilities like epilepsy. Once clicked, the button turns into a Stop button that stops the slide show when activated. You can see how it looks in Firefox in Figure 6-15.

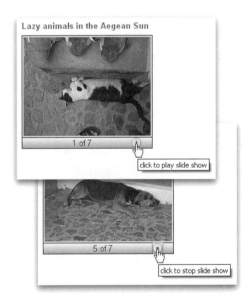

Figure 6-15. *An automatic slide show changing the Play button to a Stop button*

You start with the necessary CSS classes, which are the same as in the first slide show example with the exception of the hide class. As you won't hide any buttons this time, there is no need for it.

autoSlides.js *(excerpt)*

```
autoSlides = {

  // CSS classes
  slideClass : 'slides',
  dynamicSlideClass : 'dynslides',
  showClass : 'show',
  slideCounterClass : 'slidecounter',
```

The other properties change slightly; instead of backward and forward labels, you now need play and stop labels. The counter indicating which picture of how many is currently shown stays the same. One new property is the delay of the slide show in milliseconds.

autoSlides.js *(continued)*

```
  // Labels
  // Play and stop links, you can use any HTML here
  playLabel : '<img src="control_play_blue.png" alt="play" />',
  stopLabel : '<img src="control_stop_blue.png" alt="stop" />',
  // Counter text, # will be replaced by the current image count
  // and % by the number of all pictures
  counterLabel : '# of %',

  // Animation delay in milliseconds
  delay : 1000,
```

The init() method checks for DOM support and adds a new array called slideLists that will store all the lists that are to be turned into slide shows. This is necessary to be able to tell the function which list to apply the changes to.

autoSlides.js *(continued)*

```
  init : function() {
    if( !document.getElementById || !document.createTextNode ) {
      return;
    }
    var uls = document.getElementsByTagName( 'ul' );
    autoSlides.slideLists = new Array();
```

First, loop through all the lists in the document and check for the class to turn them into slide shows. If a list has the class, you initialize the currentSlide property to 0 and store the loop counter in a new list property called showCounter. Once again, this will be needed to tell the interval which list to change. You call the initSlideShow() method with the list as a parameter and add the lists to the slideLists array.

autoSlides.js *(continued)*

```
  for( var i = 0; i < uls.length; i++ ) {
    if( !DOMhelp.cssjs( 'check', uls[i],➥
    autoSlides.slideClass ) ){
      continue;
    }
    DOMhelp.cssjs( 'swap', uls[i], autoSlides.slideClass,_
    autoSlides.dynamicSlideClass );
    uls[i].currentSlide = 0;
    uls[i]. showIndex = i;
    autoSlides.initSlideShow( uls[i] );
    autoSlides.slideLists.push( uls[i] );
  }
},
```

The initSlideShow() method does not differ much from the method of the same name that you used in photoListInlineSlidesSafariFix.js; the only difference is that you create one link instead of two and apply the playLabel as the content of the new link:

autoSlides.js *(continued)*

```
initSlideShow : function( o ){
  var p, temp ;
  p = document.createElement( 'p' );
  DOMhelp.cssjs( 'add', p, autoSlides.slideCounterClass );
  o.parentNode.insertBefore( p, o.nextSibling );
  o.play = DOMhelp.createLink( '#', ' ' );
  o.play.innerHTML = autoSlides.playLabel;
  DOMhelp.addEvent( o.play, 'click', autoSlides.playSlide, false );
  o.count = document.createElement( 'span' );
  temp = autoSlides.counterLabel.replace( /#/, o.currentSlide + 1 );
  temp = temp.replace( /%/, o.getElementsByTagName( 'li' ).length );
  o.count.appendChild( document.createTextNode( temp ) );
  p.appendChild( o.count );
  p.appendChild( o.play );
  temp = o.getElementsByTagName( 'li' )[o.currentSlide];
  DOMhelp.cssjs('add', temp,autoSlides.showClass );
  o.play.onclick = DOMhelp.safariClickFix;
},
```

The playSlide() method is new, but it starts pretty much like the old showSlide() method. You check the target and its node name and retrieve the parent list.

autoSlides.js *(continued)*

```
playSlide : function( e ) {
  var t = DOMhelp.getTarget( e );
  while( t.nodeName.toLowerCase() != 'a'
      && t.nodeName.toLowerCase() != 'body' ){
    t = t.parentNode;
  }
  var parentList = DOMhelp.closestSibling( t.parentNode, -1 );
```

You test if the parent list already has a property called `loop`. This is the property that stores the instance of `setInterval()`. You use a property of the list instead of a variable to allow for more than one automated slide show in the same document.

You define the string to use in `setInterval()` as a call of the `showSlide()` method with the `showIndex` property of the parent list as a parameter. This is necessary as `setInterval()` is a method of the `window` object and not in the scope of the main `autoSlides` object.

You use `setInterval()` with the delay defined in the `autoSlides.delay` property and store it in the `loop` property before changing the content of the link that was activated to the Stop button.

autoSlides.js *(continued)*

```
  if( !parentList.loop ) {
    var loopCall = "autoSlides.showSlide( '" +➥
    parentList.showIndex + "' )";
    parentList.loop = window.setInterval( loopCall,➥
    autoSlides.delay );
    t.innerHTML = autoSlides.stopLabel;
```

If the list already has a property called `loop`, it means the slide show is currently running; therefore you clear it, set the `loop` property to `null`, and change the button back to the Play button. You then stop the default link behavior by calling `cancelClick()`.

autoSlides.js *(continued)*

```
  } else {
    window.clearInterval( parentList.loop );
    parentList.loop = null;
    t.innerHTML = autoSlides.playLabel;
  }
  DOMhelp.cancelClick( e );
},
```

The showSlide() method changes quite drastically, but you will see that some of the initially confusing parts of the other methods (like what the slideLists array is good for) make the method rather easy.

Remember that you define in playSlide() that the interval should call the showSlide() method with the showIndex property of the list as a parameter. You can use this index now to retrieve the list you need to loop through simply by retrieving the list from the slideLists array.

autoSlides.js *(continued)*

```
showSlide : function( showIndex ) {
  var currentShow = autoSlides.slideLists[showIndex];
```

Once you have the list, you can read out the current slide and the number of slides. Remove the showClass from the current slide to hide it.

autoSlides.js *(continued)*

```
var count = currentShow.currentSlide;
var photoCount = currentShow.getElementsByTagName('li').length;
var photo = currentShow.getElementsByTagName( 'li' )[count];
DOMhelp.cssjs( 'remove', photo, autoSlides.showClass );
```

Increment the counter to show the next slide. Compare the counter with the number of all the slides and set it to 0 if the last slide was already shown—thus restarting the slide show at the first slide.

Show the slide by retrieving the list element and adding the show class. Update the counter and reset the currentSlide property of the list to the new list element.

autoSlides.js *(continued)*

```
      count++;
      if( count == photoCount ){ count = 0 };
      photo = currentShow.getElementsByTagName( 'li' )[count];
      DOMhelp.cssjs( 'add', photo, autoSlides.showClass );
      var counterText = currentShow.count.firstChild;
      counterText.nodeValue = counterText.nodeValue.➥
      replace( /\d/, count + 1 );
      currentShow.currentSlide = count;
  }
}
DOMhelp.addEvent( window, 'load', autoSlides.init, false );
```

This complexity is just a taste of what awaits the JavaScript developer when it comes to animation and timed execution of code. Creating a smooth, stable, cross-browser animation in JavaScript is tricky and needs a lot of testing and knowledge of browser issues. Luckily, there are ready-made animation libraries available that help you with this task and have been tested for stability by a lot of developers with different operating systems and browsers. You'll get to know one of them with the examples in Chapter 11.

Navigation Methods of the Browser Window

Following is a list of methods for navigating a browser window:

- `back()`: Goes back one page in the browser history (If you use frames, this goes back to the last document without frames, not the last change inside a frame.)

- `forward()`: Goes one page forward in the browser history (If you use frames, this goes back to the last document without frames, not the last change inside a frame.)

- `home()`: Acts as if the user had clicked the home button (only for Firefox and Opera)

- `stop()`: Stops the loading of the document in the window (not supported by MSIE)

- `print()`: Starts the browser's print dialog

It is rather tempting to use these methods to provide navigation on pages that should simply link back to the previous page via something like the following:

```
<a href="javascript:window.back()">Back to previous page</a>
```

With accessibility and modern scripting in mind, this means that a user without JavaScript will have promised to him something that does not exist. A better solution is either to generate a real "back to previous page" link via server-side includes (SSIs) or to provide an actual HTML hyperlink to the right document. If neither is possible, use a placeholder and replace it with a generated link when and if JavaScript is available, as in the following example:

`exampleBackLink.html` *(to reach via* `exampleForBackLink.html`*)*

```
HTML:
<p id="back">Please use your browser's back button or
keyboard shortcut to go to the previous page</p>
JavaScript:
function backlink() {
  var p = document.getElementById( 'back' );
  if( p ) {
    var newa = document.createElement( 'a' );
    newa.setAttribute( 'href', '#' );
```

```
      newa.appendChild( document.createTextNode➥
      ( 'back to previous page' ) );
      newa.onclick = function() { window.back();return false; }
      p.replaceChild( newa, p.firstChild );
    }
  }
}
window.onload = backlink;
```

■**Caution** The danger of these methods is that you offer functionality that the browser already provides the user. The difference is that the browser does it better, as it does support more input devices. In Firefox on a PC, for example, you can print the document by pressing Ctrl+P, close the window or tab by pressing Ctrl+W, and move forward and backward in the browser history via Alt and the left or right arrow keys.

Even worse, the functionality offered with these methods is dependent on scripting support. It is up to you to decide if the preceding method—creating the links invoking these methods, which is probably the cleanest way to deal with the issue—is worth the effort, or if you should just allow the user to decide how to trigger browser functionality.

Alternatives to Opening New Windows: Layer Ads

Sometimes there is no way to avoid pop-up windows, as the site design or functionality requires them, and you just cannot make them work because of the browser issues and options explained earlier. One workaround is **layer ads**, which are basically absolutely positioned page elements put on top of the main content.

Let's try an example of those. Imagine your company wants to advertise the latest offers quite obviously when the page is loaded. The easiest way is to add the information at the end of the document and use a script to turn it into a layer ad, which means that visitors without JavaScript will still get the information, but nothing that covers the content without giving them a chance to get rid of it. The HTML can be a simple DIV with an ID (the real links have been replaced with "#" for the sake of brevity):

exampleLayerAd.html *(excerpt)*

```
<div id="layerad">
  <h2>We've got some special offers!</h2>
  <ul>
    <li><a href="#">TDK DVD-R 8x 50 pack $12</a></li>
    <li><a href="#">Datawrite DVD-R 16x 100 pack $50</a></li>
    <li><a href="#">NEC 3500A DVD-RW 16x $30</a></li>
  </ul>
</div>
```

The CSS designer can style the ad for the non-JavaScript version, and the script will add a class to allow the ad to show up above the main content. If you call the class dyn, the CSS might look like this:

layerAd.css *(excerpt)*

```
#layerad{
  margin:.5em;
  padding:.5em;
}
#layerad.dyn{
  position:absolute;
  top:1em;
  left:1em;
  background:#eef;
  border:1px solid #999;
}
#layerad.dyn a.adclose{
  display:block;
  text-align:right;
}
```

The last selector is a style for a dynamic link that the script will add to the ad, allowing the user to remove it.

The script itself does not contain any surprises. First, define the ID of the ad, the dynamic class, and the class and the text content of the "close" link as properties.

layerAd.js

```
ad = {
  adID : 'layerad',
  adDynamicClass : 'dyn',
  closeLinkClass : 'adclose',
  closeLinkLabel : 'close',
```

The init() method checks for DOM and for the ad and adds the dynamic class to it. It creates a new link and adds the text and the class of the "close" link to it. It adds an event handler to this link pointing to the killAd() method and inserts the new link before the first child node of the ad.

layerAd.js *(continued)*

```
  init : function() {
    if( !document.getElementById || !document.createTextNode ) {
      return;
    }
```

```
ad.offer = document.getElementById( ad.adID );
if( !ad.offer ) { return; }
DOMhelp.cssjs( 'add', ad.offer, ad.addDynamicClass );
var closeLink = DOMhelp.createLink( '#', ad.closeLinkLabel );
DOMhelp.cssjs( 'add', closeLink, ad.closeLinkClass );
DOMhelp.addEvent( closeLink, 'click', ad.killAd,false );
closeLink.onclick = DOMhelp.safariClickFix;
ad.offer.insertBefore( closeLink, ad.offer.firstChild );
},
```

The `killAd()` method removes the ad from the document and cancels the link's default behavior.

`layerAd.js` *(continued)*

```
killAd : function( e ) {
  ad.offer.parentNode.removeChild( ad.offer );
  DOMhelp.cancelClick( e );
}
}
DOMhelp.addEvent( window, 'load', ad.init, false );
```

You can test the effect by opening `exampleLayerAd.html` in a browser; if you have JavaScript enabled, you'll see the ad covering the content, as shown in Figure 6-16. You can get rid of it by using the "close" link.

Figure 6-16. *An example of a layer ad*

One other common use of pop-up windows is for displaying another document or file without leaving the current page. Classic examples include a long list of boring terms and conditions or a photo. Especially in the case of photos, a pop-up is a suboptimal solution, as you can open a window with the same dimensions as the picture, but there will be gaps around the image because the browser's internal styles have padding settings on the body. You could work around this problem by using a blank HTML document with a style sheet that sets the body margins and padding to 0 and adding the image to the document in the window via JavaScript. Another option is to show the photo in a newly generated and positioned element covering the main document. The demo `examplePicturePopup.html` does that; all the script needs is a class with a certain name on a link pointing to the photo.

examplePicturePopup.html *(excerpt)*

```
<a class="picturepop" href="pictures/thumbs/dog7.jpg">Sleeping Dog</a>
```

The script needs to do something that wasn't explained here before, namely reading the position of elements. You cover the main document with an element by positioning the element absolutely. As you don't know where the link pointing to the photo is in the document, you need to read its position and show the photo there.

But that is for later; first up you need to predefine properties. You need a class that triggers the script, applying a link class to the link when the photo is shown, and another class to the element containing the photo. You also need to define a prefix to be added to the link when the photo is displayed and a property acting as a shortcut reference to the newly created element.

picturePopup.js *(excerpt)*

```
pop={
  triggerClass:'picturepop',
  openPopupLinkClass:'popuplink',
  popupClass:'popup',
  displayPrefix:'Hide ',
  popContainer:null,
```

The init() method checks for DOM support and loops through all the links of the document, testing whether they have the right CSS class to trigger the pop-up. For those that do, the method adds an event handler pointing to the openPopup() method, and then stores the link's innerHTML content in a preset property.

picturePopup.js *(continued)*

```
  init : function() {
    if( !document.getElementById || !document.createTextNode ) {
      return;
    }
    var allLinks = document.getElementsByTagName( 'a' );
    for( var i = 0; i < allLinks.length; i++ ) {
      if( !DOMhelp.cssjs( 'check', allLinks[i],➥
      pop.triggerClass ) ) {
        continue;
      }
      DOMhelp.addEvent( allLinks[i], 'click', pop.openPopup, false );
      allLinks[i].onclick = DOMhelp.safariClickFix;
      allLinks[i].preset = allLinks[i].innerHTML;
    }
  },
```

The openPopup() method retrieves the event target and ensures that it is a link. It then tests whether there is already a popContainer, which would mean that the photo is shown. If this is not the case, the method adds the prefix to the link's content and adds the dynamic class to make the link look different.

picturePopup.js *(continued)*

```
openPopup : function( e ) {
  var t = DOMhelp.getTarget( e );
  if( t.nodeName.toLowerCase() != 'a' ) {
    t = t.parentNode;
  }
  if( !pop.popContainer ) {
    t.innerHTML = pop.displayPrefix + t.preset;
    DOMhelp.cssjs( 'add', pop.popContainer, pop.popupClass );
```

The method then creates a new DIV that acts as the photo container, adds the appropriate class, and adds a new image as a child node of the container DIV. It shows the image by setting the src attribute of the new image to the value of the href attribute of the original link. The newly created photo container is then added to the document (as a child of the body element). Finally, openPopup() calls the positionPopup() method with the link object as a parameter.

picturePopup.js *(continued)*

```
      pop.popContainer = document.createElement( 'div' );
      DOMhelp.cssjs( 'add', t,pop.openPopupLinkClass );
      var newimg = document.createElement( 'img' );
      pop.popContainer.appendChild( newimg );
      newimg.setAttribute( 'src', t.getAttribute( 'href' ) );
      document.body.appendChild( pop.popContainer );
      pop.positionPopup( t );
```

If the popContainer already exists, all the method does is call the killPopup() method, reset the link to its original content, and remove the class that indicates that the photo is shown. Calling cancelClick() prevents the link from simply showing the photo in the browser.

picturePopup.js *(continued)*

```
    } else {
      pop.killPopup();
      t.innerHTML = t.preset;
      DOMhelp.cssjs( 'remove', t,pop.openPopupLinkClass );
    }
    DOMhelp.cancelClick( e );
  },
```

The positionPopup() method defines two variables, x and y, initializes them both to 0, and then reads the height of the element from its offsetHeight property. It next reads the vertical and horizontal position of the element and all its parent elements and adds those to x and y. The result is the position of the element relative to the document. The method then positions the photo container below the original link by adding the height of the link to the vertical variable y and altering the popContainer style properties.

picturePopup.js *(continued)*

```
positionPopup : function( o ) {
  var x = 0;
  var y = 0;
  var h = o.offsetHeight;
  while ( o != null ) {
    x += o.offsetLeft;
    y += o.offsetTop;
    o = o.offsetParent;
  }
  pop.popContainer.style.left = x + 'px';
  pop.popContainer.style.top = y + h + 'px';
},
```

The killPopup() method removes the popContainer from the document—clearing the property by setting its value to null—and prevents the default link action from taking place by calling cancelClick().

■**Note** You can remove a node from the document by calling the removeChild() method of its parent node, with the node itself as the child node to remove. However, as you use a property that points to the node rather than checking for the node itself, you also need to set this property to null.

---

picturePopup.js *(continued)*

```
killPopup : function( e ) {
  pop.popContainer.parentNode.removeChild( pop.popContainer );
  pop.popContainer = null;
  DOMhelp.cancelClick( e );
  }
}
DOMhelp.addEvent( window, 'load', pop.init, false );
```

The result is that you can click any image pointing to a photo with the correct class, and it'll show the image below it. Figure 6-17 shows an example.

Figure 6-17. *An example of a dynamically displayed photo*

The beauty of this approach is that it is not only limited to photos. With just a simple modification, you can display other documents inside the current one. The trick is to dynamically add an IFRAME element to the photoContainer and set its src attribute to the document you want to embed. The demonstration exampleIframeForPopup.html does exactly that to show a lengthy terms-and-conditions document inside the main one.

The only differences (apart from different property names, as the method does not show a photo) are in the openPopup method where you add the new IFRAME:

iframeForPopup.js *(excerpt)*

```
var ifr = document.createElement( 'iframe' );
pop.ifrContainer.appendChild( ifr );
ifr.setAttribute( 'src', t.getAttribute( 'href' ) );
```

Figure 6-18 shows what this could look like.

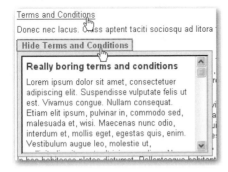

Figure 6-18. *An example of a dynamically included and displayed document*

Including other documents via IFRAME elements is an easy and well-supported method, but it is not the most accessible way. What you could do instead is use a server-side language like PHP to retrieve the content of the document and include it in the current one and use the same trick the layer ad example earlier uses. For more modern browsers, you can also do this "on the fly" using Ajax, but that will be explained in its own chapter, Chapter 8.

Summary: Windows and JavaScript

Controlling the current window and opening new ones has traditionally been a large part of JavaScript development, especially when it comes to web application development. In recent years, however, due to an increase in restrictions fueled by concerns about browser security and web surfers simply being fed up with lots of pop-ups and installing blocking software, it has become progressively harder to use new windows—even if you want to use them for a good cause. These and accessibility concerns make using multiple browser windows an increasingly unreliable method of web communication. Luckily, thanks to some of the replacement techniques discussed here (as well as Ajax, to which I devote Chapter 8), there is hardly any need for them any longer.

Things to Remember About Windows and JavaScript

- Test, test, and test again whether the window you have opened really exists before you try to do anything to it.

- Always remember that although the windows are on the same screen, they are completely separate instances of the browser. You need to go via the window.opener if you want to reach one pop-up from another or a function in the main script from any of the pop-ups you opened.

- Refrain from trying to control windows by taking away toolbars, moving them around the screen, or showing and hiding them via blur() and focus(). Most of these capabilities are still available now but are very likely to be blocked in future browsers.

- The web markup language of the future—XHTML—does not support the concept of different browser window instances (which is why the target attribute is deprecated). While you can circumvent this problem with scripting, it is still a bad idea to use XHTML STRICT and rely on several windows.

- You can simulate a lot of browser behavior or interactive elements with the window object methods—like closing and printing a window or moving back in the browser history. However, it might be better to leave this choice to the user. If you want to offer your own controls to the user, create these with JavaScript, too. Otherwise, the user will get a promise you don't keep when JavaScript is unavailable.

- If you use pop-up windows, tell visitors in the link opening the window that there will be a new window. This informs visitors with user agents that don't necessarily support multiple windows that there might be a change they have to deal with; it also prevents visitors from accidentally closing the window your web site needs. Years of unsolicited advertising and pop-ups have conditioned web surfers to immediately close new windows without even glancing at them.

- Employing timed execution of code via the `window` methods `setTimeout()` and `setInterval()` is a bit like using makeup: as a girl you learn how to put it on; as a woman you learn when to take it off. You can use both of these methods—and they are tempting to create all kind of snazzy effects—but you should think of your users, and ask yourself, "Is there really a need for animation when a static interface might lead much more quickly to the same result?"

Summary

Well done! You have reached the end of this chapter and should be well equipped now to create your own JavaScript solutions with images and windows, or—even better—window replacement techniques.

If some of the examples were a bit tough to wrap your head around, don't get frustrated, as this is a feeling you'll experience often as a JavaScript developer. And it does not mean that you don't "get it." Dozens of ways exist to solve any given problem in JavaScript. While there are much easier ways than those explained here, getting used to this kind of scripting should make you well equipped for more advanced scripting tasks like using third-party APIs or web application development.

In the next chapter, you have the chance to become better acquainted with event and property handling, as we discuss navigation and forms.

■ ■ ■

CHAPTER 7

JavaScript and User Interaction: Navigation and Forms

In this chapter, we will talk about two more common uses of JavaScript: navigation and forms. Both mean a lot of user interaction and therefore need to be planned and executed thoughtfully. The success of a web site stands and falls with the ease of its navigation, and there is nothing more frustrating on the Web than a form that is hard to use or impossible to fill out.

Note This chapter consists of a lot of code examples, and you will be asked to open some of them in a browser to test the functionality for yourself, so if you haven't been to `http://www.beginningjavascript.com` yet to download the code examples for this book, it might be a good time to do so now. I am a firm believer in hands-on training when it comes to coding, and it'll be easier for you to understand some of the functionality when you can experience it firsthand or—better yet—fiddle around with it in your own editor.

Navigation and JavaScript

Spicing up web site navigation has been one of the main tasks of DHTML since browsers first began supporting dynamic changes to the look and feel of page elements. The era of animated and fading navigation started with DHTML and has yet to end. The idea seemed to be that if the web page's navigation was very slick, tech-y, and looked and acted remotely like the LCARS interfaces on the starship *Enterprise*, the site must be great. A lot of times, visitors disagreed, and they would use a site search option, assuming one was provided, once they got bored with the navigation.

We won't talk about flashy navigation here; instead you'll see examples of what you can do with JavaScript to make page and site navigation more intuitive and less cumbersome while keeping it as accessible as possible.

The Fear of the Page Reload

A lot of JavaScript enhancements to forms and web navigation are made to prevent visitors from having to reload the page or load a lot of pages before reaching the information they came for. This is an admirable idea and can work wonderfully; however, let's not forget that JavaScript can only reach elements of the page when the whole document is loaded and deal with what is already in the document (that is, unless you use Ajax to load other content on the fly—more about that in the next chapter).

This means you can create a slick interface that only shows a slice of the overall page content with JavaScript, but it also means that visitors without JavaScript will have to deal with the whole amount of data in the document. Before you go completely nuts on enhancing pages, turn off JavaScript from time to time and see whether you'd be able to cope with the amount of data available in the document.

The benefit of smaller documents with only a bit of specialized information on them is that you can use the whole toolkit the browser offers the user: going forward and backward, bookmarking and printing. This is functionality you might break when you use JavaScript for navigation or pagination. The less desirable effect is that you have to maintain a lot more documents and visitors have to load each separately—thus also increasing the server traffic.

It is not evil to use JavaScript to enhance web sites; it is all a matter of moderation and knowing your audience.

Basics of Navigation and JavaScript

The most basic idea of navigation and JavaScript is that you don't rely on JavaScript to make your navigation work. Depending on JavaScript, page or site navigation will block out users that don't have JavaScript at their disposal and will also block out search engines.

■Tip The latter is a good argument should you ever have to explain to a nontechnical person why a bunch of `javascript:navigate('page2')` links are not a good idea. The notion of site visitors who have JavaScript disabled as a target group that is worth thinking about is not easy to explain to someone who doesn't even know how to turn it off in his browser. Explaining to him that the "big, blind millionaire" Google won't index their site is an easier selling point.

A classic example of using JavaScript seemingly to make navigation easier but with the potential of alienating quite a large a group of visitors is the use of a select box for navigation. Select boxes are great because they let you offer a lot of options without wasting screen space. Figure 7-1 shows an open select box; the closed one only uses up one line for all these options.

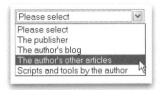

Figure 7-1. *Using a select box for navigation*

Open the demo page exampleSelectNavigation.html and select one of the options from the drop-down. If you are connected to the Web and you have JavaScript enabled, you will be immediately sent to the address you choose. Unfortunately, if you've chosen the wrong option, you don't get a chance to undo your choice. Without JavaScript, you can select an option, but nothing happens.

exampleSelectNavigation.html

```
<form>
<p>
  <select onchange="window.location = this.options[this.selectedIndex].value">
    <option value="#">Please select</option>
    <option value="http://www.apress.com">The publisher</option>
    <option value="http://wait-till-i.com">The author's blog</option>
    <option value="http://icant.co.uk">The author's other articles</option>
    <option value="http://onlinetools.org">Scripts and tools by the author</option>
  </select>
</p>
</form>
```

Keyboard access is another problem: you normally use the Tab key to access a select box and press the up and down keys to select the choice you want. In this example, you won't get that chance though, as you will be sent to the first option as soon as you press the down arrow key. The workaround is to press the Alt and down arrow keys together to expand the whole list. You can then choose your option with the up arrow and down arrow keys and hit Enter to select it. But did you know that?

The easiest solution to these problems is to never use a change, mouseover, or focus event to send data to the server or the user to a different web location. It is not accessible for a lot of visitors and can cause a lot of frustration. It is especially frustrating if there is no indicator that data is being sent and that the page will change.

Instead, offer a real Submit button, a script that does the same redirection server side, and a submit handler to redirect via JavaScript when and if it is available.

exampleSaferSelectNavigation.html *(excerpt)*

```
<form method="post" action="redir.php">
<p>
  <label for="url">Please select your destination:</label>
  <select id="url" name="url">
    <option value="http://www.apress.com">The publisher</option>
    <option value="http://wait-till-i.com">The author's blog</option>
    <option value="http://icant.co.uk">The author's other articles</option>
    <option value="http://onlinetools.org">Scripts and tools by the author</option>
  </select>
  <input type="submit" value="Make it so!" />
</p>
</form>
```

The script is pretty straightforward: you apply an event handler to the first form on submit that triggers a method. That method reads what choice the user made from the selectedIndex of the options list with the ID url and redirects the browser there via the window.location object. You'll read more about the window.location object in the next section and all about the selectedIndex and form objects in the "Forms and JavaScript" section of this chapter.

exampleSaferSelectNavigation.html *(excerpt)*

```
send = {
  init : function() {
    DOMhelp.addEvent( document.forms[0],
                      'submit', send.redirect,
                      false );
  },
  redirect : function( e ){
    var t = DOMhelp.getTarget( e );
    var url = t.elements['url'];
    window.location.href = url.options[url.selectedIndex].value;
    DOMhelp.cancelClick( e );
  }
}
DOMhelp.addEvent( window, 'load', send.init, false );
```

The server-side script to send non-JavaScript users to the other URI could be a simple header redirect in PHP:

```
<?php header( 'Location:' . $_POST[' url'] ); ?>
```

If the user has JavaScript enabled, she won't have to do the round-trip to the server; instead she'll get sent to the other web site immediately. You do this by setting the window.location.href property, which is one part of the built-in browser navigation.

Browser Navigation

Browsers give you several objects you can use for automatic redirection or navigation around the browser's history. You already encountered the `window.back()` method in the last chapter. The `window` object also provides the properties `window.location` and `window.history`.

The `window.location` object stores the URI of the current element and has the following properties (in parentheses you see the return value provided if the URI were `http://www.example.com:8080/index.php?s=JavaScript#searchresults`):

- `hash`: The name of the anchor in the URI (`#searchresults`)

- `host`: The domain name part of the URI (`www.example.com`)

- `hostname`: The domain name including subdomains and port numbers (`www.example.com:8080`)

- `href`: The whole URI string (`http://www.example.com:8080/index.php?s=JavaScript#searchresults`)

- `pathname`: The path name of the URI (`/index.php`)

- `port`: The port of the URI (`8080`)

- `protocol`: The protocol of the URI (`http:`)

- `search`: The search parameters (`?s=JavaScript`)

All of these properties can be read and written. For example, if you want the search to change to DOM scripting, you can do this via `window.location.search='?DOM scripting'`. The browser will automatically URL-encode the string to `DOM%20scripting`. You can also send the user's browser to another location by changing the `window.location.href` property.

In addition to these properties, the `window.location` has two methods:

- `reload()`: Reloads the current document (the same effect as clicking the Reload button or pressing F5 or the Ctrl and R keys simultaneously).

- `replace(URI)`: Sends the user to the URI and replaces the current URI with the other one. The current URI will not be part of the browser history any longer.

■**Caution** Notice that this is different from the `replace()` method of the `String` object, which replaces a part of a string with another.

You can use `reload()` to refresh the page in an interval to load new content from the back end without the user clicking the Reload button. This functionality is quite common in JavaScript-based chat systems.

Using `replace()` can be quite annoying, as you break the user's Back button functionality. She cannot go back to the current page when she doesn't like the one you sent her to.

The list of pages the user visited before reaching the current one is stored in the `window.history` object. This object has only one single property, called `length`, which stores the number of already visited pages. It has, however, three methods you can use:

- `back()`: Go back one page in the browser history.

- `forward()`: Go forward one page in the browser history.

- `go(n)`: Go n steps forward or back in the browser history depending on n being positive or negative. You can also reload the same page via `history.go(0)`.

The `history` object only allows you to navigate to the other pages—not read out their URIs or change them. The exception to the rule is the current page, which gets wiped from the browser history when you use `replace()`.

As already explained in the previous chapter, you effectively simulate browser functionality by sending the user to other pages via JavaScript, which might be superfluous or thoroughly confuse the user.

In-Page Navigation

You can use JavaScript to make navigation within the same page more interesting and less screen-space consuming. In HTML, you can provide in-page navigation via anchors and targets, both defined with the `<a>` tag, either with an `href` attribute for an anchor or a `name` or `id` attribute for a target.

■Note The `name` attribute for anchors is deprecated in XHTML, and it actually is enough to provide an ID to link an anchor and target pair. However, to ensure compatibility with older browsers, it might be a good idea to use it as you will in the following example.

Let's take a list of internal links in a table of contents linked to different targets further down the page as an example for in-page navigation:

exampleLinkedAnchors.html *(excerpt)*

```
<h1>X - a tool that does Y</h1>
<div id="toolinfo">
  <ul id="toolinfotoc">
    <li><a href="#info">Information</a></li>
    <li><a href="#demo">Demo</a></li>
    <li><a href="#installation">Installation</a></li>
    <li><a href="#use">Use</a></li>
    <li><a href="#license">License</a></li>
    <li><a href="#download">Download</a></li>
  </ul>
  <div class="infoblock">
    <h2><a id="info" name="info">Information about X</a></h2>
```

```
   [... content ...]
   <p class="back">
     <a href="#toolinfotoc">Back to
     <acronym title="Table of Contents">TOC</acronym></a>
   </p>
 </div>
 <div class="infoblock">
   <h2><a id="demo" name="demo">Demonstration of what
           X can do</a></h2>
   [... content ...]
   <p class="back">
     <a href="#toolinfotoc">Back to
     <acronym title="Table of Contents">TOC</acronym></a>
   </p>
 </div>
 [... more sections ...]
</div>
```

You may be thinking that the DIV elements with the class infoblock are not necessary for this in-page navigation to work. That is only partly true, as MSIE has a very annoying bug when it comes to named anchors and keyboard navigation.

If you open the demo page exampleLinkedAnchors.html in MSIE, navigate through the different menu items by hitting the Tab key, and choose the section you want by hitting the Enter key, the browser gets sent to the anchor you choose. However, MSIE does not send the keyboard focus to this anchor. If you hit the Tab key again, you don't get to the next link in the document; instead you get sent back to the menu.

You can fix this problem by—among other tricks—nesting the anchor in an element that has a defined width. This is what the DIVs are for. You can test this out on the demo page exampleLinkedAnchorsFixed.html. The practical upshot is that you can use these elements— in this case the DIVs—for CSS styling.

■**Tip** If you want to learn more about this problem and other ways to work around it, read the in-depth article on the subject written by accessibility researcher extraordinaire Gez Lemon at http:// juicystudio.com/article/ie-keyboard-navigation.php.

Now let's replicate and improve this functionality with a script. What the script should do is show the menu, but hide all the sections, and only show the one you choose to keep the page shorter and less overwhelming. The logic is pretty easy:

- Loop through the links in the menu and add click event handlers to show the sections connected with the menu item.

- In the event listener method, hide the previously shown section and show the current one.

- When initializing the page, hide all the sections and show the first one.

However, this does not take another aspect of in-page navigation into consideration: the page could have been requested with a predefined target coming from another link. Try it out by adding an anchor to the URI—for example, exampleLinkedAnchorsFixed.html#use—in your browser. You'll automatically scroll down to the "Using" section. Your script should take this use case into consideration,.

Let's start by defining the skeleton of the script. The main object of the script is called iv for inner navigation—as in is a reserved word in JavaScript, and you want to keep it short. You'll need several properties:

- A CSS class to define when the menu is JavaScript enhanced

- A CSS class to highlight the current link in the menu

- A CSS class to show the current section

■**Tip** You don't need to hide the sections via JavaScript, but you can use the CSS parent class trick described in the last chapter.

You'll need to define properties for the parent element to add the CSS class to and the ID of the menu to be able to loop through the links.

Two more properties are needed, one to store the currently shown section and one to store the currently highlighted link.

In terms of methods, you'll need an init() method, an event listener to get the current section, and a method to hide the previous section and show the current section.

innerNav.js *(skeleton)*

```
iv = {
  // CSS classes
  dynamicClass : 'dyn',
  currentLinkClass : 'current',
  showClass : 'show',

  // IDs
  parentID : 'toolinfo',
  tocID : 'toolinfotoc',

  // Global properties
  current : null,
  currentLink : null,

  init : function(){ },
  getSection : function( e ){ },
  showSection : function( o ){ }
DOMhelp.addEvent( window, 'load', iv.init, false );
```

The init() method begins with checking whether DOM is supported and all necessary elements are available. Only then you add the class to the parent element to hide all the section elements automatically, via CSS.

innerNav.js *(excerpt)*

```
  init : function(){
    if( !document.getElementById || !document.createTextNode) {
      return;
    }
    iv.parent = document.getElementById( iv.parentID );
    iv.toc = document.getElementById( iv.tocID );
    if( !iv.parent || !iv.toc ) { return; }
    DOMhelp.cssjs( 'add', iv.parent, iv.dynamicClass );
```

Store a possible URL hash in the variable loc and start looping through all the links in the menu. Replacing the # in the hash value makes it easier to use it later on, as you can use the name in a getElementById() without having to remove the hash.

innerNav.js *(continued)*

```
    var loc = window.location.hash.replace( '#', '' );
    var toclinks = iv.toc.getElementsByTagName( 'a' );
    for( var i = 0; i < toclinks.length; i++ ) {
```

Compare the current link's href attribute with loc and store the link in the currentLink property if they are the same. The string replace() method used here deletes anything but the anchor name from the href property. This is necessary because getAttribute('href') in some browsers like MSIE returns the entire link location including the file path, not only what is inside the HTML href attribute.

innerNav.js *(continued)*

```
      if( toclinks[i].getAttribute( 'href' ).➥
      replace( /.*#/, '' ) == loc ){
        iv.currentLink = toclinks[i];
      }
```

Next, add a click event pointing to getSection(). Notice that in this example script you don't need to stop the default event—on the contrary, allowing the browser to jump to the section will also change the URI in the location bar, and that in turn allows the user to bookmark the section.

innerNav.js *(continued)*

```
      DOMhelp.addEvent( toclinks[i], 'click', iv.getSection, false );
    }
```

The currentLink property is defined only when one of the links is the same as the hash in the URI. This means that if the URI has no hash, or has one that points to an anchor that isn't there, you need to define currentLink as the first anchor in the menu instead. The init() method finishes by calling the showSection() method with the currentLink as a parameter.

innerNav.js *(continued)*

```
    if( !iv.currentLink ) {
      iv.currentLink = toclinks[0];
    }
    iv.showSection( iv.currentLink );
  },
```

The event listener method getSection() does not need to do much; all it needs to do is to determine which link was clicked and send it on to showSection() as a parameter. If it weren't for the need to access window.location.hash, these two lines could have been part of the showSection() method.

innerNav.js *(continued)*

```
  getSection : function( e ) {
    var t = DOMhelp.getTarget( e );
    iv.showSection( t );
  },
```

The showSection() method retrieves the link object that was either clicked or defined in the init() method as the parameter o. The first task is to read the href attribute of this link and retrieve the anchor name by deleting everything before and including the hash sign via a regular expression. You then retrieve the section to show by reading the element with the anchor ID and going up two nodes in the node tree.

innerNav.js *(continued)*

```
  showSection : function( o ) {
    var targetName = o.getAttribute( 'href' ).➥
    replace( /.*#/,'' );
    var section = document.getElementById(targetName).➥
    parentNode.parentNode;
```

Why two nodes up? If you remember the HTML, you nested the links inside headings and nested the headings and the rest of the section inside DIV elements:

exampleLinkedAnchors.html *(excerpt)*

```
<li><a href="#demo">Demo</a></li>
 [... code snipped ...]
 <div class="infoblock">
   <h2><a id="demo" name="demo">
     Demonstration of what X can do
   </a></h2>
```

As getElementById('demo') gives you the link, one node up is the H2 and another one up is the DIV.

You then need to check whether there is an old section shown and a link highlighted, and remove the highlight and hide the section by removing the appropriate classes. Then add the classes for the current link and the current section and set the properties current and currentLink, making sure that next time showSection() is called it undoes what you did now.

innerNav.js *(continued)*

```
    if( iv.current != null ){
      DOMhelp.cssjs( 'remove', iv.current, iv.showClass );
      DOMhelp.cssjs( 'remove', iv.currentLink, iv.currentLinkClass );
    }
    DOMhelp.cssjs( 'add', section, iv.showClass );
    DOMhelp.cssjs( 'add', o,iv.currentLinkClass );
    iv.current = section;
    iv.currentLink = o;
  }
}
DOMhelp.addEvent( window, 'load', iv.init, false );
```

If you apply this script to the demo HTML page and add an appropriate style sheet, you get a much shorter page showing the different sections when you click the links. You can see this for yourself by opening exampleLinkedAnchorsPanel.html in a browser. On Windows XP in Firefox 1.5, the page looks like what you see in Figure 7-2.

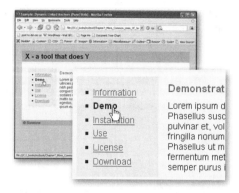

Figure 7-2. *A panel interface created from an anchor—target list*

Simply applying a different style sheet turns the page into a tabbed interface, as you can see in `exampleLinkedAnchorsTabs.html` and in Figure 7-3.

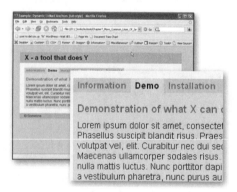

Figure 7-3. *A tabbed interface created from an anchor—target list*

This is pretty neat for a short script; however, cleaning up the link `href` and retrieving the section every time the user clicks one of the options seems repetitive.

A different approach to accomplishing the same task would be to store the links and the sections in two associative arrays and simply provide `showSection()` with the name of the anchor to show and highlight. The demo `exampleLinkedAnchorsTabsNamed.html` uses this technique and shows how to apply a `mouseover` handler for the same effect at the same time.

innerNavNamed.js

```
iv = {
  // CSS classes
  dynamicClass : 'dyn',
  currentLinkClass : 'current',
  showClass : 'show',

  // IDs
  parentID : 'toolinfo',
  tocID : 'toolinfotoc',
```

The first change is that you need only one current property as well as two new array properties called sections and sectionLinks, which will store the sections and links later on.

innerNavNamed.js *(continued)*

```
  // Global properties
  current : null,
  sections : [],
  sectionLinks : [],
  init : function() {
    var targetName,targetElement;
    if( !document.getElementById || !document.createTextNode ){
      return;
    }
    var parent = document.getElementById( iv.parentID );
    var toc = document.getElementById( iv.tocID );
    if( !parent || !toc ) { return; }
    DOMhelp.cssjs( 'add', parent, iv.dynamicClass );
    var toclinks = toc.getElementsByTagName( 'a' );
    for( var i = 0; i < toclinks.length; i++ ){
```

Add a mouseover handler in addition to the click and store the href attribute in a property called targetName for each of the links in the menu.

innerNavNamed.js *(continued)*

```
        DOMhelp.addEvent( toclinks[i], 'click', iv.getSection, false );
        DOMhelp.addEvent( toclinks[i], 'mouseover', iv.getSection,➥
        false);
        targetName = toclinks[i].getAttribute( 'href' ).➥
        replace( /.*#/,'' );
        toclinks[i].targetName = targetName;
```

Define the first link as the currently active link by storing it in the presetLink variable and determine whether the anchor points to an existing element. If it does, store the element in the sections array and the link in the sectionLinks array. Note that this results in an associative array, which means you can reach the first section via section['info'].

innerNavNamed.js *(continued)*

```
if( i == 0 ){ var presetLink = targetName; }
targetElement = document.getElementById( targetName );
if( targetElement ) {
  iv.sections[targetName] = targetElement.parentNode.parentNode;
  iv.sectionLinks[targetName] = toclinks[i];
}
}
```

Then you can obtain a possible anchor name from the URI hash and call showSection() initially either with that anchor name or with the one stored in presetLink.

innerNavNamed.js *(continued)*

```
var loc = window.location.hash.replace( '#', '' );
loc = document.getElementById(loc) ? loc : presetLink;
iv.showSection( loc );
},
```

The getSection() event () event listener calls showSection() with the value of the targetName property of the link. This property was set in the init() method earlier.

innerNavNamed.js *(continued)*

```
getSection:function( e ){
  var t = DOMhelp.getTarget( e );
  iv.showSection( t.targetName );
},
```

All of this makes showSection() a piece of cake, as all it needs to do to reset the last link and section and set the current ones is to use the arrays to reach the right elements and add or remove the CSS classes. The current section gets stored in one single property called current instead of properties for both the section and the link.

innerNavNamed.js *(continued)*

```
  showSection : function( sectionName ){
    if( iv.current != null ){
      DOMhelp.cssjs( 'remove', iv.sections[iv.current],➡
      iv.showClass);
      DOMhelp.cssjs( 'remove', iv.sectionLinks[iv.current],➡
      iv.currentLinkClass );
    }
    DOMhelp.cssjs( 'add', iv.sections[sectionName], iv.showClass );
    DOMhelp.cssjs( 'add', iv.sectionLinks[sectionName],➡
    iv.currentLinkClass );
    iv.current = sectionName;
  }
}
DOMhelp.addEvent( window, 'load', iv.init, false );
```

There are more options for in-page navigation—for example, you could offer "previous" and "next" links instead of "back" links to go through the options. If you want to see a script that does that and also offers several tabbed navigations per page, you can check out DOMtab at http://onlinetools.org/tools/domtabdata/.

Site Navigation

Web site navigation is a different kettle of fish from page internal navigation. You must be tired of reading it by now, but there is just no good argument for navigation that is dependent on JavaScript. Yes, you can use JavaScript to send the user to other locations automatically, but it is not a safe method, as browsers like Opera and Mozilla allow users to prevent that (malicious web sites used redirection in the past to send the user to spam sites). Furthermore, it strips you as the site maintainer of the opportunity to use site metrics software that counts hits and records how your visitors travel around the site, as not all metrics packages count JavaScript redirects.

For these reasons, site navigation is basically constrained to enhancing the functionality of the HTML structure of the menu and adding functionality to it via event handlers. The real redirection of the user to other pages still needs to happen via links or form submission.

One very logical HTML construct for a web site menu is a nested list:

exampleSiteNavigation.html *(excerpt)*

```
<ul id="nav">
  <li><a href="index.php">Home</a></li>
  <li><a href="products.php">Products</a>
    <ul>
      <li><a href="cms.php">CMS solutions</a>
        <ul>
          <li><a href="minicms.php">Mini CMS</a></li>
          <li><a href="ncc1701d.php">Enterprise CMS</a></li>
        </ul>
```

```
        </li>
        <li><a href="portal.php">Company Portal</a></li>
        <li><a href="mailserver.php">eMail Solutions</a>
          <ul>
            <li><a href="privatemail.php">Private POP3/SMTP</a></li>
            <li><a href="lists.php">Listservers</a></li>
          </ul>
        </li>
      </ul>
    </li>
    <li><a href="services.php">Services</a>
      <ul>
        <li><a href="training.php">Employee Training</a></li>
        <li><a href="audits.php">Auditing</a></li>
        <li><a href="bulkmail.php">Bulk sending/email campaigns</a></li>
      </ul>
    </li>
    <li><a href="pricing.php">Pricing</a></li>
    <li><a href="about_us.php">About Us</a>
      <ul>
        <li><a href="our_offices.php">Our offices</a></li>
        <li><a href="our_people.php">Our people</a></li>
        <li><a href="vacancies.php">Jobs</a></li>
        <li><a href="partners.php">Industry Partners</a></li>
      </ul>
    </li>
    <li><a href="contact.php">Contact Us</a>
      <ul>
        <li><a href="snail.php">Postal Addresses</a></li>
        <li><a href="callback.php">Arrange Callback</a></li>
      </ul>
    </li>
</ul>
```

The reason is that, even without any style sheet, the structure and the hierarchy of the navigation is obvious to the visitor. You can also style the navigation without much hassle, as all elements are contained in those higher up in the hierarchy, which allows for contextual selectors.

■Note We're not going to discuss here whether it makes sense to offer every page of the site in the navigation (as this is traditionally the job of a site map). In the next chapter, we will revisit this topic and offer it as a choice to the user.

Basic web site usability and common sense dictate that the currently shown page should not link to itself. To keep this from happening, replace the current page link with a STRONG element, which also means that users without CSS understand where they are in the navigation, and you get a chance to style the current page differently as part of the navigation without having to resort to CSS classes. Using a STRONG element instead of a SPAN also means that users without CSS get an obvious indicator which item is the current one.

For example, on the Mini CMS page, the navigation would be as follows:

exampleHighlightedSiteNavigation.html *(excerpt)*

```
<ul id="nav">
  <li><a href="index.php">Home</a></li>
  <li><a href="products.php">Products</a>
    <ul>
      <li><a href="cms.php">CMS solutions</a>
        <ul>
          <li><strong>Mini CMS</strong></li>
          <li><a href="ncc1701d.php">Enterprise CMS</a></li>
        </ul>
      </li>
    </ul>
  </li>
```

You have to do this server side, as it wouldn't make sense to highlight the current page in JavaScript (which, of course, wouldn't be hard to do by comparing all the link href attributes with the window.location.href).

Expecting this HTML structure allows you to create an Explorer-like expanding and collapsing menu. A menu item that contains other items should show or hide its child items when you click it. However, the logic of the script is probably a bit different from what you'd expect. For starters, you don't have to loop through all the links of the menu. Instead you do the following:

1. Add a CSS class to the main navigation item that hides all nested lists.

2. Loop through all UL items in the navigation (as those are the nested submenus).

3. Add a CSS class indicating that this list item contains other lists to the parent node of each UL.

4. Add a click event on the first link inside the parent node.

5. Test whether the parent node contains any STRONG elements and add the class to show the UL if there is one—thus preventing the submenu the current page is in to be hidden. You replace the parent class with an open one to show that this section is already expanded.

6. The click event listener method needs to check whether the first nested UL of the parent node has the show class and remove it if that is the case. It should also replace the open class with the parent class. If there is no show class, it should do the exact opposite.

The demo document exampleDynamicSiteNavigation.html does this, with the Mini CMS page defined as the current page to show the effect. Figure 7-4 shows how this looks in Firefox 1.5 on Windows XP.

Figure 7-4. *A tree menu with JavaScript and CSS*

The script's skeleton is rather short; you define all the necessary CSS classes as properties, the ID of the navigation as another property, and init() and changeSection() methods to apply the overall functionality and expand or collapse the sections accordingly.

siteNavigation.js *(skeleton)*

```
sn = {
  dynamicClass : 'dyn',
  showClass : 'show',
  parentClass : 'parent',
  openClass : 'open',
  navID : 'nav',
  init : function() {},
  changeSection : function( e ) {}
}
DOMhelp.addEvent( window, 'load', sn.init, false );
```

The init() method defines a variable called triggerLink and checks for DOM support and whether the necessary navigation element is available before applying the dynamic class to hide the nested elements.

siteNavigation.js *(excerpt)*

```
init : function() {
  var triggerLink;
  if( !document.getElementById || !document.createTextNode ) {
    return;
  }
  var nav = document.getElementById( sn.navID );
  if( !nav ){ return; }
  DOMhelp.cssjs( 'add', nav, sn.dynamicClass );
```

It then loops through all the nested UL elements and stores a reference to the first link inside the parent node as triggerLink. It applies a click event calling the changeSection() method and adds the parent class to the parent node.

siteNavigation.js *(continued)*

```
var nested = nav.getElementsByTagName( 'ul' );
for( var i = 0; i < nested.length; i++ ){
  triggerLink = nested[i].parentNode.getElementsByTagName('a')[0];
  DOMhelp.addEvent( triggerLink, 'click', sn.changeSection,➥
  false );
  DOMhelp.cssjs( 'add', triggerLink.parentNode, sn.parentClass );
  triggerLink.onclick = DOMhelp.safariClickFix;
```

The code tests whether the parent node contains a STRONG element and adds the show class to the UL and the open class to the parent node if that is the case. This prevents the current section from being hidden.

siteNavigation.js *(continued)*

```
if(nested[i].parentNode.getElementsByTagName( 'strong' ).➥
length > 0 ){
  DOMhelp.cssjs( 'add', triggerLink.parentNode, sn.openClass);
  DOMhelp.cssjs( 'add', nested[i], sn.showClass);
}
}
},
```

All the event listener method changeSection() needs to do is to get the event target, test whether the first nested UL of the parent node has the show class applied to it, and remove that UL if that is the case. Furthermore, it needs to change the open class of the parent node to parent and vice versa.

siteNavigation.js *(continued)*

```
  changeSection : function( e ){
    var t = DOMhelp.getTarget( e );
    var firstList = t.parentNode.getElementsByTagName('ul')[0];
    if(DOMhelp.cssjs( 'check', firstList, sn.showClass ) ) {
      DOMhelp.cssjs( 'remove', firstList, sn.showClass )
      DOMhelp.cssjs( 'swap', t.parentNode, sn.openClass,➡
      sn.parentClass );
    } else {
      DOMhelp.cssjs( 'add', firstList,sn.showClass )
      DOMhelp.cssjs( 'swap', t.parentNode, sn.openClass,➡
      sn.parentClass );
    }
    DOMhelp.cancelClick( e );
  }
}
DOMhelp.addEvent( window, 'load', sn.init,false );
```

This script, applied to the right HTML and styled with an appropriate style sheet, will give you the expanding and collapsing navigation. The relevant parts of the CSS are as follows:

siteNavigation.css *(excerpt)*

```
#nav.dyn li ul{
  display:none;
}
#nav.dyn li ul.show{
  display:block;
}
#nav.dyn li{
  padding-left:15px;
}
#nav.dyn li.parent{
  background:url(plus.gif) 0 5px no-repeat #fff;
}
#nav.dyn li.open{
  background:url(minus.gif) 0 5px no-repeat #fff;
}
```

You can show and hide the nested UL elements by setting the values of their display properties to block and none, respectively. This also takes the contained links out of the normal tabbing order: keyboard users won't have to tab through all the links in the nested lists if they want to reach the next element on the same hierarchical level without expanding the section. If they hit Enter first to expand the section, they will be able to navigate through the submenu links with the Tab key.

All LI elements get a left padding to allow for an indicator image to show that the section has child links or that it is open. The LI elements with the class open or parent get a background image to indicate their state.

All of this is pretty nice, but what if you want to provide a link to the parent pages of the nested sections? The solution is to add a new linked image before each of the parent links that does the showing and hiding and leaving the link as it is.

The demo page exampleIndicatorSiteNavigation.html shows what this looks like and how it works. The script does not have to change that much:

siteNavigationIndicator.js *(excerpt)*

```
sn = {
  dynamicClass : 'dyn',
  showClass : 'show',
  parentClass : 'parent',
  openClass : 'open',
```

The first change is that you need two new properties that provide the images to be added to the parent nodes of the nested lists. These will be added via innerHTML to make it easy for the maintainer to replace them with other images or even text if desired.

siteNavigationIndicator.js *(continued)*

```
  parentIndicator : '<img src="plus.gif" alt="open section"➥
  title="open section">',
  openIndicator:'<img src="minus.gif" alt="close section"➥
  title="close section">',
  navID : 'nav',
  init : function() {
    var parentLI, triggerLink;
    if( !document.getElementById || !document.createTextNode ){
      return;
    }
    var nav = document.getElementById( sn.navID );
    if( !nav ){ return; }
    DOMhelp.cssjs( 'add', nav,sn.dynamicClass );
    var nested = nav.getElementsByTagName( 'ul' );
    for( var i = 0; i < nested.length; i++ ) {
```

Instead of taking the first link in the parent node as the trigger link, you create a new link element, set its href attribute to a simple hash to make it clickable, and add the parent indicator image defined earlier as its content. Then insert the linked image as the first child of the parent node.

siteNavigationIndicator.js *(continued)*

```
parentLI = nested[i].parentNode;
triggerLink = document.createElement( 'a' );
triggerLink.setAttribute( 'href', '#' )
triggerLink.innerHTML = sn.parentIndicator;
parentLI.insertBefore( triggerLink, parentLI.firstChild );
```

The rest of the init() method stays almost as it was, with the difference that you not only apply the classes when the parent node contains a STRONG element, but also replace the "parent" indicator image with the "open" one.

siteNavigationIndicator.js *(continued)*

```
DOMhelp.addEvent( triggerLink, 'click', sn.changeSection,➥
false);
triggerLink.onclick = DOMhelp.safariClickFix;
DOMhelp.cssjs( 'add', parentLI, sn.parentClass );
if( parentLI.getElementsByTagName( 'strong' ).length > 0) {
  DOMhelp.cssjs( 'add', parentLI, sn.openClass );
  DOMhelp.cssjs( 'add', nested[i], sn.showClass );
  parentLI.getElementsByTagName( 'a' )[0].innerHTML =➥
  sn.openIndicator
  }
 }
},
```

The difference in the changeSection() method is that you need to ensure that the event target was a link and not the image by comparing the node name of the target with A.

siteNavigationIndicator.js *(continued)*

```
changeSection : function( e ){
  var t = DOMhelp.getTarget( e );
  while( t.nodeName.toLowerCase() != 'a' ) {
    t = t.parentNode;
  }
```

The rest of the method stays the same with one difference—you change the content of the link in addition to applying the different classes.

siteNavigationIndicator.js *(continued)*

```
    var firstList = t.parentNode.getElementsByTagName( 'ul' )[0];
    if( DOMhelp.cssjs( 'check', firstList, sn.showClass ) ) {
      DOMhelp.cssjs( 'remove', firstList, sn.showClass );
      DOMhelp.cssjs( 'swap', t.parentNode, sn.openClass,➡
      sn.parentClass);
      t.innerHTML = sn.parentIndicator;
    } else {
      DOMhelp.cssjs( 'add', firstList, sn.showClass )
      DOMhelp.cssjs( 'swap', t.parentNode, sn.openClass,➡
      sn.parentClass );
      t.innerHTML = sn.openIndicator;
    }
    DOMhelp.cancelClick( e );
  }
}
DOMhelp.addEvent( window, 'load', sn.init, false );
```

All of this is just one example of enhanced site navigation and is probably the easiest one to use. Making a multilevel drop-down navigation menu accessible, for example, that also works for mouse and keyboard users alike is an immense task that is not within the scope of this book, as it is very advanced DOM scripting.

■Note A very good explanation of why dynamic menus should not work by tabbing through the links but instead offer cursor-based navigation appears on the Mozilla.org site, where a lot of very gifted developers work on the issue (while breaking some HTML rules that prove to be in the way of creating dynamic pages in an accessible manner): http://developer.mozilla.org/en/docs/Key-navigable_custom_DHTML_widgets. There is also commercial script called Ultimate Drop Down Menu (http://www.udm4.com) that gets it right.

Pagination

Pagination means that you cut down a large set of data into several pages. This is normally done on the back end, but you can use JavaScript to make it quicker to check a long list of elements.

A demo of pagination is examplePagination.html, which appears in Firefox 1.5 on Windows XP as shown in Figure 7-5.

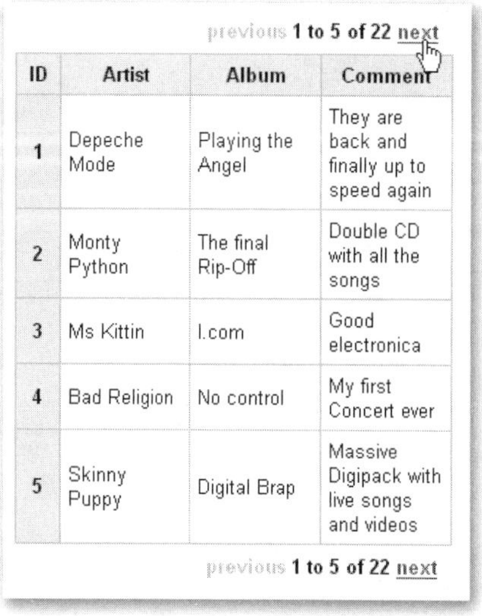
previous 1 to 5 of 22 next

ID	Artist	Album	Comment
1	Depeche Mode	Playing the Angel	They are back and finally up to speed again
2	Monty Python	The final Rip-Off	Double CD with all the songs
3	Ms Kittin	I.com	Good electronica
4	Bad Religion	No control	My first Concert ever
5	Skinny Puppy	Digital Brap	Massive Digipack with live songs and videos

previous 1 to 5 of 22 next

Figure 7-5. *Paginating a large set of data rows*

The content to be manipulated consists of a set of rows of the same HTML table, which has the class paginated.

examplePagination.html *(excerpt)*

```
<table class="paginated">
<thead>
  <tr>
    <th scope="col">ID</th>
    <th scope="col">Artist</th>
    <th scope="col">Album</th>
    <th scope="col">Comment</th>
  </tr>
</thead>
<tbody>
  <tr>
    <th>1</th>
    <td>Depeche Mode</td>
    <td>Playing the Angel</td>
    <td>They are back and finally up to speed again</td>
  </tr>
  <tr>
    <th>2</th>
    <td>Monty Python</td>
```

```
      <td>The final Rip-Off</td>
      <td>Double CD with all the songs</td>
    </tr>
    [... and so on ...]
  </tbody>
</table>
```

We used pagination in the last chapter in the slide show example, although the example showed one item at a time. The logic of pagination with several items is much more complex, but this example should give you an insight to the tricks you can use.

- You hide all the table rows via CSS.

- You define how many rows should be shown on each page.

- You show the first rows and generate the pagination menu.

- This menu has a "previous" and "next" link and a counter telling the user which slice of the data is to be shown and how many items there are in total.

- If the current slice is the first, the "previous" link should be inactive; if it is the last, the "next" link should be inactive.

- The "next" link increases the start value of the slice by the amount defined, and the "previous" link decreases the start value.

You will use several properties and five methods in this example. It is a good idea to comment the properties to make it easier for future maintainers to alter them to their needs.

pagination.js *(skeleton)*

```
pn = {
  // CSS classes
  paginationClass : 'paginated',
  dynamicClass : 'dynamic',
  showClass : 'show',
  paginationNavClass : 'paginatedNav',
  // Pagination counter properties
  // Number of elements shown on one page
  Increase : 5,
  // Counter: _x_ will become the current start position
  //          _y_ the current end position and
  //          _z_ the number of all data rpws
  Counter : ' _x_ to _y_ of _z_ ',
  // "previous" and "next" links, only text is allowed
  nextLabel : 'next',
  previousLabel : 'previous',
```

You use one method to initialize the script, one to generate the extra links and elements that you need, one to navigate around the "pages" (that is, hide the current result set and show the next), one to show the current page, and one to alter the pagination menu.

```
init : function(){},
createPaginationNav : function( table ){},
navigate : function( e ){},
showSection : function( table, start ){},
changePaginationNav : function( table, start ){}
}
DOMhelp.addEvent( window, 'load', pn.init, false );
```

Grab a coffee and some cookies, as this is quite a script ahead of you; don't worry though—most of it is simple logic.

The init() method checks whether DOM is supported and starts looping through all table elements in the document. It tests whether the table has the right class (defined in the pn.paginationClass property) and whether it has more rows than you want to show on each "page" (defined in the pn.increase property). If one of these is not the case, it skips the rest of the method—effectively not adding any menu.

pagination.js *(excerpt)*

```
init : function() {
  var tablebody;
  if( !document.getElementById || !document.createTextNode ){
    return;
  }
  var ts = document.getElementsByTagName( 'table' );
  for(var i = 0;i < ts.length; i++ ){
    if( !DOMhelp.cssjs( 'check', ts[i],➡
    pn.paginationClass ) ){
      continue;
    }
    if( ts[i].getElementsByTagName( 'tr' ).length <➡
    pn.increase+1 ){
      continue;
    }
```

As the data rows you want to hide don't include the header row, but only those contained in the table body, you need to tell the other methods this.

The easiest option is to store only the relevant rows in a property of the table. You grab the first TBODY in the table and store all of its rows in a datarows property. You also store the number of all rows in datarowsize and initialize the current property as null.

This property will store the start of the page you want to show. By storing the rows and the number of rows as properties, you make it easier for other methods to retrieve information from the table without having to read out this information again from the DOM.

pagination.js *(excerpt)*

```
tablebody = ts[i].getElementsByTagName( 'tbody' )[0];
ts[i].datarows = tablebody.getElementsByTagName( 'tr' );
ts[i].datarowsize = ts[i].datarows.length;
ts[i].current = null;
```

Apply the dynamic class to the table and thus hide all the table rows. Call the
createPaginationNav() method with a reference to the current table as a parameter
to add the "previous" and "next" links, and call showSection() with the table reference
and 0 as parameters to show the first result set.

pagination.js *(excerpt)*

```
    DOMhelp.cssjs( 'add', ts[i], pn.dynamicClass );
    pn.createPaginationNav( ts[i] );
    pn.showSection( ts[i], 0 );
  }
},
```

The createPaginationNav() method does not contain any surprises; all it does is create
the links and the counter and add the event handlers pointing to the navigate() method. You
start by creating a new paragraph element and adding the pagination menu class to it.

pagination.js *(excerpt)*

```
createPaginationNav : function( table ){
  var navBefore, navAfter;
  navBefore = document.createElement( 'p' );
  DOMhelp.cssjs('add', navBefore, pn.paginationMenuClass );
```

Add a new link to the paragraph with the previousLabel property value as the text content
and a new SPAN element that will display the number of the current result set in between the
"previous" and "next" links. You preset the counter with 1 as the start value, the number of elements shown on each page as defined in pn.increase as the end value, and the number of all
data rows as the total number. The last element to add to the new paragraph is the "next" link.
You add the new paragraph immediately before the table via parentNode and insertBefore().

pagination.js *(excerpt)*

```
navBefore.appendChild( DOMhelp.createLink( '#',➡
pn.previousLabel ) );
navBefore.appendChild( document.createElement( 'span' ) );
counter=pn.counter.replace( '_x_', 1 );
counter=counter.replace( '_y_', pn.increase );
counter=counter.replace( '_z_', table.datarowsize-1 );
navBefore.getElementsByTagName( 'span' )[0].innerHTML = counter;
navBefore.appendChild( DOMhelp.createLink( '#', pn.nextLabel ) );
table.parentNode.insertBefore( navBefore, table );
```

It would be good to show the same menu below the table as well. Instead of re-creating all these elements once more, it is enough to clone the paragraph and insert it after the table via parentNode, insertBefore(), and nextSibling. Then, store the "previous" and "next" links of each paragraph as their own table properties to make it easier to change them in other methods.

pagination.js *(excerpt)*

```
navAfter = navBefore.cloneNode( true );

table.parentNode.insertBefore( navAfter, table.nextSibling );
table.topPrev = navBefore.getElementsByTagName( 'a' )[0];
table.topNext = navBefore.getElementsByTagName( 'a' )[1];
table.bottomPrev = navAfter.getElementsByTagName( 'a' )[0];
table.bottomNext = navAfter.getElementsByTagName( 'a' )[1];
```

You couldn't apply the event handlers earlier, as cloneNode() does not clone any handlers. Now you can apply all the handlers and the fixes for Safari to each of the links. The last change for this method is to store the counters in properties to make it easier for the other methods to update them.

pagination.js *(excerpt)*

```
DOMhelp.addEvent( table.topPrev, 'click', pn.navigate, false);
DOMhelp.addEvent( table.bottomPrev, 'click', pn.navigate, false);
DOMhelp.addEvent( table.topNext, 'click', pn.navigate, false);
DOMhelp.addEvent( table.bottomNext, 'click', pn.navigate, false);
table.bottomNext.onclick = DOMhelp.safariClickFix;
table.topPrev.onclick = DOMhelp.safariClickFix;
table.bottomPrev.onclick = DOMhelp.safariClickFix;
table.topNext.onclick = DOMhelp.safariClickFix;
table.topCounter = navBefore.getElementsByTagName( 'span' )[0];
table.bottomCounter = navAfter.getElementsByTagName( 'span' )[0];
},
```

The event listener method navigate() needs to check which link invoked it. The first step is to retrieve the event target via getTarget() and make sure it is a link by comparing its node name with A (remember, Safari likes to send the text node inside the link as the event target instead).

pagination.js *(excerpt)*

```
navigate : function( e ){
  var start, table;
  var t = DOMhelp.getTarget( e );
  while( t.nodeName.toLowerCase() != 'a' ){
    t = t.parentNode;
  }
```

It then needs to check whether the link is active or not by testing whether it has an href attribute (you will later turn the "next" or "previous" link off by removing the href attribute). If there is none, it shouldn't do anything. The next task is to find the table from the link that is activated. As there is navigation above and below the table, you need to check whether either the previous or the next sibling node has the node name of table and define the variable table accordingly.

pagination.js *(excerpt)*

```
if( t.getAttribute( 'href' ) == null ||➡
  t.getAttribute( 'href' ) == '' ){ return; }
if( t.parentNode.previousSibling &&➡
  t.parentNode.previousSibling.nodeName.➡
  toLowerCase() == 'table' ) {
  table = t.parentNode.previousSibling;
} else {
  table = t.parentNode.nextSibling;
}
```

Then determine whether the activated link was either one of the "next" links or one of the "previous" links, and define start as the current property of the table plus or minus the defined increase accordingly. You call showSection() with the retrieved table and the start values as parameters.

pagination.js *(excerpt)*

```
if(t == table.topNext || t == table.bottomNext ){
  start = table.current + pn.increase;
} else if ( t == table.topPrev || t == table.bottomPrev ){
  start = table.current - pn.increase;
}
pn.showSection( table, start );
},
```

The showSection() method calls the changePaginationNav() method to update the links and the counter and tests whether there is already a current parameter on the table. If there is one, this means data rows exist that need to be removed. You get rid of them by looping through the section of the data rows stored in the datarows property and removing the CSS class defined in showClass().

pagination.js *(excerpt)*

```
showSection : function( table, start ){
  var i;
  pn.changePaginationNav( table, start );
  if( table.current != null ){
    for( i=table.current; i < table.current+pn.increase; i++ ){
      if( table.datarows[i] ) {
        DOMhelp.cssjs( 'remove', table.datarows[i], pn.showClass );
      }
    }
  }
}
```

You then loop from start to start plus the predefined increase, and add the CSS class to show these rows in the table. Notice that you need to test whether these rows exist; otherwise, you might try to reach rows that aren't there on the last page. (Imagine a list of 22 elements; clicking the "next" link on the 16–20 page would try to show elements 21 to 25). To make sure the right slice gets shown the next time the method gets called, all that is left is to define the current property as the start value.

pagination.js *(excerpt)*

```
    for( i = start; i < start + pn.increase; i++ ){
      if( table.datarows[i] ) {
        DOMhelp.cssjs( 'add', table.datarows[i], pn.showClass );
      }
    }
    table.current = start;
  },
```

As hinted earlier, the changePaginationNav() method renders the "previous" link on the first page and the "next" link on the last page inactive. The trick to making links appear but not clickable is to remove the href attribute.

On the first page, the start value minus the predefined increase would result in a negative number, which is easy to test. When the number is larger than 0, you add the href attribute again.

pagination.js *(excerpt)*

```
changePaginationNav : function( table, start ){
  if(start - pn.increase < 0 ) {
    table.bottomPrev.removeAttribute( 'href' );
    table.topPrev.removeAttribute( 'href' );
  } else {
    table.bottomPrev.setAttribute( 'href', '#' );
    table.topPrev.setAttribute( 'href', '#' );
  }
```

If start plus the increase is bigger than the number of rows, you need to remove the "next" link; otherwise, you need to make it active.

pagination.js *(excerpt)*

```
  if(start + pn.increase > table.rowsize - 2 ) {
    table.bottomNext.removeAttribute( 'href' );
    table.topNext.removeAttribute( 'href' );
  }else{
    table.bottomNext.setAttribute( 'href', '#' );
    table.topNext.setAttribute( 'href', '#' );
  }
```

Update the counter with the appropriate values (start needs a 1 added to it to make it easier to understand for humans, and you need to test that the last value is not larger than the number of existing rows), and you have created a paginated interface from a normal data table.

pagination.js *(excerpt)*

```
  var counter = pn.counter.replace( '_x_', start+1 );
  var last = start + pn.increase;
  if( last > table.datarowsize ){ last = table.datarowsize; }
  counter = counter.replace( '_y_', last )
  counter = counter.replace( '_z_', table.datarowsize )
  table.topCounter.innerHTML = counter;
  table.bottomCounter.innerHTML = counter;
  }
}
DOMhelp.addEvent( window, 'load', pn.init, false );
```

The logic of pagination stays the same, even if you decide to show and hide list items or other HTML constructs. You can make it even more complex by showing numbered steps in between the "previous" and the "next" links instead of the counter, but I leave that to you to have a go at it.

Summary of Navigation with JavaScript

Powering a site's navigation with JavaScript is a very tempting use of your skills, as it is "out there" and still quite amazing for "wowing" clients with a fancy interface. The main thing to remember is that you should turn off JavaScript from time to time and see whether your interface still works. The same applies to not using your mouse but trying the keyboard instead.

You can use JavaScript to make large amounts of data like deeply nested navigation menus easier to grasp and presented to the user in bite-size chunks. However, don't forget that some users will get all of the navigation without your script cutting it up into smaller servings. It might be a good idea to make menu interfaces that use the whole site map as their data source optional rather than a given. We will take a look at how to do that in the next chapter.

Things to Remember About JavaScript Navigation

- Don't send the user to another location or send form data without him clicking or activating an interface element. It is more confusing than helpful and may even be considered a security threat (if you can do it, anyone can send the user to a site).

- Hiding data does not make it disappear; while you can make a lot of data easy to digest with a slick interface, some users will still get the whole lot in one serving, and all users—including those on slow connections—will have to download all of the data.

- It is much safer to piggyback on existing web navigation patterns than to invent new ones. For example, it was quite easy to turn a working in-page navigation using links and anchors into a tabbed interface. Creating all the necessary tabs via JavaScript would have been a lot more hassle.

Forms and JavaScript

On the following pages, you'll learn how to access, read, and change forms and their elements. We will not go into the details of validating forms here, as I have devoted Chapter 9 to the topic of data validation.

We will, however, touch on basic form usability as well as some bad practices and why they should be avoided. First of all, let's take a look at the form used in some examples in this chapter and later on in the book:

exampleForm.html *(excerpt)*

```
<form method="post" action="send.php">
<fieldset>
  <legend>About You</legend>
  <p><label for="Name">Your Name</label></p>
  <p><input type="text" id="Name" name="Name" /></p>
  <p><label for="Surname">Your Surname</label></p>
  <p><input type="text" id="Surname" name="Surname" /></p>
  <p><label for="email">Your email</label></p>
```

```
  <p><input type="text" id="email" value="you@example.com"➡
  name="email" /></p>
</fieldset>
<fieldset>
  <legend>Your message</legend>
  <p><label for="subject">Subject</label>
  <select id="subject" name="subject">
    <option value="generalEnquiry" selected="selected">➡
    General question</option>
    <option value="Webdesign">Webdesign</option>
    <option value="Hosting">Hosting</option>
    <option value="Training">Training</option>
    <option value="Partnership">Partnership</option>
    <option value="other">Other</option>
  </select></p>
  <p><label for="otherSubject">specify other subject</label>
  <input type="text" id="otherSubject" name="otherSubject" /></p>
  <p><label for="Message">Your Message</label></p>
  <p><textarea id="Message" name="Message" cols="20" rows="5"></textarea></p>
</fieldset>
<fieldset>
  <legend>Email options</legend>
  <p><input type="checkbox" name="copyMeIn" id="copyMeIn" />
  <label for="copyMeIn">Send me a copy of this email to
  the above address</label></p>
  <p><input type="checkbox" name="newsletter" value="yes"➡
  id="newsletter" />
  <label for="newsletter">Sign me up for the newsletter</label></p>
  <p>Newsletter format:
  <input type="radio" name="newsletterFormat" id="newsHtml"➡
  value="html" checked="checked" />
  <label for="newsHTML">HTML</label>
  <input type="radio" name="newsletterFormat" id="newsPlain"➡
  value="plain"/>
  <label for="newsPlain">Text</label></p>
  <p class="submit"><input type="submit" value="Send Form" /></p>
</fieldset>
</form>
```

■Note As you can see, this is a valid form for a HTML 4 STRICT document, and all elements are closed for XHTML compliance should you want to go that way. Notice also that in XML-compliant HTML you need to write single attributes like `selected` and `checked` as `selected="selected"` and `checked="checked"`, respectively.

The form features fieldsets for grouping elements into logical units and labels for connecting explanation texts with specific form elements. This helps a lot with form accessibility, as it provides logical organization and avoids ambiguity.

Basics of Forms with JavaScript

Reaching and altering forms in JavaScript can be achieved in several different ways. As always, there is the DOM scripting way of simply reaching the forms and their elements via `getElementsByTagName()` and `getElementById()`, but there is also an object called `forms` that contains all the forms in the current `document`.

This object allows you to reach the forms in the `document` in three different ways:

- Via their `index` number where `index` is an integer, for example, `document.forms[2]` for the third form.

- Via their name defined in the `name` attribute as an object, for example `document.forms.myForm`.

- Via their name defined in the `name` attribute as a string, for example `document.forms['myForm']`. This is necessary when the name contains special characters or spaces, and you cannot notate it as an object.

Form Properties

The `forms` object itself has only one property, `length`, and it stores the number of forms in the document.

Each of the forms, however, has more properties you can use, all of which can be read and changed:

- `action`: The script the form data is sent to when the form is submitted

- `encoding`: The encoding of the form as defined in the `enctype` attribute of the `FORM` element

- `method`: The submission method of the form—either `POST` or `GET`

- `name`: The name of the form as defined in the `name` attribute (not in the `id`!)

- `target`: The target the form data should be sent to (only important if you use frames or multiple windows)

Form Methods

The `Form` object has only two methods:

- `reset()`: Resets the form to its initial state, which means that all the entries and choices the user made get undone, and the form shows the initial values defined in the `value`, `selected`, or checked `attributes` of the individual elements. Be aware of the difference—`reset()` does not clear the form, but restores it to its initial state. This is the same effect a user gets when he activates a Reset button in the form.

- `submit()`: Submits the form.

Both methods simulate browser functionality—namely activating a Reset or a Submit button—and you should make sure that you don't use them to take away necessary interactivity from the user. There is a good reason that forms get submitted when the user clicks a Submit button or hits Enter on the keyboard—it is the most accessible way, and if you hijack this functionality and submit the form when users interact with other elements, you may force them to submit the form prematurely.

Form Elements

Every form in the `forms` collection has as a property an object called `elements`, which in essence is an array of all the form elements inside this form (as opposed to all HTML elements). You can reach the elements the same way you initially reach the forms, via the index number, the object name, or the name as a string in square brackets:

- `var elm = document.forms[0].elements[2];`

- `var elm = document.forms.myForm.elements.myElement;`

- `var elm = document.forms.myForm.elements['myElement'];`

As you can see in the last example, you can mix and match the notations. You can also use variables instead of the index numbers or the strings inside the brackets.

The `elements` collection itself has one read-only property called `length`. You could, for example, use this property to loop through all elements in a form and read out their type:

```
var myForm = document.forms[0];
var formElements = myForm.elements;
var all = formElements.length;
for( var i = 0; i < all; i++ ) {
  alert( formElements[i].type );
}
```

Each element inside the collection has several properties; which ones are supported is dependent on the type of the element. I'll now list all the properties and list the elements that support this property in parentheses. We'll go through the different elements in detail later on in this chapter:

- `checked`: Boolean if the element was checked or not (buttons, check boxes, radio buttons)

- `defaultChecked`: Boolean if the element was initially checked (check boxes, radio buttons)

- `value`: The value of the element as defined in the `value` attribute (all elements but select boxes)

- `defaultValue`: The initial value of the element (text boxes, text areas)

- `form`: The form the element resides in (read only—all elements)

- `name`: Name of the element (all elements)

- `type`: The type of the element (read only—all elements)

One special element type is the select box, which comes with a collection of its own, a property called `options`—but more on this later. Each element has a range of methods that is also dependent on the type of element. None of these methods expect any parameters.

- `blur()`: Takes the focus of the user agent away from the element (all elements)

- `focus()`: Puts the focus of the user agent on the element (all elements)

- `click()`: Simulates the user clicking the element (buttons, check boxes, file upload fields, Reset and Submit buttons)

- `select()`: Selects and highlights the text content of the element (password fields, text fields, and text areas)

■**Note** Notice that `click()` seems at first a bit odd, but can be really helpful if you work on web applications, and the middle tier of your development environment does things to the submitting process of forms like Java Spring and .NET do. This is not a JS beginner's environment though, and so falls outside the scope of this book.

HTML Attributes Not Contained in the Elements Collection

In addition to the properties of the `elements` collection, you can read and set (browser settings permitting of course) the attributes of the element in question once you have reached it via the `forms` and `elements` collections. For example, you could change the size of a text field by changing its `cols` and `rows` attributes:

```
var myTextBox = document.forms[0].elements[2];
if ( myTextBox.type == 'textarea' ){
  myTextBox.rows = 10;
  myTextBox.cols = 30;
}
```

■**Tip** Notice that it is a good idea to check the type of the element you are manipulating before trying to set attributes on it, in case they are not available for this element. A SELECT element, for example, does not have `cols` or `rows` attributes.

Globally Supported Properties

All form elements initially supported the type, name, form, and value properties. One recent change is that file upload fields do not support setting value any longer, as it would allow a malicious scripter to inject her own files to upload to your server when a user on an infected computer uploads something.

Using form can be quite handy to reach the parent form when you access an element directly via DOM methods. For example, if you access the e-mail field in the example form via the DOM:

```
var mail = document.getElementById( 'email' );
```

You can reach the form to change one of its properties or submit it either via mail.form or via mail.parentNode.parentNode.parentNode.

exampleForm.html *(excerpt)*

```
<form method="post" action="send.php">
<fieldset>
  [... code snipped ...]
  <p><input type="text" id="email" value="you@example.com" name="email" /></p>
</fieldset>
  [... code snipped ...]
</form>
```

Depending how deep the element is nested in the form, using form can save you a lot of trouble counting the nodes and actually makes the script easier to maintain because you are independent of the HTML. If you want to use node traversal exclusively, you could also use a recursive loop that checks the nodeName of the parent node to achieve the same independence of the HTML markup:

```
var mail = document.getElementById( 'email' );
parentForm = mail.parentNode;
while( parentForm.nodeName.toLowerCase() != 'form' ) {
  parentForm = parentForm.parentNode;
}
```

While this is independent of the user agent, it might be overkill in most web sites, as you can assume that most browsers do offer the forms and elements collections (you can, of course, test for them to make sure). Using the forms and elements collections also means you support non–DOM-2 browsers like Netscape 4 or MSIE 4.

Using `blur()` and `focus()`

You can use `blur()` to take the user agent's focus away from an element or `focus()` to set it. The danger of this is that `blur()` does not take any target it should set the focus to, which means that user agents might focus on the next element, the location bar of the browser, or whatever else they please. For a sighted user with a mouse, this is not much of an issue; however, blind users relying on assistive technology or keyboard users will have a problem finding their way around the document again.

You might encounter something like this when you look through the code of some web sites:

```
<a href="#" onclick="dothings();" onfocus="this.blur()">Home</a>
```

Developers used to do this to stop browsers from showing a blue box (MSIE on Mac) or a dotted border (MSIE/Mozilla on PC) around the current link. This is a very bad idea, as a keyboard user wouldn't know which element she is currently able to reach when hitting Enter.

There are some legitimate reasons to use `focus()`; however, in most cases, it is not a good idea to alter the automatic order of form entry. Not every user can see the form, and even users who can see might not look at it.

Especially in longer forms that expect a lot of different data to enter, you'll find that people don't look on the screen, but touch-type as they read the data from a printout or their credit card, passports, and so on. It is pretty frustrating to check the form in between and realize you didn't fill out the right fields or you are still stuck at an error message that popped up earlier.

Text Fields, Text Areas, Hidden and Password Fields

Text fields, text areas, hidden fields, and password fields are probably the most common fields you will have to deal with, as they are the ones that users enter text content in.

In addition to the global form element properties, they also support the element properties `value` and `defaultValue`. The difference is that if a user changes the content of the element, it does change the `value` property but not the `defaultValue`. This also means that when you change the `value` of the field, the change is visible, but when you change the `defaultValue`, it isn't. If you want to change the element's default value and make it visible, you need to call the `reset()` method immediately afterwards. In the example document, you have a default value on the e-mail field:

```
<p><input type="text" id="email" value="you@example.com"➥
name="email" /></p>
```

You could read the value and the default value like this:

```
var mail= document.getElementById( 'email' );
alert( mail.defaultValue );
alert( mail.value );
```

When the user hasn't changed anything on the field, both values would be you@example.com. However, if the user were to enter me@otherexample.com in the field, the two values become different.

It is tricky to find an example for defaultValue that does not mean you have to do something with JavaScript that should be the job of the back end. One example could be to test whether the current domain is German and change the default of the e-mail field to a German e-mail address. The following code should be executed when the document has loaded:

```
var mail = document.getElementById( 'email' );
if( window.location.host.indexOf( '.de' ) != -1 ) {
  mail.defaultValue = 'email@adresse.de';
  mail.form.reset();
}
```

Notice that you need to call reset() to make the change visible. You can see the change happening in exampleFormGermanPreset.html (we cheated there to make it visible by excluding the host test).

Note For TEXTAREA elements, you read and write the value and defaultValue just like for any other form text element. However, the HTML tag has no value attribute—the initial and the changed value is the text contained in between the opening and closing tag.

Text elements allow for a method called select(), which highlights all the text inside them to ease copying and pasting of text examples. This is often seen as a feature in webzines or online documentation systems.

Check Boxes

Check boxes are a great way to offer an unambiguous "yes" or "no" choice. They are very easy to read out on the server side (the form sends the name of the box with the value of the check box if there is one or "on" if there is none, and doesn't send the name at all when the user hasn't checked the box) and much easier to use than, for example, a radio button group or a select box with "yes" and "no" options.

In addition to the global element properties described earlier, check boxes have the properties checked and defaultChecked, both Boolean values indicating whether the option was chosen. You can read and write both of these properties, but you need to reset the form to make changes to defaultChecked visible.

One common use of JavaScript in connection with check boxes is offering the user the opportunity to check all check boxes or reverse the choices made in a lot of check boxes, one example being in web-based e-mail systems, as shown in Figure 7-6. The logic of these functions is pretty simple: you loop through all elements, test the type of each one, and change the checked attribute accordingly. You can see a demo of this in exampleFormCheckboxes.html.

Figure 7-6. *Bulk changing of check boxes via JavaScript*

There are three buttons in the example that call the same function—changeBoxes()—when the user clicks them. Each button supplies a different numeric value for the function's sole parameter—1 for select all, -1 for invert, and 0 for select none.

exampleFormCheckboxes.html *(excerpt)*

```
<input type="button" onclick="changeBoxes(1)" value="select all" />
<input type="button" onclick="changeBoxes(-1)" value="invert selection" />
<input type="button" onclick="changeBoxes(0)" value="select none" />
```

This allows you to keep the function to change the check boxes simple. Simply loop through all the elements in the first form found in the page. If the element type is not checkbox, continue the loop without executing the rest of it.

If the element is a check box, determine whether action is smaller than 0 and reverse the check box state by changing checked to false when it is true and vice versa. If the action is 0 or larger, simply set the checked property to the value of action.

exampleFormCheckboxes.html *(excerpt)*

```
function changeBoxes( action ) {
  var f = document.forms[0];
  var elms = f.elements;
  for( var i = 0; i < elms.length; i++ ) {
    if( elms[i].type != 'checkbox' ){ continue; }
    if( action < 0 ){
      elms[i].checked = elms[i].checked ? 0 : 1;
    } else {
      elms[i].checked = action;
    }
  }
}
```

If this is confusing, remember that the checked property is a Boolean value. This means when it is true or 1, it is checked, and when it is false or 0, it is unchecked. If you were to use only the true or false keywords, you'd have to add another case in the else condition (via the ternary notation in this case):

```
function changeBoxes(action) {
  var f = document.forms[0];
  var elms = f.elements;
  for( var i = 0; i < elms.length; i++ ){
    if( elms[i].type != 'checkbox' ){ continue; }
    if( action < 0 ){
      elms[i].checked = elms[i].checked ? false : true;
    } else {
      elms[i].checked = action == 1 ? true : false;
    }
  }
}
```

Using the ternary operator, you could even reduce the whole check box logic part of the script to one line:

```
function changeBoxes( action ) {
  var f = document.forms[0];
  var elms = f.elements;
  for( var i = 0; i < elms.length; i++ ){
    if( elms[i].type != 'checkbox' ){ continue; }
    elms[i].checked = action < 0 ? (elms[i].checked ? 0 : 1 ) :➥
    action;
  }
}
```

As a lot of complex form code is not necessarily created by client-side-oriented developers, there is a high chance you might encounter constructs like this, which is why we took the opportunity here to show it to you.

Radio Buttons

Radio buttons have their name because they look like the dials on old radios, in case you wondered. They act like check boxes, with the difference being that they belong to one group with the same name, and the user can only choose one exclusively. Radio buttons are very easy to use for mouse and keyboard users alike, and they are a good replacement for short select boxes in case you ever run into problems using a select box.

They have the same Boolean checked and defaultChecked properties as check boxes, but will automatically set the checked property of the other choices to false when you set one. Again, you can read and write both checked and defaultChecked, and you need to reset the form to make changes to defaultChecked appear visually. As the example HTML only has a radio group of two options, let's choose a different example:

exampleFormRadioGroup.html *(excerpt)*

```
<form method="post" action="send.php">
  <fieldset>
    <legend>Step 1 of 3 - Your favourite Character </legend>
    <p>
      <input type="radio" name="character" id="charC"
       value="Calvin" checked="checked" />
      <label for="charC">Calvin</label>
    </p>
    <p>
      <input type="radio" name="character"
       id="charH" value="Hobbes" />
      <label for="charH">Hobbes</label>
  </p>
  <p>
    <input type="radio" name="character"
     id="charSd" value="Susie Derkins" />
    <label for="charSd">Susie Derkins</label>
  </p>
  <p>
    <input type="radio" name="character"
     id="charS" value="Spaceman Spiff" />
    <label for="charS">Spaceman Spiff</label>
  </p>
  <p>
    <input type="radio" name="character"
     id="charSm" value="Stupendous Man" />
    <label for="charSm">Stupendous Man</label>
  </p>
  </fieldset>
  <p class="submit"><input type="submit" value="Next Step" /></p>
</form>
```

■**Note** This is also a good opportunity to show the difference between name and id. While a group of radio buttons all share the same name (in this case character), they each must get a unique id to allow the labels to be connected with them. Labels are not only handy for assistive technology like screen readers, but also make the form much easier to use, as users can click the names next to the check boxes to select them.

The demo HTML includes some buttons to show the output of the JavaScript; you can test it out by opening it in a browser. The script shows how you can deal with radio buttons:

formRadioGroup.js

```
function setChoice( n ) {
  var f = document.forms[0];
  f.character[n].checked = true;
}
function getChoice() {
  var f = document.forms[0];
  var choices = f.elements.character;
  for(var i = 0; i < choices.length; i++ ){
    if( choices[i].checked ){ break; }
  }
  alert( 'Favourite Character is: ' + choices[i].value );
}
```

You can access the radio button group as an array with the shared name (in this case character). Setting an option of a radio group is pretty straightforward: the setChoice() function takes a number as a parameter (n), reads the first form (forms[0]), and sets the checked property of the n-th character item to true.

formRadioGroup.js *(excerpt)*

```
function setChoice( n ) {
  var f = document.forms[0];
  f.character[n].checked = true;
}
```

If you click the "set choice to Hobbes" button in the example, you see that the highlighted radio button changes as shown in Figure 7-7.

Figure 7-7. *Changing the selected option in a radio group*

Reading the currently selected choice is just as easy: you select the first form, store the characters list in a new variable called `choices`, and loop through it. Then, you test the `checked` property of each of the elements in the array and break the loop when you find one that returns `true`. This is the currently selected radio choice: there can be only one that is selected in any group of radio buttons sharing the same `name`.

`formRadioGroup.js` *(continued)*

```
function getChoice() {
  var f = document.forms[0];
  var choices = f.elements.character;
  for( var i = 0; i < choices.length; i++ ) {
    if( choices[i].checked ){ break; }
  }
  alert( 'Favourite Character is: ' + choices[i].value );
}
```

Buttons

There are three kinds of buttons in HTML: two that work without scripting, and one that was included in the specifications to work only in conjunction with scripts.

> *Authors may create three types of buttons:*
>
> *submit buttons: When activated, a submit button submits a form. A form may contain more than one submit button.*
>
> *reset buttons: When activated, a reset button resets all controls to their initial values.*
>
> *push buttons: Push buttons have no default behavior. Each push button may have client-side scripts associated with the element's event attributes. When an event occurs (e.g., the user presses the button, releases it, etc.), the associated script is triggered.*
>
> —http://www.w3.org/TR/REC-html40/interact/forms.html#buttons

This makes "push buttons"—which are either the input-type button or the button element—the perfect trigger element for JavaScript-only functionality.

The Reset and Submit buttons, on the other hand, are very important parts of the form and shouldn't be tampered with unless you really have a good reason for the change. One recurring request is to change the value or the state of the Submit button when the form was submitted to prevent impatient users from clicking the button twice. You could do this via a `click` handler; however, the better option is to use a `submit` handler on the form, as this would also trigger the change when the form is submitted via the Enter key. Figure 7-8 shows how this might look.

Figure 7-8. *Changing the style and text content of a Submit button when the form gets sent*

All you need to do to achieve this functionality is assign an event handler to the window that calls an init() function and another one that calls a change() function when the form is submitted.

This function loops through all the form elements (after retrieving the form via getTarget()) and checks whether the element is an image or a Submit button. If this is the case, it disables the button via the disabled attribute and changes the button value to Please wait:

exampleChangeSubmitButton.html *(excerpt)*

```
submitChange = {
  init : function() {
    DOMhelp.addEvent( document.forms[0], 'submit',➥
    submitChange.change,false);
  },
  change : function( e ){
    var t = DOMhelp.getTarget( e );
    for( var i = 0; i < t.elements.length; i++ ){
      if( !/submit|image/.test( t.elements[i].type ) ) { continue; }
        t.elements[i].disabled = true;
        t.elements[i].value = 'Please wait...';
      }
    }
  }
}
DOMhelp.addEvent( window, 'load', submitChange.init ,false );
```

An image button defined via <input type="image"> acts like a Submit button, the only difference being that it doesn't submit its name to the back end but two sets of name-value pairs, consisting of the original name followed by .x and .y and the coordinates the user clicked as the values. That way you can perform different actions depending on where the button was clicked. This information is not readable via JavaScript, only on the back end.

From a JavaScript point of view, there is not much more you can do with an image input, except that you can provide a rollover state for it.

Select Boxes

Select boxes are probably the most complex and most versatile of form elements. Designers love them, as it lets them store a lot of options for the user to choose from in a small screen space (on the other hand, designers also hate them because they cannot style them with CSS properly).

Each select box has a list object called `options` that has several properties:

- `length`: The number of all options inside this select box.

- `selected`: Boolean if the option is selected by the user.

- `selectedIndex`: The index number of the selected element. If no element was selected, this returns -1 (which actually is a property of the `SELECT` element but is appropriate to mention here).

- `text`: The text content of the option.

- `value`: The value of the option.

Note Notice that `text` and `value` are properties of each of the options contained in the select box; you cannot read out the chosen value by reading the value property of the select box object itself—as there is no such thing.

There are two kinds of select boxes: single-choice select boxes that only allow one exclusive choice and multiple-choice select boxes that allow the user to choose more than one option by holding down Ctrl and highlighting the options he desires.

Note Multiple-choice select boxes are a nightmare to use for users with assistive technology or keyboard users, which is why you might want to consider using a list of check boxes instead. This will also make it easier to read out the choice on the server side.

Reading out single-choice select boxes is pretty easy. For example, take the select box in the demo form:

exampleSelectChoice.html *(excerpt)*

```
<p>
  <label for="subject">Subject</label>
  <select id="subject" name="subject">
    <option value="generalEnquiry" selected="selected">General➥
    question</option>
    <option value="Webdesign">Webdesign</option>
    <option value="Hosting">Hosting</option>
    <option value="Training">Training</option>
    <option value="Partnership">Partnership</option>
    <option value="other">Other</option>
  </select>
</p>
```

The quickest way to reach the select box is to use the name of the element instead of the index. The reason is that the element type of select boxes could be either select-one or select-multiple depending on whether or not the multiple attribute is set. Once you get to the correct object, you can use its selectedIndex property to read out the chosen option and display the value or the text of the option by using the selectedIndex as the list counter:

exampleSelectChoice.html *(excerpt)*

```
function checkSingle() {
  var f = document.forms[0];
  var selectBox = f.elements['subject'];
  var choice = selectBox.selectedIndex;
  alert( 'You chose ' + selectBox.options[choice].text )
}
```

In the case of multiple-choice select boxes, this isn't enough, as the user might have chosen more than one option (selectedIndex will return only the first choice).

Instead of using `selectedIndex`, you'll have to loop through all the options and test the `selected` property of each one:

exampleSelectChoice.html *(excerpt)*

```
function checkMultiple() {
  var f = document.forms[0];
  var selectBox = f.elements['multisubject'];
  var choices=[];
  for( var i = 0; i < selectBox.options.length; i++ ) {
    if( selectBox.options[i].selected == 1) {
      choices.push( selectBox.options[i].text );
    }
  }
  alert( choices.join(',') );
}
```

You can reach the select box via its `name` in the `elements` collection, and create a new array called `choices` (the [ ] is a shortcut notation for `new Array()`). Loop through each of the `options` of the select box and check whether its `selected` property is `true`. Where that is the case, push the option's `text` value as a new array item into `choices`. Then convert the array to a string using the array's `join()` method and display it.

This way of reading the values would also work with a single-choice select box; however, it might be overkill depending on the number of options available. You can put both methods together in a more generic function by reading out the choices depending on the type of the element:

exampleSelectChoice.html *(excerpt)*

```
function getSelectValue( fieldName ) {
  var f = document.forms[0];
  var selectBox = f.elements[fieldName];
  if( selectBox.type == 'select-one' ) {
    var choice = selectBox.selectedIndex;
    alert( 'You chose ' + selectBox.options[choice].text );
  } else {
    var choices = [];
    for( var i = 0;i < selectBox.options.length; i++ ){
      if( selectBox.options[i].selected == 1 ) {
        choices.push( selectBox.options[i].text );
      }
    }
    choices.join( ',' );
    alert( choices );
  }
}
```

Adding, Replacing, and Removing Options

Select boxes are unique as form elements go, insofar as they allow you to add or remove options programmatically. You can add a new option by using the `Option` constructor and including it in the list of options:

```
extraOption = new Option(value, text, defaultSelected, selected);
```

If you want, for example, to add "DOM scripting" as a subject to the list, you can do so like this:

exampleSelectChoice.html *(excerpt)*

```
function addOption(fieldName) {
  var f = document.forms[0];
  var selectBox = f.elements[fieldName];
  var extraOption = new Option('DOM scripting', 'domscripting', 0, 0);
  selectBox.options[ selectBox.options.length ] = extraOption;
}
```

You can remove an option by setting it equal to `null`:

exampleSelectChoice.html *(excerpt)*

```
function removeOption(fieldName,i) {
  var f = document.forms[0];
  var selectBox = f.elements[fieldName];
  selectBox.options[i] = null;
}
```

Replacing options is as easy; simply set the old option to the new one:

exampleSelectChoice.html *(excerpt)*

```
function replaceOption( fieldName, i ) {
  var f = document.forms[0];
  var selectBox = f.elements[fieldName];
  var extraOption = new Option( 'DOM scripting', 'domscripting',➡
  0 ,0 );
  selectBox.options[i] = extraOption;
}
```

Inserting an option before another option is a bit more problematic, as you need to copy all the options before you rewrite the options collection. The function `insertBeforeOption()` takes two parameters: the name of the form element and the index of the option you want to insert the new option before. You start by defining two loop counters called `i` and `j` and a blank array called `opts` before finding the select box and creating the new option.

exampleSelectChoice.html *(excerpt)*

```
function insertBeforeOption( fieldName, n ) {
  var i = 0, j = 0, opts = [],
  var f = document.forms[0];
  var selectBox = f.elements[fieldName];
  var extraOption = new Option('DOM scripting',➥
  'domscripting', 0,0);
```

Then store the options of the select box in a variable called old and loop through them, creating a new option for each of them and assigning their properties to the new option.

exampleSelectChoice.html *(continued)*

```
  var old = selectBox.options;
  for( i = 0; i < old.length; i++ ) {
    opts[i] = new Option(old[i].text, old[i].value,➥
    old[i].defaultSelected, old[i].selected );
  }
```

The new list will be one element longer, which is why you increase the length property before looping through the new list. You test whether the loop counter is the same as the parameter sent to the function and insert the new option if this is the case.

exampleSelectChoice.html *(continued)*

```
  old.length++;
  for( i = 0; i < old.length; i++ ) {
    if( i == n ) {
      old[i] = extraOption;
```

Otherwise, you set the option to the old option and increase the j counter variable. Notice you need a second counter here because you cannot change the variable i during the loop. As the new option list will be one item bigger, you need to use j to get the value stored in the opts array.

exampleSelectChoice.html *(continued)*

```
    } else {
      old[i] = opts[j];
      j++;
    }
  }
}
```

Depending on the number of options in the select box, this could become a rather slow and demanding script. You can achieve the same effect a lot quicker and with less code by using the DOM:

exampleSelectChoice.html *(excerpt)*

```
function insertBeforeOptionDOM( fieldName, i ) {
  var selectBox = document.getElementById( fieldName );
  if( !selectBox ){ return false; }
  var opt = selectBox.getElementsByTagName( 'option' );
  var extraOption = document.createElement( 'option' );
  extraOption.setAttribute( 'value', 'domscripting' );
  extraOption.appendChild( document.createTextNode(➡
  'DOM Scripting' ) );
  selectBox.insertBefore( extraOption, selectBox.options[i] );
}
```

Select boxes are a big part of web application development and have traditionally been the interface for sorting two lists by moving elements back and forth.

Interactive Forms: Hiding and Showing Dependent Elements

One really cool thing about JavaScript and forms is that you can make forms a lot more engaging and dynamic than they are "out-of-the-box." It is tempting to make everything interact with each other and immediately send a form without expecting the user to click a Submit button or press Enter. The danger of this is not only do you sacrifice support for user agents other than visual ones, but also users may send data prematurely.

When it comes to simply changing the interface or the number of options displayed in a form, it is quite safe to use change handlers. Let's use the demo form as an example. You might have noticed that there are some fields that have a logical connection: the "other subject" text field only makes sense when the "Other" option has been selected, and the choice to receive the newsletter as HTML or plain text comes into play only when the user has chosen to subscribe to the newsletter.

exampleDynamicForm.html *(excerpt)*

```
<form method="post" action="send.php">
  [... code snipped ...]
  <p><label for="subject">Subject</label>
  <select id="subject" name="subject">
    <option value="generalEnquiry" selected="selected">General➥
    question</option>
    <option value="Webdesign">Webdesign</option>
    <option value="Hosting">Hosting</option>
    <option value="Training">Training</option>
    <option value="Partnership">Partnership</option>
    <option value="other">Other</option>
  </select></p>
  <p><label for="otherSubject">specify other subject</label>
  <input type="text" id="otherSubject" name="otherSubject" /></p>
  [... code snipped ...]
  <p><input type="checkbox" name="newsletter" value="yes"➥
  id="newsletter" />
  <label for="newsletter">Sign me up for the newsletter</label></p>
  <p>Newsletter format:
  <input type="radio" name="newsletterFormat" id="newsHtml"➥
  value="html" checked="checked" />
  <label for="newsHTML">HTML</label>
  <input type="radio" name="newsletterFormat" id="newsPlain"➥
  value="plain"/>
  <label for="newsPlain">Text</label></p>
```

With a script you can hide these options and make them appear only when the user has selected the appropriate option. Figure 7-9 shows how that looks in a browser.

Figure 7-9. *Showing and hiding form elements depending on user choices*

You define a class to apply to the elements you want to hide and the IDs of the two dynamic elements as properties of a main object called df.

dynamicForm.js

```
df = {
  hideClass : 'hide',
  letterOption : 'newsletter',
  subjectOption : 'subject',
```

The init() method checks for DOM support and whether the necessary elements are available.

dynamicForm.js *(continued)*

```
init : function() {
  if( !document.getElementById || !document.createTextNode ){
   return;
  }
  df.news = document.getElementById( df.letterOption );
  df.subject = document.getElementById( df.subjectOption );
  if( !df.subject || !df.news ){ return; }
```

Next you need to find the elements to hide. By using the DOMhelp method closestSibling(), you can make sure you don't try to hide line breaks but the elements that you actually want to reach. Store the elements in properties of the main object to make them accessible to the event handler methods.

You can hide the elements by adding the hiding class to them and assign a click event handler that points to the letterChange() method to the check box and a change handler that points to subjectChange() to the select box.

dynamicForm.js *(continued)*

```
df.newsOpt = DOMhelp.closestSibling( df.news.parentNode, 1 );
df.subjectOpt = DOMhelp.closestSibling( df.subject.➡
parentNode, 1 );
DOMhelp.cssjs( 'add', df.newsOpt, df.hideClass );
DOMhelp.cssjs( 'add', df.subjectOpt, df.hideClass );
DOMhelp.addEvent( df.news, 'click', df.letterChange, false );
DOMhelp.addEvent( df.subject, 'change', df.subjectChange, false );
},
```

You retrieve the check box via getTarget() in the letterChange() method before testing its checked property. If the property is checked, you remove the hiding class; otherwise you add it.

dynamicForm.js *(continued)*

```
letterChange : function( e ){
  var t = DOMhelp.getTarget( e );
  var action = t.checked ? 'remove' : 'add';
  DOMhelp.cssjs( action, df.newsOpt, df.hideClass );
},
```

The subjectChange() method works the same way; you retrieve the target and check whether the fifth option is the selected one (that is, whether selectedIndex is equal to 4). If it is, you remove the hiding class from the optional element; otherwise you add it. As an extra, the method sets the focus of the browser to the newly shown element so that users can immediately start typing.

dynamicForm.js *(continued)*

```
  subjectChange : function( e ) {
    var t = DOMhelp.getTarget( e );
    var action = t.selectedIndex == 5 ? 'remove' : 'add';
    DOMhelp.cssjs( action, df.subjectOpt, df.hideClass );
    if(action == 'remove' ) {
      df.subjectOpt.getElementsByTagName( 'input' )[0].focus();
    }
  }
}
}
DOMhelp.addEvent(window, 'load', df.init, false );
```

Showing and hiding the connected elements is one way to make parts of a form connected to other options. A different approach is to keep them visible but add a `disabled` attribute. This makes them impossible to change for the user, and the browser shows them grayed out.

This is a bit less versatile than just hiding elements, as the `disabled` attribute is only applicable to `input`, `textarea`, `select`, `option`, `optgroup`, and `button`. Figure 7-10 shows how the form looks with disabled elements in Firefox on Windows.

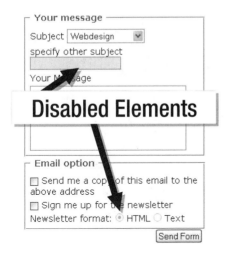

Figure 7-10. *Disabling elements instead of hiding them*

The main difference in the script is that you have to target each `input` element you want to disable individually. In the case of the radio buttons, this means that you have to go through a loop. The changes in the script are highlighted in bold and should be self-explanatory:

dynamicFormDisable.js

```
df = {
  hideClass : 'hide',
  letterOption : 'newsletter',
  subjectOption : 'subject',
  init : function() {
    if( !document.getElementById || !document.createTextNode ){
     return;
    }
    df.news = document.getElementById( df.letterOption );
    df.subject = document.getElementById( df.subjectOption );
    if(!df.subject || !df.news){ return; }
    df.newsOpt = DOMhelp.closestSibling( df.news.parentNode, 1 );
    df.newsOpt = df.newsOpt.getElementsByTagName( 'input' );
    for( var i = 0; i < df.newsOpt.length; i++ ){
      df.newsOpt[i].disabled = 1;
    }
    df.subjectOpt = DOMhelp.closestSibling( df.subject.parentNode, 1);
    df.subjectOpt = df.subjectOpt.getElementsByTagName( 'input' )[0];
    df.subjectOpt.disabled = 1;
    DOMhelp.addEvent( df.news, 'click', df.letterChange, false );
    DOMhelp.addEvent( df.subject, 'change', df.subjectChange, false );
  },
  letterChange : function( e ){
    var i;
    var t = DOMhelp.getTarget( e );
    var disable = t.checked ? null: 1 ;
    for( i = 0; i < df.newsOpt.length; i++ ) {
      df.newsOpt[i].disabled = disable;
    }
  },
  subjectChange : function( e ){
    var t = DOMhelp.getTarget( e );
    if( t.selectedIndex == 5 ) {
      df.subjectOpt.disabled = null;
      df.subjectOpt.focus();
    } else {
      df.subjectOpt.disabled = 1;
    }
  }
}
DOMhelp.addEvent( window, 'load', df.init, false );
```

The practical upshot of using `disabled` is that these elements cannot be reached via tabbing any longer either—something that is still possible with elements that are hidden (unless you hide them by setting `display` to `none` as shown earlier in the site navigation section).

Custom Form Elements

Given enough skill and testing time, you can use JavaScript to extend the normal form controls browsers provide the user with your own custom controls and even make them keyboard accessible. Especially in web application development, this might be a true necessity.

I won't go into developing your own custom elements here, but I will touch on the subject in Chapter 11 again. For now, you can take a look at what the development teams at Yahoo (`http://developer.yahoo.com/yui/slider/examples/slider.html`) and Mozilla (`http://www.mozilla.org/access/dhtml/#examples`) have come up with and give out for free.

Summary of Forms and JavaScript

I hope this gave you insight as to what is possible with forms and JavaScript. You have learned about the different properties and methods of forms themselves and each of the elements that they may contain with their individual properties and methods. You've seen in detail how to deal with select boxes and how you could make a form more dynamic by hiding elements that are dependent on others and only showing them when the other elements are activated or have the right value.

Things to Remember About Forms and JavaScript

- Try not to go overboard on what you can do with forms. See whether the form is still usable with a keyboard once you're done spicing it up. In particular, longer forms are more likely to be filled out by tabbing from field to field rather than by clicking the different elements and then editing them.

- Don't automatically submit a form with an event handler—forms can be submitted by clicking the Submit button or by hitting Enter. Don't take these options away from the user.

- While the older form collections `forms` and `elements` are not up-to-date DOM scripting techniques (as they are HTML dependent, whereas all the other DOM methods could also be applied to an XML string), they might be the easier option to use on generic or generated forms where you cannot control the IDs or the number of elements. Looping through one `elements` list is a lot easier than looping through all child elements of a form and comparing them with the possible element names or looping through the `input`, `textarea`, and `select` element collections individually.

Summary

You now should be able to handle the most common uses of JavaScript and come back to this and the previous chapter when you need to refresh your memory of how to deal with images, windows, navigation, and forms.

In the next chapter, we will leave the world of browser and client-side scripting and focus on how we can make JavaScript talk to the back end and server-side scripts. This will also enable you to take a look at that new kid on the scripting block: Ajax.

■ ■ ■

CHAPTER 8

Back-End Interaction
with Ajax

You finally reached the chapter where I am going to talk about the new amazing JavaScript-related phenomenon, Ajax. The good news is that you can use Ajax to create really nice, slick interfaces, and you can extend JavaScript's reach much further than the browser and the currently displayed document.

The not-so-good news is that Ajax depends on the XMLHTTPRequest, XHR object for short (or its Microsoft equivalent), and that one has "HTTP" written all over it. What this means is that you cannot use any Ajax examples without a server, and furthermore you will have to have some basic knowledge of server-side scripting to use Ajax (unless you use one of the out-of-the-box packages available—more on those in the "Summary" section of the chapter).

It also means that using Ajax robs JavaScript of one of its strengths: to be able to create interfaces that work offline and on the file system of a computer or even from a CD or memory stick. However, the benefits of Ajax make up for this.

If you don't want to transfer files back and forth between your local computer and a remote computer to test your code, the best option is to install a local server. This is not as tough as it seems at first glance, as nowadays there are a lot of prepackaged servers available (it was a nightmare in the 1990s, especially on Windows).

My personal favorite is XAMPP, which can be downloaded at http://www.apachefriends.org/. You can get an installer and follow the instructions to have your own server up and running in a matter of minutes.

XAMPP installs Apache 2, MySQL, PHP, and all the add-ons you will ever need and is available for many platforms. It also comes with an FTP and e-mail server, a statistics package, and many more options, and it is constantly kept up-to-date by the maintainers of Apache Friends (http://www.apachefriends.org). Oh and yes, it is free, of course.

■**Tip** Again, to avoid frustration with the rest of the chapter, you should try out for yourself the many code examples in this chapter to see what I am talking about. The difference in comparison with the other chapters is that the code examples will not work locally on a computer on the file system; they require a server, as Ajax needs the HTTP protocol to work. If you don't want to install a server but you are online, you can go to this book's homepage at http://www.beginningjavascript.com/ where you'll be able to see all the code examples in action.

When and if you install XAMMP, you can unpack the chapter examples in a directory—called, for example, `jsbook`—in the `htdocs` directory of the server installation, which could be `c:\xammp\htdocs\`. To see the examples, you open a browser and type in **http://localhost/jsbook/** as the location.

Tip In addition to the official help FAQs at `http://www.apachefriends.org/en/faq-xampp.html`, there is also a nice step-by-step explanation of how to install XAMPP (and WordPress) on a computer running Windows XP available at `http://www.tamba2.org.uk/wordpress/xampp/`.

Household Cleaning Liquid, Football Club, or Flash Gordon's Spacecraft: What Is Ajax?

Ajax stands for Asynchronous JavaScript and XML, a term that was coined by Jesse James Garrett at Adaptive Path in February 2005 (`http://www.adaptivepath.com/publications/essays/archives/000385.php`). It describes a methodology of developing web applications in a way different from the traditional one.

According to the article, traditional web apps and sites work synchronously—every time you follow a link, or when you submit a form, the browser sends the data to the server, the server (hopefully) responds, and the whole page gets refreshed.

Note This is not necessarily true, as older web apps like the Microsoft Outlook web interface work with frames and only reload smaller parts of the whole interface that way, but let's not be picky; and for heaven's sake let frames be a thing of the past when web connection speeds were below the 56K of a standard modem.

Ajax applications work *asynchronously*, which means that you send data back and forth between the user agent and the server without reloading the whole page. You replace only the parts of the page that change. You can also send several requests out and go on scrolling and using the page while the other parts load in the background.

One good comparison is that Ajax is to traditional web pages what instant messaging is to e-mails: immediate feedback, with no long waiting times and with more options to communicate. Figure 8-1 shows the flow of Ajax applications in comparison to traditional web sites and web applications.

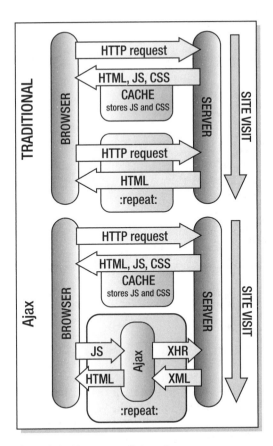

Figure 8-1. *Ajax vs. traditional request*

At first glance, this appears to add an extra layer of complexity to the whole matter. However, the really cool thing about it is that the communication between the Ajax engine and the browser happens via JavaScript and not via page reloads.

In practical terms, this means for the end user less waiting for pages to load and render, and easier interaction with the page, as you can request data and still read the text or look at the other content on the page.

This makes for a much slicker interface, as you could, for example, give feedback on a login form without changing the whole site while being able to test for the right entries on the server or in a database.

Let's have a go at a simple example. The demo file `exampleXHR.html` uses Ajax (well, without the X, as there is no XML involved) to load and display files from the server when the user clicks a link as shown in Figure 8-2.

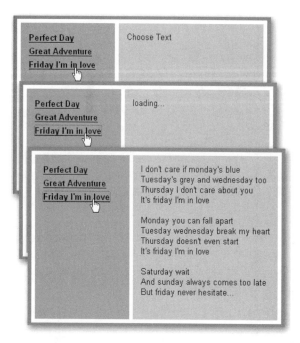

Figure 8-2. *Loading external files via Ajax*

The magic wand behind all of this is an object called XMLHttpRequest, or XHR for short. This is a nonstandard object insofar as it is not part of an official standard on the W3C site (it is a working draft at the moment: http://www.w3.org/TR/XMLHttpRequest/), but it is supported across all modern browsers (Safari, Mozilla/Firefox, Opera). MSIE does not support XHR, but uses an ActiveX control instead. The good news is that the ActiveX control works the same way.

■**Caution**　The problem with this is when a user has JavaScript enabled but ActiveX disabled in MSIE, he won't be able to experience your Ajax efforts. Keep this in mind if you create Ajax solutions and get user bug reports.

Let's go through the example step by step so you can see what the different parts do. The HTML contains links pointing to text files and calls the `simplexhr.doxhr` method with two parameters: an ID of an HTML element to send the text to and the URL of the text:

exampleXHR.html *(excerpt)*

```
<li>
    <a href="perfect_day.txt"
       onclick="simplexhr.doxhr( 'txtcontainer1', this.href );➥
       return false;">
       Perfect Day
    </a>
</li>
<li>
    <a href="great_adventure.txt"
       onclick="simplexhr.doxhr( 'txtcontainer1', this.href );➥
       return false;">
       Great Adventure
    </a>
</li>
```

Note Notice that these links are not totally unobtrusive and up to the standard of the rest of the code examples in this book, but at least they work without JavaScript—the browser will simply show the text files when scripting is not available. It is very tempting, especially when using out-of-the-box Ajax libraries, to create scripting-dependent links. No matter how cool the technology is, this is never a good idea.

---

simpleXHR.js

```
simplexhr = {
  doxhr : function( container, url ) {
   if( !document.getElementById || !document.createTextNode) {
     return;
   }
   simplexhr.outputContainer = document.getElementById( container );
   if( !simplexhr.outputContainer ){ return; }
```

The script starts by checking for the DOM and whether the element you want to write content into is available. If it is, it gets stored in a property called outputContainer to make it available for all other methods in the script.

simpleXHR.js *(continued)*

```
var request;
try{
  request = new XMLHttpRequest();
} catch ( error ) {
  try {
    request = new ActiveXObject( "Microsoft.XMLHTTP" );
  } catch ( error ) {
    return true;
  }
}
```

Define a new variable called request and use the try and catch construct to see which XHR version is supported. Try assigning a new XMLHttpRequest() for Mozilla and Safari; if that is not supported, an error occurs that triggers the catch statement (you can learn more about try and catch() in the appendix of this book). This one tries to assign the Microsoft ActiveX object instead. If that is not available either, the method returns true, which means the browser will just follow the link and show the text in the browser.

If the assignment was successful, you have a new XMLHttpRequest object at your disposal.

■**Note** For a complete list of methods, handlers, and properties of the XMLHttpRequest object, you can consult the documentation at XULPlanet (http://www.xulplanet.com/references/objref/XMLHttpRequest.html) or Microsoft (http://msdn.microsoft.com/library/en-us/xmlsdk/html/xmobjpmexmlhttprequest.asp), respectively.

The first step is to call the open() method to start the connection with the server and retrieve or send data. The open() method takes five parameters, three of which are optional:

```
request = open(requestMethod, url[, sync, [name, [password]]]);
```

- The requestMethod parameter can be (among some other options that would exceed the scope of this chapter) either GET or POST, and corresponds to the method attribute of a FORM element. The GET method is much easier, but also less secure, just as it is with forms and server-side data handling (data sent via GET is visible in the URL and can be easily manipulated there by others).

- The url parameter is the location of the file on your server.

Note XMLHttpRequest does not allow you to load content from other servers, as that would be a big security problem. Imagine any JavaScript embedded into an e-mail or web site being able to send off any data from your computer or retrieve more code from a server. There is a way to load third-party content, though, by using a proxy script on the server—more on that later in the XML example.

- The sync parameter is optional and is a Boolean that defines whether the request should be sent asynchronously or synchronously. It is hard-wired to true—which means the request will be sent asynchronously. Synchronous requests would lock up the browser.

- The name and password parameters are optional and only necessary when the file you try to call requires user authentication.

In this case, you will retrieve files only from the server, and to do that you use GET as the request method and the file's location as the url parameter, omitting the optional parameters.

simpleXHR.js *(continued)*

```
request.open( 'get', url );
```

The readyState property of the request object contains a numeric value that describes what is happening to the connection. It is incremented throughout the connection attempt. The different possible values for readyState and their corresponding request states are as follows:

- 0: There is no connection—it is uninitialized.

- 1: The connection is loading.

- 2: The data was loaded.

- 3: The connection is interactive.

- 4: The connection is complete—the data was sent and retrieved.

Every time the status changes, XHR triggers a readystatechange event. You can use the corresponding onreadystatechange event handler to invoke a method in which you can test against the possible values of readyState and take the appropriate action.

simpleXHR.js *(continued)*

```
request.onreadystatechange = function() {
  if( request.readyState == 1 ) {
    simplexhr.outputContainer.innerHTML = 'loading...';
  }
}
```

Once the request is initialized (readyState equals 1), it is a very good idea to give the user some feedback that there are things happening in the background. In this example, the script displays a "loading..." message inside the HTML output element as shown in Figure 8-3.

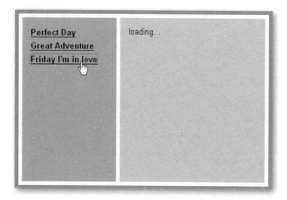

Figure 8-3. *Notifying the user that the request was sent and is under way*

The other states cannot be read safely cross-browser, which is why we skip 2 and 3 and check whether the request was finished by comparing readyState with 4.

simpleXHR.js *(continued)*

```
    if( request.readyState == 4 ) {
      if ( /200|304/.test( request.status ) ) {
        simplexhr.retrieved(request);
      } else {
        simplexhr.failed(request);
      }
    }
```

When the request is complete, you check another property called status, which stores the status of the request. The status is the standard HTTP response code of the request. It is 0 when the connection cannot be established and 404 when the file is not found.

Note For a complete list of standard HTTP response codes, see http://www.w3.org/Protocols/rfc2616/rfc2616-sec10.html.

If the status is either 200 (all OK) or 304 (not modified), the file has been retrieved and you can do something with it. In the case of this demo script, you call the retrieved() method. If the status is any other value, you call failed().

simpleXHR.js *(continued)*

```
    }
    request.send( null );
    return false;
  },
```

The send() method sends your request to the server and can take request parameters to send to the server-side script being invoked. If you don't have any parameters to send, it is safest to set it to null. (Internet Explorer accepts send() without any parameters, but this can cause problems in Mozilla browsers.) Finally, setting the method's return value to false stops the link from being followed.

simpleXHR.js *(continued)*

```
  failed : function( requester ) {
    alert( 'The XMLHttpRequest failed. Status: ' + requester.status );
    return true;
  },
```

If the request didn't succeed, the `failed()` method shows an `alert()` dialog telling the user about the problem. (This is not very clever or pretty, but should do for the moment.) Returning `true` after the user has clicked the dialog's OK button causes the link to be followed. You can test this by opening the file `exampleXHR.html` locally in a browser (without the `http://` protocol) and clicking the links. As there is no HTTP transmission, any request will fail with code `0` as shown in Figure 8-4.

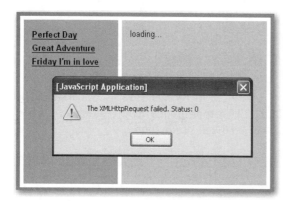

Figure 8-4. *Notifying the user that the* `XMLHttpRequest` *failed*

However, if all went well with the request, the `retrieved()` method takes over:

`simpleXHR.js` *(continued)*

```
retrieved : function( requester ) {
  var data = requester.responseText;
  data = data.replace( /\n/g, '<br />' );
  simplexhr.outputContainer.innerHTML = data;
  return false;
  }
}
```

This method enables you to obtain and use the data sent back from the `XMLHttpRequest`. The data can be read out in two different formats: `responseText` and `responseXML`, the difference between these being the type of output—`responseText` returns a string, and `responseXML` will return an XML object. You can use all the usual string properties and methods on `responseText` (`length`, `indexOf()`, `replace()`, etc.), and all the DOM methods on `responseXML` (`getElementsByTagName()`, `getAttribute()`, and so on).

In this example, you merely retrieve text and use the `String.replace()` method to convert all line breaks, `\n`, into `BR` elements. Then you can write out the changed string as `innerHTML` to the `outputContainer` and return `false` to stop the normal link behavior.

In many cases, it is sufficient to use `responseText` and write out data via `innerHTML`. It is also a lot quicker and less work for the user's browser and CPU than using XML and DOM to convert the objects back into HTML.

■Note The Ajax acronym doesn't really work for these examples, as the process lacks the XML component. For this reason, this approach is known as AHAH and is defined as a **microformat** with code examples at http://microformats.org/wiki/rest/ahah.

Et Tu, Cache?

Normally the browser cache is our friend. The browser stores downloaded files in it, which means the user doesn't have to download our scripts over and over again. However, in the case of Ajax, caching can cause problems.

Safari is the main offender, as it caches the response status and does not trigger the changes (remember that the status returns the HTTP code 200, 304, or 404) any longer. However, avoiding issues with caching is pretty simple: before calling the send() method, add another header to the request. This header tells the browser to test whether the data has changed since a certain date. Which date you set doesn't matter, as long as it is in the past, for example, at the time of this writing:

```
request.setRequestHeader( 'If-Modified-Since', 'Thu, 06 Apr 2006➥
00:00:00 GMT' );
request.send( null );
```

Putting the X Back into Ajax

If you use responseXML, you can use DOM methods to turn the received XML into HTML. The demo exampleXMLxhr.html does this. As a data source, take the album collection used in the pagination example in the last chapter in XML format:

albums.xml *(excerpt)*

```
<?xml version="1.0" encoding="utf-8"?>
<albums>
  <album>
    <id>1</id>
    <artist>Depeche Mode</artist>
    <title>Playing the Angel</title>
    <comment>They are back and finally up to speed again</comment>
  </album>
  <album>
    <id>2</id>
    <artist>Monty Python</artist>
    <title>The final Rip-Off</title>
    <comment>Double CD with all the songs</comment>
  </album>
  [... more albums snipped ...]
</albums>
```

You want to retrieve this data via XHR and display it as a table in the page. Figure 8-5 shows the different stages of the request.

Figure 8-5. *Retrieving and showing XML data as a table*

The main part of the script does not have to change:

simpleXMLxhr.js

```
simplexhr = {
  doxhr : function( container, url ) {
    if( !document.getElementById || !document.createTextNode ){
      return;
    }
    simplexhr.outputContainer = document.getElementById( container );
    if( !simplexhr.outputContainer ) { return; }
    var request;
    try {
      request = new XMLHttpRequest();
    } catch( error ) {
      try {
        request = new ActiveXObject( "Microsoft.XMLHTTP" );
      } catch ( error ) {
        return true;
      }
    }
    request.open( 'get', url,true );
```

```
  request.onreadystatechange = function() {
    if(request.readyState == 1) {
      simplexhr.outputContainer.innerHTML = 'loading...';
    }
    if(request.readyState == 4) {
      if( request.status && /200|304/.test( request.status ) ) {
        simplexhr.retrieved( request );
      } else {
        simplexhr.failed( request );
      }
    }
  }
  request.setRequestHeader( 'If-Modified-Since',➥
  'Wed, 05 Apr 2006 00:00:00 GMT' );
  request.send( null );
  return false;
},
```

The difference is in the retrieved() method that reads the data via responseXML and writes out a data table using the XML as the source of content. Remove the loading message and use the DOM createElement() and createTextNode() methods to create the main table:

simpleXMLxhr.js *(continued)*

```
retrieved : function( requester ) {
  var data = requester.responseXML;
  simplexhr.outputContainer.removeChild(➥
  simplexhr.outputContainer.firstChild );
  var i, albumId, artist, albumTitle, comment, td, tr, th;
  var table = document.createElement( 'table' );
  var tablehead = document.createElement( 'thead' );
  table.appendChild( tablehead );
  tr = document.createElement( 'tr' );
  th = document.createElement( 'th' );
  th.appendChild( document.createTextNode( 'ID' ) );
  tr.appendChild( th );
  th=document.createElement( 'th' );
  th.appendChild( document.createTextNode( 'Artist' ) );
  tr.appendChild( th );
  th = document.createElement( 'th' );
  th.appendChild( document.createTextNode( 'Title' ) );
  tr.appendChild( th );
  th=document.createElement( 'th' );
  th.appendChild( document.createTextNode( 'Comment' ) );
  tr.appendChild( th );
  tablehead.appendChild( tr );
  var tablebody = document.createElement( 'tbody' );
  table.appendChild( tablebody );
```

Notice that when you create tables on the fly, MSIE will not display them unless you nest the rows and cells in a TBODY element. Firefox won't mind.

Next, loop over all the album elements of the data that was retrieved.

simpleXMLxhr.js *(continued)*

```
var albums = data.getElementsByTagName( 'album' );

for( i = 0 ; i < albums.length; i++ ) {
```

For each album, you read the contents of the XML nodes by their tag name and retrieve their text content via firstChild.nodeValue.

simpleXMLxhr.js *(continued)*

```
tr = document.createElement( 'tr' );
albumId = data.getElementsByTagName( 'id' )[i].➡
firstChild.nodeValue;
artist = data.getElementsByTagName('artist')[i].➡
firstChild.nodeValue;
albumTitle = data.getElementsByTagName('title')[i].➡
firstChild.nodeValue;
comment = data.getElementsByTagName('comment')[i].➡
firstChild.nodeValue;
```

You use this information to add the data cells to the table via createElement(), createTextNode(), and appendChild().

simpleXMLxhr.js *(continued)*

```
td = document.createElement( 'th' );
td.appendChild( document.createTextNode( albumId ) );
tr.appendChild( td );
td = document.createElement( 'td' );
td.appendChild( document.createTextNode( artist ) );
tr.appendChild( td );
td = document.createElement( 'td' );
td.appendChild( document.createTextNode( albumTitle ) );
tr.appendChild( td );
td = document.createElement( 'td' );
td.appendChild( document.createTextNode( comment ) );
tr.appendChild( td );
tablebody.appendChild( tr );
}
```

Add the resulting table as a new child element to the output container, and return `false` to stop the link from loading the XML as a new document. The `failed()` method stays the same.

`simpleXMLxhr.js` *(continued)*

```
      simplexhr.outputContainer.appendChild( table );
      return false;
    },
    failed : function( requester ) {
      alert( 'The XMLHttpRequest failed. Status: ' + requester.status );
      return true;
    }
}
```

You can see that by doing the "right thing" in terms of DOM scripting, scripts can get rather convoluted. You could cut down the amount of code by using tool methods to create the table rows, but that would mean even more processing, as the methods would have to be called from within a loop.

If you know the XML structure like you do in this example, it is probably a lot faster and easier to use `innerHTML` and string methods to convert the data. The demo `exampleXHRxmlCheat.html` does exactly that. Most of the script stays the same, but the `retrieved()` method is a lot shorter:

`simpleXMLxhrCheat.js` *(excerpt)*

```
  retrieved : function( requester ){
    var data = requester.responseText;
    simplexhr.outputContainer.removeChild(➥
    simplexhr.outputContainer.firstChild);
    var headrow = '<tr><th>ID</th><th>Artist</th><th>➥
    Title</th><th>Comment</th></tr>';
    data = data.replace( /<\?.*\?>/g, '' )
    data = data.replace( /<(\/*)id>/g, '<$1th>' )
    data = data.replace( /<(\/*)(artist|title|comment)>/g, '<$1td>' )
    data = data.replace( /<(\/*)albums>/g, '<$1table>' )
    data = data.replace( /<(\/*)album>/g, '<$1tr>' );
    data = data.replace( /<table>/g, '<table>' + headrow );
    simplexhr.outputContainer.innerHTML = data;
    return false;
  },
```

You retrieve the data as `responseText`, remove the "loading…" message, and then create a header table row as a string and store it in the variable `headrow`. Since `responseText` is a string, you can use the `String.replace()` method to change the XML elements.

Start by removing the XML prologue by deleting anything beginning with `<?` and ending with `?>`.

■**Note** This example uses regular expressions, which you may not know yet, but which we will talk about in more detail in the next chapter. It suffices to say that regular expressions are delimited with slashes and match a certain pattern of text. If there are parentheses inside the slashes, these strings will be stored in variables starting with $; these can be used in the replacement string to stand in for the substrings that match the pattern. For example, the regular expression pattern /<(\/*)id>/g matches everything that starts with a <, followed by an optional / (which is stored as $1 if it is found), followed by the string id and the closing > character. The second parameter, <$1th>, writes out either <th> or </th>, depending on the original id tag being the opening or closing tag. Rather than use regular expressions, you could perform simple string replacement instead:

```
data = data.replace('<id>', '<th>');
data = data.replace('</id>', '</th>');
```

Replace the other elements according to this scheme: every albums element becomes a table, every album a tr, every id a th; artist, title, and comment become a td each. Append the headrow string to <table> and store the end result in the outputContainer element using innerHTML.

Replacing XML with JSON

While XML is the undisputed champion of data transfer formats—it is text based and you can ensure validity and systems being able to talk to each other via DTDs, XML Schemata, or RELAX NG—Ajax fans have become more and more aware that it can be quite a drag to convert XML to JavaScript objects.

Instead of reading an XML file as XML and parsing it via the DOM or reading it as text and using regular expressions, it would be a lot easier and less straining to the system to have the data in a format that JavaScript can use directly. This format is called **JSON** (http://json.org/) and is basically a dataset in object literal notation. The demo exampleJSONxhr.html uses the XML of the earlier example as JSON:

```
<albums>
  <album>
    <id>1</id>
    <artist>Depeche Mode</artist>
    <title>Playing the Angel</title>
    <comment>They are back and finally up to speed again</comment>
  </album>
  <album>
    <id>2</id>
    <artist>Monty Python</artist>
    <title>The final Rip-Off</title>
    <comment>Double CD with all the songs</comment>
  </album>
  <album>
    <id>3</id>
```

```
    <artist>Ms Kittin</artist>
    <title>I.com</title>
    <comment>Good electronica</comment>
  </album>
</albums>
```

Converted to JSON, this is as follows:

albums.json

```
{
  'album':
  [
    {
      'id' : '1',
      'artist' : 'Depeche Mode',
      'title' : 'Playing the Angel',
      'comment' : 'They are back and finally up to speed again'
    },
    {
      'id' : '2',
      'artist' : 'Monty Python',
      'title' : 'The final Rip-Off',
      'comment' : 'Double CD wiid all the songs'
    },
    {
      'id' : '3',
      'artist' : 'Ms Kittin',
      'title' : 'I.com',
      'comment' : 'Good electronica'
    }
  ]
}
```

The benefit is that the data is already in a format that JavaScript can understand, and all you need to do to convert it to objects to display is to use the eval method on the string:

exampleJSONxhr.js *(excerpt)*

```
  retrieved : function( requester ) {
    simplexhr.outputContainer.removeChild(➥
    simplexhr.outputContainer.firstChild);
    var content = '<table><thead>';
    content += '<tr><th>ID</th><th>Artist</th>';
    content += '<th>Title</th><th>Comment</th>';
    content += '</tr></thead><tbody>';
    var data = eval( '(' + requester.responseText + ')' );
```

This will give you all the content as objects that you can access via either property notation or associative array notation (the latter is shown in the id example, the former in all the others):

exampleJSONxhr.js *(excerpt)*

```
var albums = data.album;
for( var i = 0; i < albums.length; i++ ) {
  content += '<tr><td>' + albums[i]['id'] + '</td>';
  content += '<td>' + albums[i].artist + '</td>';
  content += '<td>' + albums[i].title + '</td>';
  content += '<td>' + albums[i].comment + '</td></tr>';
}
Content += '</tbody></table>';
simplexhr.outputContainer.innerHTML = content;
return false;
},
```

For files on your own server, using JSON instead of XML is a lot quicker (in tests it proved up to ten times faster); however, using eval() can be dangerous if you use JSON from a third-party server, as it executes any JavaScript code and not only JSON data.

You can avoid this danger by using a parser that makes sure that only data gets converted into objects and malicious code does not get executed. An open-source version is available at http://www.json.org/js.html. We'll come back to JSON in Chapter 11.

Using Server-Side Scripts to Reach Third-Party Content

As mentioned earlier, it is impossible for security reasons to use XHR to load content from other servers. If you want to retrieve for example RSS feeds from other servers, you need to use a server-side script that loads them for you.

Note This is a common myth about Ajax: it does not replace server-side code but is backed up by it and offers a slicker interface to it. XHR in itself can only retrieve data from the same server or send information to server-side scripts. You couldn't, for example, access a database in JavaScript—unless the database provider offers an output as JavaScript, and you include it in its own script tag.

The server-side component is a pass-through or proxy script that takes a URL, loads the content of the document, and sends it back to the XHR. The script needs to set the right header to tell the XHR that the data it returns is XML. If the file cannot be found, the script returns an XML error string instead. The following example uses PHP, but any server-side language can perform the same task:

loadrss.php

```php
<?php
// Set the XML header
header('Content-type: text/xml');
// Define an error message in case the feed cannot be found
$error='<?xml version="1.0"?><error>Cannot find feed</error>';
// Clear the contents
$contents = '';
// Read the url variable from the GET request
$rssurl = $_GET['url'];
// Test if the url starts with http to prevent surfers
// from calling and displaying local files
if( preg_match( '/^http:/', $rssurl ) ) {
  // Open the remove file, and store it contents
  $handle = @fopen( $rssurl, "rb" );
    if( $handle == true ){
      while ( !feof($handle ) ) {
        $contents .= fread( $handle, 8192 );
      }
      fclose( $handle );
    }
}
// If the file has no channel element, delete contents
if( !preg_match( '/<channel/', $contents ) ){ $contents = ''; }
// Return either the contents or the error
echo $contents == '' ? $error : $contents;
?>
```

The demo `exampleExternalRSS.html` uses this script to retrieve the latest headlines in RSS format from the Yahoo web site.

The relevant part in the HTML is the link that calls the doxhr() method with the element to output the news in and the RSS URI as parameters:

exampleExternalRSS.html *(excerpt)*

```
<p>
  <a href="http://rss.news.yahoo.com/rss/topstories"
     onclick="return readrss.doxhr('newsContainer',this.href)">
     Get Yahoo news
  </a>
</p>
<div id="newsContainer"></div>
```

■**Note** RSS is an acronym for Really Simple Syndication, and it is in essence XML with content in it that you want to share with the world—typically news headlines. The specifications for RSS are available at http://blogs.law.harvard.edu/tech/rss, and you can read more about its benefits at Wikipedia: http://en.wikipedia.org/wiki/RSS_%28file_format%29.

The important detail in this example is that RSS is a standardized format, and you know the XML structure—even if you get it from a third-party web site. Every valid RSS document contains—among many other things—an items element with nested item elements. Each of these contains at least a title describing and a link pointing to the full piece of information. You can use these to show a list of clickable headlines that send the user to the Yahoo site where she can read the full news article as shown in Figure 8-6.

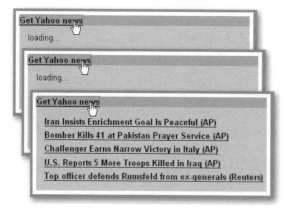

Figure 8-6. *Retrieving and showing RSS feed data*

The script is once again a simple XHR. The difference is that instead of linking to the URL directly, you pass it to the PHP script as a GET parameter:

externalRSS.js

```
readrss = {
  doxhr:function( container, url ) {
    [... code snipped as it is the same as in the last example ...]
    request.open('get', 'loadrss.php?url=' + encodeURI( url ) );
    request.setRequestHeader( 'If-Modified-Since',➥
    'Wed, 05 Apr 2006 00:00:00 GMT' );
    request.send( null );
    return false;
  },
```

The retrieved() function needs to change. First, it deletes the "loading..." message from the output container and retrieves the data in XML format using responseXML. Since the PHP script returns an error message in XML format, you need to test whether the returned XML contains an error element. If this is the case, read the node value of the first child of the first error element and write it to the outputContainer surrounded by a paragraph tag.

externalRSS.js *(continued)*

```
  retrieved : function( requester ) {
    readrss.outputContainer.innerHTML = '';
    var data = requester.responseXML;
    if( data.getElementsByTagName( 'error' ).length > 0 ) {
      var error = data.getElementsByTagName('error')[0].➥
      firstChild.nodeValue;
      readrss.outputContainer.innerHTML = '<p>' + error + '</p>';
```

If there is no error element, retrieve all the item elements contained in the returned XML and check the length of the resulting list. If there is less than one item, return from the method, and allow the link to load the XML document in the browser. This is a necessary step to ensure that the RSS returned was valid—as you didn't check this in the server-side script.

externalRSS.js *(continued)*

```
  } else {
    var items = data.getElementsByTagName( 'item' );
    var end = items.length;
    if( end < 1 ){ return; }
```

If there are items to be displayed, you define the necessary variables and loop through them. As some RSS feeds have lots of entries, it makes sense to constrain how many you display; in this case, you choose 5. You read the `link` and the `title` for each `item` and add a new list item with an embedded link with this information as its `href` attribute and text content, respectively. Notice that this example simply assembles a string of HTML; you could, of course, go the "cleaner" way and create elements and apply text nodes.

externalRSS.js *(continued)*

```
var item, feedlink, name, description, content = '';
for( var i = 0; i < 5; i++ ) {
  feedlink = items[i].getElementsByTagName('link').item(0).➡
   firstChild.nodeValue;
  name = items[i].getElementsByTagName('title').item(0).➡
  firstChild.nodeValue;
  item = '<li><a href="' + feedlink+'">' + name + '</a></li>';
  content += item;
}
```

Insert the final content string inside a UL tag within the outputContainer, and you have clickable headlines with fresh Yahoo news.

externalRSS.js *(continued)*

```
readrss.outputContainer.innerHTML = '<ul>' + content + '</ul>';
    return false;
}
```

The rest of the script remains unchanged; the failed() method only displays an alert when the XHR doesn't succeed.

externalRSS.js *(continued)*

```
},
failed : function( requester ) {
  alert( 'The XMLHttpRequest failed. Status: ' + requester.status );
  return true;
}
}
```

XHR on Slow Connections

One problem that might occur is that the connection of an XHR can take a long time, and the user sees a loading message with nothing happening at all. You can avoid this issue by using window.timeout() to stop the execution after a certain amount of time. The demo exampleXHRtimeout.html shows an example using this technique.

The default setting for the request is 10 milliseconds, which will cause the timeout as shown in Figure 8-7. You can use the second link in the example to set the timeout to

10 seconds and try again, and—pending your connection not being dead slow or Yahoo being down—you will get the headlines.

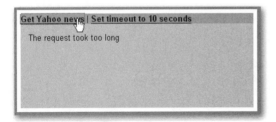

Figure 8-7. *Allowing an* XHR *connection to time out*

The differences in the script are that you need a property to define how long to wait before a timeout is triggered, one to store the window.timeout, and a Boolean property that defines whether there was a timeout or not. The latter has to be inside the doxhr() method, as it needs to get initialized every time doxhr() is called.

XHRtimeout.js

```
readrss = {
  timeOutDuration : 10,
  toolong : false,
  doxhr : function( container, url ) {
    readrss.timedout = false;
    if( !document.getElementById || !document.createTextNode ){
      return;
    }
    readrss.outputContainer = document.getElementById( container );
    if( !readrss.outputContainer ){ return; }
    var request;
    try {
      request = new XMLHttpRequest();
    } catch( error ) {
      try {
        request = new ActiveXObject( "Microsoft.XMLHTTP" );
      } catch( error ) {
        return true;
      }
    }
  }
```

In the onreadystatechange event listener, you add the timeout and assign it to the toolong property of the main object. Inside the timeout you define an anonymous function that checks the readyState and compares it with 1. This is the scenario when the defined time has passed, and the request is still on the first stage rather than the fourth and final one. When this happens, call the abort() method of the request, set the timedout property to true, and write out a message to the display element that the request took too long.

XHRtimeout.js *(continued)*

```
request.onreadystatechange = function() {
  if( request.readyState == 1) {
      readrss.toolong = window.setTimeout( function(){
        if( request.readyState == 1 ) {
          readrss.timedout = true;
          request.abort(); // Stop, Hammer Time!
          readrss.outputContainer.innerHTML = 'The request➥
          took too long';
         }
        },
       readrss.timeOutDuration
      );
     readrss.outputContainer.innerHTML = 'loading...';
  }
```

When the request has successfully ended and there wasn't any timeout (which is stored in the timedout property), you clear the timeout.

XHRtimeout.js *(continued)*

```
    if( request.readyState == 4 && !readrss.timedout ) {
    window.clearTimeout( readrss.toolong );
    if( /200|304/.test( request.status ) ) {
        readrss.retrieved( request );
      } else {
        readrss.failed( request );
      }
    }
  }
  request.open( 'get', 'loadrss.php?url='+encodeURI( url ) );
  request.setRequestHeader( 'If-Modified-Since',➥
  'Wed, 05 Apr 2006 00:00:00 GMT' );
  request.send( null );
  return false;
},
```

The rest of the script stays the same.

A Larger Ajax Example: Connected Select Boxes

Let's take a look at a larger Ajax example—I call it that although you won't be using XML. Connected select boxes are a classic example of what JavaScript can do for you to make an interface faster. One common use for them is the flight offer web site, where you choose one airport in a select box and the page immediately shows you the destination airports that are available from this airport in a second select box. Traditionally, this is achieved by keeping all the airport connection data in JavaScript arrays and manipulating the options arrays of the select elements. Changing the first airport select box would automatically change the second one to the available destinations.

This is very nice when you have a mouse and you have JavaScript available; however, it can be pretty frustrating when one of the two is missing, or even impossible when neither is available. This example will show how you can create interdependent select boxes that work without a mouse and JavaScript, and will not reload the whole page when JavaScript is available.

The trick is to make the functionality work on the server side and then add the JavaScript and XHR tricks to stop the whole page from reloading. As you don't know whether the user really can cope with this, you can even make it optional instead of a given.

■**Note** This approach to Ajax is more accessibility aware than the original one. The reason is that you don't want to make the biggest DHTML mistake once again—using a technology without considering those who cannot deal with it. Jeremy Keith coined this approach **HIJAX** in his DOM scripting book, but it hasn't gotten as much public awareness as the Ajax term has by now. Ajax is hot, and it is tough to put a slight dent into people's expectations by pointing out that you cannot rely on it being possible for all users.

The first step is to create a server-side script that does all the functionality. As this is not a book about PHP, we won't get into too much detail here. Suffice to say that the main document exampleSelectBoxes.php includes a smaller PHP script, selectBoxes.php. The latter contains all the airport data as arrays (but could as easily go to a database to retrieve them) and writes out the different states of the interface depending on the user selecting a choice and sending the form as shown in Figure 8-8.

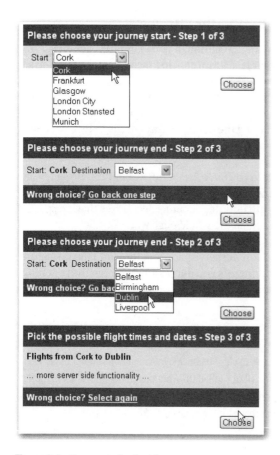

Figure 8-8. *Connected select boxes*

The main page features the form with a DIV with an id you can use for the XHR output:

exampleSelectBoxes.php *(excerpt)*

```
<form action="exampleSelectBoxes.php" method="post">
  <div id="formOutput">
   <?php include('selectBoxes.php');?>
  </div>
  <p class="submit"><input type="submit" name="select"
  id="select" value="Choose" /></p>
</form>
```

■Note Notice that this example uses POST as the method to send the data. This will make your XHR code a bit harder, but it is a good idea to try this, as most web applications will work with POST instead of GET.

The PHP script will return an HTML interface you can hook into at each stage of the process:

- If there hasn't been any form data sent yet, it displays one select box with the ID `airport` listing all the airports in the dataset.

- If there was an airport chosen and sent to the server, the script displays the chosen airport inside a strong element and as a hidden form field. It also displays the possible destination airports for this choice as a select box with the ID `destination`. Furthermore, it creates a link pointing back to the main document to start a new selection with the ID `back`.

- If the user chooses an airport and a destination and sent them back to the server, the script just hints at more functionality, as you don't need more for this example. However, it offers the link back to the initial page.

If JavaScript is available, the script should do the following:

- Create a new check box in the form that allows to user to turn on Ajax functionality—in this case only reloading the section of the form that is created by `selectBoxes.php`.

- If that check box has been selected, the script should override the normal submit process of the form with a function called by an event handler. As a loading indicator, it should change the text of the Submit button to "loading".

- It should also add a search parameter to the link back to the first stage to ensure that when the user hits that link, he won't have to select the check box again.

Let's start with the skeleton of the script. You need a label for the check box, a class for the paragraph containing it (not really necessary, but it allows for styling), and the IDs of the form elements container and the link back to the start of the process.

As methods, you need an `init()` method, the main XHR method with the retrieval and failure handlers, and `cancelClick()` and `addEvent()` for event handling.

`selectBoxes.js` *(skeleton)*

```
dynSelect = {
  AJAXlabel : 'Reload only the results, not the whole page',
  AJAXofferClass : 'ajax',
  containerID : 'formOutput',
  backlinkID : 'back',
  init : function(){},
  doxhr : function( e ){},
  retrieved : function( requester, e ){},
  failed : function( requester ){},
  cancelClick : function( e ){},
  addEvent : function(elm, evType, fn, useCapture ){}
}
dynSelect.addEvent( window, 'load', dynSelect.init, false );
```

Now start to flesh out the skeleton:

selectBoxes.js

```
dynSelect = {
  AJAXlabel : 'Only reload the results, not the whole page',
  AJAXofferClass : 'ajax',
  containerID : 'formOutput',
  backlinkID : 'back',
```

The init() method tests whether the W3C DOM is supported, retrieves the first form, and stores the Submit button with the ID select in a property—this is necessary to remove the button on the last step. It then creates a new paragraph and applies the class for the Ajax trigger defined earlier.

selectBoxes.js *(continued)*

```
  init : function(){
    if( !document.getElementById || !document.createTextNode ){
     return;
    }
    var f = document.getElementsByTagName( 'form' )[0];
    dynSelect.selectButton = document.getElementById( 'select' );
    var p = document.createElement( 'p' );
    p.className = dynSelect.AJAXofferClass;
```

Next on the agenda is the check box to offer the option to turn on Ajax. Set the name and ID of the check box to xhr and determine whether the current URI already has the ?ajax search string. If it has, preset the check box to already selected (this is necessary to ensure that the link back to the first step does not stop the Ajax enhancements from working).

selectBoxes.js *(continued)*

```
    dynSelect.cb = document.createElement( 'input' );
    dynSelect.cb.setAttribute( 'type', 'checkbox' );
    dynSelect.cb.setAttribute( 'name', 'xhr' );
    dynSelect.cb.setAttribute( 'id', 'xhr' );
    if( window.location.search != '' ) {
      dynSelect.cb.setAttribute( 'defaultChecked', 'checked' );
      dynSelect.cb.setAttribute( 'checked', 'checked' );
    }
```

Add the check box to the new paragraph, and a label with the appropriate text following it. The new paragraph becomes the first child node of the form, and you apply an event handler that triggers the dohxhr() method when the form is submitted.

selectBoxes.js *(continued)*

```
    p.appendChild( dynSelect.cb );
    var lbl = document.createElement( 'label' );
    lbl.htmlFor = 'xhr';
    lbl.appendChild( document.createTextNode( dynSelect.AJAXlabel ) );
    p.appendChild( lbl );
    f.insertBefore( p, f.firstChild );
    dynSelect.addEvent(f, 'submit', dynSelect.doxhr, false );
  },
```

The dohxr() method tests whether the check box has been ticked and simply returns when it isn't. If it is, you define two variables for the current airport and the current destination and store the output element in a property. You test whether the output container exists and return if it doesn't.

selectBoxes.js *(continued)*

```
  doxhr : function( e ) {
    if( !dynSelect.cb.checked ){ return; }
    var airportValue, destinationValue;
    dynSelect.outputContainer = document.getElementById(➥
    dynSelect.containerID );
    if( !dynSelect.outputContainer ){ return; }
```

Here is the XHR code, defining the correct object and setting the onreadystage event listener.

selectBoxes.js *(continued)*

```
    var request;
    try {
      request = new XMLHttpRequest();
    } catch( error ) {
      Try {
        request = new ActiveXObject( "Microsoft.XMLHTTP" );
      } catch( error ) {
        return true;
      }
    }
    request.onreadystatechange = function() {
      if( request.readyState == 1 ) {
        dynSelect.selectButton.value = 'loading...';
      }
```

```
   if( request.readyState == 4 ) {
     if( request.status && /200|304/.test( request.status ) ) {
       dynSelect.retrieved( request );
     } else{
       dynSelect.failed( request );
     }
   }
 }
}
```

Determine whether the document contains the airport and destination select boxes; if so, store their current states in the variables `airportValue` and `destinationValue`. Notice that you need to check the type of the airport field in the second stage of the flight selection process, since it is a hidden field.

selectBoxes.js *(continued)*

```
var airport = document.getElementById( 'airport' );
if( airport != undefined ) {
  if( airport.nodeName.toLowerCase() == 'select' ) {
    airportValue = airport.options[airport.selectedIndex].value;
  } else {
    airportValue = airport.value;
  }
}
var destination = document.getElementById( 'destination' );
if( destination ) {
  destinationValue = destination.options➡
  [destination.selectedIndex].value;
}
```

Since the form is sent using POST and not GET, you need to define the request a bit differently. First of all, you need to assemble the request parameters as a string (this is the trail of variables on the URI when the send method is GET, e.g., http://www.example.com/index.php?search=DOM&values=20&start=10).

selectBoxes.js *(continued)*

```
var parameters = 'airport=' + airportValue;
if( destinationValue != undefined ) {
  parameters += '&destination=' + destinationValue;
}
```

Next, open the request. In addition to the modified header to prevent caching, you also need to tell the server that the content type is `application/x-www-form-urlencoded`; then you transmit the length of all the request parameters as the value to accompany `Content-length`. You also need to tell the server to close the connection once it has finished retrieving all the data. Unlike `GET` requests, `send()` needs a parameter when you `POST`, which is the URI-encoded parameters.

`selectBoxes.js` *(continued)*

```
request.open( 'POST', 'selectBoxes.php' );
request.setRequestHeader( 'If-Modified-Since',➡
'Wed, 05 Apr 2006 00:00:00 GMT' );
request.setRequestHeader( 'Content-type',➡
'application/x-www-form-urlencoded' );
request.setRequestHeader( 'Content-length', parameters.length );
request.setRequestHeader( 'Connection', 'close' );
request.send( encodeURI( parameters ) );
```

■**Note** Don't beat yourself up if you don't know all that is going on here; it is after all server and HTTP code, and you are just starting with JavaScript. Chances are you will never really have to grasp what all that means, as long as you use it this way.

If you are on the page before the last one and both an airport and a destination are available, remove the Submit button to prevent errors.

■**Note** This is a cosmetic step for this example. A real application should work through the following steps, too, but you don't need to go that far now.

Finally, invoke `cancelClick()` to prevent normal form submission.

`selectBoxes.js` *(continued)*

```
if( airport && destination ) {
  var sendButton = document.getElementById( 'select' );
  sendButton.parentNode.removeChild( sendButton );
}
dynSelect.cancelClick( e );
},
```

The `retrieved()` method doesn't differ much from the other examples. Undo what you have done in the previous step by changing the Submit button's value back to `Select` before retrieving the `responseText` of the request and replacing the old form elements with the new ones. Add `?ajax` to the `href` of the link pointing back to the first step to make sure that activating this link will not turn off the previously selected functionality (by now you know the user wants the Ajax interface).

`selectBoxes.js` *(continued)*

```
retrieved : function( requester, e ) {
  dynSelect.selectButton.value = 'Select';
  var content = requester.responseText;
  dynSelect.outputContainer.innerHTML = content;
  var backlink = document.getElementById( dynSelect.backlinkID );
  if( backlink ) {
    var url = backlink.getAttribute( 'href' );
    backlink.setAttribute( 'href', url+'?ajax' );
  }
  dynSelect.cancelClick( e );
},
```

The rest of the script consists of the familiar `failed()`, `cancelClick()`, and `addEvent()` utility methods.

`selectBoxes.js` *(continued)*

```
failed : function( requester ){
  alert('The XMLHttpRequest failed. Status: ' + requester.status);
  return true;
},
cancelClick : function( e ){
  [... code snipped ...]
},
addEvent: function( elm, evType, fn, useCapture ){
  [... code snipped ...]
}
}
dynSelect.addEvent( window, 'load', dynSelect.init, false );
```

This example shows that Ajax is very dependent on server code. If you know what you will get back, then it is easy to create a useful and attractive interface.

You can also use the Ajax approach in an unobtrusive and optional manner to make older effects more eye-catching and targeted better to those who want them. In the previous chapter, you developed a dynamic navigation that collapsed and expanded nested links, and I promised you that we'd come back to that example, which we do in the following section.

Optional Dynamic Ajax Menus

One of the problems dynamic navigation has is that you may offer the user too many choices. It is pretty tempting to consider a menu easy to use when you can see it collapsed, and you can collapse and expand sections to navigate through it, but it is a different story when you turn off JavaScript and CSS and you see all the links at once. Now also consider the kind of visitors who listen to your web site because they cannot see, or those who need to zoom only a part of the screen to navigate around the page.

Wouldn't it be much more useful to give visitors the choice to enable an enhanced dynamic menu and give only the minimum necessary menu structure to those who choose otherwise?

Recall the menu structure you used in the previous chapter:

navigation.php

```
<ul id="nav">
  <li><a href="index.php">Home</a></li>
  <li><a href="products.php">Products</a>
    <ul>
      <li><a href="cms.php">CMS solutions</a>
        <ul>
          <li><a href="minicms.php">Mini CMS</a></li>
          <li><a href="ncc1701d.php">Enterprise CMS</a></li>
        </ul>
      </li>
      <li><a href="portal.php">Company Portal</a></li>
      <li><a href="mailserver.php">eMail Solutions</a>
        <ul>
          <li><a href="privatemail.php">Private POP3/SMTP</a></li>
          <li><a href="lists.php">Listservers</a></li>
        </ul>
      </li>
    </ul>
  </li>
  <li><a href="services.php">Services</a>
```

```
  <ul>
    <li><a href="training.php">Employee Training</a></li>
    <li><a href="audits.php">Auditing</a></li>
    <li><a href="bulkmail.php">Bulk sending/email campaigns</a></li>
  </ul>
</li>
<li><a href="pricing.php">Pricing</a></li>
<li><a href="about_us.php">About Us</a>
  <ul>
    <li><a href="our_offices.php">Our offices</a></li>
    <li><a href="our_people.php">Our people</a></li>
    <li><a href="vacancies.php">Jobs</a></li>
    <li><a href="partners.php">Industry Partners</a></li>
  </ul>
</li>
<li><a href="contact.php">Contact Us</a>
  <ul>
    <li><a href="snail.php">Postal Addresses</a></li>
    <li><a href="callback.php">Arrange Callback</a></li>
  </ul>
</li>
</ul>
```

I've already said that displaying the menu item corresponding to the current page as a STRONG element is a very good idea. Let's take that idea further and strip down the menu to what is actually necessary. What this means is that you'll remove all the nested elements from menu items other than the current one (or its parent). For example, on the company portal page this would be as follows:

```
<ul id="nav">
  <li><a href="index.php">Home</a></li>
  <li><a href="products.php">Products</a>
    <ul>
      <li><a href="cms.php">CMS solutions</a></li>
      <li><strong>Company Portal</strong></li>
      <li><a href="mailserver.php">eMail Solutions</a></li>
    </ul>
  </li>
  <li><a href="services.php">Services</a></li>
  <li><a href="pricing.php">Pricing</a></li>
  <li><a href="about_us.php">About Us</a></li>
  <li><a href="contact.php">Contact Us</a></li>
</ul>
```

For a top-level item like that corresponding to the products page, the code will be even less:

```
<ul id="nav">
  <li><a href=".index.php">Home</a></li>
  <li><strong>Products</strong></li>
  <li><a href="services.php">Services</a></li>
  <li><a href="pricing.php">Pricing</a></li>
  <li><a href="about_us.php">About Us</a></li>
  <li><a href="contact.php">Contact Us</a></li>
</ul>
```

You could easily do this in JavaScript by now; however, that would defeat the purpose of the exercise, as visitors without JavaScript would still get the full menu.

Instead, you'll use a server-side script in PHP that does this for you. On every page this script

- Loads the navigation template

- Checks through all the links and replaces the one that matches the current file name with a STRONG element (via regular expressions)

- Checks whether there is an ?ajax parameter sent via GET and if not removes all nested lists that are not inside an LI item that also contains a STRONG element

We will not go into the details of the script here, as this is not a PHP book; if you want to have a look, the script is called globals.php and is located in the navigation folder of the code download for this chapter.

Using this script, you can offer users a fully functional menu without any unnecessary links, as shown in Figure 8-9.

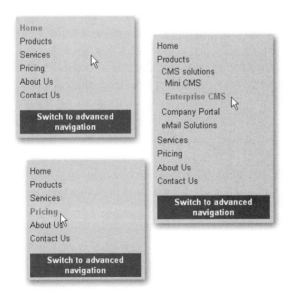

Figure 8-9. *The basic navigation without JavaScript*

You can now use JavaScript to offer the user a more advanced navigation menu that shows the complete site map and loads the content via XHR instead of reloading the whole page. To achieve this, you can reuse the dynamic navigation script developed in the previous chapter and add one line that triggers the collapsing and expanding functionality only when there is a search parameter called ajax in the URI for the current page:

siteNavigationIndicator.js *(changes)*

```
sn={
  init : function() {
    if( window.location.search.indexOf( 'ajax' ) == -1 ){ return; }
    [... code snipped ...]
  },
```

The main script will have to do the following:

- Add a new list item to the navigation with a link that allows the user to turn Ajax functionality on or off (select a basic or an enhanced navigation).

- If there is no ajax parameter in the URI, stop and let the back end create and change the navigation.

- Otherwise, attach event handlers on all the links in the navigation, loading the linked documents in an output container via XHR instead of reloading the page.

- Replace the old STRONG element with a link pointing to the right document and the XHR handler when another link is activated.

- Replace that other link with a STRONG element and expand and highlight the menu section in which the link is located.

■**Note** This means that you need to know which document the links replacing the STRONG elements should point to. You can do this by storing the file name (without the .php extension, since class names cannot contain full stops) in the class attribute of the STRONG. This is not the cleanest of options, but other than using invalid HTML with a made-up attribute, it is the only way. The PHP script provides you with that functionality on the highlighted menu item.

You start with a bunch of properties—the ID of the menu, the trigger as a blank property, and its ID and labels for both states. The trigger will become a list item in the menu that turns the Ajax functionality and the enhanced navigation on or off. Depending on the state, the different labels will be the link text. Furthermore, you define the ID of the output element and the message displayed when the XHR is loading the content.

XHRSiteNav.js

```
Xhrsitenav = {
  navID : 'nav',
  trigger : null,
  triggerID : 'AJAXtrigger',
  triggerLabel : 'Switch to advanced navigation',
  downLabel : 'Switch to basic navigation',
  output : 'content',
  loadingMessage : '<img src="../indicator_big.gif"➥
  alt="loading..." />',
```

The init() method needs to test for all the necessary elements, call createTrigger() to add the link to the menu, and not do anything else when there is no ajax search parameter in the current URL.

XHRSiteNav.js *(continued)*

```
init : function() {
  if( !document.getElementById || !document.createTextNode ) {
    return;
  }
  xhrsitenav.nav = document.getElementById( sn.navID );
  if( !xhrsitenav.nav ) { return; }
  xhrsitenav.outputContainer = document.getElementById(➥
  xhrsitenav.output );
  if( !xhrsitenav.outputContainer ){ return; }
  xhrsitenav.createTrigger();
  if( window.location.search.indexOf( 'ajax' ) == -1 ){ return; }
```

Loop through all the links but the last one and those links having only a hash mark (#) as the href attribute; assign a click event handler pointing to the xhr method for each one. Since the last link is the trigger, you need to skip the last one; the links having only # as their href attribute values are the ones added by the dynamic menu script.

XHRSiteNav.js *(continued)*

```
var navlinks = xhrsitenav.nav.getElementsByTagName( 'a' );
for( var i = 0; i < navlinks.length - 1; i++ ){
  if( navlinks[i].href == '#' ){ continue; }
  DOMhelp.addEvent( navlinks[i], 'click', xhrsitenav.xhr, false );
  navlinks[i].onclick = DOMhelp.safariClickFix;
}
```

You then take the link inside the trigger and remove anything after and including the question mark. This means that if the user clicks the link, it'll turn off both the Ajax and the dynamic menu functionality. You also change the link text to the label text for the basic navigation.

XHRSiteNav.js *(continued)*

```
var triggerlink = xhrsitenav.trigger.getElementsByTagName( a')[0];
triggerlink.href = triggerlink.href.replace( /\?.*/, '' );
triggerlink.innerHTML = xhrsitenav.downLabel;
},
```

The xhr() method needs to get the current link via getTarget() and ensure the event target is a link by comparing it with the right nodeName.

XHRSiteNav.js *(continued)*

```
xhr : function( e ){
  var t = DOMhelp.getTarget( e );
  while( t.nodeName.toLowerCase() != 'a' ) {
    t = t.parentNode;
  }
```

It uses parentNode to retrieve the list item the link resides in and checks whether the item contains a STRONG element. If there is a STRONG element, xhr() highlights the current section via the parameters defined in the dynamic menu script. It calls removeOldHighlight() to undo any other highlights and retrieve the url to load into the content container element.

XHRSiteNav.js *(continued)*

```
var parentLI = t.parentNode;
if( t.parentNode.getElementsByTagName('ul').length > 0 ) {
  var firstList = t.parentNode.getElementsByTagName( 'ul' )[0];
  DOMhelp.cssjs( 'add', firstList, sn.showClass )
  DOMhelp.cssjs( 'swap', parentLI, sn.openClass, sn.parentClass );
  parentLI.getElementsByTagName( 'a' )[0].innerHTML =➡
  sn.openIndicator;
}
var url = xhrsitenav.removeOldHighlight( t );
```

The remainder of xhr()and its helper methods, retrieved() and failed(), are unchanged from the other examples in this chapter.

XHRSiteNav.js *(continued)*

```
    var request;
    try {
      request = new XMLHttpRequest();
    } catch(error) {
      try {
        request = new ActiveXObject('Microsoft.XMLHTTP');
      } catch(error) {
        return true;
      }
    }
    request.open( 'get', url, true );
    request.onreadystatechange = function() {
      if( request.readyState == 1 ){
        xhrsitenav.outputContainer.innerHTML =➥
        xhrsitenav.loadingMessage;
      }
      if( request.readyState == 4 ) {
        if( request.status && /200|304/.test( request.status ) ) {
          xhrsitenav.retrieved( request );
        } else {
          xhrsitenav.failed( request );
        }
      }
    }
    request.setRequestHeader( 'If-Modified-Since', ➥
    'Wed, 05 Apr 2006 00:00:00 GMT');
    request.send( null );
    DOMhelp.cancelClick( e );
    return false;
  },
  retrieved : function( requester, e ) {
    var data = requester.responseText;
    xhrsitenav.outputContainer.innerHTML = data;
    DOMhelp.cancelClick( e );
    return false;
  },
  failed : function( requester ) {
    alert( 'The XMLHttpRequest failed. Status: ' + requester.status );
    return true;
  },
```

The createTrigger() method checks whether there is already a trigger defined and creates a new one if necessary. The trigger is the list item containing the link that allows the user to switch between the different navigation states. There shouldn't be any surprises in this method—it could have been part of the init() method, after all. It might be a good idea to keep functionality like this in own methods, should other scripts need to add the trigger once more.

XHRSiteNav.js *(continued)*

```
createTrigger : function() {
  if( !xhrsitenav.trigger ) {
    xhrsitenav.trigger = document.createElement( 'li' );
    xhrsitenav.trigger.id = xhrsitenav.triggerID;
    var loc = xhrsitenav.shorturl( window.location.href );
    var newlink = DOMhelp.createLink( loc + '?ajax=1',➡
    xhrsitenav.triggerLabel );
    xhrsitenav.trigger.appendChild( newlink );
    xhrsitenav.nav.appendChild( xhrsitenav.trigger );
  }
},
```

The removeOldHighlight() method is called by the xhr() method. It replaces the current STRONG element inside the navigation with a link and vice versa. For the STRONG element that gets replaced by a link, the method sets the href attribute to the STRONG element's class name suffixed with ".php" and attaches the event handler to call xhr() when the user clicks the link.

XHRSiteNav.js *(continued)*

```
removeOldHighlight : function( o ) {
  var highlight = xhrsitenav.nav.getElementsByTagName('strong')[0];
  var current = highlight.className + '.php';
  var newlink = document.createElement( 'a' );
  newlink.appendChild( document.createTextNode➡
  ( highlight.innerHTML ) );
  newlink.setAttribute( 'href', current );
  DOMhelp.addEvent( newlink, 'click', xhrsitenav.xhr, false );
  newlink.onclick = DOMhelp.safariClickFix;
  highlight.parentNode.replaceChild( newlink, highlight );
```

For the link retrieved as the parameter o, the method calls a helper method named shorturl() that cleans out excess data from the link's href (you only need the file name, not the whole path that href returns). It then creates a new STRONG element, removes the .php file extension, and stores the resulting string in the STRONG element's className property. It prefixes the url with the name of the directory where the content pages are stored, and returns the complete url to xhr() in order to load the correct content.

XHRSiteNav.js *(continued)*

```
    var shorturl = xhrsitenav.shorturl( o.getAttribute( 'href' ) );
    var st = document.createElement( 'strong' );
    st.className = shorturl.replace( '.php', '' );
    st.innerHTML = o.innerHTML;
    o.parentNode.replaceChild( st, o );
    var url = 'content/' + shorturl;
    return url;
  },
```

The shorturl() helper method removes anything before the last slash from the string it got as a parameter and returns the result.

XHRSiteNav.js *(continued)*

```
  shorturl : function( url ) {
    return url.replace( /.*\//g, '' );
  }
}
DOMhelp.addEvent(window, 'load', xhrsitenav.init, false );
```

If the user chooses the enhanced navigation, he'll get a tree menu that loads the content in the page without reloading the whole document as shown in Figure 8-10.

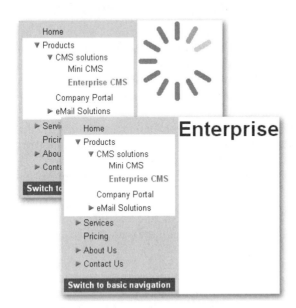

Figure 8-10. *The enhanced* XHR *navigation*

This is an example of how you can make high-end JavaScript functionality optional instead of hoping that visitors can deal with it. It is not a very common approach, as it adds an extra level of complexity to the interface; but depending on the audience of your product, it might give a good impression and also tells visitors that once they have chosen the advanced navigation, they cannot expect it to offer the same experience as a static one does—for example, Back button functionality and bookmarking.

Summary

I hope this has given you an insight into what can be done with JavaScript and `XMLHttpRequest` to create dynamic connections between the back end and the browser without reloading the page.

As cool as Ajax is, there are some things to keep in mind:

- Primarily, Ajax was invented as a methodology to develop web applications, and not web sites. It might be overkill to "Ajax-ify" every small form and menu.

- Ajax is a connector between client-side scripting and the back end; it is only as powerful as the back-end script or the information is.

- Ajax is confined to scripts and data sources on the same server as the script using it, unless you use a pass-through script on the server or you have a third-party service that offers data in JSON format, such as `http://del.icio.us` does.

- It is very tempting and easy to create an Ajax application that looks impressive but is very obtrusive—relying on the mouse and on JavaScript being available. Creating an Ajax interface that is accessible is a much harder task.

Ajax is currently "hot," and a lot of very gifted developers are working on frameworks and libraries that can help you to create Ajax applications quickly without having to know all the ins and outs of it—using them may even prevent you from repeating mistakes these developers have made themselves in the past. The number of libraries available is staggering, and it can be hard to tell which one is the right one for the task at hand.

Leland Scott has done an amazing job researching dozens of different Ajax libraries on the Web and comparing them in terms of cross-browser and cross-platform compatibility: `http://www.musingsfrommars.org/2006/03/ajax-dhtml-library-scorecard.html`.

Here is a sampling of the best-known and most popular libraries with some information as to their capabilities and goals:

- **DOJO** (`http://www.dojotoolkit.org/`) is one of the most mature and most popular DHTML/Ajax toolkits now available. The only issue is that there is not a huge examples section.

- **prototype** (`http://prototype.conio.net/`) is a very powerful and much appreciated framework; however, it comes with neither documentation nor examples, which is why several prototype spin-offs are more likely to be usable for you as follows:

    - **script.aculo.us** (`http://script.aculo.us/`) is probably the best-documented library available. Dozens of examples and explanations help you find your way around the library quite quickly.

- • **moofx** (`http://moofx.mad4milk.net/`) was especially developed with size in mind. The entire library is only 3KB and offers lots of visual tricks and effects, along with a basic Ajax engine.

- • **Rico** (`http://openrico.org/rico/home.page`) was developed with web applications in mind and features a panel bar, a data grid, and some effects, as well as an Ajax engine of its own.

- **S@rdalya** (`http://www.sarmal.com/sardalya/Default.aspx`) is a newer library that is very modular. It is constantly being updated. S@dalya's developer is also very active on evolt's thelist mailing list (`http://lists.evolt.org/`).

- **The Yahoo User Interface library** (`http://developer.yahoo.com/yui/index.html`), created and maintained by Yahoo, provides good documentation and examples, making it easy to take your first steps with Ajax. You'll find a support mailing list at `http://groups.yahoo.com/group/ydn-javascript/`.

- **Sarissa** (`http://sarissa.sourceforge.net/doc/`) helps when you need to work with XML; it allows you to convert XML to strings easily, and from one XML document to another, using XSLT.

In the next chapter, we will finally take a closer look at regular expressions and how to use them to validate data. You will learn how to create a contact form as an example application and maybe reuse some of the XHR functionality achieved here to make it slicker than your usual run-of-the-mill contact form.

■■■

CHAPTER 9

Data Validation Techniques

In this chapter, you will learn about using JavaScript to validate data entered by the user or coming from other systems. You already heard a lot about this in Chapter 2, which dealt with decisions involving data, and we will use some of that knowledge and extend it here.

I'll start with a quick introduction of the pros and cons of JavaScript validation and go on to explaining different techniques, starting with string and mathematical validation techniques and building up gradually to the developer's Swiss Army Knife: pattern matching with regular expressions.

You will then get to know different means of spotting what parts of a form need validating, how to ease the maintenance of form validation, and how to display validation output. We'll finish with an Ajax example of how to suggest possible values.

Historically, JavaScript books for beginners will tell you about all the ins and outs of client-side validation and what you can do to validate data before it is sent to the server. I deliberately kept this to the bare minimum. The reason is that it simply is not safe to rely on JavaScript validation (as you'll see in the upcoming section), and you can spend hours writing functions to validate when you really should rely on the server-side component of your web site to do the validation and use JavaScript as a first sanity check of the data coming from the user. You will learn about techniques to use server-side component validation rules in JavaScript though.

Pros and Cons of Client-Side JavaScript Validation

Validating user entries via JavaScript is great for several reasons:

- It saves the user a page reload when he enters incorrect data; and you can save the state of the variables, so the user does not have to enter all the data again, just the incorrect data.

- It cuts down on server traffic, as there is no round-trip to the back end in case of an error.

- It makes the interface more responsive, as it gives the user immediate feedback.

On the other hand, validating with JavaScript has several issues:

- It cannot be trusted as the one and only means of validation (JavaScript could not be available or could even be deliberately turned off to circumvent your validation measures).

- It promotes the notion that validating input is an easy process—it isn't, yet it is very crucial to the security and usability of your product. A lot of web forms are no fun to use because the usability aspect of validation has not been taken care of. Entering data is hard enough, so don't make it harder for the user than necessary by expecting the data in formats that are not easily understandable or by using methods of error reporting that are in the user's way (for example, alert messages and client-side validation that makes it impossible to send the form without JavaScript) rather than preventing him from making mistakes.

- It could happen that the user agent does not notify the user of dynamic changes to the document—this is the case with very old screen readers for users with visual impairments.

- Unless you share validation rules on the client and server side (you'll get an example of how to do that during the course of the chapter), it means twice the maintenance should a validation rule change.

- If you don't want to make your validation rules visible—say to prevent spam or for authentication purposes—there is no way to do that in JavaScript.

A Quick Reminder About Protecting Content with JavaScript

Validation is one thing, protecting content with a password or obfuscating it via encryption is another. If you look around the web, you will find a lot of examples that promise that you can protect a web page from being available with a JavaScript password. Normally these scripts are something like this:

examplePassword.html

```
var pw = prompt( 'Enter Password', '' );
if( pw != 'password123' ) {
  alert( 'Wrong password' );
  window.location = 'boo.html' ;
} else {
  window.location = 'creditCardNumbers.html';
}
```

The one and only cracking skill needed to work around this protection is to look at the page source, or—if the protection is in its own JavaScript file—open that in a browser or text editor. In some cases, where there is no redirection to the correct page, but only to the wrong one, simply turning off JavaScript will get you through.

There are seemingly more clever protection methods that use the password as a part of the file name:

```
var pw = prompt( 'Enter Password' , '' );
window.location = 'page' + pw + '.html';
```

These can be cracked by finding out which files are available on the server—because either the directory listing hasn't been turned off (which is amazingly often the case—for proof just perform a Google search on "index of /mp3"—including the quotation marks) or the page can be found in counter statistics or in the cache of either the browser or Google.

The same applies to obfuscating (making something unreadable by encrypting or replacing words) content and scripts. Anything that was protected by JavaScript can be cracked with it—given enough time and determination. Just don't waste your time with it.

■**Note** JavaScript is a language that is executed on the client computer most of the time, which makes it far too easy for a malicious attacker to work around your protection methods. In the case of right-click prevention scripts to protect images and text from being copied, you will most likely alienate normal visitors and get nothing but a dry chuckle out of real attackers.

Packing JavaScript with something like Dean Edward's packer (http://dean.edwards.name/packer/) to make really heavy scripts shorter is another issue though, and might be a good idea at times—for example, if you want to use a large library script on a high-traffic site.

The One-Size-Fits-All Validation Myth

Validation of user entry can be pretty straightforward—for example, ensuring that a field in a form has some data in it, a select box option has been chosen, or a check box was ticked. However, when it comes to more complex forms of data like dates and times, there is just no catch-all validation approach. A lot of ready-made scripts are available on the Web, and every development framework or IDE comes with out-of-the-box generic form validation solutions that promise to solve any problem for you.

The sad fact is that most of them are rather convoluted or just don't hold up to their promise. Good web forms are as much a user interface and usability matter as they are a technical issue. Knowing your audience and their environment is very important. This is why I don't give you a lot of "silver bullet" examples of validation here, but explain which tools to use to write your own validation scripts.

The biggest mistake a lot of client-side validation tutorials and ready-made solutions make is not considering localization.

- My birthday in American notation is 4/26/1975, in Europe 26/04/1975; others might write it as 26. April 1975 or Apr. 26, 1975.

- Numbers are displayed as 1,000.95 in England and America, whereas Germans write and enter 1.000,95.

- Americans and the English write 1pm or 1am, whereas other Europeans go for 13.00 or 1.00.

- English post codes have syntax like N16 5UN, American ZIP codes 12345 and an optional -1234, whereas in Germany the post codes used to be four digits before the reunion and are now five digits.

- Testing whether telephone numbers are only numerical is not enough, as people might provide the optional country codes or extension numbers, like +44 (0)208 11111-1122.

Interestingly, enough back-end solutions and frameworks like .NET, Spring, and Mono have these issues sorted out for you already, and you can define your displays and validation rules in localization files. This means that if you work in an environment that uses these, it might be a good idea to share validation rules with the back end. We will come back to this in the "Sharing Validation Rules" section.

Basic JavaScript Validation with String and Numeric Methods

The easiest form of validating user entry is using string and numeric methods. I've covered a lot of these in Chapter 2 when I talked about data types and conditions, but I'll recap them here.

String Validation Methods

The string methods most useful for validation are the following:

- `charAt(n)`: Returns the character at the nth position in the string, starting at 0.

- `charCodeAt(n)`: Returns the Latin-1 ASCII character value at the nth position in the string starting at 0.

- `indexOf(search)`: Returns the position of search inside the main string. Returns -1 if the search cannot be found.

- `lastIndexOf(search)`: Returns the last position of search inside the main string. Returns -1 if the search cannot be found.

- `slice(start,end)`: Returns the part of the string in between start and end. If you don't provide an end value, it returns the rest of the string.

- `split(search)`: Splits the string into an array with the parts of the main string surrounding search as the elements. The search term itself is not part of this array.

- substr(start,n): Returns the string that is n characters long beginning at start.

- substring(start,end): Returns the part of the string in between start and end.

The other, more powerful, string methods, search, replace, and match, work with regular expressions. I will talk about those shortly.

You can use the string methods, for example, to check whether a value is a valid number:

exampleCheckNumberString.html *(excerpts)*

```
<form onsubmit="return isNumber()">
  <p>
    <label for="total">Total</label>
    <input type="text" name="total" id="total" />
  </p>
  <p><input type="submit" value="send" /></p>
</form>

function isNumber() {
  var currentCode;
  var total = document.getElementById( 'total' );
  if( !total ) { return false; }
  total = total.value;
  if( total.length == 0 ) {
    alert( 'Field is empty' );
    return false;
  }
  if( total.indexOf( '-' ) != -1 && total.substring( 0,1 ) != '-' ||
      total.lastIndexOf( '-' ) != total.indexOf( '-' ) ) {
    alert( 'A number can only have a minus at the beginning' );
    return false;
  }
  if( total.indexOf( '.' ) != -1 &&
      total.lastIndexOf( '.' ) != total.indexOf( '.' ) ) {
    alert( 'A number can only have one decimal point' );
    return false;
  }
  for( var i = 0; i < total.length; i++ ) {
    currentCode = total.charCodeAt( i );
    if( currentCode != 45 && currentCode !=46  &&
        currentCode < 48 || currentCode > 57 ) {
      alert( 'Only Numbers are allowed' );
      return false;
    }
  }
  return true;
}
```

Let's go through the script and see what is going on there.

`exampleCheckNumberString.html`

```
function isNumber () {
  var currentCode;
  var total = document.getElementById( 'total' );
  if( !total ){ return false; }
  total = total.value;
```

You define a variable called `currentCode` and get the value of the form element with the ID `total`.

`exampleCheckNumberString.html` *(continued)*

```
  if( total.length == 0 ) {
    alert( 'Field is empty' );
    return false;
  }
```

Next, you test whether a value was entered for the field by verifying that the `length` of the value is not 0; if it is, you stop the form submission by returning `false` after displaying an error message.

`exampleCheckNumberString.html` *(continued)*

```
  if( total.indexOf( '-' ) != -1 && total.substring( 0,1 ) != '-' ||
      total.lastIndexOf( '-' ) != total.indexOf( '-' ) ) {
    alert( 'A number can only have a minus at the beginning' );
    return false;
  }
```

As valid numbers should only have a minus as the first nondigit character (theoretically, it could also be a + or a ., but who would enter that?), you test whether the value contains a minus (`indexOf()` does not return -1) and whether it is the first character using `substring()`. This is not enough though, as the user might have entered -12-12, which means you must also check whether the `lastIndexOf()` is different from `indexOf()`. This can only be the case when there is more than one minus sign. If there is more than one minus or it is not at the beginning, you show an error and return `false`.

`exampleCheckNumberString.html` *(continued)*

```
  if( total.indexOf( '.' ) != -1  &&
      total.lastIndexOf( '.' ) != total.indexOf( '.' ) ) {
    alert( 'A number can only have one decimal point' );
    return false;
  }
```

The same logic applies to the decimal point; there can be only one in a valid number.

exampleCheckNumberString.html *(continued)*

```
for( var i = 0; i < total.length; i++ ) {
  currentCode = total.charCodeAt( i );
  if( currentCode != 45 && currentCode != 46 &&
      currentCode < 48 || currentCode > 57 ) {
    alert( 'Only Numbers are allowed' );
    return false;
  }
}
```

Use the charCodeAt() method to test whether there are any invalid characters in the value. Only minus signs (45), decimal points (46), or the number characters 0 to 9 (48 to 57) are allowed. Loop through the string one character at a time and if there is any character whose ASCII code is outside this range, display an error message and return false;.

exampleCheckNumberString.html *(continued)*

```
  return true;
}
```

If all went well, you return true, which sends the form data to the server.

A more complex example is to test for valid e-mail syntax. An e-mail must contain only one @, and the preceding user name part may not start with a period or a hyphen and may not end with a period. The domain part after the @ may not start or end with a period or hyphen. Both parts may only contain the characters from a to z, 0 to 9, periods, underscores, and hyphens.

exampleCheckEmailString.html

```
function isEmail() {
  var mail = document.getElementById( 'email' );
  var error = '';
  if( !mail ){ return false; }
  var mailstring = mail.value;
```

You start by checking for the necessary form field and retrieving its value. Define a variable called error to store error messages. In this example, you need this only to constrain line length, but in the form example at the end of the chapter, we will come back to this.

exampleCheckEmailString.html *(continued)*

```
  if( mailstring.length == 0 ) {
    error = 'You didn\'t enter a value';
    alert( error );
    return false;
  }
```

Test whether the user entered an e-mail by comparing the value length with 0; display an alert and cancel the form submission if there is nothing in the field.

exampleCheckEmailString.html *(continued)*

```
if( mailstring.indexOf( '@' ) == -1 ) {
  error = 'This email has no @ sign';
  alert( error );
  return false;
} else if( mailstring.lastIndexOf( '@' ) != mailstring.➥
          indexOf( '@' ) ) {
  error = 'An email may only contain one @ sign.';
  alert( error );
  return false;
}
```

Test whether the e-mail contains an @ sign using indexOf() and that it only has one of these by comparing the values returned by indexOf() and lastIndexOf().

exampleCheckEmailString.html *(continued)*

```
var chunks = mailstring.split( '@' );
var n = chunks[0];
```

Split the e-mail string at the @ sign to retrieve the user name and the domain parts to check them separately. You define n as the first "chunk," which is the user name.

exampleCheckEmailString.html *(continued)*

```
if( n.substring( 0,1 ) == '.' || n.substring( 0,1 ) == '-' ||
    n.substr( n.length-1, 1 ) == '.' ) {
  error = 'The user name may not start with a period or hyphen';
  error += ' and may not end with a period';
  alert(error);
  return false;
}
```

As the user name may not start with a period or a hyphen, nor end with a period, you test these conditions via substring() and substr().

■**Note** This shows that using substr() is the shorter option when testing for characters at the end of the string. To test for the last character, use string.substr(string.length-1, 1) and not string.substring(string.length-1, string.length).

Display an error and stop the form from submitting if the email is invalid.

exampleCheckEmailString.html *(continued)*

```
if( !checkValidCharacters( n ) ) {
  error = 'The email name contains invalid characters';
  alert( error );
  return false;
}
```

The name may only contain numbers, letters, dashes, underscores, and periods. The utility function checkValidCharacters() takes care of validating this and returns true or false accordingly. If there are invalid characters in the user name, you advise the user of this and cancel the form submission.

exampleCheckEmailString.html *(continued)*

```
n = chunks[1];
if( n.substring( 0, 1 ) == '.' || n.substring( 0, 1 ) == '-' ||
    n.substr( n.length-1, 1 ) == '-' ||
    n.substr( n.length-1, 1 ) == '.' ) {
  error = 'The domain name may not start or end with a hyphen ➥
            or period';
  alert( error );
  return false;
}
```

Then take the second "chunk," which is the domain part of the e-mail, and make sure that neither the start nor the end of the string is a hyphen or a period. Otherwise, alert the user and cancel the form submission.

exampleCheckEmailString.html *(continued)*

```
if( !checkValidCharacters( n ) ) {
  error = 'The domain name contains invalid characters';
  alert( error );
  return false;
}
return true;
}
```

Test the domain for invalid characters and return true—thus sending the form data to the server—if everything is OK.

exampleCheckEmailString.html *(continued)*

```
function checkValidCharacters( n ) {
  for( var i = 0; i < n.length; i++ ) {
    currentCode = n.charCodeAt( i );
    if( currentCode == 45 || currentCode == 46 ||
        currentCode == 95 ||
        ( currentCode > 96 && currentCode < 123 ) ||
        ( currentCode > 47 && currentCode < 58 ) ) {
      continue;
    } else {
      return false;
    }
  }
  return true;
}
```

In the utility function checkValidCharacters(), you loop through the entire length of the string (sent as the parameter n) and make sure that the charCode of each of the characters in the string does not fall outside the range of permitted characters. The function returns false if the character is neither a hyphen (45) nor a period (46) nor an underscore (96) nor any character from a to z (97 to 122) nor any character from 0 to 9 (48 to 57). Otherwise, it returns true.

The number checking example seems a bit convoluted, and indeed it is. For numeric validation and comparison, you are normally a lot better off using numeric validation methods.

Numeric Validation Methods

- Number(): Tries to convert the value of the variable inside the parentheses into a number.

- isNaN(n): Tests whether n is a number (float or integer) and returns true if it isn't.

- parseFloat(n): Tries to convert n to a floating point number. It parses the string character by character from left to right, until it encounters a character that cannot be used in a number. It then stops at that point and evaluates this string as a number. If the first character cannot be used in a number, the result is NaN - Not A Number.

- parseInt(n): Converts n to an integer by removing any fractional part without rounding the number up or down. Any nonnumeric characters passed to the function will be discarded. If the first character is not +, –, or a digit, the result is NaN.

Whenever the validation in question is a mathematical one, like testing for a real number, the mathematical methods are much easier to use. The isNumber() function mentioned earlier is a lot simpler if you rewrite it to use isNaN(), which is a method that returns true when its parameter is not a number:

exampleCheckNumberMath.html *(excerpt)*

```
function isNumber() {
  var total = document.getElementById( 'total' );
  if( !total ){ return false; }
  total = total.value;
  if( total.length == 0 ) {
    alert( 'Field is empty' );
    return false;
  }
  if( isNaN( total ) ) {
    alert( 'Please enter a number' );
    return false;
  }
  return true;
}
```

A more complex example is to check whether a date is the right format. The big problem with dates is that they don't follow a straight algorithm; things would be a lot easier if there were 10 days to a month, 10 months in a year, and so on. As it stands, you need to check for a lot of details:

- Is the month between 1 and 12?

- Does the day exist in the month—for example, 31.04.2000? (It doesn't.)

- Is the year a leap year, which makes the 29th of February possible?

Let's go through an example step by step:

exampleCheckDateMath.html *(excerpt)*

```
function isValidDate() {
  var leap;
  var datestring = document.getElementById( 'date' );
  if( !datestring ){ return false; }
  datestring = datestring.value;
  if( datestring.length == 0 ) {
    alert( 'Field is empty' );
    return false;
  }
```

You start with predefining a variable for leap years, reading the value of the date field, and check whether there is any content in the field.

exampleCheckDateMath.html *(continued)*

```
if( datestring.length != 10 && datestring.indexOf( '/' )== -1  ||
    datestring.indexOf( '/' ) != 2 ||
    datestring.lastIndexOf( '/' ) != 5){
  alert( 'The date is not in the format dd/mm/yyyy' );
  return false;
}
```

You continue to check whether the date is in the right format by checking the string length and ensuring that the slashes are at the right positions.

exampleCheckDateMath.html *(continued)*

```
var chunks = datestring.split( '/' );
var day = chunks[0];
var month = chunks[1];
var year = chunks[2];
```

You then split the date into day, month, and year to validate them separately.

exampleCheckDateMath.html *(continued)*

```
if( ( month < 1 ) || ( month > 12 ) ) {
  alert( 'The month must be in between 01 and 12' );
  return false;
}
```

The month is pretty easy; all you need to test is whether it is larger than 1 and smaller than 12.

exampleCheckDateMath.html *(continued)*

```
if( day < 1 ) {
  alert('The day cannot be negative');
  return false;
}
```

The first day check is to weed out negative days, which could have slipped through the earlier formatting test.

exampleCheckDateMath.html *(continued)*

```
if( (year % 4 == 0) || (year % 100 == 0) || (year % 400 == 0) ) {
  leap = 1;
}
if( (month == 2) && (leap == 1) && (day > 29) ) {
  alert( 'This month does not have that many days' );
  return false;
}
if( (month == 2) && (leap != 1) && (day > 28) ) {
  alert( 'This month does not have that many days' );
  return false;
}
```

For February, you need to check whether the date is a leap year or not. Leap years are those that can be divided by 4, 100, or 400 without resulting in a floating point number. Therefore, you check the modulo (%) of these calculations and compare it with 0. If the year is a leap year, February can have 29 days; otherwise it can only have 28.

exampleCheckDateMath.html *(continued)*

```
if( ( day > 31 ) && ( ( month == "01" ) || ( month == "03" ) ||
    ( month == "05" ) || ( month == "07" ) || ( month == "08" ) ||
    ( month == "10" ) || ( month == "12" ) ) ) {
  alert( 'This month does not have that many days' );
  return false;
}
if( ( day > 30 ) && ( ( month == "04" ) || ( month == "06" ) ||
    (month == "09" ) || ( month == "11" ) ) ) {
  alert( 'This month does not have that many days' );
  return false;
}
return true;
}
```

For the rest of the months, you need to determine whether the day entered is over 30 or 31 and whether the month has that many days. As JavaScript has no knuckles to count on, you need to hard-wire these comparisons. If all goes well, you return true to send the form off to the server.

It seems cumbersome to have to hard-wire all these comparisons, and indeed it is. If you remember, JavaScript has a Date object that has all this logic already in it. Therefore, you can harness this to make the validation of a form a lot shorter:

exampleCheckDateObj.html *(excerpt)*

```
function isValidDate() {
  var datestring = document.getElementById( 'date' );
  if( !datestring ){ return false; }
  datestring = datestring.value;
  if( datestring.length == 0 ) {
    alert( 'Field is empty' );
    return false;
  }
  if( datestring.length != 10 && datestring.indexOf( '/' ) == -1 ||
  datestring.indexOf( '/' ) != 2 || datestring.lastIndexOf( '/' ) != 5 ) {
    alert( 'The date is not in the format dd/mm/yyyy' );
    return false;
  }
```

You start the same way, testing whether the field exists, whether data has been entered, and whether the entry is in the right format.

exampleCheckDateObj.html *(continued)*

```
  var chunks = datestring.split( '/' );
  var testDate = new Date( chunks[2], chunks[1]-1, chunks[0] );
  if( testDate.getDate() == chunks[0] ) {
    if ( testDate.getMonth()+1 == chunks[1] ) {
      if( testDate.getFullYear() == chunks[2] ) {
        return true;
      } else {
        alert( "This is not a valid year." );
      }
    } else {
      alert( "This is not a valid month." );
    }
  } else {
    alert( "This is not a valid date." );
  }
  return true;
}
```

You split the date into its components and create a new Date with these settings (notice that you need to subtract 1 from the month). Then compare the values that the getter methods of the Date object return with the day, the month, and the year, and alert the user of an error if these don't match—the Date methods do all the testing for you! You need to add 1 to the month to match the human/computer readable offset, though.

■Tip Get yourself well acquainted with the JavaScript `Math` and `Date` objects. A lot of times you don't have to come up with clever code yourself, but you can piggyback on functionality they already provide you with.

Regular Expressions

Regular expressions help you match a string against a character pattern and are great for validation of user entry or changing document content. They are not confined to JavaScript, and are present in other languages like Perl, PHP, and UNIX server scripts. They are amazingly powerful, and if you talk to Perl or PHP enthusiasts and server administrators, you'll be amazed how often they can replace a 50-line `switch/case` or `if/else` construct you wrote in JavaScript with a single regular expression. Many editing environments also feature "find" and "search and replace" functionality, allowing the use of regular expressions.

Regular expressions are the cat's pajamas once you get your head around them; however, at first sight a construct like `/^[\w]+(\.[\w]+)*@([\w]+\.)+[a-z]{2,7}$/i` (which checks whether a string is a valid e-mail syntax) can strike fear into the faint of heart. The good news is that it is not as tough as it looks.

Syntax and Attributes

Imagine you want to search for the string "cat" in text. As a regular expression, you can define this in two different formats:

```
// String notation; notice that you must not use quotation marks!
var searchTerm = /cat/;
// Object constructor
var searchTerm = new RegExp( 'cat' );
```

If you use this expression on a string via the `match()`, `search()`, `exec()`, or `test()` method, it'll return anything that has "cat" in it—regardless of the location in the string—like **cat**alog, con**cat**enation, or s**cat**.

If you want to only match the word "cat" as a string without anything else around it, you need to use a ^ to indicate the start and $ for the end:

```
var searchTerm = /^cat$/;
var searchTerm = new RegExp( '^cat$' );
```

You can also omit either the start indicator, ^, or the end indicator, $. This would match **cat**, **cat**alog, or **cat**astrophe:

```
var searchTerm = /^cat/;
var searchTerm = new RegExp( '^cat' );
```

This would find pole**cat** or wild**cat:**

```
var searchTerm = /cat$/;
var searchTerm = new RegExp('cat$' );
```

If you want to find "cat" regardless of case—for example, to match "cat", "Catherine", or "CAT"—you need to use the i attribute following the second slash. This causes the case to be ignored:

```
var searchTerm=/cat/i;
var searchTerm=new RegExp('cat','i');
```

If you have a string that could have the word "cat" in it several times, and you want to get all matches as an array, you need to add the parameter g for "global":

```
var searchTerm = /cat/g;
var searchTerm = new RegExp('cat','g');
```

By default, regular expressions match patterns only in single-line strings. If you want to match a pattern in a multiline string, use the parameter m for "multiline." You can also mix them, and the order is not important:

```
var searchTerm = /cat/gim;
var searchTerm = new RegExp( 'cat', 'mig' );
```

Wildcard Searches, Constraining Scope, and Alternatives

The period character (.) plays the role of the joker card in regular expressions; it stands for "any character." (This can be confusing, as in advanced web searches or on the DOS and UNIX command line it is the asterisk, *.)

```
var searchTerm = /c.t/gim;
var searchTerm = new RegExp( 'c.t', 'mig' );
```

This matches "cat", "cot", "CRT", and even nonsense strings like "c#t" and "c!T", or those including spaces like "c T" or "c\tt". (Remember that \t is the tab character.)

This might be too much flexibility for your needs, which is why you can use square brackets to limit the scope of the choices only to those you want to offer:

```
var searchTerm = /c[aou]t/gim;
var searchTerm = new RegExp( 'c[aou]t', 'mig' );
```

You can match "cat", "cot", or "cut" in all upper- and lowercase versions with this regular expression. You can also provide ranges within the brackets like a-z to match all lowercase letters, A-Z to match all uppercase letters, and 0-9 to match digits.

■**Caution** Notice that regular expressions match the characters of the numbers, not their value. A regular expression with [0-9] would return 0200 as a valid four-digit number.

If you want, for example, to find any word all in lowercase, followed immediately by a word in uppercase, you'll use

```
var searchTerm = /[a-z][A-Z]/g;
var searchTerm = new RegExp( '[a-z][A-Z]', 'g' );
```

You can use the ^ character inside the brackets to exclude an option from the search. If you wanted to avoid "cut", for example, you can use

```
var searchTerm = /c[^u]t/g;
var searchTerm = new RegExp( 'c[^u]t', 'g' );
```

Brackets only match one character at a time, which is why you couldn't match something like "cost", "coast", or "cast" with this expression. If you want to match several options, you can use the pipe character (|) inside parentheses, which functions like a logical OR:

```
var searchTerm = /c(^u|a|o|os|oas|as)t/g;
var searchTerm = new RegExp( 'c(^u|a|o|os|oas|as)t', 'g' );
```

This now matches "cat", "cot", "cost", "coast", and "cast", but not "cut" (because of the ^u).

Restricting the Number of Characters with Quantifiers

In many cases, you want to allow for a range of characters, like a to z, but you want to restrict their number. For this you can use **quantifiers** in regular expressions, as listed in Table 9-1.

Table 9-1. *Quantifier Notations in Regular Expressions*

Notation	Number of Times Possible
*	0 or 1 time(s)
+	1 or more time(s)
?	0 or 1 time(s)
{n}	n times
{n,m}	n to m times

Note Adding the ? after each of these means that the regular expression should match them but as few times as possible.

For example, if you wanted to match the syntax of a serial number that consists of two groups of four characters, each separated with dashes, you'd use

```
var searchTerm = /[a-z|0-9]{4}\-[a-z|0-9]{4}/gim;
var searchTerm = new RegExp( '[a-z|0-9]{4}\-[a-z|0-9]{4}', 'mig' );
```

■**Note** Notice that you need to escape characters that are to be used literally, and not with any special meaning they might have in a regular expression pattern, like the dash in this case. You can do this by preceding the character with a backslash, \. Characters that need to be escaped are -, +, /, (,), [,], *, {, }, and ?. For example, /c.t/ matches "cat" or "cot" or "c4t", whereas /c\.t/ only matches "c.t".

Word Boundaries, Whitespace, and Other Shortcuts

All of these different options can result in pretty convoluted regular expressions, which is why there are some shortcut notations available. You may remember the special character notation for whitespace in Chapter 2, like \n for a line break and \t for a tab character. The same are available for regular expressions, as Table 9-2 shows.

Table 9-2. *Shortcut Notations for Regular Expressions*

Notation	Equivalent Notation	Meaning
\d	[0-9]	Only integers
\D	[^0-9]	All characters but integers
\w	[a-zA-Z0-9_]	All alphanumeric characters and the underscore
\W	[^a-zA-Z0-9_]	All nonalphanumeric characters
\b	N/A	Word boundary
\B	N/A	Not word boundary
\s	[\t\n\r\f\v]	All whitespace
\S	[^\t\n\r\f\v]	No whitespace

For example, if you want to test for a US Social Security number, which is a nine-digit number with dashes following the third and the fifth digits (e.g., 456-33-1234), you can use the following regular expression, with optional dashes (using the ? quantifier), as the user might not enter them:

```
var searchTerm = /[0-9]{3}\-?[0-9]{2}\-?[0-9]{4}/;
var searchTerm = new RegExp( '[0-9]{3}\-?[0-9]{2}\-?[0-9]{4}', '' );
```

Alternatively, you can use the shortcut notation for digits:

```
var searchTerm = /\d{3}\-?\d{2}\-?\d{4}/;
var searchTerm = new RegExp( '\\d{3}\-?\\d{2}\-?\\d{4}', '' );
```

Be aware that if you use the shortcut notations inside quotation marks or in the constructor notation, you'll need to precede them with double backslashes, not single ones, as you need to escape them! With this knowledge, you should be well equipped to write your own regular expressions. As proof, let's go back to the example in the beginning paragraph of this section:

```
var validEmail = /^[\w]+(\.[\w]+)*@([\w]+\.)+[a-z]{2,7}$/i
```

E-mails can be pretty straightforward, like me@example.com, or more complex, like chris.heilmann.webdev@example.museum. This regular expression should return both as valid e-mails.

It tests whether the string starts with a group of one or more word characters, ^[\w]+, followed by a group of 0 or more word characters preceded by a period, (\.[\w]+)*, before the @ sign. After the @ sign, the string might have one or more groups of one or more word characters followed by a period, ([\w]+\.)+, and it'll end in a string that has in between two and seven characters. This last string is the domain, which could be something short like de or longer like name or museum. Notice that by allowing several words followed by a period, you also make sure that e-mails like user@open.ac.uk are recognized.

Methods Using Regular Expressions

There are several methods that take regular expressions as parameters. The expression itself—the things inside the slashes or the RegExp constructor—is called a **pattern**, as it matches what you want to retrieve or test for.

- pattern.test(string): Tests whether the string matches the pattern and returns true or false.

- pattern.exec(string): Matches the string and the pattern one time and returns an array of matches or null.

- string.match(pattern): Matches the string and the pattern and returns the resulting matches as an array of strings or null.

- string.search(pattern): Matches the string and the pattern and returns the positions of the positive matches. If the string does not match any of the pattern, the search returns -1.

- string.replace(pattern, replaceString): Matches the string against the pattern and replaces every positive match with replaceString.

- string.split(pattern, limit): Matches the string against the pattern and splits it into an array with the substrings surrounding the pattern matches as array items. The optional limit parameter cuts down the number of array elements.

The Power of Parenthesis Grouping

You might remember that to group an expression, you use parenthesis, (). This not only groups the pattern, but also stores the results in special variables you can use later on. This is especially handy when you use it in conjunction with the replace() method. The results are stored in variables named $1 through $9, which means you can use up to nine parenthetical groupings in each regular expression. If you want to exclude a group from this, you precede it with ?:.

For example, if you have a list of names in the format *Surname, Name* and you want to convert each entry in the list into *Name Surname* format, you can do the following:

exampleNameOrder.html

```
names=[
  'Reznor, Trent',
  'Eldritch, Andrew',
  'Clark, Anne',
  'Almond,Marc'
];
for( i = 0; i < names.length; i++ ) {
  alert(names[i].replace( /(\w+)+,\s?(\w+)/g, '$2 $1' ) );
}
```

The pattern matches any word preceding the comma (followed by an optional white-space character) and the following word, and stores both in variables. The replacement string reverses the order by using the $ variables.

A more complex example is to print the URL of every external link of a content area behind the link:

exampleShowURL.html

```
showURLs = function(){
  var ct = document.getElementById( 'content' );
  var searchTerm = '(<a href="((?:http|https|ftp):\/\/';
  searchTerm    += '(?:[\\w]+\.)+[a-z]{2,7})">';
  searchTerm    += '(?:\\w|\\s|\\.)+<\/a>)';
  var pattern = new RegExp( searchTerm, 'mgi' );
  ct.innerHTML = ct.innerHTML.replace( pattern, '$1 ($2)' );
}
```

You start the pattern with a set of parentheses to store the whole construct in the variable $1 and match the start of a link <a href=". You follow up with a set of parentheses surrounding what is inside the href attribute, which is a URL starting with either http, https, or ftp, not storing this group in a variable (as this set of parentheses is preceded by ?:), followed by a colon and two slashes (that need to be escaped), followed by a URL ending in a domain (this is the same pattern used in the e-mail checking example).

You close the parentheses, storing everything inside the link's href attribute in $2, and match everything inside the link element (which could be one or more words, whitespace, or a period) but don't store it in a variable. Then close the main group after the closing </a> and use replace to replace every link with the pattern matches, which in effect will turn <a href=http://www.example.com">example</a> into <a href=http://www.example.com"> example</a> (http://www.example.com).

Regular Expression Resources

As with any programming language, there are dozens of ways to reach the same goal, and I don't want to just give examples to copy and paste when getting your head around regular expressions will get you so much further.

There are many online resources that list patterns according to their task:

- The Regular Expression Library (`http://regexlib.com/`) has a searchable database of patterns.

- At Regular-Expressions.info, (`http://www.regular-expressions.info/`), you'll find a very extensive tutorial on regular expressions.

- RegEx Advice (`http://regexadvice.com/`) has a good forum and blogs on regular expressions.

In terms of books, there's *Regular Expressions Pocket Reference* by Tony Stubblebine (O'Reilly, 2003) and the very extensive *Mastering Regular Expressions* by Jeffrey Friedl (O'Reilly, 2002).

For the more UNIX-inclined user, there is *Regular Expression Recipes: A Problem-Solution Approach* by Nathan A. Good (Apress, 2004).

Summary of Validation Methods

In real-life scripting situations, you are never likely to stick to one of the preceding methods, but use a mixture of them all to reach your goal as quickly as possible. There are no fixed rules for what to use when, but some hints and benefits might be good to remember:

- Regular expressions only match characters; you cannot do calculations with them (at least not in JavaScript; PHP offers the e switch, which evaluates matches as PHP code).

- Regular expressions have the benefit of being language independent—you can use the same rules on the server and the client side (you'll see an example of that later in the "Sharing Validation Rules" section). Both the string and the mathematical methods are fixed to JavaScript and may not be the same in other languages.

- It is very easy to match large ranges of options in regular expressions, with strings that can get messy very quickly, unless the ranges are following a simple rule, like A to Z or 0 to 9.

- If you have to validate numbers, most of the time it is not worth the effort using string or regular expression validation; just stick to testing the values mathematically. Strings are too forgiving, as you cannot compare values and do calculations with them. The only options you have are determining the string length and testing for special characters.

- There is no shame in using out-of-the-box patterns and methods developed by others. Many of these have been tested by dozens of developers in different development environments.

Form Validation Techniques

We'll now talk about some of the techniques you can use with forms, spotting which fields need validation and how to tell the user that something is amiss. The list of examples is by far not complete—newer technologies, better browsers, and behavior patterns of users change constantly, and what might be a utopian idea right now may be normal in a year's time, or even already normal with some users. The best option you have in choosing which measures are correct is to watch your users and get their feedback. Don't make too many assumptions—there are more than enough hardly usable forms out there.

Designating Mandatory Fields

There are several methods you can use to designate form elements as mandatory and requiring validation. We'll now discuss the most common ones and the issues associated with each of them before we continue with different examples of how to give validation feedback.

▉Note Chris Campbell at Particletree published a similar list some time ago called "A Guide to Unobtrusive JavaScript Validation" (`http://particletree.com/features/a-guide-to-unobtrusive-javascript-validation/`). The article and the comments are a very good read if you want to know more.

The Hidden Field Method

The traditional approach to identifying required fields uses a hidden field called `mandatory` or something similar, which lists all mandatory fields by name. This allows you to use the same information for both server-side and client-side processing. One very common form mailing script, Matt Wright's `formmail.pl` (`http://www.scriptarchive.com/formmail.html`), uses this method.

Validating such a form with client-side JavaScript requires simply getting the value of this hidden field, splitting it up using the comma or other delimiter character into an array, and testing whether each and every one of the fields exist before sending its ID to the validation method:

`exampleHiddenFieldForm.html` *(excerpt)*

```
<p class="submit">
  <input type="submit" name="send" value="Send Form" />
  <input type="hidden" name="mandatory" id="mandatory"
    value="email,Message,subject,Name" />
</p>
```

hiddenFieldForm.js *(excerpt)*

```
init:function() {
  [... code snipped ...]
  var mandatory = document.getElementById('mandatory');
  if( !mandatory ){ return; }
  hfv.mandatory = mandatory.value.split( ',' );
  [... code snipped ...]
},
send:function(e) {
  [... code snipped ...]
  for( var i = 0; i < hfv.mandatory.length; i++ ) {
    if( !document.getElementById( hfv.mandatory[i] ) ) { continue; }
    hfv.checkValue( hfv.mandatory[i] );
  }
  [... code snipped ...]
},
```

The send() method loops over all the items of the array that was generated by splitting the value of the field with the name mandatory at the comma and checks whether an element with the ID of the current item value exists before sending it to a tool method called checkValue().

The Indicator Element Method

Basic usability dictates that mandatory fields should be clear to the user, which is why the HTML needs to have an indicator to mark mandatory fields, traditionally in the form of an asterisk after the label text.

This is something you could use as a means of spotting which fields are mandatory. You loop through all the SPAN elements in the form and test whether their class is mandatory. If this is the case, you grab the ID of the element to validate from the for attribute of its LABEL (notice that the name of the property is not for but htmlFor!):

exampleAsteriskForm.html *(excerpts)*

```
<p>
  <label for="Name">Your Name
  <span class="mandatory">*</span></label>
</p>
<p>
  <label for="Message">Your Message
  <span class="mandatory">*</span></label>
</p>
```

asteriskForm.js *(excerpt)*

```
init:function() {
  hfv.mandatory = [];
  [... code snipped ...]
  hfv.f = document.getElementsByTagName( 'form' )[0];
  var msgs = hfv.f.getElementsByTagName( 'span' );
  for( var i = 0; i < msgs.length; i++) {
    if( DOMhelp.cssjs( 'check', msgs[i], 'mandatory' ) ) {
      hfv.mandatory.push( msgs[i].parentNode.htmlFor );
    }
  }
  [... code snipped ...]
},
```

The CSS Classes Method

Another approach is to give the fields that are mandatory appropriate CSS classes and test for these.

exampleClassesForm.html *(excerpts)*

```
<p>
   <input type="text" id="Name" name="Name" class="mandatory" />
</p>
<p>
   <input type="text" id="email" name="email" class="mandatory" />
</p>
```

In the script, you'll have to loop through all form fields and check whether they have the right class. You could also use the DOM-2 methods, but then you need several loops, checking for INPUT, SELECT, and TEXTAREA elements.

classesForm.js *(excerpt)*

```
hfv.f = document.getElementsByTagName( 'form' )[0];
  var msgs = hfv.f.elements;
  for( var i = 0; i < msgs.length; i++) {
    if( DOMhelp.cssjs( 'check', msgs[i], 'mandatory' ) ) {
    hfv.mandatory.push( msgs[i].id );
  }
}
```

The Custom Attribute Method

The very experimental custom attribute method was explained by Peter-Paul Koch (http://www.quirksmode.org) in his "JavaScript Triggers" article on A List Apart (http://

www.alistapart.com/articles/scripttriggers/) in February 2005. We won't go into an example here, but what it means is that you come up with nonstandard attributes for elements like

```
<input type="text" name="name" id="name" required="true" />
```

You can then use getAttribute() in your script to check for these attributes and act accordingly. You can even extend this idea to allow for maintenance of the validation rules in HTML:

```
<input type="text" name="name" id="name" required="true"
error="Please enter a Name at least 5 characters long"
 pattern="/.{5}/" />
```

The main issue of this method is that you reinvent HTML, and you will have to come up with a custom DTD for it. David Eisenberg explains how to do that in "Validating a Custom DTD" (http://www.alistapart.com/articles/customdtd/).

Failures of These Methods

All of these methods have the same problem: you keep validation rules in HTML and JavaScript and in the back-end script separately, which means double maintenance. Furthermore, all but the "hidden field" method make the HTML cater to JavaScript exclusively, as the back-end script cannot determine which fields are mandatory by means of a class or a SPAN.

Sharing Validation Rules

A much cleaner approach is to keep all the validation rules and feedback messages in one spot. You could use XML to store the information and use XHR to retrieve it, but this is rather error-prone. An easier solution is to use JSON:

```
validationRules : {
  'Name' : {
    'error' : 'Please enter a name',
    'pattern' : /.{10}/i
  },
  'subject' : {
    'error' : 'Please choose a subject',
    'pattern' : /.{5}/i
  },
  'Message' : {
    'error' : 'Please enter a message at least 20 characters long',
    'pattern' : /.{20}/i
  },
  'email' : {
    'error' : 'Please enter a valid email',
    'pattern' : /^[\w-]+(\.[\w-]+)*@([\w-]+\.)+[a-zA-Z]{2,7}$/i
  }
}
```

You can retrieve all the mandatory elements by looping through the JSON object:

```
for( i in validationRules ) {
  // i will be Name, subject, Message, email
  if( !document.getElementById( i ) ) { continue; }
    toplist.checkValue( i );
}
```

Retrieving the patterns and error messages is as easy; an alert(validationRules['email']['error']) would result in an alert stating "Please enter a valid email".

You can also generate the JSON string on the back end. For example, in PHP:

```
validationRules.php

<?php
$validationRules = array (
  'Name' => array (
    'error' => 'Please enter a name',
    'pattern' => '/.{10}/i'
  ),
  'subject' => array (
    'error' => 'Please choose a subject',
    'pattern' => '/.{10}/i'
  ),
  'Message' => array (
    'error' => 'Please enter a message at least 20 characters long',
    'pattern' => '/.{20}/i'
  ),
  'email' => array (
    'error' => 'Please enter a valid email',
    'pattern' => '/^[\w-]+(\.[\w-]+)*@([\w-]+\.)+[a-zA-Z]{2,7}$/i'
  )
);
if( isset( $_GET['json'] ) ) {
  header( 'Content-type:text/javascript' );
  echo 'validationRules = {';
    foreach( array_keys( $validationRules ) as $a ) {
      echo '\''.$a.'\' : {'."\n";
        foreach( array_keys ( $validationRules[$a] ) as $b ) {
          if( $b == 'pattern' ) {
            echo '\'' . $b . '\' : ' . $validationRules[$a][$b].➦
                 ',' . "\n";
```

```
        } else {
          echo '\'' . $b . '\' : \'' . $validationRules[$a][$b].➥
              '\',' . "\n";
        }
      }
    }
    echo '},' . "\n";
  }
  echo '};';
}
?>
```

Don't worry if the syntax is confusing; what is important to know is that if a different PHP script includes this one, it'll get the validation rules as a PHP array; but if you include the PHP script with a json parameter as a JavaScript, you'll have the validationRules object at your disposal. This is what the part in bold does by sending a text/javascript header to the browser and writing out the array data in the right format. Without the text/javascript header, the browser would not recognize the string returned from the PHP as JavaScript, so you can see it is a very important aspect of writing out JavaScript using server-side languages.

Using this functionality is as easy as including the PHP script as a JavaScript in the head of the document:

```
<script type="text/javascript" src="validationRules.php?json=1"></script>
```

We'll use this in a second in the first example on how to give users validation feedback

Giving Users Validation Feedback

We've already covered some methods of giving feedback in Chapter 4 and in Chapter 7, and we will now go through one form validation example in detail and list the necessary changes to the script in the other options.

We will not repeat the most obvious and probably oldest method—JavaScript alerts—as they've been covered, and you should know by now how to use them. Instead, let's take a look at some prettier examples.

Showing a List of Erroneous Fields

In this method, you show the user a list of fields that contain errors. This is a traditional feedback of back-end scripts, which show the list above the form after the page has loaded. As you don't reload the page when you validate with JavaScript, it might be a better idea to show the list where the user is—at the bottom of the form above the Submit button. Figure 9-1 shows how that might look. You can see the example for yourself by opening exampleTopList.html on your localhost—which must be a server running PHP, like XAMPP or Apache, as explained earlier in Chapter 8.

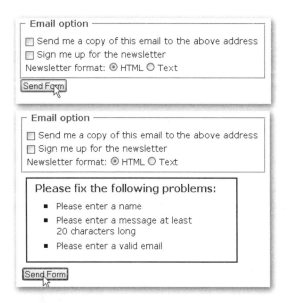

Figure 9-1. *Showing a list of erroneous fields above the Submit button*

You start by embedding the rule set in the head of the HTML:

exampleTopList.html *(excerpt)*

```
<script type="text/javascript" src="validationRules.php?json=1"></script>
```

You should plan your script starting with the skeleton of properties and methods:

topList.js *(skeleton)*

```
toplist = {
  error:[],
  errorMessage : null,
  errorClass : 'error',
  errorTitle : 'Please fix the following problems:',
  sendButtonID : 'send',
  init:function(){},
  send:function( e ){},
  flushErrors:function(){},
  checkValue:function( o ){ }
}
```

You'll need an error array that will store all the errors that occurred in the form. You pre-define an errorMessage as null, which will become the message above the Submit button. The errorTitle and the errorClass will be shown above the list of errors and the class applied to define the look and feel. The sendButtonID is necessary to find the Submit button.

The methods are pretty standard for a form submission script: an init() method to apply the event handler when the form is submitted, an event listener send() method, a method to remove older error messages (as the user will not reload the page but may enter data several times because the script stops the page from reloading when there is an error), and a tool method to check the value of each mandatory form field.

I'll now go through the script step by step and explain what the different methods do.

toplist.js

```
toplist = {
  error:[],
  errorMessage : null,
  errorClass : 'error',
  errorTitle : 'Please fix the following problems:',
  sendButtonID : 'send',
  init:function() {
    toplist.sendButton = document.getElementById( toplist.➥
    sendButtonID );
    if( !toplist.sendButton ) { return; }
    toplist.f = document.getElementsByTagName( 'form' )[0];
    DOMhelp.addEvent( toplist.f, 'submit', toplist.send, false );
  },
```

There are no surprises in the init() method; you check whether the Submit button exists, retrieve the first form in the document, and apply a submit handler pointing to send.

toplist.js (continued)

```
  send:function( e ) {
    toplist.flushErrors();
    for( var i in validationRules ) {
      if( !document.getElementById( i ) ) { continue; }
      toplist.checkValue( i );
    }
```

Call the flushErrors() method to remove any error messages that might already be visible and loop through the validationRules JSON object. Determine whether each of the mandatory elements exists and call the checkValue() method with the element's ID as a parameter.

toplist.js (continued)

```
    if( toplist.error.length > 0 ) {
      toplist.errorMessage = document.createElement( 'div' );
      toplist.errorMessage.className = toplist.errorClass;
      var errorTitle = document.createElement( 'h2' );
      errorTitle.appendChild( document.➥
      createTextNode( toplist.errorTitle ) );
      toplist.errorMessage.appendChild( errorTitle );
      entry = document.createElement( 'ul' );
      toplist.errorMessage.appendChild( entry );
      toplist.errorList = entry;
```

The utility method `checkValue()` adds new elements to the error array if there are problems with some of the fields, which is why you check whether its `length` is larger than 0 before you start assembling the error message.

Next, create a DIV, store it in the `errorMessage` property, and apply the `error` class to it to make it style-able. Create an H2 and add the text stored in the `errorTitle` property as the text content of this heading. Add the heading to the `errorMessage` DIV, create a new UL element, and add the UL to `errorMessage`. Then store the newly created UL in the `errorList` property.

`toplist.js` *(continued)*

```
for( i = 0; i < toplist.error.length; i++ ) {
    entry = document.createElement( 'li' );
    entry.appendChild( document.➥
    createTextNode( toplist.error[i] ) );
    toplist.errorList.appendChild( entry );
  }
```

Loop through the `error` array and create a new list item containing the text of each error before appending it as a child node to the `errorList` UL.

`toplist.js` *(continued)*

```
    var sendPara = toplist.sendButton.parentNode;
    sendPara.parentNode.insertBefore( toplist.errorMessage, sendPara );
    DOMhelp.cancelClick( e );
  }
},
```

Now, retrieve the parent element of the form's Send button and insert the error message as a new sibling element in front of it. Since there was an error, cancel the form submission by calling `cancelClick()`.

`toplist.js` *(continued)*

```
flushErrors : function() {
  toplist.error = [];
  if( toplist.errorMessage ) {
    toplist.errorMessage.parentNode.removeChild(➥
    toplist.errorMessage );
    toplist.errorMessage = null;
  }
},
```

The `flushErrors()` method redefines the `error` array as an empty array and tests whether there is already an existing `errorMessage`. If there is, it removes the document node and sets the object to `null`.

toplist.js *(continued)*

```
checkValue : function( o ) {
  var elm = document.getElementById( o );
  switch( elm.type ) {
    case 'text' :
      if( !validationRules[o][ 'pattern' ].test( elm.value ) ) {
        toplist.error.push( validationRules[o][ 'error' ] );
      }
    break;
    case 'textarea' :
      if( !validationRules[o][ 'pattern' ].test( elm.value ) ) {
        toplist.error.push( validationRules[o][ 'error' ] );
      }
    break;
```

The checkValue() method does the real validation tasks, and starts by retrieving the element with the ID that was sent as a parameter. There is no need to test whether the element exists, as you've already done that in the send method. You retrieve the element type and start a switch statement that tests for the different form elements accordingly.

In the cases of text and textarea as the type, you take the element's value attribute and test it against the pattern stored in the validationRules object. If the pattern does not match, you add a new item to the error array with the error message associated with the element ID as the value.

■**Note** The parameter o is the ID of the element, which means if you use validationRules['Name'] ['pattern'], for example, you get /.{10}/i as the result, which is a regular expression pattern that tests whether the name is at least ten characters long. If you use validationRules['Name']['error'], you get 'Please enter a name', which is the error message you put into the new item of the error array.

---

toplist.js *(continued)*

```
    case 'select-one' :
      var curelm = elm.options[ elm.selectedIndex ].value;
      if( elm.selectedIndex == 5 ) {
        curelm = document.getElementById( 'otherSubject' ).value;
      }
      if( !validationRules[o][ 'pattern' ].test( curelm ) ) {
        toplist.error.push( validationRules[o][ 'error' ] );
      }
    break;
    }
  }
}
DOMhelp.addEvent( window, 'load', toplist.init, false );
```

In the case of the select box—which in this example is a single select box, therefore the type is select-one—you need to retrieve the value of the selected option via the options array and the selectedIndex property. As the form offers an "other" option, you need to check whether it was chosen and take the value of the text field otherSubject instead.

Both the select value and the other subject gets tested with the pattern stored in the validationRules object and added as an error if it doesn't match. Add an event handler to the window executing the init() method when the window has finished loading, and *voilà*, you've created a form that is validated using JavaScript and shows a list of errors until the user has entered the correct sort of data in all mandatory fields.

Replacing the Main Form with a Clickable Error Message

A different approach is to hide the form when the validation brings up errors and show a warning message with a link back to the form, as illustrated in Figure 9-2. You can see the example for yourself by opening exampleHideForm.html on your localhost.

Figure 9-2. *Hiding the form and offering a link back to it*

The differences are not that many:

hideform.js *used in* exampleHideForm.html

```
toplist = {
  error:[],
  errorMessage : null,
  errorClass : 'error',
  errorTitle : 'Please fix the following problems:',
  errorLink : 'Back to form',
  errorLinkClass : 'errorlink',
  init:function() {
  [... code snipped ...]
  },
```

You need two new properties: one to store the link text and another to define a CSS class to style the link to close the message.

hideform.js *(continued)*

```
    send:function( e ) {
      toplist.flushErrors();
      for( var i in toplist.validationRules ) {
       [... code snipped ...]
      }
      if( toplist.error.length > 0 ) {
       [... code snipped ...]
        for( i = 0; i < toplist.error.length; i++ ) {
         [... code snipped ...]
        }
        entry = document.createElement( 'li' );
        var closeLink = DOMhelp.createLink( '#', ➥
        toplist.errorLink );
        DOMhelp.addEvent( closeLink, 'click', ➥
        toplist.flushErrors, false );
        closeLink.onclick = DOMhelp.safariClickFix;
        entry.appendChild( closeLink );
        entry.className = toplist.errorLinkClass;
        toplist.errorList.appendChild( entry );
        toplist.f.style.display = 'none';
        toplist.f.parentNode.insertBefore( toplist.errorMessage, toplist.f );
        DOMhelp.cancelClick( e );
      }
    },
```

In the send() method, you need to add an additional list item and create a link with the errorLink property as text. You apply a click handler pointing to the flushErrors() method, add the CSS class, and add the new list item to the errorList. You hide the main form by setting its style display property to none (alternatively, you could have added a dynamic CSS class to hide the form).

hideform.js *(continued)*

```
    flushErrors : function() {
      toplist.error = [];
      if( toplist.errorMessage ) {
        toplist.errorMessage.parentNode.➥
        removeChild( toplist.errorMessage );
        toplist.errorMessage = null;
      }
      toplist.f.style.display = 'block';
    },
    [... code snipped ...]
  DOMhelp.addEvent( window, 'load', toplist.init, false );
```

The flushErrors() message now needs to set the display property of the form back to block, and indicate that all the changes are necessary and the rest of the script stays as it was.

Highlighting Erroneous Fields Individually

Especially with larger forms, it makes a lot more sense to display error messages directly next to the fields that have an error. Figure 9-3 shows what that looks like, and you can see it yourself by opening exampleErrorFields.html on your localhost.

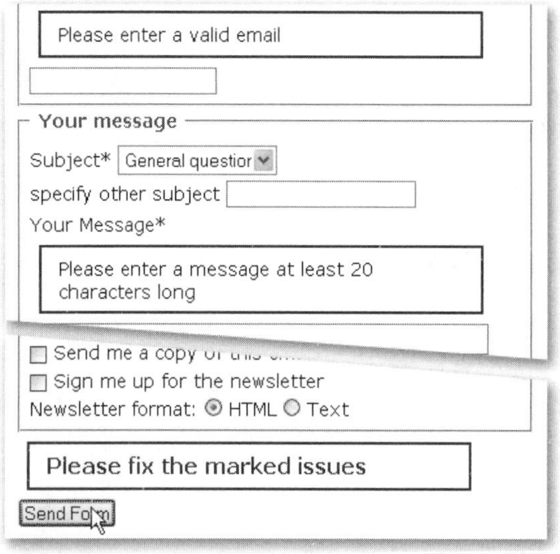

Figure 9-3. *Highlighting individual error fields*

The script is slightly different; the send, flushErrors(), and checkValue() methods have to change, and you need a new method called addErrorMessage() that adds the error message where the error occurred.

errorFields.js

```
ef = {
  error:[],
  errorMessage : null,
  errorClass : 'error',
  errorTitle : 'Please fix the marked issues',
  init : function() {
    ef.sendButton = document.getElementById( 'send' );
    if( !ef.sendButton ){ return; }
    ef.f = document.getElementsByTagName( 'form' )[0];
    DOMhelp.addEvent( ef.f, 'submit', ef.send, false );
    ef.f.onsubmit = function(){ return false; }
  },
```

The properties and the init() method stay the same as in the toplist example.

errorFields.js *(continued)*

```
send:function( e ) {
  ef.flushErrors();
  for( var i in validationRules ) {
    if( !document.getElementById( i ) ) { continue; }
    ef.checkValue( i );
  }
  if( ef.error.length > 0 ) {
    ef.errorMessage = document.createElement( 'div' );
    ef.errorMessage.className = ef.errorClass;
    var errorTitle = document.createElement( 'h2' );
    errorTitle.appendChild( document.➥
    createTextNode( ef.errorTitle ) );
    ef.errorMessage.appendChild( errorTitle );
    var sendPara = ef.sendButton.parentNode;
    sendPara.parentNode.insertBefore( ef.errorMessage, sendPara );
    DOMhelp.cancelClick( e );
  }
},
```

The send method is a lot shorter, as you don't need to create the error list; just the main errorMessage element with the heading in it.

errorFields.js *(continued)*

```
checkValue : function( o ) {
  var elm = document.getElementById( o );
  switch( elm.type ) {
    case 'text ' :
      if( !validationRules[o][ 'pattern' ].test( elm.value ) ) {
        ef.error.push( validationRules[o][ 'error' ] );
        ef.addErrorMsg( elm, validationRules[o][ 'error' ] );
      }
    break;
    case 'textarea' :
      if( !validationRules[o][ 'pattern' ].test( elm.value ) ) {
        ef.error.push( validationRules[o][ 'error' ] );
        ef.addErrorMsg( elm, validationRules[o][ 'error' ] );
      }
    break;
    case 'select-one' :
      var curelm = elm.options[elm.selectedIndex].value;
      if( elm.selectedIndex == 5 ) {
        curelm = document.getElementById( 'otherSubject' ).value;
      }
```

```
        if( !validationRules[o]['pattern'].test( curelm ) ) {
          ef.error.push( validationRules[o][ 'error' ] );
          ef.addErrorMsg( elm, validationRules[o]['error'] );
        }
      break;
    }
  },
```

The changes in the checkValue() method are that in addition to adding the error to the error array, you also call the new addErrorMsg() method with the element and the error text as parameters.

errorFields.js *(continued)*

```
addErrorMsg : function( o, msg ) {
    var errorMsg = document.createElement( 'span' );
    errorMsg.className = ef.errorClass;
    errorMsg.appendChild( document.createTextNode( msg ) );
    o.parentNode.insertBefore( errorMsg, o );
  },
```

The addErrorMsg method creates a new SPAN element, adds the error class to make it style-able, and adds the error text as a text node. It then inserts the new SPAN before the element with the error.

errorFields.js *(continued)*

```
  flushErrors:function() {
    var elm;
    ef.error = [];
    if( ef.errorMessage ) {
      ef.errorMessage.parentNode.removeChild( ef.errorMessage );
      ef.errorMessage = null;
    }
    for( var i in validationRules ) {
      elm = document.getElementById( i );
      if( !elm ) { continue; }
      if( elm.previousSibling &&
        elm.previousSibling.nodeName.toLowerCase() == 'span' &&
        elm.previousSibling.className == ef.errorClass ) {
        elm.parentNode.removeChild( elm.previousSibling );
      }
    }
  }
}
DOMhelp.addEvent(window, 'load', ef.init, false );
```

These changes mean that there is no single new element showing the errors but one at each erroneous field. This means that the flushErrors() method needs to loop through all mandatory fields and check whether there is a previous sibling node that is a SPAN and has the right class applied to it. If all of this is true, it removes that node.

Instant Validation Feedback

All of the preceding examples validate when the form is submitted, which is—as mentioned in earlier chapters—the most accessible way of validating forms. However, it does not hurt to make forms a bit more interactive if you still validate on submission. If the user realizes her errors and remedies them immediately, the submission validation will not trigger any errors anyways. The demo exampleDynamicFields.html validates fields immediately after you change them, and you can test it by opening it on your localhost.

The script needs a new method called sendField() and some minor changes in the init() method:

dynamicFields.js

```
df = {
  error : [],
  errorMessage : null,
  errorClass : 'error',
  errorTitle : 'Please fix the marked issues',
  init : function() {
    var elm;
    df.sendButton = document.getElementById( 'send' );
    if( !df.sendButton ) { return; }
    df.f = document.getElementsByTagName( 'form' )[0];
    DOMhelp.addEvent( df.f, 'submit', df.send,false );
    df.f.onsubmit = function() { return false; }
    for( var i in validationRules ) {
      elm = document.getElementById( i );
      if( !elm ){ continue; }
      DOMhelp.addEvent( elm, 'blur', df.sendField, false );
    }
  },
```

In addition to the submit handler on the form, you need to loop through all the mandatory fields and add a blur handler to the field pointing to sendField() as the event listener. If you only want feedback when the user changes the field rather than when he leaves it, you could also use a change handler.

dynamicFields.js *(continued)*

```
sendField : function( e ) {
  var t = DOMhelp.getTarget( e );
  if( t.previousSibling &&
      t.previousSibling.nodeName.toLowerCase() == 'span'  &&
      t.previousSibling.className == df.errorClass ) {
    t.parentNode.removeChild( t.previousSibling );
  }
  df.checkValue( t.id );
},
```

The sendField() method needs to retrieve the current element via getTarget(). It then removes any error message that might already be visible the same way flushErrors() does it and calls checkValue() with the ID of the element as a parameter. That is all there is to it.

dynamicFields.js *(continued)*

```
send : function( e ) {
  [... code snipped ...]
},
flushErrors : function() {
  [... code snipped ...]
},
checkValue : function( o ) {
  [... code snipped ...]
},
addErrorMsg : function( o, msg ) {
  [... code snipped ...]
}
}
DOMhelp.addEvent( window, 'load', df.init, false );
```

The rest of the script remains unchanged.

Other Dynamic Validation Methods

It is very tempting to make every field validate immediately when the user changes it, and you can do a lot with Ajax and the proper back-end datasets or functionality. One great example is to include suggestions of what data is valid while you enter a form.

Google Suggest (http://www.google.com/webhp?complete=1) was one of the first examples of web forms to do that. It offers you searches other users have already done with the number of possible results as shown in Figure 9-4.

Figure 9-4. *Google Suggest showing possible results while you type*

Offering suggestions this way is not hard to do, and you can use the knowledge from the previous chapters to create a suggestion form element. The demo exampleContactSuggest.html does just that. It uses Ajax to read an XML file containing contact names and compares them with what the user enters while she types. Figure 9-5 shows one possible outcome.

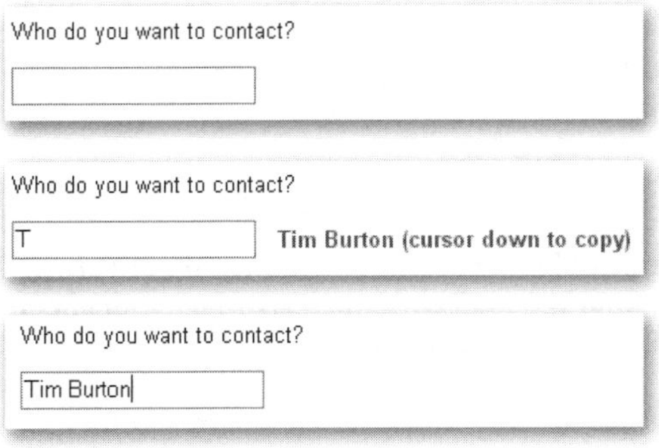

Figure 9-5. *Offering data dynamically from an XML dataset*

The XML data is very simple:

contacts.xml

```xml
<?xml version="1.0" encoding="utf-8"?>
<contacts>
  <name>Bill Gates</name>
  <name>Linus Torvalds</name>
  <name>Douglas Coupland</name>
  <name>Ridley Scott</name>
  <name>George Lucas</name>
  <name>Dan Akroyd</name>
  <name>Sigourney Weaver</name>
  <name>Tim Burton</name>
  <name>Katie Jane Garside</name>
  <name>Winona Ryder</name>
</contacts>
```

In a real-life example you might want to add a contact element around each name and add other data, like e-mail, extension, and department.

The script uses the XHR you've seen in the last chapter mixed with some regular expressions:

contactSuggest.js

```javascript
cs = {
  init : function() {
    if( !document.getElementById || !document.createTextNode ) {
      return;
    }
    cs.f = document.getElementById( 'contact' );
    if( !cs.f ) { return; }
    cs.output = document.createElement( 'span' );
    cs.f.parentNode.insertBefore( cs.output, cs.f.nextSibling )
    DOMhelp.addEvent( cs.f, 'keyup', cs.check, false );
  },
```

You test for DOM support and whether there is a field with the ID contact. If both are a given, you create a new SPAN element and add it after the field with the ID contact. You add an event handler on keyup that triggers the check() event listener method.

contactSuggest.js *(continued)*

```javascript
check : function( e ) {
  if( window.event ) {
    var key = window.event.keyCode;
  } else if( e ) {
    var key = e.keyCode;
  }
  if( key == 8 ) { return; }
  if( key == 40 ) {
    cs.f.value = cs.output.innerHTML.replace( /\s\(.*\)$/, '' );
    cs.output.innerHTML = '';
    return;
  }
  cs.doxhr( 'contacts.xml' );
},
```

This method finds out which key was pressed, and returns when it is the Backspace (8). If the user hit the down arrow key (40), it removes anything starting with a space and ending in a parenthesis from the content of the SPAN and copies it into the form field. It then deletes the content of the SPAN and returns. If the user pressed any other key, the check() method invokes the doxhr() method with contacts.xml as the URI to load.

contactSuggest.js *(continued)*

```javascript
doxhr : function( url ) {
  var request;
  try{
    request = new XMLHttpRequest();
  } catch ( error ){
    try{
      request = new ActiveXObject("Microsoft.XMLHTTP");
    } catch ( error ) {
      return true;
    }
  }
  request.open( 'get', url, true );
  request.onreadystatechange = function() {
    if( request.readyState == 4) {
      if (request.status && /200|304/.test( request.status ) ) {
        cs.retrieved( request );
```

```
          } else {
            cs.failed( request );
          }
        }
      }
      request.setRequestHeader( 'If-Modified-Since', ➡
                               'Wed, 05 Apr 2006 00:00:00 GMT' );
      request.send( null );
      return false;
    },
```

There is no change to the xhr() method; you create an XMLHttpRequest and load the URI sent as a parameter.

contactSuggest.js *(continued)*

```
  retrieved : function( requester ) {
    var v;
    var pattern = new RegExp( '^'+cs.f.value, 'i' );
    var data = requester.responseXML;
    var names = data.getElementsByTagName( 'name' );
    for( var i = 0; i < names.length; i++ ) {
      v = names[i].firstChild.nodeValue;
      if( pattern.test( v ) ) {
        cs.output.innerHTML = v + ' (cursor down to copy)';
        break;
      }
    }
  },
```

The retrieved method creates a regular expression that tests whether something starts with the value of the contact field. It reads the content of contacts.xml from responseXML, retrieves all the names using getElementsByTagName(), and loops through them. If any of the names matches the pattern, it writes the text content of the name followed by the message "(cursor down to copy)" into the SPAN and stops the loop.

contactSuggest.js *(continued)*

```
  failed : function( requester ) {
    alert( 'The XMLHttpRequest failed. Status: ' + requester.status );
    return true;
  }
}
DOMhelp.addEvent( window, 'load', cs.init, false );
```

If there is an error, the user is informed via an alert. When the window has finished loading the document, the method `cs.init()` is called.

For a small number of contacts, using XHR is probably not worth the effort, and you'd be better off importing the data in JSON format and spare yourself the server round-trips every time the user hits a key. However, this example could also use a database to retrieve the right contact.

Summary

I hope that you feel quite confident to write your own form validation scripts and regular expressions after this chapter. It is not that hard to do, but as said before, it is too easy to take validation lightly or assume too many givens.

Form validation is as much a usability problem as it is a technical issue. You have to make sure that your validation methods make sense in the technical environment you are dealing with and that the solution fits the regulations of the product. Many online forms these days have to adhere to accessibility guidelines or sometimes even bespoke regulations (for example, when you work on local government sites). If your validation mechanism requires the user to see the form or use a mouse, then you will not be able to fulfill these guidelines.

It is very tempting to use the most modern approach and make everything dynamic in web sites these days. Be aware of restrictions and usage patterns of the audience you want to reach, and ensure that everything works without JavaScript, and you'll make both your clients and yourself happy.

In the next chapter, we'll take on a larger project and create a dynamic image gallery powered by the back end and spiced up with CSS, JavaScript, and Ajax.

■■■

CHAPTER 10

Modern JavaScript Case Study: A Dynamic Gallery

In this chapter, you will learn how to develop a JavaScript-enhanced thumbnail gallery backed up by a PHP script. You'll start with techniques of static galleries and how to enhance them and move on to a gallery that uses PHP and Ajax to pull images dynamically from the server.

■Note You can download the demo code of this chapter or see the results online at `http://www.beginningjavascript.com`. As the chapter contains image galleries, the download is on the larger side, but it allows you to see all the code—including the server-side PHP—on your local server.

Basics of Thumbnail Galleries

Let's start at the basics first and plan our thumbnail gallery. I pondered for a long time whether I should include one in this book, as it has become almost cliché for JavaScript and CSS books to have galleries as examples. However, I wrote this chapter to give an example of how you can spice up a very common solution like a thumbnail gallery with modern scripting and CSS and stay independent of the both of them. Many examples—especially CSS-only galleries—look great and work in modern browsers; however, they don't degrade well and don't really deliver what a thumbnail gallery is supposed to deliver.

What Is a Thumbnail Gallery and What Should It Do?

The idea of a thumbnail gallery goes back to the times when browsers started to support images, and connection speeds on the Web could be measured in the single kilobits. The job of such a gallery was and still is to give an overview of what images are available by providing a smaller preview of each image in the gallery. "Smaller" means smaller in dimensions but also—and most importantly—smaller in file size. This means that a visitor who is only interested in one picture in your gallery does not need to download all images, only the one he is interested in—saving both him time and you server traffic. A lot of CSS-only or JavaScript/HTML thumbnail galleries fail to do this and assume that every user wants to download the lot to see one image. You can offer downloading of all the images, but it should be an option rather than a requirement. The worst thumbnail galleries resize photos via HTML attributes or CSS to thumbnails, thus forcing visitors to download the large images to see them as bad-quality thumbnails. Resizing images by altering their dimensions in CSS, via JavaScript, or by (ab)using HTML attributes does not result in good-quality thumbnails; it is simply laziness and a bad idea.

If you want to offer thumbnail galleries in their original sense, you need to generate smaller thumbnail pictures of the large images you want to show. You can do that either as a batch process before you upload the gallery or on the fly via scripting on the server.

■Tip There are a lot of thumbnail-generation and batch-generation tools available. Good—and most importantly free—ones are Google's Picasa (available at `http://picasa.google.com/`) and IrfanView (available at `http://www.irfanview.com/`). Generating thumbnails on the server can be easily achieved with PHP and the GD library. I've written an article how to do that, available at `http://icant.co.uk/articles/phpthumbnails/`, and there is a great premade PHP class called `phpThumb()` available at `http://phpthumb.sourceforge.net/`. As this is a book about JavaScript, I will not get into the details of image generation via PHP, although it is amazingly handy for online galleries.

Static Thumbnail Galleries

Traditional thumbnail galleries offer the small thumbnail images inside a table or a list. Each of the thumbnails links to a page with the large image that in return links back to the thumbnail gallery or offers previous and next image links.

If there are a lot of images, the thumbnail pages may be paginated, showing a certain number of thumbnails at a time and offering navigation forward and backward through the whole collection. With purely static galleries, this means you have to generate all the thumbnail pages, and one for each photo, which is a lot of work initially and a lot of files to transfer to the server on every update of the gallery.

Faking Dynamic Galleries with JavaScript

You can use JavaScript to turn a static thumbnail gallery into a seemingly dynamic gallery by applying event handlers to all the thumbnails. When a thumbnail is clicked, you cover the thumbnails with a new element containing the large image. Keep the gallery accessible to non-JavaScript users by linking the thumbnail to the large picture and simply showing this in the browser:

exampleFakeDynamic.html *(excerpt)*

```
<ul id="thumbs">
  <li>
    <a href="galleries/animals/dog2.jpg">
      <img src="galleries/animals/tn_dog2.jpg" alt="tn_dog2.jpg" />
    </a>
  </li>
  <li>
    <a href="galleries/animals/dog3.jpg">
      <img src="galleries/animals/tn_dog3.jpg" alt="tn_dog3.jpg" />
    </a>
  </li>
  <li>
    <a href="galleries/animals/dog4.jpg">
      <img src="galleries/animals/tn_dog4.jpg" alt="tn_dog4.jpg" />
    </a>
  </li>
  [... more thumbnails ...]
</ul>
```

■**Tip** You might as well use tables or definition lists for thumbnail galleries, as tables degrade better because they remain multicolumn constructs even in non-CSS browsers and definition lists are semantically correct, too. For the examples in this chapter, I used a simple list to keep things easy and allow the thumbnails to take up as much space as is available on the screen.

You can test the effect by opening the demo exampleFakeDynamic.html. Let's go through the functionality step by step, starting with a skeleton for the script:

fakeDynamic.js *(skeleton)*

```
fakegal = {
  // IDs
  thumbsListID : 'thumbs',
  largeContainerID : 'photo',
  // CSS classes
  closeClass : 'close',
  nextClass : 'next',
  prevClass : 'prev',
  hideClass : 'hide',
  showClass : 'show',
  // Labels
  closeLabel : 'close',
  prevContent : '<img src="last.gif" alt="previous photo" />',
  nextContent : '<img src="next.gif" alt="next photo" />',

  init : function(){  },
  createContainer : function(){},
  showPic : function(e){  },
  setPic : function(pic){ },
  navPic : function(e){  }
DOMhelp.addEvent( window, 'load', fakegal.init, false );
```

You need

- The ID of the element containing all the thumbnails

- An ID to assign to the large picture container

- CSS classes for the link to remove the large picture

- The links to navigate through the large pictures

- Classes to show and hide elements

- A label to tell the user that the link hides the large picture

- Labels for the next and previous picture links

In terms of methods, you need

- A method to initialize the functionality

- A utility method that initially creates the image container

- A method to show the picture

- A method to set the picture to be shown

- A method to navigate to the next or previous picture

The method setting the picture to be shown, setPic(), is necessary because both the showing method, showPic(), and the navigation method, navPic(), change the image in the container.

fakeDynamic.js

```
fakegal = {
  // IDs
  thumbsListID : 'thumbs',
  largeContainerID : 'photo',
  // CSS classes
  closeClass : 'close',
  nextClass : 'next',
  prevClass : 'prev',
  hideClass : 'hide',
  showClass : 'show',
  // Labels
  closeLabel : 'close',
  prevContent : '<img src="last.gif" alt="previous photo" />',
  nextContent : '<img src="next.gif" alt="next photo" />',
  init:function() {
    if( !document.getElementById || !document.createTextNode ) {
      return;
    }
    fakegal.tlist = document.getElementById( fakegal.thumbsListID );
    if( !fakegal.tlist ){ return; }
    var thumbsLinks = fakegal.tlist.getElementsByTagName( 'a' );
    fakegal.all = thumbsLinks.length;
    for(var i = 0 ; i < thumbsLinks.length; i++ ) {
      DOMhelp.addEvent( thumbsLinks[i], 'click', ➥
      fakegal.showPic, false );
      thumbsLinks[i].onclick = DOMhelp.safariClickFix;
      thumbsLinks[i].i = i;
    }
    fakegal.createContainer();
  },
```

The init() method tests whether DOM is supported and retrieves the element that contains the thumbnails. It then loops through all the links after storing the number of all links in a property called all (this is necessary later on to avoid a next link on the last image). It applies an event handler pointing to showPic() to each link in the thumbnail list and stores its index number in a new property called i before calling createContainer() to add the necessary image container element to the document.

fakeDynamic.js *(continued)*

```
createContainer : function() {
  fakegal.c = document.createElement( 'div' );
  fakegal.c.id = fakegal.largeContainerID;
```

You start the createContainer() method by creating a new DIV element, storing it in a property called c, and assigning the large image container ID to it.

fakeDynamic.js *(continued)*

```
var p = document.createElement( 'p' );
var cl = DOMhelp.createLink( '#', fakegal.closeLabel );
cl.className = fakegal.closeClass;
p.appendChild( cl );
DOMhelp.addEvent( cl, 'click', fakegal.setPic, false );
cl.onclick = DOMhelp.safariClickFix;
fakegal.c.appendChild(p);
```

Create a new paragraph and insert a link into it with the closeLabel as text content. Assign an event handler pointing to setPic() to the link, apply the Safari fix, and add the paragraph to the container element.

fakeDynamic.js *(continued)*

```
var il = DOMhelp.createLink( '#', '' );
DOMhelp.addEvent( il, 'click', fakegal.setPic, false );
il.onclick = DOMhelp.safariClickFix;
fakegal.c.appendChild( il );
```

Now add another—empty—link to the container with an event handler calling setPic(). This link will later surround the large picture, making it clickable and thus possible for keyboard users to get rid of it.

fakeDynamic.js *(continued)*

```
    fakegal.next = DOMhelp.createLink( '#', '' );
    fakegal.next.innerHTML = fakegal.nextContent;
    fakegal.next.className = fakegal.nextClass;
    DOMhelp.addEvent( fakegal.next, 'click', fakegal.navPic, false );
    fakegal.next.onclick = DOMhelp.safariClickFix;
    fakegal.c.appendChild( fakegal.next );

    fakegal.prev = DOMhelp.createLink( '#', '' );
    fakegal.prev.innerHTML = fakegal.prevContent;
    fakegal.prev.className = fakegal.prevClass;
    DOMhelp.addEvent( fakegal.prev, 'click', fakegal.navPic, false );
    fakegal.prev.onclick = DOMhelp.safariClickFix;
    fakegal.c.appendChild( fakegal.prev );
```

Two more links need to be added to show the previous and the next image, respectively, both with event handlers pointing to navPic().

fakeDynamic.js *(continued)*

```
    fakegal.tlist.parentNode.appendChild( fakegal.c );
  }
```

Add the new container to the parent node of the thumbnail list, and the show can begin.

fakeDynamic.js *(continued)*

```
  showPic : function( e ) {
    var t = DOMhelp.getTarget(e);
    if( t.nodeName.toLowerCase() != 'a' ) {
      t = t.parentNode;
    }
    fakegal.current = t.i;
    var largePic = t.getAttribute( 'href' );
    fakegal.setPic( largePic );
    DOMhelp.cancelClick( e );
  },
```

In the event listener method showPic(), retrieve the target and determine whether it really is a link by testing the nodeName. Then store the i property that was assigned to each thumbnail link in the init() method as the value of a new property, current, of the main object to tell all other methods which picture is currently shown. Retrieve the link's href attribute and call the setPic() method with the href as a parameter before stopping the browser from following the link via cancelClick().

fakeDynamic.js *(continued)*

```
  setPic : function( pic ) {
    var a;
    var picLink = fakegal.c.getElementsByTagName('a')[1];
    picLink.innerHTML = '';
```

The setPic() method takes the second link inside the image container (which is the link after the closing link) and removes any content that this link might have by setting its innerHTML property to an empty string. This is necessary to avoid more than one picture showing at a time.

fakeDynamic.js *(continued)*

```
    if( typeof pic == 'string' ) {
      fakegal.c.className = fakegal.showClass;
      var i = document.createElement( 'img' );
      i.setAttribute( 'src' , pic );
      picLink.appendChild( i );
```

You compare the type of the parameter pic with string, since the method may be called with a URL as the parameter or without it. If there is a parameter that is a valid string, you add the show class to the container to show it to the user and add a new image to it with the pic parameter as its source.

fakeDynamic.js *(continued)*

```
    } else {
      fakegal.c.className = '';
    }
```

If there isn't a parameter of the type string, you remove any class from the picture container, thus hiding it.

fakeDynamic.js *(continued)*

```
    a = fakegal.current == 0 ? 'add' : 'remove';
    DOMhelp.cssjs( a, fakegal.prev, fakegal.hideClass );
    a = fakegal.current == fakegal.all-1 ? 'add' : 'remove';
    DOMhelp.cssjs( a, fakegal.next, fakegal.hideClass );
  },
```

Test to see whether the current property of the main object is equal to 0, and hide the previous picture link if this is the case. Do the same with the next picture link and compare current with the number of all thumbnails (stored in all). Hide or show each link by adding or removing the hide class.

fakeDynamic.js *(continued)*

```
navPic : function( e ) {
  var t = DOMhelp.getTarget( e );
  if( t.nodeName.toLowerCase() != 'a' ) {
    t = t.parentNode;
  }
  var c = fakegal.current;
  if( t == fakegal.prev ) {
    c -= 1;
  } else {
    c += 1;
  }
  fakegal.current = c;
  var pic = fakegal.tlist.getElementsByTagName('a')[c];
  fakegal.setPic( pic.getAttribute( 'href' ) );
  DOMhelp.cancelClick( e );
  }
}
DOMhelp.addEvent( window, 'load', fakegal.init, false );
```

Retrieve a reference to the link that was clicked (by getting the event target via DOMhelp's getTarget() and ensuring the nodeName is A), and determine whether the link is the previous link by comparing this node to the one stored in the prev property. Increment or decrement current depending on which link was activated. Then call setPic() with the href attribute of the new current link and prevent the browser from following the activated link by calling cancelClick().

All that is left is to add a style sheet; the result might appear as shown in Figure 10-1.

Figure 10-1. *Using JavaScript to simulate a server-controlled dynamic image gallery*

Displaying Captions

Thumbnail galleries are visual constructs, but it is still a good idea to think about alternative text and image captioning. Not only will these make your gallery accessible to blind users, but they also allow for searching the thumbnail data and indexing it through search engines.

Many tools like Google's Picasa allow for dynamic captioning and addition of alternative text. You could use XHR to create something similar, but as this is a book about JavaScript, and how to store the entered data on the server would need some explanation, it is not a relevant example. Instead, let's modify the "fake" gallery so that it displays captions.

You'll use the image's title attribute as a caption for the image; this means that the static HTML needs proper alternative text and title data.

exampleFakeDynamicAlt.html *(excerpt)*

```
<ul id="thumbs">
  <li>
    <a href="galleries/animals/dog2.jpg">
      <img src="galleries/animals/tn_dog2.jpg"
      title="This square is mine"
      alt="Dog in a shady square" />
    </a>
  </li>
  <li>
    <a href="galleries/animals/dog3.jpg">
      <img src="galleries/animals/tn_dog3.jpg"
      title="Sleepy bouncer"
      alt="Dog on the steps of a shop" />
    </a>
  </li>
  [... More thumbnails ...]
</ul>
```

The script itself does not have to change much; basically all it needs is an extra paragraph in the generated image container and alterations of the methods to send the caption and alternative text data to the large image container.

fakeDynamicAlt.js

```
fakegal = {
  // IDs
  thumbsListID : 'thumbs',
  largeContainerID : 'photo',
  // CSS classes
  closeClass : 'close',
  nextClass : 'next',
  prevClass : 'prev',
  hideClass : 'hide',
  closeLabel : 'close',
  captionClass : 'caption',
  // Labels
  showClass : 'show',
  prevContent : '<img src="last.gif" alt="previous photo" />',
  nextContent : '<img src="next.gif" alt="next photo" />',
```

The first change is a cosmetic one: you add a new CSS class that will be applied to the caption.

fakeDynamicAlt.js *(continued)*

```
  init : function() {
    if( !document.getElementById || !document.createTextNode ) {
      return;
    }
    fakegal.tlist = document.getElementById( fakegal.thumbsListID );
    if( !fakegal.tlist ) { return; }
    var thumbsLinks = fakegal.tlist.getElementsByTagName( 'a' );
    fakegal.all = thumbsLinks.length;
    for( var i = 0; i < thumbsLinks.length; i++ ) {
      DOMhelp.addEvent( thumbsLinks[i], 'click',➥
      fakegal.showPic, false );
      thumbsLinks[i].onclick = DOMhelp.safariClickFix;
      thumbsLinks[i].i = i;
    }
    fakegal.createContainer();
  },
  showPic : function( e ) {
    var t = DOMhelp.getTarget( e );
    if( t.nodeName.toLowerCase() != 'a' ) {
      t = t.parentNode;
    }
    fakegal.current = t.i;
    var largePic = t.getAttribute( 'href' );
    var img = t.getElementsByTagName( 'img' )[0];
    var alternative = img.getAttribute( 'alt' );
    var caption = img.getAttribute('title');
    fakegal.setPic( largePic, caption, alternative );
    DOMhelp.cancelClick( e );
  },
```

The init() method remains unchanged, but the showPic() method needs to read the alternative text and the title attribute of the image, in addition to the href attribute of the link, and send all three of them as parameters to setPic().

fakeDynamicAlt.js *(continued)*

```
setPic : function( pic, caption, alternative ) {
  var a;
  var picLink = fakegal.c.getElementsByTagName( 'a' )[1];
  picLink.innerHTML = '';
  fakegal.caption.innerHTML = '';
  if( typeof pic == 'string' ) {
    fakegal.c.className = fakegal.showClass;
    var i = document.createElement( 'img' );
    i.setAttribute( 'src', pic );
    i.setAttribute( 'alt' ,alternative );
    picLink.appendChild( I );
  } else {
    fakegal.c.className = '';
  }
  a = fakegal.current == 0 ? 'add' : 'remove';
  DOMhelp.cssjs( a, fakegal.prev, fakegal.hideClass );
  a = fakegal.current == fakegal.all-1 ? 'add' : 'remove';
  DOMhelp.cssjs( a, fakegal.next, fakegal.hideClass );
  if( caption != '' ) {
   var ctext = document.createTextNode( caption );
    fakegal.caption.appendChild( ctext );
  }
},
```

The setPic() method now takes three parameters instead of one—the source of the large picture, the caption, and the alternative text. The method needs to delete any caption that may already be visible, set the alternative text attribute of the large picture, and display the new caption.

fakeDynamicAlt.js *(continued)*

```
  navPic : function( e ) {
    var t = DOMhelp.getTarget( e );
    if( t.nodeName.toLowerCase() != 'a' ) {
      t = t.parentNode;
    }
    var c = fakegal.current;
    if( t == fakegal.prev ) {
      c -= 1;
    } else {
      C += 1;
    }
    fakegal.current = c;
    var pic = fakegal.tlist.getElementsByTagName( 'a' )[c];
    var img = pic.getElementsByTagName( 'img' )[0];
    var caption = img.getAttribute( 'title' );
    var alternative = img.getAttribute( 'alt' );
    fakegal.setPic( pic.getAttribute('href'), caption, alternative );
    DOMhelp.cancelClick( e );
  },
```

The navPic() method, just like the init() method, needs to retrieve the alternative text, the caption, and the source of the large picture and send them to setPic().

fakeDynamicAlt.js *(continued)*

```
  createContainer : function() {
    fakegal.c = document.createElement( 'div' );
    fakegal.c.id = fakegal.largeContainerID;

    var p = document.createElement( 'p' );
    var cl = DOMhelp.createLink( '#', fakegal.closeLabel );
    cl.className = fakegal.closeClass;
    p.appendChild( cl );
    DOMhelp.addEvent( cl, 'click', fakegal.setPic, false );
    cl.onclick = DOMhelp.safariClickFix;
    fakegal.c.appendChild( p );

    var il = DOMhelp.createLink( '#', '' );
    DOMhelp.addEvent( il, 'click', fakegal.setPic, false );
    il.onclick = DOMhelp.safariClickFix;
    fakegal.c.appendChild( il );
```

```
    fakegal.next = DOMhelp.createLink( '#', '' );
    fakegal.next.innerHTML = fakegal.nextContent;
    fakegal.next.className = fakegal.nextClass;
    DOMhelp.addEvent( fakegal.next, 'click', fakegal.navPic, false );
    fakegal.next.onclick = DOMhelp.safariClickFix;
    fakegal.c.appendChild( fakegal.next );

    fakegal.prev = DOMhelp.createLink( '#', '' );
    fakegal.prev.innerHTML = fakegal.prevContent;
    fakegal.prev.className = fakegal.prevClass;
    DOMhelp.addEvent( fakegal.prev, 'click', fakegal.navPic, false );
    fakegal.prev.onclick = DOMhelp.safariClickFix;
    fakegal.c.appendChild( fakegal.prev );

    fakegal.caption = document.createElement( 'p' );
    fakegal.caption.className = fakegal.captionClass;
    fakegal.c.appendChild( fakegal.caption );

    fakegal.tlist.parentNode.appendChild( fakegal.c );
  }
}
DOMhelp.addEvent( window, 'load', fakegal.init, false );
```

The `createContainer()` method needs only one small change, which is creating a new paragraph in the container to host the caption.

As you can see, creating dynamic galleries with JavaScript means generating a lot of HTML elements and reading and writing of attributes. It is up to you to decide whether it is worth the hassle or not. This gets even worse when you want to offer pagination of the thumbnails.

Instead of doing all of this in JavaScript, you could do it on the back end (for example, with PHP or ASP.NET) and offer a fully functional gallery to all users, and only improve it via XHR and JavaScript.

Dynamic Thumbnail Galleries

Real dynamic thumbnail galleries use URL parameters, instead of lots of static pages, and create the pagination and show the thumbs or the large images depending on these parameters.

The demo `examplePHPgallery.php` works that way, and Figure 10-2 shows what this might look like.

Figure 10-2. *A dynamic PHP-driven thumbnail gallery example with thumbnail pagination and previous and next image preview on the large picture page*

This gallery is fully functional and accessible without JavaScript, but you may not want to reload the whole page every time the user clicks a thumbnail. Using XHR, you can offer both. Instead of using the original PHP document, you use a cut-down version that only generates the content you need, in this case `gallerytools.php`. I won't go into details of the PHP script; suffice to say that it does the following for you:

- It reads the contents of a folder the link in the main menu points to, checks it for images, and returns ten at a time as a HTML list with thumbnails linked to the large images.

- It adds a pagination menu that shows which ten of how many images in total are displayed and offers previous and next links.

- If any of the thumbnails is clicked, it returns the HTML of the large image and a menu showing the next and the previous thumbnail.

You use this output to overwrite the HTML output of the original PHP script as shown in the demo examplePHPXHRgallery.php. Without JavaScript, it does the same as examplePHPgallery.php; however, when JavaScript is available, it will not reload the whole document, but only refresh the gallery itself. You achieve this by replacing the links in the content section with links to gallerytools.php and XHR calls instead of reloading the whole page.

dyngal_xhr.js

```
dyngal = {
  contentID : 'content',
  originalPHP : 'examplePHPXHRgallery.php',
  dynamicPHP : 'gallerytools.php',
   init : function() {
     if( !document.getElementById || !document.createTextNode ) {
       return;
     }
     dyngal.assignHandlers( dyngal.contentID );
   },
```

You start by defining your properties:

- The ID of the element that contains the content that should be replaced with the HTML returned from gallerytools.php

- The file name of the original script

- The file name of the script that returns the data you call via XHR

The init() method tests for DOM support and calls the assignHandlers() method with the content element ID as a parameter.

Note In this case, you only replace one content element; however, as there may be situations where you want to replace numerous different sections of the page, it is a good idea to create separate methods for tasks like these.

---

dyngal_xhr.js *(continued)*

```
assignHandlers : function( o ) {
   if( !document.getElementById( o ) ){ return; }
   o = document.getElementById( o );
   var gLinks = o.getElementsByTagName( 'a' );
   for(var i = 0; i < gLinks.length; i++ ) {
     DOMhelp.addEvent( gLinks[i], 'click', dyngal.load, false );
     gLinks[i].onclick = DOMhelp.safariClickFix;
   }
},
```

The assignHandlers() method tests whether the element with the ID that was sent as a parameter exists, and then loops through all the links in the element. Next, it adds an event handler pointing to the load method and applies the Safari fix to prevent that browser from following the original link (remember—the preventDefault() method used in cancelClick() is supported by Safari, but does not stop the link from being followed due to a bug in Safari).

dyngal_xhr.js *(continued)*

```
load : function( e ) {
  var t = DOMhelp.getTarget( e );
  if( t.nodeName.toLowerCase() != 'a' ) {
    t = t.parentNode;
  }
  var h = t.getAttribute( 'href' );
  h = h.replace( dyngal.originalPHP, dyngal.dynamicPHP );
  dyngal.doxhr( h, dyngal.contentID );
  DOMhelp.cancelClick( e );
},
```

In the load method, you retrieve the event target and make sure it is a link. You then read the href attribute of the link and replace the original PHP script name with the dynamic one that only returns the content you need. You call the doxhr() method with the href value and the content element ID as parameters and stop the link propagation by calling cancelClick().

dyngal_xhr.js *(continued)*

```
doxhr : function( url, container ) {
  var request;
  try{
    request = new XMLHttpRequest();
  } catch( error ) {
    try {
      request = new ActiveXObject("Microsoft.XMLHTTP");
    } catch ( error ) {
      return true;
```

```
        }
      }
      request.open( 'get', url, true );
      request.onreadystatechange = function() {
        if( request.readyState == 1 ) {
          container.innerHTML = 'Loading...';
        }
        if( request.readyState == 4 ) {
          if( request.status && /200|304/.test( request.status ) ) {
            dyngal.retrieved( request, container );
          } else {
            dyngal.failed( request );
          }
        }
      }
      request.setRequestHeader( 'If-Modified-Since',➥
      'Wed, 05 Apr 2006 00:00:00 GMT');
      request.send( null );
      return false;
    },
    retrieved : function( request, container ) {
      var data = request.responseText;
      document.getElementById(container).innerHTML = data;
      dyngal.assignHandlers( container );
    },
    failed : function( request ) {
      alert( 'The XMLHttpRequest failed. Status: ' + requester.status );
      return true;
    }
  }
}
DOMhelp.addEvent( window, 'load', dyngal.init, false );
```

The XHR methods are the same as those you used in Chapter 8. The only difference is that you need to call the `assignHandlers()` method again, as you replaced the original content and as a result lost the event handlers on the links.

■**Note** PHP and JavaScript are a powerful combination. Once you have mastered JavaScript, it might be a good idea to look into PHP, as without knowledge of a server-side language Ajax is less fun. PHP can do what JavaScript cannot—reach files on the server and read their names and properties, and even reach content from third-party servers. PHP syntax is similar to that of JavaScript in some respects, and the nature of the language makes it easy to take the first steps without having to deal with compilers or command-line inter-faces to build your scripts.

Creating an Image Badge from a Folder

Let's have a go at another small gallery example using PHP and JavaScript/XHR before we look at some ready-made third-party code and online services in the next chapter.

If you already use Flickr (http://www.flickr.com) or you read blogs a lot, you may have encountered **Flickr badges**, which are small galleries showing the latest photos the maintainer of the site has uploaded to the system. Figure 10-3 shows my blog as an example.

Figure 10-3. *My latest photos on Flickr as a badge on my blog*

Let's spice up the idea of a badge by allowing the user to navigate through the thumbnails with previous and next links and showing the large photo by clicking the thumbnail. The demo exampleBadge.html does this, and Figure 10-4 shows how it looks with two badge galleries in Firefox on Windows XP.

Figure 10-4. *Two image folders as badge galleries*

When creating scripts like these, it is a good idea to keep the HTML as easy as possible. The less you expect from the maintainer, the more likely it is that people will use your script. In this case, all the maintainer needs to do to add a badge gallery to the HTML document is to add an element with the class badge and a link pointing to the folder containing the images:

exampleBadge.html *(excerpt)*

```
<p class="badge"><a href="galleries/animals/">Animals</a></p>
<p class="badge"><a href="galleries/buildings/">Buildings</a></p>
```

As JavaScript cannot check a folder on the server for files, you need a PHP script to do this for you. The file badge.php does so and returns thumbnails as list items.

■**Note** The following is a quick explanation of the PHP script. This is not JavaScript, but I hope you appreciate some insight into the workings of the tools the upcoming badge script uses.

---

badge.php

```php
<?php
$c = preg_match( '/\d+/', $_GET['c'] ) ? $_GET['c'] : 5;
$s = preg_match( '/\d+/', $_GET['s'] ) ? $_GET['s'] : 0;
$cd = is_dir( $_GET['cd'] ) ? $_GET['cd'] : '';
```

You define three variables: $c, which stores the number of thumbnails to be shown; $s, which is the index of what is currently the first thumbnail in the list of all thumbnails; and $cd, which is the folder URL on the server. The $_GET array of PHP stores all the parameters of the URL, which means that if the URL were to be badge.php?c=3&s=0&cd=animals, $_GET['c'] would be 3, $_GET['s'] would be 0, and $_GET['cd'] would be animals. You can use regular expressions to make sure that $c and $s are integers and preset to 5 and 0, respectively, and the is_dir() function of PHP to make sure that $cd really is an available folder.

badge.php *(continued)*

```php
if( $cd != '' ) {
  $handle = opendir($cd);
   if( preg_match( '/^tn_.*(jpg|jpe|jpeg)$/i', $file ) ) {
      $images[] = $file;
   }
 }
 closedir( $handle );
```

If the folder is available, you start reading out each file in the folder with the opendir() method and test whether the file is a thumbnail by matching its name with the pattern ^tn_.*(jpg|jpe|jpeg)$ (starts with tn_ and ends with either jpg, jpe, or jpeg). If the file is a thumbnail, add it to the images array. When there are no files left in the folder, close the folder by calling the closedir() method.

badge.php *(continued)*

```php
  $imgs = array_slice( $images, $s, $c );
  if( $s > 0 ) {
    echo '<li class="badgeprev">';
    echo '<a href="badge.php?c='.$c;
    echo '&amp;s=' . ( $s-$c ) . '&amp;cd='.$cd.'">';
    echo 'previous</a></li>';
  } else {
    echo '<li class="badgeprev"><span>previous</span></li>';
  }
```

You use the `array_slice()` method of PHP to reduce the array down to the chosen images ($c images starting at $s) and test whether $s is larger than 0. If it is, write out a list element with the class `badgeprev` that has the right parameters in the link's `href` attribute. If it isn't, write out a SPAN inside the list item instead of a link.

badge.php *(continued)*

```
for( $i=0; $i<sizeof($imgs); $i++ ) {
  echo '<li><a href="'.str_replace('tn_','',$cd.$imgs[$i]).'">'.
  '<img src="' . $cd . $imgs[$i] . '" alt="' . $imgs[$i] .
  '" /></a></li>';
}
```

Loop through the images and display an IMG element inside a link pointing to the large image for each array item. You can retrieve the link to the large image by removing the `tn_` string of the array element's value with `str_replace()`.

badge.php *(continued)*

```
if( ( $c+$s ) <= sizeof( $images ) ) {
  echo '<li class="badgenext">';
  echo '<a href="badge.php?c=' . $c . '&amp;s=' . ($s + $c);
  echo '&amp;cd=' . $cd . '">next</a></li>';
} else {
  echo '<li class="badgenext"><span>next</span></li>';
}
}
?>
```

Test whether $c and $s together are less than the number of all images in the folder and display a link if it is or a SPAN if it isn't.

As you can see, the programming syntax and logic of JavaScript and PHP is pretty similar, which is one of the reasons for the success of PHP. Let's now create the JavaScript that uses this PHP script to turn the links into image badges.

badge.js

```
badge = {
  badgeClass : 'badge',
  containerID : 'badgecontainer',
```

You define the CSS class used to specify the badge links and the ID of the image container showing the large picture as properties of the main object `badge`.

badge.js *(continued)*

```
init : function() {
  var newUL, parent, dir, loc;
  if( !document.getElementById || !document.createTextNode ) {
    return;
  }
  var links = document.getElementsByTagName( 'a' );
  for( var i = 0; i < links.length; i++ ) {
    parent = links[i].parentNode;
    if( !DOMhelp.cssjs( 'check', parent, badge.badgeClass ) ) {
      continue;
    }
```

You test for DOM support and loop through all links in the document, testing whether a particular link's parent node has the badge class assigned to it. If it doesn't, you skip this link.

badge.js *(continued)*

```
    newUL = document.createElement( 'ul' );
    newUL.className = badge.badgeClass;
    dir=links[i].getAttribute( 'href' );
    loc = window.location.toString().match( /(^.*\/)/g );
    dir = dir.replace( loc, '' );
    badge.doxhr( 'badge.php?cd=' + dir, newUL );
    parent.parentNode.insertBefore( newUL, parent );
    parent.parentNode.removeChild( parent );
    i--;
  }
}
```

You create a new list element and add the badge class to it. You retrieve the link's href attribute, read the window location, and remove anything in the window.location before the last / from the href attribute value. This is necessary to make the script work in Microsoft Internet Explorer.

■Note You might remember that the link is `<a href="galleries/animals/">Animals</a>`, and if you have the script on your localhost, for example, at `http://localhost/book/mybook/Chapter10_A_Dynamic_gallery/exampleBadge.html`, Mozilla returns the href attribute value as `galleries/animals/`. MSIE, however, returns `http://localhost/book/mybook/Chapter10_A_Dynamic_gallery/galleries/animals/`, and you need to remove the excess data, as `badge.php` expects only the folder name as the URL.

You call the doxhr() method with the correct URL and the newly created list as parameters, and add the list before the parent element of the current link. You then remove the link's parent element with the DOM method removeChild() and decrease the loop counter by one (you loop through all the links of the document, which means that when you remove one of them, the counter needs to decrease to stop the loop from skipping the following link).

badge.js *(continued)*

```
    badge.container = document.createElement( 'div' );
    badge.container.id = badge.containerID;
    document.body.appendChild( badge.container );
  },
```

You create a new DIV as the container for the large image, set its ID, and add it to the body of the document.

badge.js *(continued)*

```
  doxhr : function( url, container ) {
    var request;
    try {
      request = new XMLHttpRequest();
    } catch ( error ) {
      try {
        request = new ActiveXObject("Microsoft.XMLHTTP");
      } catch ( error ) {
        return true;
      }
    }
    request.open( 'get', url, true );
    request.onreadystatechange = function() {
      if( request.readyState == 1 ) {
      }
      if( request.readyState == 4 ) {
        if( request.status && /200|304/.test( request.status ) ) {
          badge.retrieved( request, container );
        } else{
          badge.failed( request );
        }
      }
    }
    request.setRequestHeader( 'If-Modified-Since', ➥
    'Wed, 05 Apr 2006 00:00:00 GMT');
    request.send( null );
    return false;
  },
  retrieved : function( request, container ) {
    var data = request.responseText;
    container.innerHTML = data;
    badge.assignHandlers( container );
  },
```

```
failed : function( requester ) {
  alert('The XMLHttpRequest failed. Status: ' + requester.status);
  return true;
},
```

The Ajax/XHR methods remain largely unchanged, the only difference being that when the data is successfully retrieved, the assignHandlers() method is called with the list item as a parameter.

badge.js *(continued)*

```
assignHandlers : function( o ) {
  var links = o.getElementsByTagName('a');
  for( var i = 0; i < links.length; i++ ) {
    links[i].parent = o;
    if( /badgeprev|badgenext/.test( links[i].parentNode.➡
    className ) ) {
      DOMhelp.addEvent( links[i], 'click', badge.load, false );
    } else {
      DOMhelp.addEvent( links[i], 'click', badge.show, false );
    }
  }
},
```

The assignHandlers() method loops through all the links in the element sent as the parameter o. It stores this element as a new property in each link called parent and tests whether the link has the class badgeprev or badgenext, which, as you may remember, are added by badge.php to the previous and next links. If the CSS class is there, assignHandlers() adds an event handler pointing to the load method; otherwise it adds an event handler pointing to the show method, as some links need to navigate through the thumbnails and others need to show the large image.

badge.js *(continued)*

```
load : function( e ) {
  var t = DOMhelp.getTarget( e );
  if( t.nodeName.toLowerCase() != 'a' ) {
    t = t.parentNode;
  }
  var dir = t.getAttribute( 'href' );
  var loc = window.location.toString().match( /(^.*\/)/g );
  dir = dir.replace( loc, '' );
  badge.doxhr( 'badge.php?cd=' + dir, t.parent );
  DOMhelp.cancelClick( e );
},
```

The load method retrieves the event target and makes sure it is a link. It retrieves the href attribute value of the event target and cleans it up before calling the doxhr method with the element stored in the link's parent property as the output container. You stop the link from being followed by calling DOMhelp's cancelClick().

badge.js *(continued)*

```
show : function( e ) {
  var t = DOMhelp.getTarget( e );
  if( t.nodeName.toLowerCase() != 'a' ) {
    t = t.parentNode;
  }
  var y = 0;
  if( self.pageYOffset ) {
    y = self.pageYOffset;
  } else if ( document.documentElement &&
              document.documentElement.scrollTop ) {
    y = document.documentElement.scrollTop;
  } else if( document.body ) {
    y = document.body.scrollTop;
  }
  badge.container.style.top = y + 'px';
  badge.container.style.left = 0 + 'px';
```

In the show method you once again retrieve the event target and test that it is a link. You then position the large image container on the screen. As you don't know where in the document the badge will be, the safest method to show the image is to read out the scroll position of the document. To achieve this, you need to do bit of object detection for different browsers.

■**Note** Firefox, Safari, and Opera store the current vertical scrolling position in a property of the window object called pageYOffset, MSIE without a proper HTML DOCTYPE stores it in the body.scrollTop of the document object, and MSIE with a proper HTML DOCTYPE and Firefox store it in the documentElement.scrollTop property of the document object.

You test for all these eventualities and position the image container accordingly by setting the left and top properties of its style attribute collection. This way you can always be sure that the large image will be visible in the user's browser window.

badge.js *(continued)*

```
    var source = t.getAttribute( 'href' );
    var newImg = document.createElement( 'img' );
    badge.deletePic();
    newImg.setAttribute( 'src', source );
    badge.container.appendChild( newImg );
    DOMhelp.addEvent( badge.container, 'click', badge.deletePic,➡
    false );
    DOMhelp.cancelClick( e );
  },
```

You read the href attribute of the link and create a new IMG element. You remove any large image that may already be shown by calling the deletePic() method and set the new image's src attribute to the href of the link. You add the new image as a child node to the image container, apply an event handler that calls deletePic() when the user clicks the image, and stop the link from being followed by calling cancelClick().

badge.js *(continued)*

```
  deletePic : function() {
    badge.container.innerHTML = '';
  }
}
DOMhelp.addEvent( window, 'load', badge.init, false );
```

All the deletePic method needs to do is to set the innerHTML property of the container element to an empty string, thus removing the large image.

Summary

In this chapter, you learned how to enhance already existing HTML structures or dynamic server-side scripts for thumbnail galleries with JavaScript either to become dynamic or to appear more dynamic by not loading the whole document when the user chooses another image or thumbnail subset.

Galleries are always fun to create and to come up with new and flashier solutions for, and I hope that by learning some of the tricks presented in this chapter you feel confident to play around with them and come up with your own gallery ideas.

■ ■ ■

CHAPTER 11

Using Third-Party JavaScript

As you'll have gathered by now, when you create a JavaScript application, you don't need to reinvent the wheel and recode all the functionality from scratch every time—JavaScript has many, many functions available for you to use, and you can create your own reusable functions and objects, too. But it goes even further than that—you can also make use of third-party code libraries and APIs, and there are many available on the Web these days. But it's knowing where, why, and how that's the key, and that's where this chapter comes in.

In this chapter, we will take a look at some ready-made content and code available on the Web these days. We'll quickly talk about the different kinds of resources you can find on the Web to make your JavaScript development easier: content in RSS format, REST services, APIs, code generators, and libraries. We'll take a look at a code library and try some examples, check how to add an interactive map to your web site in a matter of minutes using the Google Maps API, and take a closer look at Yahoo's User Interface Library.

What the Web Offers You

We are currently living in pretty exciting times as developers. Over the last few years, the outlook of companies in terms of sharing content and technology has changed drastically. In the past, every company guarded its content and code as if it were made of platinum, and getting any information about the workings of a system or how to communicate with it was a painful and long-winded process including price negotiations, nonworking demonstrations, Power-Point presentations, preview code, and other marketing collateral.

A lot of these closed source ideas still prevail, and even maintainers of personal web sites wonder how they can make sure nobody can save their images or copy their code and content. We've discussed the issues and misconceptions of this approach over the last chapters and will not dwell on it. Instead, we will look at the modern outlook of forward-thinking companies who are going in quite the opposite direction. For example, many content providers like media agencies have realized that when they offer their news in lightweight, easy-to-syndicate formats like RSS, people will use them to display headlines on their web sites and drive traffic and users to their sites.

Furthermore, e-commerce companies like eBay, PayPal, and Amazon realize that if they allow programmatic access to their services, people will sell more things online, as they can offer content-specific products on their web sites without having to send their visitors to third-party web sites. And last but not least, companies have started realizing that if you share the technologies you use with the world, you get a lot of quality feedback, you get your products tested in the most adverse environments (as every developer's computer and connection is different), and you attract a lot of talent that you may want to hire at a later stage. With a developer network, you see immediately what a person can do instead of having to rely on his CV.

As a developer, this means that if you take a look around the Web, you find an amazing amount of content and technology to play with for free. A good proof of concept is the web site Don't Meet Your Heroes (`http://www.dontmeetyourheroes.com`), which is full of web design and web development content that is always up to date due to being syndicated from various RSS feeds from different blogs and magazines. The site therefore offers a lot to the reader, and the maintainers don't need to spend time writing or researching the content. If the maintainers stumble upon a nice piece of content, it is simple to add, and they also offer a facility for visitors to recommend a resource. The maintainers don't have much to do, the owners of the listed resource pages get more readers, and the visitors of the site find up-to-date content already collated for them in one spot. Everybody wins.

The Web is also littered with countless third-party JavaScript libraries, which can be downloaded and plugged into your applications, allowing you access to a lot of powerful functionality with very little effort. We'll look at some examples of these later on in the chapter by looking at jQuery and the Yahoo User Interface Library.

Code Snippets, RSS Feeds, APIs, and Libraries

Probably the oldest type of third-party JavaScript available on the Web are scripts you simply embed into a web site. These could be

- Counters recording how many people visit your site, like StatCounter (`http://www.statscounter.com/`)

- Advertising programs like Google AdSense (`https://www.google.com/adsense/`)

- Previews of your own content added to a product like the Flickr or Yahoo Answers badge

- Search tools like TheFreeDictionary's double-click script (double-click any word in your web site to search for it in TheFreeDictionary—`http://www.thefreedictionary.com/lookup.htm#script`)

Another example is script generators that create JavaScripts for you depending on parameters you define. Google AdSense has this feature, and there are dozens of free script generators out on the Web (some are listed at `http://www.scriptsearch.com/JavaScript/Scripts/Generators/`). You'd want to handle these script generators especially with care, as a lot of them are outdated and create obtrusive code.

This is a general issue with premade third-party JavaScript. Most such scripts need to be embedded in the body of the document rather than the head and are optimized for performance rather than valid syntax or unobtrusiveness. Many counter scripts also use browser sniffing to determine the user agent (reading out the `navigator` data instead of using object detection) and are therefore rather inaccurate.

RSS Feeds and REST APIs

I've covered RSS feeds in Chapter 8 already, but it is worth mentioning them again here, as it is amazing what kind of information you can find on the Web for you to use:

- There are hardly any news agencies that don't offer RSS feeds of the latest happenings. Prominent examples of those that do are CNN (http://www.cnn.com/services/rss), Reuters (http://today.reuters.com/rss/newsrss.aspx), and the very geeky The Register (http://www.theregister.co.uk/odds/about/feeds/).

- You can get image feeds from Flickr, for example, pictures of San Francisco (http://flickr.com/photos/tags/sanfrancisco/) and from blogs that deal mainly with images like Cute Overload (http://mfrost.typepad.com/cute_overload/rss.xml).

- You can get Podcast information at Podcast Networks (http://www.podcast.net/) and Odeo (http://odeo.com/) in case you want to offer something for those who like to listen rather than read.

The really great service several web sites offer is REST APIs, which allow you to get exactly the information you need.

■**Note** An API (http://www.webopedia.com/TERM/A/API.html) is an **application program interface**, which is a set of routines and tools to build software applications. Basically, you have a set of methods, objects, and properties to use that allow you to piggyback on the functionality of another program or even operating system. In a sense, you've used an API in this book a lot—the browser API that allows you to access the window object with all its methods and the DOM, which allows you to alter and read the document. We'll get to an API example later on in this chapter when we talk about Google Maps.

I could fill an entire book by going into detail about REST, so a detailed discussion is out of scope here. If you are interested, you can read up on it at Wikipedia (http://en.wikipedia.org/wiki/Representational_State_Transfer). What REST APIs do is allow you to define in the URL whatever kind of information you want. This could be as simple as adding different data to the URL, for example, to reach different entries of Wikipedia:

- http://en.wikipedia.org/wiki/Javascript

- http://en.wikipedia.org/wiki/DOM_scripting

Or it can become rather sophisticated, where the API allows you to define the output format of the data and other parameters, for example in Yahoo Search: http://api.search.yahoo.com/WebSearchService/V1/webSearch?appid=YahooDemo&query=webstandards. This searches for the term "webstandards" in the Yahoo Database and returns an XML string of results. By default, it returns ten results; however, you can limit it to two by adding a parameter: http://api.search.yahoo.com/WebSearchService/V1/webSearch?appid=YahooDemo&query=webstandards&results=2.

The API also allows for other parameters like the start of the search result section you want to see or the output format. For example, if you want the results 10 to 15 for the search term "web-standards" in JSON format, you can have that: `http://api.search.yahoo.com/WebSearchService/V1/webSearch?appid=YahooDemo&query=webstandards&results=5&start=10&output=json`.

You can use this information directly in JavaScript by sending a callback function name as a parameter to the API:

```
<script type="text/javascript">
  function results(d) {
    for(i in d.ResultSet.Result) {
      alert( d.ResultSet.Result[i].Title );
    }
}</script>
<script type="text/javascript" ➥
src="http://api.search.yahoo.com/➥
WebSearchService/V1/webSearch?appid=YahooDemo➥
&query=webstandards&results=5&start=10&➥
output=json&callback=results"></script>
```

In short, a REST API allows you to retrieve information from a system in the easiest form, by assembling a static URL, and in the most complex form, to send parameters to customize the output format of that data and call different methods to retrieve different kind of data.

Examples of REST APIs

One example of a REST API is Yahoo's HotJobs, which allows you to put together a URL to retrieve job offers tailored to your location in the following format: `http://hotjobs.yahoo.com/rss/version/country/state/city/category/keywords`.

For example:

- This URL searches for JavaScript jobs all across the US and returns an RSS feed: `http://hotjobs.yahoo.com/rss/0/USA/-/-/-/javascript`.

- This URL returns any jobs in Los Angeles, CA: `http://hotjobs.yahoo.com/rss/0/USA/CA/Los+Angeles/-/-`.

- And this example returns new media and Internet jobs in San Jose: `http://hotjobs.yahoo.com/rss/0/USA/CA/San+Jose/NEW/-`.

Another example is Upcoming.org, which is a shared event calendar that lists gigs, exhibitions, and other social events and offers a REST API. For example, you could find all the upcoming events in the following places:

- **London, England**: `http://upcoming.org/metro/uk/london/london/`

- **New York City**: `http://upcoming.org/metro/us/ny/nyc/`

The BBC currently offers a prototype of a REST API at `http://www0.rdthdo.bbc.co.uk/services/api/` that will be part of their other developer offers at `http://backstage.bbc.co.uk/` once it has matured enough. This API allows you to browse the BBC program schedule in RSS format. BBC has an Ajax example application available at `http://www0.rdthdo.bbc.co.uk/services/api/examples/ajax/doc.html`.

■**Note** You can find more information about REST (Ajax related) in a couple of Christian Gross's books—*Ajax Patterns and Best Practices* (Apress, 2006) and *Ajax and REST Recipes* (Apress, to be published late 2006).

Using a Library: Short, Shorter, jQuery

One of the main reasons for code libraries is that developers want to make it easier for other developers to achieve day-to-day coding tasks. You've done that in this book with the DOM-help library by creating utility methods to work around browser inconsistencies and solve reoccurring tasks. What you haven't done is provide your own coding syntax or any other means of reaching elements in the page than the DOM. If you had done that, you could have come up with much shorter code, but also sacrificed the recognition effect of "normal" Java-Script syntax and made development dependent on the knowledge of the library.

There is a trend, however, in JavaScript development to go that route, and many of the large libraries like Rico (`http://openrico.org/`) and prototype (`http://prototype.conio.net/`) become more and more daunting in terms of learning the library-specific code syntax and rules in order to achieve a task. Probably the most daring approach in this direction is jQuery (`http://jquery.com/`), which comprises a single JavaScript file weighing in at only 16K that you add to the head of your documents. It provides you with an amazing amount of utility methods to achieve web-specific tasks. The code you have to write to work with jQuery is very confusing to JavaScript beginners or developers who haven't dabbled in languages like Ruby, Python, or Java yet. However, it is very powerful all the same once you get your head around it.

The concept of jQuery is to offer quick access to any element of the document, and to get this access you have a utility method called $ (of all things) that takes either

- A DOM construct, for example, `$( document.body )`

- A CSS selector, for example, `$( 'p a' )`, which is every link inside a paragraph in the document

- An XPath expression, for example, `$(" //a[@rel='nofollow'] ")`, which matches every link in the document with an attribute called `rel` that has the value of `nofollow`

■Note XPath is a W3C standard language to reach parts of an XML document, normally used in connection with XSLT or XPOINTER (`http://www.w3.org/TR/xpath`). As modern HTML should conform to XML syntax rules (all tags closed, all elements lowercase, attribute values in quotation marks, and single attributes defined as name/value pairs), you can use XPath to find parts of the HTML document, too. Together with XSLT, it is a very powerful tool to convert one XML format to another.

The other trick jQuery has up its sleeve to achieve very short code is a concept called **chainable methods,** which you already know from the DOM. You can add each method to the last one by concatenating them with a full stop. Instead of

```
$p = $( 'p' );
$p.addClass( 'test' );
$p.show();
$p.html('example' );
```

You can use

```
$( 'p' ).addClass( 'test' ).show().html( 'example' );
```

Both of these examples do the same: take every paragraph of the document, add a CSS class called test, show the paragraph (in case it was hidden), and change the HTML content of the paragraph to "example". What jQuery provides you with is an amazing number of these very short-named methods that are tailored to fulfill day-to-day web application development tasks. There is good documentation and examples available on the jQuery site (`http://jquery.com/docs/`) and on Mark Constable's site (`http://markc.renta.net/jquery/`).

Let's take a look at an example. If you are a developer and you write tutorials, you often have to show code examples in HTML pages. You wrap them in PRE and CODE elements to make whitespace in the code appear in the right format, like this:

exampleJQuery.html *(excerpt)*

```
<h1>Showing and hiding a code example with jQuery</h1>
<p>The code</p>
<pre><code>
  [... code example ...]
</code></pre>
<p>The CSS</p>
<pre><code>
  [... code example ...]
</code></pre>
```

Let's now write a script in jQuery that will generate links preceding the code examples that allow for expanding and collapsing the examples instead of simply showing them, as demonstrated in Figure 11-1.

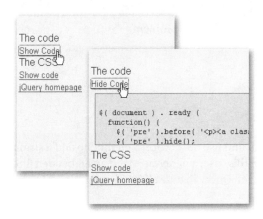

Figure 11-1. *Showing and hiding code examples with jQuery*

```
jqueryTest.js
$( document ) . ready (
  function() {
    $( 'pre' ).before( '<p><a class="trigger"➥
    href="#">Show code</a></p>' );
    $( 'pre' ).hide();
    $('a.trigger').toggle (
      function() {
        $(this.parentNode.nextSibling).slideDown('slow');
        $(this).html( 'Hide Code' );
      },
      function() {
        $(this.parentNode.nextSibling).slideUp('slow');
        $(this).html( 'Show Code' );
      }
    )
  }
)
```

As you can see, the code is amazingly short, but also rather complex in terms of syntax. Let's go through the example bit by bit so you can understand what is going on:

```
jqueryTest.js (excerpt)

$( document ) . ready (
  function() {
```

The $(document).ready () method is an event handler that calls the function provided as a parameter (in this case an anonymous function) when the document is ready to be manipulated. This means that everything that follows in this script is executed when the document has loaded—and that means only the document and not all the embedded assets in it like images.

As you may remember, we talked in Chapter 5 about the ugly effect of the page content showing up before you can hide it. This method works around that problem.

jqueryTest.js *(continued)*

```
$( 'pre' ).before( '<p><a class="trigger"➥
href="#">Show code</a></p>' );
$( 'pre' ).hide();
```

You take every PRE element in the document and use the before() method to add a string of HTML in the DOM tree before this element, in this case, a paragraph with an embedded link with the class trigger. You use the hide() method of jQuery to hide all PRE elements (hide() sets the CSS attribute display to none).

jqueryTest.js *(continued)*

```
$('a.trigger').toggle (
```

You use the CSS selector a.trigger to match all links with the class trigger (which hopefully are only the ones the script added via the before() method) and use the toggle() method. This method alternately executes the two functions provided as parameters when the user clicks the element. The first parameter is an anonymous function that shows the previously hidden code example and changes the link text to "Hide Code" and vice versa.

jqueryTest.js *(continued)*

```
function() {
  $(this.parentNode.nextSibling).slideDown('slow');
  $(this).html( 'Hide Code' );
},
```

You can use several jQuery methods to show and hide elements, the most basic being show() and hide(). A more advanced effect is produced using slideDown() and slideUp(), which show the element in a line-by-line animation. Both of these methods take a parameter that indicates the speed of the animation, which can be slow, normal, or fast. In order to reach the PRE element to show or hide, you need to use the $(this) construct, which returns the event target of toggle(). This means you can use this.parentNode.nextSibling to reach the PRE as the links are nested in a paragraph. You can change the content of the link itself via $(this) and the html() method, which takes a string of HTML as the sole parameter and changes the element's innerHTML property.

jqueryTest.js *(continued)*

```
    function() {
      $(this.parentNode.nextSibling).slideUp('slow');
      $(this).html( 'Show Code' );
    }
  )
}
)
```

The other case of toggle() in this example uses slideUp() to slowly hide the code example and changes the text of the link back to "Show Code".

A really great extension for jQuery (implementations or extensions for jQuery are called **plug-ins**) is the Ajax plug-in. This plug-in allows for dead-easy Ajax implementations via the load(), $.get(), and $.post() methods as explained at http://jquery.com/docs/ajax/. For example, if you want to create the PRE elements and load the real code examples into them when the user clicks a link, this is pretty easy to do. Check the demo exampleJQueryAjax.html to see the following script in action:

jqueryTestAjax.js

```
$( document ) . ready (
  function() {
    $('a.codeExample').each (
      function( i ) {
        $( this ).after( '<pre class="codeExample">➡
        <code></code></pre>' );
      }
    )
    $( 'pre.codeExample' ).hide();
    $('a.codeExample').toggle (
      function() {
        if( !this.old ){
          this.old = $(this).html();
        }
        $( this ).html('Hide Code');
        parseCode( this );
      },
      function() {
        $( this ).html( this.old );
        $( this.nextSibling ).hide();
      }
```

```
      )
      function parseCode(o){
        if(!o.nextSibling.hascode){
            $.get (o.href,
              function(code){
                code=code.replace(/&/mg,'&#38;');
                code=code.replace(/</mg,'&#60;');
                code=code.replace(/>/mg,'&#62;');
                code=code.replace(/\"/mg,'&#34;');
                code=code.replace(/\r?\n/g,'<br>');
                code=code.replace(/<br><br>/g,'<br>');
                code=code.replace(/ /g,' ');
                o.nextSibling.innerHTML='<code>'+code+'</code>';
                o.nextSibling.hascode=true;
              }
            );
        }
        $(o.nextSibling).show();
      }
    }
  )
```

Let's go through this script step by step:

jqueryTestAjax.js *(excerpt)*

```
$( document ) . ready (
  function() {
```

You start once again with the ready() method and an anonymous function (you might as well create a named function and call it via the ready() method).

jqueryTestAjax.js *(continued)*

```
    $('a.codeExample').each (
      function( i ) {
        $( this ).after( '<pre class="codeExample">➡
        <code></code></pre>' );
      }
    )
    $( 'pre.codeExample' ).hide();
```

You use one of jQuery's iterator methods, each(), to loop through all links that have the CSS class codeExample. You then create PRE elements with the class codeExample and embedded CODE elements after each of these links via the after() method and the $(this) selector before hiding all PRE elements with the codeExample class using jQuery's hide() method.

jqueryTestAjax.js *(continued)*

```
$('a.codeExample').toggle (
  function() {
    if( !this.old ){
      this.old = $(this).html();
    }
    $( this ).html('Hide Code');
    parseCode( this );
  },
  function() {
    $( this ).html( this.old );
    $( this.nextSibling ).hide();
  }
)
```

You use toggle() to show and hide the code examples; however, unlike the last script, you store the original text of the link in a property called old when you show the code and replace the link text with "Hide Code". You then invoke the function parseCode() with the link as a parameter when you show the code. When you hide the code, you restore the original link text by setting the link text back to the value stored in the old parameter before hiding the PRE element with jQuery's hide() method.

jqueryTestAjax.js *(continued)*

```
function parseCode(o){
  if(!o.nextSibling.hascode){
      $.get (o.href,
         function(code){
```

This function tests whether the PRE element following the link (which is its next sibling) has a property called hascode, which you will set once the code has been loaded for the first time. This is necessary to avoid the script loading the code every time the user clicks the link, instead loading it only once. You then use the $.get() method with the link's href attribute value and an anonymous function as parameters. This will effectively send an XHR request that loads the linked document and invokes the function once the document has been loaded. You send a parameter called code, which will contain the content of the document that was loaded via XHR.

jqueryTestAjax.js *(continued)*

```
            code=code.replace( /&/mg, '&#38;' );
            code=code.replace( /</mg, '&#60;' );
            code=code.replace( />/mg, '&#62;' );
            code=code.replace( /\"/mg, '&#34;' );
            code=code.replace( /\r?\n/g, '<br>' );
            code=code.replace( /<br><br>/g, '<br>' );
            code=code.replace( / /g, ' ' );
            o.nextSibling.innerHTML = '<code>'+code+'</code>';
            o.nextSibling.hascode = true;
```

You then use regular expressions to replace all ampersands, tag brackets, and quotation marks with their numbered HTML entities, line breaks with <br>, and spaces with their HTML entity before adding the result inside a CODE element as the innerHTML property of the PRE element. You set the hascode property to true to ensure that the next time the user clicks the link to show the code, the $.get() construct is skipped.

jqueryTestAjax.js *(continued)*

```
            }
          );
        }
        $(o.nextSibling).show();
      }
    }
)
```

All that is left to do is to show the PRE element using jQuery's show() method. Notice that you need to do that outside the $.get() construct to make sure the code gets shown the second and consecutive times the user chooses to show the code.

Dangers of jQuery and Other Libraries Using Their Own Syntax

It is amazing how many day-to-day web application and web development tasks you can fulfill easily and quickly with jQuery. However, if you were to hand this document over to a third-party developer for maintenance, she'd have to know about jQuery or she would be completely lost. This is one of the dangers of using libraries. Instead of relying on JavaScript syntax and rules, you add an extra layer of necessary knowledge to the process. It is up to you to decide whether the benefits the library offers are worth that.

The other issue is that a lot of code library examples are not unobtrusive, but were made to show what the library can do. It is very tempting to expect JavaScript to be available when using and explaining libraries. Make sure you don't make this mistake. Libraries are there to make the development process quicker and easier, not make us dependent on them or repeat mistakes we've done with libraries in the past already—creating applications and web sites that don't work without JavaScript.

Next we'll look at using the Google Maps API to create mapping applications.

Using an API: Adding a Map to Your Site with Google Maps

Google Maps (`http://maps.google.com`) is probably the web application that got the whole Ajax craze rolling. It provides the user with maps that can be moved around, zoomed, and—the implementation permitting—even annotated. You can show the location you want to see as maps, as satellite pictures, or as a mixture of both.

Google allows web developers to use Google Maps on their own web sites by means of an API. In order to use the API, you need to sign up for a free developer key at its homepage: `http://www.google.com/apis/maps/`. Here you will also find the documentation and many examples of how to use Google maps. The key will enable you to use maps on a single domain or subfolder in this domain. The examples in this chapter use a key that works with localhost, which means you need to run them in your local server via `http://localhost/` and not from the file system.

Once you have obtained the developer key, you can link to the JavaScript that contains all the map's code in the head of your document. The "your key" in bold should be replaced with the key you obtained from Google—if you try the example code on a different server than localhost, you will have to change the key in the example files.

```
<script src="http://maps.google.com/maps?file=api_
&amp;v=2&amp;key=your key" type="text/javascript">
</script>
```

■**Caution** This URL might change in the future, so be sure to check the API homepage should your examples fail to work out all of a sudden. The part that is likely to change is the v parameter in the URL, which is the version of the API.

The next step you need to take is to get the latitude and longitude value of the location you want to display. If you are in the US, you are in luck, as there is a free service that converts addresses to these values available at `http://geocoder.us/`. For example, if you want to show the location of Paramount Studios in Hollywood, California, which is located at 5555 Melrose Avenue, you can get the data from `http://geocoder.us/demo.cgi?address=5555+Melrose+Ave%2C+Hollywood%2C+CA`.

The result is

```
Address
5555 Melrose Ave
Los Angeles CA 90038
Latitude
34.083517 °
N 34 ° 5' 0.7"
Longitude
-118.321951 °
W 118 ° 19' 19.0"
```

An even easier solution is to use the REST APIs at `http://www.localsearchmaps.com` (explained at `http://emad.fano.us/blog/?p=277`) and `http://www.zeesource.net/maps/geocoding.do`. The former returns code that is compatible with the Google Maps API (sadly enough at the moment outdated code for the old API, but this might have changed by the time this book comes out), and the latter returns a series of comma-separated lines with the longitude and latitude information—both return worldwide information, not only for the US.

When you have the information, you can start adding your own map to your web site. As an example for an international location, let's use my street in the north of London, England. The coordinates of my street are 51.5623° latitude and –0.0934° longitude. Using this information and the methods provided for you by the API, it is easy to show a map of my area.

You start with an HTML element to contain the map. You can add content in this element that is displayed when JavaScript is not available or the browser isn't supported. This content could be any HTML, text, or even a static image of the same map. The latter is a nice option to ensure backwards compatibility; you just need to ensure not to tell the user anywhere in the text that the map is dynamic, because it might not be.

exampleGoogleMaps.html *(Excerpt)*

```
<div id="map">
  <p>Here you should see an interactive map, but you
  either have scripting disabled or your browser
  is not supported by Google Maps.</p>
</div>
```

Make sure that you give that element dimensions in the CSS, as otherwise the map will behave erratically.

googleMaps.css

```
#map{
  width:400px;
  height:300px;
  border:1px solid #999;
  margin:1em;
}
```

To add the map to your HTML document, embed the following script (either inline or in a SCRIPT element) after you add the main Google Maps code as explained earlier.

googleMaps.js

```
function addMap() {
  if ( GBrowserIsCompatible() ) {
    var mapContainer = document.getElementById( 'map' );
    var map = new GMap2( mapContainer );
    var point = new GLatLng( 51.5623, -0.0934 );
    map.setCenter( point, 13 );
  }
}
window.onload = addMap;
window.onunload = GUnload;
```

The GBrowserIsCompatible() function of the API tests whether the browser can support Google Maps and returns true if that is the case. You call your own function addMap() when the document has finished loading and the function GUnload() provided by the API when the window gets closed (as closing the window triggers the unload event). The latter is necessary because the maps use a lot of event handling, which might slow down MSIE because of its memory-leak issues.

■**Tip** You can learn more about MSIE's memory leaking and workarounds at http://javascript. weblogsinc.com/2005/03/07/javascript-memory-leaks/.

You add the map by calling the GMap2() method, which creates a new map object. The method takes the element to insert the map into as the parameter, in this case the element with the ID map. You can add as many maps as you want to a document.

You define a new point with the GLatLng() method that takes the latitude and longitude values as parameters. You then center the map at this point via the setCenter() method, which takes the point to center the map and the zoom level (1 to 17) as parameters. This is all it takes to have an interactive map as shown in Figure 11-2 on your page.

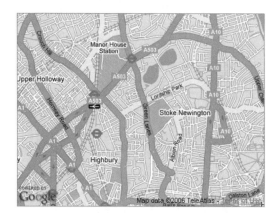

Figure 11-2. *A plain map with Google Maps*

Without the usual controls shown on http://maps.google.com and other dynamic map web sites (zooming, panning, changing the type of the map), this map could be confusing to users, as nothing indicates that this is an interactive map rather than a static image. Therefore, it makes sense to add the controls using the addControl() method of the API.

googleMapsControls.js

```
function addMap() {
  if ( GBrowserIsCompatible() ) {
    var mapcontainer = document.getElementById('map');
    var map = new GMap2( mapcontainer );
    map.addControl( new GSmallMapControl() );
    map.addControl( new GMapTypeControl() );
    map.addControl( new GScaleControl() );
    map.addControl( new GOverviewMapControl() );
    var point = new GLatLng( 51.5623, -0.0934 );
    map.setCenter( point, 13 );
  }
}
window.onload = addMap;
window.onunload = GUnload;
```

The addControl() method takes an instance of the control's object as its sole parameter. This example adds a GSmallMapControl(), which consists of the arrows that pan the map around and the + and – buttons to zoom in and out. The GMapTypeControl() creates the three buttons to show the map, a satellite photo, or a hybrid—which means a satellite photo with road names. The GScaleControl() displays the scale of the map on the bottom left next to the Google logo, and last but not least the GOverviewMapControl() provides the overview rectangle on the bottom right. The outcome is shown in Figure 11-3.

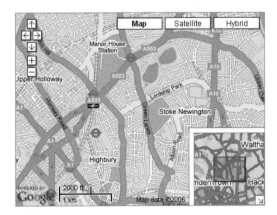

Figure 11-3. *A map with controls*

At the time of writing, the overview control invoked by GOverviewMapControl() has one problem: the API places the control outside the map on the bottom-right corner of the screen. In order to make the overview appear on the map, you need to apply the following fix:

googleMapsControlsFixed.js

```
function addMap() {
  if ( GBrowserIsCompatible() ) {
    var mapContainer = document.getElementById('map');
    var map = new GMap2( mapContainer );
    map.addControl( new GSmallMapControl() );
    map.addControl( new GMapTypeControl() );
    map.addControl( new GScaleControl() );
    map.addControl( new GOverviewMapControl() );
    var point = new GLatLng( 51.5623, -0.0934 );
    map.setCenter( point, 13 );
    var overview = document.getElementById('map_overview');
    mapContainer.style.position = 'relative';
    overview.style.position = 'absolute';
    mapContainer.appendChild(overview);
  }
}
window.onload = addMap;
window.onunload = GUnload;
```

The API creates the overview control element as a `<div>` with the ID map_overview. It does that with any map; if the map has the ID myMap, the ID of the overview control would be myMap_overview. You can use this information to position the control absolutely and the main map DIV relatively, and append the overview control as a child to mapContainer. This will keep the control inside the main map.

The map now displays the area that I live in, but you cannot tell where I am. To highlight points in the map, you can use the GMarker() method, which needs a point as the parameter. The addOverlay() method of the map adds the marker at the position of the point.

googleMapsMarker.js

```javascript
function addMap() {
  if ( GBrowserIsCompatible() ) {
    var mapContainer = document.getElementById('map');
    var map = new GMap2( mapContainer );
    var point = new GLatLng( 51.5623, -0.0934 );
    map.setCenter( point, 13 );
    var marker = new GMarker( point );
    map.addOverlay( marker );
  }
}
window.onload = addMap;
window.onunload = GUnload;
```

This change shows a red marker icon at the location you define as the point, as shown in Figure 11-4. You can set as many markers on a map as you want.

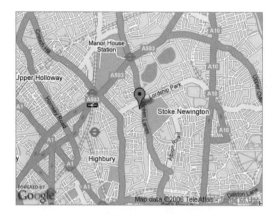

Figure 11-4. *A map with a marker*

The API also allows you to add event handlers to the map and each of its elements. For example, if you want to show an information window when the user clicks the marker (as markers are clickable by default), you can use the GEvent.addListener() method. This method takes the element to add an event, the event, and the function to call as parameters, much like addEvent() does. In the function that adds the message, you create a new text node of the document and use the openInfoWindow() method of the map with the point and the new text node as parameters to display the information window as shown in Figure 11-5.

exampleGoogleMapsMarkerEvent.js

```
function addMap() {
  if ( GBrowserIsCompatible() ) {
    var mapContainer = document.getElementById('map');
    var map = new GMap2( mapContainer );
    var point = new GLatLng( 51.5623, -0.0934 );
    map.setCenter( point, 13 );
    var marker = new GMarker( point );
    map.addOverlay( marker );
    GEvent.addListener( marker, 'click', addMessage );
  }
  function addMessage() {
    var message = 'This is where Chris lives';
    var msgNode = document.createTextNode( message );
    map.openInfoWindow( point, msgNode );
  }
}
window.onload = addMap;
window.onunload = GUnload;
```

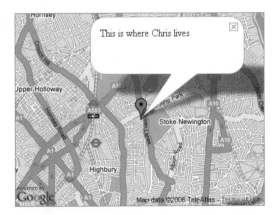

Figure 11-5. *A map with a marker and an information window*

■**Tip** You can use HTML inside the information window, just use the openInfoWindowHtml() method instead of openInfoWindow().

Another really cool option of Google maps is that you can set the zoom level with the setZoom() method, and you can move the map center to another location by using the panTo() method. Furthermore, the openInfoWindowHtml() method allows you to define a function to call when the user closes the information window, and you don't need to use your own event handler for that (technically, this is of course also done with an event handler, but the API does that for you). The syntax of this functionality is a bit odd: you add a JSON object as the last parameter to the openInfoWindowHtml() method, that, among others, has a property called onCloseFn, which has the name of the function that should get called when the user closes the window as a value.

Let's use setZoom(), panTo(), and openInfoWindowHtml() with the third parameter to create an interactive map that opens a window when the user clicks the initial marker, zooms the map out when he closes that window, moves the map to a different location, and opens another window there.

googleMapsPan.js

```
function addMap() {
  if ( GBrowserIsCompatible() ) {
    var mapContainer = document.getElementById('map');
    var map = new GMap2( mapContainer );
    var home = new GLatLng( 51.5623, -0.0934 );
    var work = new GLatLng( 51.5138, -0.1284 );
    var homeMarker = new GMarker( home );
    var workMarker = new GMarker( work );
    var homeMessage = 'This is where Chris lives';
    var workMessage = 'This is where Chris works';
    map.setCenter( home, 13 );
    map.addOverlay( homeMarker );
    map.addOverlay( workMarker );
    function addMessage() {
      map.openInfoWindowHtml( home, homeMessage,
                             { onCloseFn : goToWork } );
    }
    function goToWork() {
      map.setZoom( 12 );
      map.panTo( work )
      map.openInfoWindowHtml( work, workMessage,
                             { onCloseFn : backToHome } );
    }
    function backToHome(){
      map.panTo( home )
      map.openInfoWindowHtml( home, homeMessage,
                             { onCloseFn : goToWork } );
      map.setZoom( 13 );
    }
```

```
    GEvent.addListener( homeMarker, 'click', addMessage );
  }
}
window.onload = addMap;
window.onunload = GUnload;
```

The result is shown in Figure 11-6.

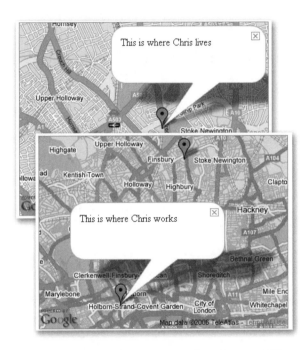

Figure 11-6. *Panning from one map location to a different one*

The example needs to zoom out one level to pan smoothly to the other location. If the
point you give panTo( ) as a parameter is outside the currently visible map, the API will simply
render a new map with this location as the center. If you keep both start and end point on the
same map, it will animate the map and move there smoothly.

Let's go through the script step by step:

googleMapsPan.js *(excerpt)*

```
function addMap() {
  if ( GBrowserIsCompatible() ) {
    var mapContainer = document.getElementById('map');
    var map = new GMap2( mapContainer );
```

You test whether the browser supports Google maps and define mapContainer as the element that gets converted into a map. You create a new map by calling the GMap2( ) constructor
with mapContainer as the parameter.

googleMapsPan.js *(continued)*

```
var home = new GLatLng( 51.5623, -0.0934 );
var work = new GLatLng( 51.5138, -0.1284 );
var homeMarker = new GMarker( home );
var workMarker = new GMarker( work );
var homeMessage = 'This is where Chris lives';
var workMessage = 'This is where Chris works';
```

You define two new points using latitude and longitude information retrieved from one of the services mentioned earlier and define two markers using GMarker(). One is where I live and the other one is where I work. You define two messages telling the web page visitor what these points are.

googleMapsPan.js *(continued)*

```
map.setCenter( home, 13 );
map.addOverlay( homeMarker );
map.addOverlay( workMarker );
```

You show the map by calling the setCenter() method with the home point and a zoom level of 13 as parameters. You then use the addOverlay() method to display markers on the map for each point—home and work.

googleMapsPan.js *(continued)*

```
function addMessage() {
  map.openInfoWindowHtml( home, homeMessage,
                          { onCloseFn : goToWork } );
}
```

Next, you need to define some functions before adding the handlers that will invoke them—otherwise the API won't work. The addMessage() function uses the openInfoWindowHtml() method to show the message that the first marker is where I live when the user clicks the marker. Notice the difference from the first marker example: this time you need to use { onCloseFn : goToWork } as the third parameter to add a handler that will invoke the goToWork() function when the user closes the message window.

Note The syntax of this parameter is pretty confusing, and the only reason I can think of for this is the Google developers wanted the third parameter to be as flexible as possible without having to add another parameter in the specs. As it is now, it is an object with literal notation, and onCloseFn is one of the possible properties. There are more, which you can look up in the API documentation at http://www.google.com/apis/maps/documentation/.

---

googleMapsPan.js *(continued)*

```
function goToWork() {
  map.setZoom( 12 );
  map.panTo( work )
  map.openInfoWindowHtml( work, workMessage,
                          { onCloseFn : backToHome } );
}
function backToHome(){
  map.panTo( home )
  map.openInfoWindowHtml( home, homeMessage,
                          { onCloseFn : goToWork } );
  map.setZoom( 13 );
}
```

The goToWork() function uses the setZoom() method to set the zoom level of the map to 12 to ensure that both the home and the work marker are on the same visible section of the map. This makes the API scroll the map smoothly to the other section when you call panTo() with the work point as the sole parameter. Once the API pans the map to the work location, you show an information window that invokes backToHome() when the user closes it, again using the third parameter of openInfoWindowHtml().

The backToHome() function does the same but in reverse. It tells the API to pan the map back to the home point, open an information window there that invokes goToWork() when the user closes it, and set the zoom level of the map back to 13.

googleMapsPan.js *(continued)*

```
    GEvent.addListener( homeMarker, 'click', addMessage );
  }
}
window.onload = addMap;
window.onunload = GUnload;
```

This example should get you going and give you a small insight into the world of Google Maps. The API offers a lot more options, like defining different-looking markers, your own overlays, and more methods to play with. The documentation is available at http://www.google.com/apis/maps/documentation/ and seems to be thoroughly maintained to stay up to date with the changes in the API.

■**Note** Maps are hot at the moment, and a lot of developers use Yahoo Maps or Google Maps to create so-called **mashups**. These are applications that mix (mash together) several online applications that offer APIs to create a new one. Examples are maps that show events, current news, or weather conditions at certain locations. You can find a whole list of mashups of the different map APIs at http://www.programmableweb.com/.

Full Service: The Yahoo Developer Network and User Interface Library

Yahoo, being one of the oldest Internet content and service providers, has taken an interesting step by offering the Yahoo Developer Network to web developers. The network homepage is http://developer.yahoo.com, and there you can find a listing of all Yahoo APIs, RSS feeds, and REST services. The really interesting approach is that the REST results are also available in JSON format in many cases, which means that you can embed them as data in a SCRIPT element without having to use Ajax at all. There is also a JavaScript developer center at http://developer.yahoo.com/javascript/, which lists services, articles, and code examples on how to use what Yahoo and its companies can offer you.

The Developer Network also includes design patterns, which supply information on how to approach a certain web design task and solutions for it, and a library to develop JavaScript-enhanced web sites and applications from the ground up—including premade CSS for different layouts and font-sizing issues. This library is called the Yahoo User Interface Library, or YUI for short, and you can download it at http://developer.yahoo.com/yui/. In the download zip file, you can find the library files in the build folder, the documentation in the docs folder, and examples in the examples folder. The library consists of several components that each have to be included as their own <script> tags. The components are available either as readable Java-Script files, for example yahoo.js, or as file-size-optimized versions with file names ending in -min, for example, yahoo-min.js. The latter have no whitespace and are compacted to result in much smaller files.

Currently, the library consists of the following components:

- An Animation component to animate and fade elements in and out

- A Connection Manager to create Ajax applications

- A DOM component to reach and change elements and dynamically apply CSS classes

- A Drag & Drop component

- An Event component for event handling

- An Autocomplete control for form fields

- A Calendar control to pick dates for forms

- A Container control that creates scriptable page elements that can be positioned to cover the current document

- A Menu control to create dynamic menus

- A Slider control

- A Treeview control

Let's have a go at using some of these to replicate and enhance some of the solutions already discussed in the other chapters.

Bouncy Headlines Using YUI

Let's use the YUI and its components to create a fancier example of clickable headlines. The demo exampleBouncyHeadlines.html uses the DOM, the Event, and the Animation components to show and hide the content below the headlines in an animation when the user clicks the headlines. The animation reveals the content, pushing the rest down the page, smoothly fading it in from white to the final color. Figure 11-7 shows what this looks like.

Figure 11-7. *Smooth animation and fading of content using YUI libraries*

At first glance, the script does look rather overwhelming, but it is pretty easy to use the library scripts once you understand what they do. I will just mention the features here, not all the options you have, as those would fill a chapter on its own; the YUI documentation will be kept up to date, and you can read about changes and new options there.

bouncyHeadlines.js

```
YAHOO.namespace('bh');
bh = {
  triggerClass:'show',
  init : function() {
    var listitems, i, content;
    bh.headings = document.getElementById('headlines');
    if( !bh.headings ){ return; }
    listitems = bh.headings.getElementsByTagName( 'h3' );
    for( i = 0; i < listitems.length; i++ ) {
      content = listitems[i].parentNode.➥
      getElementsByTagName( 'p' )[0];
      content.defaultHeight = content.offsetHeight;
      listitems[i].content=content;
      YAHOO.util.Event.addListener( listitems[i], 'click',➥
      bh.toggle);
    }
```

```
    },
    toggle : function() {
      var attributes, anim;
      var c = this.content;
      if( c.shown ) {
        attributes = {
          height: { from : c.defaultHeight, to : 0},
          opacity: { from : 1, to : 0 }
        };
        anim = new YAHOO.util.Anim( c, attributes, .6,➥
        YAHOO.util.Easing.easeBoth );
        anim.animate();
        anim.onComplete.subscribe( bh.toggleCustom );
      } else {
        YAHOO.util.Dom.addClass( c, 'shown' );
        attributes = {
          height: { from:0, to:c.defaultHeight },
          opacity: { from:0, to:1 }
        };
        anim = new YAHOO.util.Anim( c, attributes, .6,➥
        YAHOO.util.Easing.backOut );
        anim.animate();
        anim.onComplete.subscribe( bh.toggleCustom );
      }
    },
    toggleCustom:function() {
      var c=this.getEl();
      c.shown = c.shown ? false : true;
    },
    hideContents : function() {
      YAHOO.util.Dom.addClass( 'headlines', 'dynamic' );
    }
}
YAHOO.util.Event.onAvailable( 'headlines', bh.hideContents );
YAHOO.util.Event.addListener( window, 'load', bh.init );
```

You start with defining a namespace for your main object and the object itself (in this case, call it bh for bouncy headlines). The namespace definition is optional; however, it provides an extra level of ensuring your script does not interfere with others and that it was built upon the YUI and may be part of a larger application at a later stage. You define a property called triggerClass, which is the class to show the news item once the user clicks the headline.

bouncyHeadlines.js *(excerpt)*

```
YAHOO.namespace('bh');
bh = {
  triggerClass:'show',
```

You start the initialization method init() by defining the variables listitems, i, and content and store the element with the ID headlines in the property headings of the main object bh. If there is no element with the ID headlines, you stop the rest of the script from executing using return; otherwise you define listitems as the array of all H3 elements inside the element with the ID headlines.

bouncyHeadlines.js *(continued)*

```
  init : function() {
    var listitems, i, content;
    bh.headings = document.getElementById('headlines');
    if( !bh.headings ){ return; }
    listitems = bh.headings.getElementsByTagName( 'h3' );
```

You loop through all the list items and define content as the first paragraph element inside the parent node of the current headline. You read out the height of the paragraph by reading out the offsetHeight property and store it in a new property of the paragraph element called defaultHeight. This is necessary to tell the animation method later on how high the paragraph was initially and what to set it to at the end of the animation. You store the paragraph as a new property called content to the list item, to make it easy to retrieve it in other methods, and add an event that triggers the listener method toggle() when the user clicks the headline.

bouncyHeadlines.js *(continued)*

```
    for( i = 0; i < listitems.length; i++ ) {
      content = listitems[i].parentNode.➥
      getElementsByTagName( 'p' )[0];
      content.defaultHeight = content.offsetHeight;
      listitems[i].content=content;
      YAHOO.util.Event.addListener( listitems[i], 'click',➥
      bh.toggle);
    }
  },
```

In the toggle() method, you'll see why the addListener() method of the YUI is great. Instead of having to use the event object e, retrieving the element that was activated via getTarget() and hacking around browser issues, all you need to retrieve the object that triggered the event is the this keyword, as YUI's addListener() sets this one for you automatically, which is one of the things that Scott Andrew LePera's addListener() function fails to do. You define the variables attributes and anim and retrieve the paragraph to animate via this.content—as this returns the headline that was clicked, and you store the paragraph in a property called content. You read out the property shown of the paragraph—which will indicate whether the paragraph is visible or not—and if the property is not set, you add the CSS class shown to the paragraph to make it visible. Adding and removing classes is achievable via the addClass() method of the DOM utilities inside the YUI, which takes the element and the class name as arguments.

bouncyHeadlines.js *(continued)*

```
toggle : function() {
  var attributes, anim;
  var c = this.content;
  if( !c.shown ) {
    YAHOO.util.Dom.addClass( c, 'shown' );
```

You can then start animating the paragraph. Animating an object with the YUI is dead easy: you set the attributes of the animation as a JSON object with each attribute having either a from and to property or a by property. The former animates the object from one state to the other, and the latter animates the object by a certain amount (in case you just want to change it instead of having a fixed start and end value). In this example, you'll animate the height of the paragraph from 0 to the original height and the opacity from 0 to 1, effectively making the paragraph show line by line and getting darker as it does so. You retrieve the end value of the height animation by reading out the defaultHeight property of the paragraph you defined in the init() method earlier.

bouncyHeadlines.js *(continued)*

```
    attributes = {
      height: { from : 0, to : c.defaultHeight },
      opacity: { from:0, to:1 }
    };
```

Once you've set the attributes, you can invoke a new animation object via the Anim() utility method of the YUI. This method takes four parameters—the object to animate, the animation attributes (that you just defined), the duration of the animation (in this case 600 milliseconds), and the method to provide the values needed to animate the object. The latter could be several properties of the Easing utility of the YUI, which provides values that ensure a smooth animation. Animating objects on a screen does not only mean increasing a variable from a start value to an end value; if you start an animation slowly and get faster in your iterations or start faster and slow down towards the end, it will look a lot smoother and more natural. Calculating these transitions and making sure they work smoothly with different monitors and computers can be tricky work, and the YUI developers have done that for you already. The Easing utility has several objects that contain these values:

- easeIn, easeOut, and easeBoth, which begin slower, end slower, or both respectively

- backIn backOut, and backBoth, which begin below the start value or above the end value and return to the correct values smoothly

To show the paragraph, you can use backOut to make it appear smoothly, show some extra pixel lines below it, and snap back to the right height until the real value is reached. You start the animation by invoking the animate() method of the animation object (in this case anim). The anim object also has an onComplete event that you can subscribe to via onComplete.subscribe() and tell it to invoke the toggleCustom() method when the animation reached the final values.

bouncyHeadlines.js *(continued)*

```
anim = new YAHOO.util.Anim( c, attributes, .6,➡
YAHOO.util.Easing.backOut );
anim.animate();
anim.onComplete.subscribe( bh.toggleCustom );
```

If the paragraph is already visible (indicated by the shown property being set), you animate it the other way around. You start at an opacity value of 1 and at a paragraph height of defaultHeight and decrease both until they reach 0. Instead of backOut, use easeBoth to make the disappearance of the paragraph less jumpy.

bouncyHeadlines.js *(continued)*

```
  } else {
    attributes = {
      height: { from : c.defaultHeight, to : 0},
      opacity: { from : 1, to : 0 }
    };
    anim = new YAHOO.util.Anim( c, attributes, .6,➡
YAHOO.util.Easing.easeBoth );
    anim.animate();
    anim.onComplete.subscribe( bh.toggleCustom );
  }
},
```

The toggleCustom() event listener method needs to retrieve the element that was animated (the paragraph) and toggle its shown property. As the onComplete.subscribe() method runs within the scope of the animation object you created as a new instance using the YAHOO.util.Anim() constructor, you can retrieve the object and all its properties and methods using the this keyword. This means you can retrieve the element using the getEl() method, which is part of every animation object that was created with the YUI Anim() method.

bouncyHeadlines.js *(continued)*

```
toggleCustom:function() {
  var c=this.getEl();
  c.shown = c.shown ? false : true;
},
```

The last thing your script needs is a method that initially hides all the paragraphs and calls the init() method. You hide the paragraphs by adding a new CSS class to the headlines element using addClass().

bouncyHeadlines.js *(continued)*

```
hideContents : function() {
  YAHOO.util.Dom.addClass( 'headlines', 'dynamic' );
  bh.init();
  }
}
```

Instead of calling the hideContents() method to initially hide the paragraphs using a normal load event on the window, the YUI has another trick up its sleeve: the onAvailable() method, which tries to reach the element with the ID you provide as a property before the window has finished loading and calls the function provided as a second parameter once the element is available. The practical upshot of this is that you can hide the paragraphs without having to resort to hacks like inline CSS as discussed in Chapter 5.

bouncyHeadlines.js *(continued)*

```
YAHOO.util.Event.onAvailable( 'headlines', bh.hideContents );
```

I hope that this example has given you a quick overview of the power of the DOM, Event, and Animation components of the YUI. Each has its own examples and full documentation in the zip file you download from the homepage and are well worth trying out and amending yourself.

Replacing Pop-Up Windows Using the YUI Connection Manager and Container Components

Let's take a look at two more components of the YUI library: Connection Manager, which deals with Ajax calls, and Container, which allows for modular windows and elements that cover the page. The Connection Manager is a very powerful part of the YUI as it allows you to create Ajax requests in a really easy syntax:

- You define a handler object that has two properties, success and failure, both of which point the Ajax request to functions provided as the property values.

- You define the functions to respond to these handlers, and you can use all the response data of an XHR call like you've seen in Chapter 8.

- You instantiate the XHR with the YAHOO.util.Connect.asyncRequest() method, which takes the request method, the URL, and the handler object as parameters.

The following short example loads the file `demotext.html` when the window has finished loading:

`exampleXUIAjax.html` *(excerpt)*

```
var handlers = {
  success: success,
  failure: failure
}
function success( t ) {
  alert( t.responseText );
}
function failure( t ) {
  alert( 'There was an error: ' + t.statusText);
}
window.onload = function() {
  call = YAHOO.util.Connect.asyncRequest('GET', 'demotext.html',➥
  handlers);
}
```

You can monitor the connection's status via the `YAHOO.util.Connect.isCallInProgress()` method, which returns `true` when the call is still in progress. If you want to time out a connection after a certain number of seconds, you could use the `YAHOO.util.Connect.abort()` method together with a `window.timeOut()`. Both the `isCallInProgress()` and the `abort()` methods take the variable name of the connection (in the preceding example `call`) as a parameter.

The Container tools allow you to create dynamic elements that have a certain relationship to the current document. You can create modules, which are scriptable page elements; overlays, which cover the document; tooltips, which appear when you hover over an element; panels, which can be moved around by the user like a new browser window; and dialogs, which replace the window methods `alert()`, `confirm()`, or `prompt()` or even allow for their own forms to cover the document. The really amazing feature of Container is that it fixes a lot of problems you encounter when you try to hand-roll your own dialogs or panels:

- You can center the modules automatically on the currently visible part of the browser.

- The user can move the modules around by dragging the header of the panel, but you can prevent her from shifting the panel outside the currently visible document section.

- You can apply effects to make the panel appear and disappear smoothly.

- You can apply drop shadows to the panels.

- You can apply a fix to prevent form elements in the document from being visible although the element covers them. This is a very common problem with overlay elements in MSIE.

Let's take both library components and some DOM trickery to simulate a browser pop-up window that resides in the same document, loads and displays a document via Ajax, and allows the user to move it around and close it. Figure 11-8 shows the result.

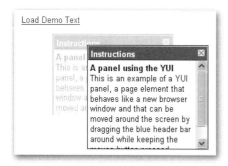

Figure 11-8. *Simulating a pop-up window with YUI library components*

As this is a rather top-of-the-difficulty-stage exercise, you need to include almost all components of the library in the HTML document:

examplePopUpReplace.html

```
<!DOCTYPE HTML PUBLIC "-//W3C//DTD HTML 4.01//EN"
"http://www.w3.org/TR/html4/strict.dtd">
<html dir="ltr" lang="en">
<head>
  <meta http-equiv="Content-Type" content="text/html;
  charset=utf-8">
  <title>Example: Using YUI to replace pop-up windows</title>
  <script type="text/javascript" src="yahoo-min.js"></script>
  <script type="text/javascript" src="event-min.js"></script>
  <script type="text/javascript" src="dom-min.js"></script>
  <script type="text/javascript" src="dragdrop-min.js"></script>
  <script type="text/javascript" src="container-min.js"></script>
  <script type="text/javascript" src="connection-min.js"></script>
  <script type="text/javascript" src="animation-min.js"></script>
  <script type="text/javascript" src="popUpReplace.js"></script>
  <style type="text/css">
    @import 'reset-min.css';
    @import 'fonts-min.css';
    @import 'popUpReplace.css';
  </style>
</head>
```

```
<body>
  <a href="demotext.html"
    onclick="makeRequest(this);return false">Load Demo Text</a>
  <div id="win">
    <div class="hd"></div>
    <div class="bd"></div>
  </div>
</body>
</html>
```

Notice that this example is not really unobtrusive: you are using an inline `onclick` handler and creating HTML that is scripting dependent—the `<div>` with the ID of `win` will become your simulated pop-up. You could create these easily via the DOM and the Event library components, but let's concentrate on using Connection Manager and Container now. The `onclick` handler sends the link as a parameter to the function `makeRequest()`, which reads out the link's `href` attribute and starts a new Ajax request with the `handleSuccess()` and `handleFailure()` functions as event handlers.

`examplePopUpReplace.js`

```
function makeRequest( o ) {
  var sUrl = o.href;
  var request = YAHOO.util.Connect.asyncRequest( 'GET', sUrl,
    {
      success : handleSuccess,
      failure : handleFailure
    }
  );
}
```

The `handleSuccess()` method retrieves the content of the linked document and checks whether the `responseText` is not undefined before creating the simulated pop-up with a new instance of the `YAHOO.widget.Panel()` constructor method. This method takes two parameters: the ID of the element that should be turned into a panel, and the panel attributes as a JSON object. The ID of the panel is `win` in this case.

`examplePopUpReplace.js` *(continued)*

```
function handleSuccess( o ) {
  if( o.responseText !== undefined ) {
    panel = new YAHOO.widget.Panel (
      "win",
```

There is an amazing number of properties a panel can have, and they are all listed in the documentation at `http://developer.yahoo.com/yui/container/panel/#config`. In this example, let's choose an effect to fade the panel in and out smoothly and set the effect duration to half a second. The `constraintoviewport` property defines whether the user should be allowed to drag the panel outside the currently visible browser section or not. Setting it to true ensures that there won't be any ugly scrollbars when the user drags the panel too far to the right or down. The Panel() method automatically allows the user to drag the panel around when you set draggable to true and creates a link to hide the panel when you set close to true. As you'll be changing the content of the panel, it is a good idea to hide it by setting the visible property to false. When you defined all the parameters, you can invoke the render() method of the new panel to create all the necessary HTML elements and apply all the event handlers.

examplePopUpReplace.js *(continued)*

```
    {
      effect : {
        effect : YAHOO.widget.ContainerEffect.FADE,
        duration : 0.5
      },
      constraintoviewport : true,
      close : true,
      visible : false,
      draggable : true
    }
  );
  panel.render();
```

The parameter o that the function handleSuccess() retrieved from the Ajax call contains all the connection data, and you can retrieve the text content of the document that was loaded via o.responseText. Before you can use this data to populate the simulated pop-up panel, you need to clean it out, as you only need the title information for the panel's title bar and the body content for the content. Everything else, from DOCTYPE to styles and script blocks, has to go. You could use regular expressions for that, but there is another way. First of all, you need to replace the BODY element in the text with a <div> with an ID of popupbody. This is necessary because setting the data as it is as innerHTML to an element would remove the BODY element—since there can be only one BODY in a browser window. To replace the BODY element with the <div>, you use regular expressions.

examplePopUpReplace.js *(continued)*

```
  var content  = o.responseText;
  content = content.replace( /<body>/, ➥
  '<div id="popupbody">' );
  content  = content.replace( /<\/body>/, '</div>' );
```

You next retrieve the second <div> inside the element with an ID of win (which is the panel body) and set its innerHTML property to the changed content. Then you can easily retrieve the title via getElementsByTagName() and the body content via getElementById().

examplePopUpReplace.js *(continued)*

```
  var win = document.getElementById('win');
  var windowbody = win.getElementsByTagName('div')[1];
```

```
windowbody.innerHTML=content;
var title = win.getElementsByTagName( 'title' )[0].innerHTML;
var body = document.getElementById( 'popupbody' ).innerHTML;
```

You set the panel's body and header content using the setBody() and setHeader() methods (the former conveniently overrides the rest of the content you don't need) and show the panel by invoking the show() method.

examplePopUpReplace.js *(continued)*

```
    panel.setBody( body );
    panel.setHeader( title );
    panel.show();
  }
}
```

All that is left to do is to define the handleFailure() method that tells the user when the linked document could not be loaded.

examplePopUpReplace.js *(continued)*

```
function handleFailure( o ){
  if( o.responseText !== undefined ) {
    alert( 'Couldn\'t load the content: ' + o.statusText );
  }
}
```

Yahoo User Interface Library Summary

The YUI is a really interesting library to use, especially because it offers much more than just a lot of methods that make your life easier like other libraries do, as it tries to give a lot of documentation and examples and also CSS layout and typography resources to quickly put together a JavaScript-enhanced web site or web application that works with all modern browsers.

The number of people involved in the library and the discussions on the mailing list are sure to make the library even better over time and make testing new components a lot easier. Right now the library is still young, and the documentation is daunting at times, but it is pretty easy to ask a question on the mailing list, and many developers are eager to help you out—in more problematic cases or when you have a request or an idea to extend the library, you will also quite surely find a Yahoo web developer dealing with the library to answer you—probably in the future even me. In comparison with other libraries, especially jQuery, you need to produce a lot more code in YUI to achieve several effects; however, what YUI does is keep the syntax to JavaScript standards and does not change the way you do loops or iterations. At first sight, YUI-driven code can look very complex, and the number of YAHOO.something.somethingElse statements can be confusing. The longer you work with it, the easier it becomes on the eye, and you start appreciating the way methods and properties are named according to what they do or what part of the library they belong to.

Summary

I hope this chapter has given you a taste of what is out there at the moment, and I am sure that this is simply the beginning of a longer experience of shared content, information, and services. Many developers spend a lot of time creating wonderful code just to realize that there is already another product out there that does exactly the same, but better; however, that is not much of a problem—it is through communication and trial and error that we become better in what we do.

You can learn a lot and help the community a great deal by keeping your eyes open and looking at the services available out there, especially giving feedback from your point of view as to how easy some services or libraries are to use. It is far too tempting to consider one's own code perfect, and it is sometimes not until someone else shows you how to break it that you realize it's not. This works both ways. And you shouldn't be put off by your shortcomings—keep at it, and you will get better. Don't be shy—keep participating in the JavaScript community.

Debugging JavaScript

In this appendix, I will introduce you to some tricks and tools to debug your JavaScript code. It is very important to get acquainted with debugging tools, as programming consists to a large extent of trying to find out what went wrong a particular time. Some browsers help you with this problem; others make it harder by having their debugging tools hidden away or returning cryptic error messages that confuse more than they help. Some of my favorites include philosophical works like "Undefined is not defined" or the MSIE standard "Object doesn't support this property or method."

Common JavaScript Mistakes

Let's start with some common mistakes that probably every JavaScript developer has made during his career. Having these in the back of your head when you check a failing script might make it a lot quicker to spot the problem.

Misspellings and Case-Sensitivity Issues

The easiest mistakes to spot are misspellings of JavaScript method names or properties. Classics include getElementByTagName() instead of getElementsByTagName(), getElementByID() instead of getElementById() and node.style.colour (for the British English writers). A lot of times the problem could also be case sensitivity, for example, writing keywords in mixed case instead of lowercase.

```
If( elm.href ) {
  var url = elm.href;
}
```

There is no keyword called If, but there is one called if. The same problem of case sensitivity applies to variable names:

```
var FamilyGuy = 'Peter';
var FamilyGuyWife = 'Lois';
alert( 'The Griffins:\n'+
       familyGuy + ' and ' +
       FamilyGuyWife );
```

This will result in an error message stating "familyGuy is not defined", as there is a variable called FamilyGuy but none called familyGuy.

Trying to Access Undefined Variables

We talked about it in the first chapter of the book—you define variables either by declaring them with or without an additional var keyword (the latter is necessary to define the scope of the variable).

```
Stewie = "Son of Peter and Lois";
var Chris = "Older Son of Peter and Lois";
```

If you try to access a variable that hasn't been defined yet, you'll get an error. The alert() in the following script throws an error as Meg is not defined yet.

```
Peter = "The Family Guy";
Lois = "The Family Guy's Wife";
Brian = "The Dog";
Stewie = "Son of Peter and Lois";
Chris = "Older Son of Peter and Lois";
alert( Meg );
Meg = "The Daughter of Peter and Lois";
```

This is easy when it is an obvious example like this one, but how about trying to guess where the bug in the following example is?

exampleFamilies.html

```
function getFamilyData( outptID, isTree, familyName ) {
  var father, mother, child;
  switch( familyName ) {
    case 'Griffin':
      father = "Peter";
      mother = "Lois";
      child = "Chris";
    break;
    case 'Flintstone':
      father = "Fred";
      mother = "Wilma";
      child = "Pebbles";
    break;
  }
  var out = document.getElementById( outputID );
  if( isTree ) {
    var newUL = document.createElement( 'ul' );
    newUL.appendChild( makeLI( father ) );
    newUL.appendChild( makeLI( mother ) );
    newUL.appendChild( makeLI( child ) );
    out.appendChild( newUL );
```

```
  } else {
    var str = father + ' ' + mother + ' ' + child;
    out.appendChild( document.createTextNode( str ) );
  }
}
getFamilyData( 'tree', true, 'Griffin' );
```

Microsoft Internet Explorer tells you that there is an error in line 23—"'outputID' is undefined," as shown in Figure A-1.

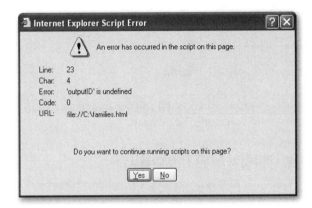

Internet Explorer Script Error

⚠ An error has occurred in the script on this page.

Line: 23
Char: 4
Error: 'outputID' is undefined
Code: 0
URL: file://C:\families.html

Do you want to continue running scripts on this page?

[Yes]   [No]

Figure A-1. *MSIE showing an error on line 23*

However, if you look at the code in line 23 as shown in Figure A-2, nothing seems to be wrong.

```
 9 □ function getFamilyData(outptID,isTree,familyName){
10      var father,mother,child;
11 □    switch(familyName){
12        case 'Griffin':
13          father = "Peter";
14          mother = "Lois";
15          child = "Chris";
16        break;
17        case 'Flintstone':
18          father = "Fred";
19          mother = "Wilma";
20          child = "Pebbles";
21        break;
22      }
23      var out=document.getElementById(outputID);
24 □    if(isTree){
25        var newUL=document.createElement('ul');
26        newUL.appendChild(makeListElement(father));
```

Figure A-2. *The code shown in UltraEdit with a highlight on line 23*

The culprit is a typo in the function parameter, highlighted in Figure A-3, which means that outputID is not defined but outptID is.

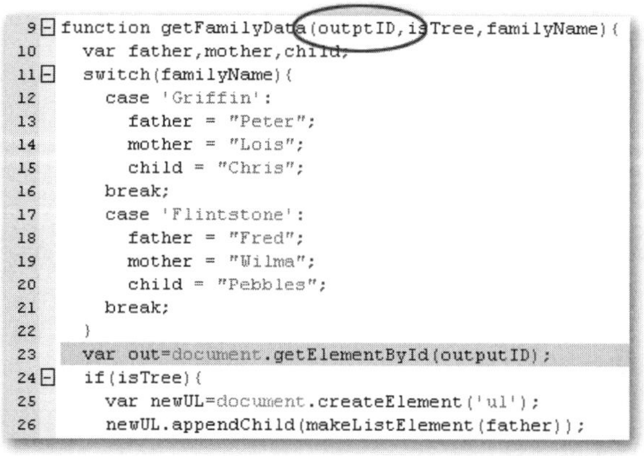

```
 9☐ function getFamilyData(outptID, isTree, familyName) {
10      var father,mother,child;
11☐    switch(familyName){
12        case 'Griffin':
13          father = "Peter";
14          mother = "Lois";
15          child = "Chris";
16        break;
17        case 'Flintstone':
18          father = "Fred";
19          mother = "Wilma";
20          child = "Pebbles";
21        break;
22      }
23      var out=document.getElementById(outputID);
24☐    if(isTree){
25        var newUL=document.createElement('ul');
26        newUL.appendChild(makeListElement(father));
```

Figure A-3. *The misspelled function parameter that caused the error*

Typos in parameters are a very confusing bug, as browsers tell you the error occurred in the line where the variable is used and not where you made the mistake.

Incorrect Number of Closing Braces and Parentheses

Another very common mistake is not closing curly braces or keeping an orphaned closing brace in the code when deleting some lines. Say, for example, you don't need the isTree option any longer and you remove it from the code:

exampleCurly.html

```
function getFamilyData( outputID, familyName ) {
  var father, mother, child;
  switch( familyName ) {
    case 'Griffin':
      father = "Peter";
      mother = "Lois";
      child = "Chris";
    break;
    case 'Flintstone':
      father = "Fred";
      mother = "Wilma";
      child = "Pebbles";
    break;
  }
  var out = document.getElementById( outputID );
  var newUL = document.createElement( 'ul' );
  newUL.appendChild( makeListElement( father ) );
  newUL.appendChild( makeListElement( mother ) );
  newUL.appendChild( makeListElement( child ) );
```

```
  out.appendChild( newUL );
  }
}
getFamilyData( 'tree', true, 'Griffin' );
```

The orphan closing brace shown in bold will cause a "syntax error in line 30." The same problem occurs when you don't close all the braces in a construct, a mistake that can easily happen when you don't indent your code:

exampleMissingCurly.html

```
function testRange( x, start, end ) {
if( x <= end && x >= start ) {
if( x == start ) {
alert( x + ' is the start of the range');
}
if( x == end ) {
alert(x + ' is the end of the range');
}
if( x! = start && x != end ) {
alert(x + ' is in the range');
} else {
alert(x + ' is not in the range');
}
}
```

Running this example will cause an "expected '}' in line 27" error, which is the last line of the script block. This means that somewhere inside the conditional construct we forgot to add a closing curly brace. Where the missing brace is supposed to be is rather hard to find, but a lot easier when the code is properly indented.

exampleMissingCurlyFixed.html

```
function testRange( x, start, end ) {
  if( x <= end && x >= start ) {
    if( x == start ) {
      alert(x + ' is the start of the range');
    }
    if( x == end ) {
      alert(x + ' is the end of the range');
    }
    if( x != start && x != end ) {
      alert(x + ' is in the range');
    }
  } else {
    alert( x + ' is not in the range' );
  }
}
```

The previously missing curly brace is shown in bold (following the "is in the range" alert() message).

Not closing or closing too many parentheses is another common problem. This happens when you nest functions in if() conditions and later on delete some of them. For example:

```
if (all = parseInt(getTotal()){ doStuff(); }
```

This causes an error, as you forgot to close the parentheses of the condition itself.

```
if (all = parseInt(getTotal())){ ... }
```

It can also happen when you nest too many methods and returns:

```
var elm=grab(get(file).match(/<id>(\w+)<\/id>/)[1];
```

This one lacks the closing parentheses after the [1]:

```
var elm=grab(get(file).match(/<id>(\w+)<\/id>/)[1]);
```

In general, this kind of concatenation of functions is not good coding style, but there are situations where you will encounter examples like this one. The trick is to count the opening and the closing parentheses from left to right—good editors also highlight opening and closing parentheses automatically.

You could also write a utility function to do this for you, which in itself is a test of your attention to detail when it comes to coding syntax:

```
exampleTestingCodeLine.html

function testCodeLine( c ) {
  if( c.match( /\(/g ).length !=
      c.match( /\)/g) .length ) {
    alert( 'closing ) missing' );
  }
}
c = "var elm=grab(get('demo.xml')" +
  ".match( /<id>(\w+)<\/id>/ )[1] );";
testCodeLine( c );
```

Concatenation Gone Wrong

Concatenation is happening a lot when you use JavaScript to output HTML. Make sure that you don't forget the + signs in between the different parts to concatenate to a whole.

```
father = "Peter";
mother = "Lois";
child = "Chris";
family = father+" "+mother+" "child;
```

The preceding lacks one addition sign before the child variable:

```
father = "Peter";
mother = "Lois";
child = "Chris";
family = father+" "+mother+" "+child;
```

Another obstacle is to make sure you don't concatenate the wrong data types.

```
father = "Peter";
fAge = 40;
mother = "Lois";
mAge = 38;
child = "Chris";
cAge = 12;
family = father + ", " + mother +
        " and " + child + " Total Age: " +
        fAge + mAge + cAge;
alert( family );
```

This will not show the desired result, but this instead:

```
Peter, Lois and Chris Total Age: 403812
```

The mistake is that you concatenate strings and numbers as the + operator works from left to right. You need to add parentheses around the age term:

```
father = "Peter";
fAge = 40;
mother = "Lois";
mAge = 38;
child = "Chris";
cAge = 12;
family = father + ", " + mother +
        " and " + child + " Total Age: " +
        (fAge + mAge + cAge);
alert(family);
```

This results in the desired outcome:

```
Peter, Lois and Chris Total Age: 90
```

Assigning Instead of Testing the Value of a Variable

When testing the value of a variable, it is all too easy to assign it instead of testing it: all you need to do is forget an equal sign.

```
if(Stewie = "talking") {
  Brian.hear();
}
```

This will entice Brian to hear all the time, not only when Stewie has something to say; however, adding one equal sign does make Brian hear only when Stewie talks:

```
if(Stewie == "talking") {
  Brian.hear();
}
```

Tracing Errors with `alert()` and "Console" Elements

The easiest way to trace errors is to use `alert()` wherever you want to test a certain value. The `alert()` method will stop the script execution (with the exception of Ajax calls that might still be going on in the background) and provide you with information about the value of a certain variable, and you can deduce if that value is correct or if it is the cause of the error. In some instances, using an `alert()` is not the right option, for example, if you want to trace the change of several values while looping through an array. Depending on the size of the array, this can become tedious, as you need to press Enter every time you want to get rid of the `alert()` and commence to the next array item. A workaround for this problem is coming up with your own debugging console or logging elements. Most JavaScript libraries come with a logging sublibrary (DOJO has dojo.logging, at `http://manual.dojotoolkit.org/index.html#infrastructure`; Mochikit has Logging, at `http://mochikit.com/doc/html/MochiKit/Logging.html`), and the DOMhelp library we put together in this book is no exception. You can use the `initDebug()`, `setDebug()`, and `stopDebug()` methods to simulate a debugging console. Simply add a style for the element with the ID DOMhelpdebug and use the methods to show the element and write content to it. For example:

exampleDebugTest.html *(excerpt)*

```
#DOMhelpdebug{
  position:absolute;
  top:0;
  right:0;
  width:300px;
  height:200px;
  overflow:scroll;
  background:#000;
  color:#0F9;
  white-space:pre;
  font-family:courier,monospace;
```

```
    padding:1em;
}
html>body #DOMhelpdebug{
  position:fixed;
  min-height:200px;
  height:200px;
  overflow:auto;
}
```

exampleDebugTest.html *(excerpt)*

```
<script type="text/javascript"
 src="../DOMhelp.js"></script>
<script type="text/javascript">
  function DOMDebugTest(){
    DOMhelp.initDebug();
    for(var i = 0; i < 300; i++ ) {
      DOMhelp.setDebug( i + ' : ' + ( i % 3 == 0 ) + '\n' );
    }
  }
  DOMhelp.addEvent( window, 'load', DOMDebugTest, false );
</script>
```

This example loops through the numbers 0 to 299 and displays whether the number can be divided by 3 without resulting in a floating point number. Instead of hitting Enter 300 times, all you need to do to see the results is to scroll in the "console window" you created with the earlier styles.

Error Handling with `try` and `catch()`

You can test scripts using the `try ... catch` construct. Simply add the code you want to test inside a `try` condition and if there is an error, the code inside `catch()` will be executed. For example:

exampleTryCatch.js

```
try{
  alert( 'this is a code example' );
  alert( myVariable );
} catch( exceptionObject ) {
  // Predefine empty output
  var errorString = '';
  for( i in exceptionObject ) {
    errorString += i + ':' + exceptionObject[i] + '\n';
  }
  alert( errorString );
}
```

The catch() method retrieves an Exception object as a parameter when an error occurs inside the try statement. You can give this object any variable name; in this example we call it exceptionObject. Depending on the error and the browser, this object will have different properties, and the properties that are the same across browsers will have different values. On MSIE 6 on Windows XP, the preceding code shows the bug—which is the second alert() trying to display an undefined variable—the following way:

```
name:TypeError
message:'myVariable' is undefined
number:-2146823279
description:'myVariable' is undefined
```

On Firefox 1.5.0.3 on Windows XP:

```
message:myVariable is not defined
fileName:file:///c:/exampleTryCatch.html
lineNumber:11
stack:@file:///c:/exampleTryCatch.html:11
name:ReferenceError
```

On Opera 8.54 on Windows XP:

```
message:Statement on line 4: Reference to undefined variable: myVariable
Backtrace:
  Line 4 of inline#1 script in
  file://localhost/C:/exampleTryCatch.html
  alert(myVariable);
opera#sourceloc:4
```

If you try a different error, you will get the same properties, but different values. Let's try to call a function that doesn't exist by misspelling alert().

exampleTryCatchTypo.js

```
try{
  allert( 'this is a code example' );
}
catch( exceptionObject ) {
  var errorString = '';
  for( i in exceptionObject ) {
    errorString += i + ':' + exceptionObject[i] + '\n';
  }
  alert( errorString );
}
```

The results on MSIE 6 are the following:

```
name:TypeError
message:Object expected
number:-2146823281
description:Object expected
```

On Firefox 1.5.0.3:

```
message:allert is not defined
fileName:file:///c:/exampleTryCatchTypo.html
lineNumber:10
stack:@file:///c:/exampleTryCatchTypo.html:10
name:ReferenceError
```

On Opera 8.54:

```
message:Statement on line 3: Reference to undefined variable: allert
Backtrace:
Line 3 of inline#1 script in
file://localhost/C://exampleTryCatchTypo.html
allert("this is a code example");
opera#sourceloc:3
```

Using try and catch in a debugging process can be very helpful, and depending on the browser, you can easily spot the problem.

Note Notice that Opera reports the line number of the code inside the SCRIPT element, while Firefox reports the line number of the whole HTML document. MSIE leaves you in suspense where the error might have occurred when using try and catch().

However, as the construct in itself is JavaScript, you cannot debug JavaScript syntax errors with it:

exampleTryCatchFailing.js

```
try{
  alert( 'this is a code example' ) );
} catch( exceptionObject ) {
  var errorString = '';
  for( i in exceptionObject ) {
    errorString += i + ':' + exceptionObject[i] + '\n';
  }
  alert( errorString );
}
```

The extra closing parenthesis after the first alert() is a syntax error that will cause the browser to show its built-in error messaging and stop the script from executing instead of executing the code inside the catch construct.

Sequential Uncommenting

Another very easy way to trace an error is to comment out the whole script and uncomment it function by function or—if it is a single function—line by line. Test the script every time you uncomment a line by reloading it in a browser, and you will quickly get to the one that causes the error. This can take time though, and it would be much easier to know roughly where the error occurs, which is why you need to rely on your browser to give you this information.

Error Reporting in Browsers

Browsers help you to different degrees to debug your code. Following is a roundup of different browsers and their means of displaying errors and locating their origin. As I wanted to give an overview of different browsers you can use, I will not go into much further detail about the different add-ons for each of them. Instead, I will provide you with some information and URLs where to get these add-ons and to read their documentation for yourself. The reason for this is not laziness on my behalf, but the fact that the number of browser add-ons and debugging tools for JavaScript increased a lot in the last year, with the advent of Ajax making JavaScript interesting again to a broader audience. Therefore, detailed explanations of a certain tool might be outdated once this book hits the shops.

Microsoft Internet Explorer 6

MSIE6 is probably still the most common browser on Windows these days. If you're a developer, though, it doesn't help you much—most of the time it throws errors other browsers don't.

Older versions of MSIE (4 and 5 on PC) showed a report window every time a JavaScript error occurred. This feature has been turned off in newer versions; you can turn it back on in the Browsing section of the Advanced tab under Tools ➤ Internet Options as shown in Figure A-4.

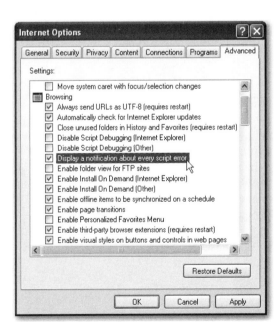

Figure A-4. *Turning on error reporting in Microsoft Internet Explorer*

As the error messages provided by MSIE can be rather cryptic, like "Object does not support this method or property," and if MSIE is your only option for development, you might want to download the free Microsoft script debugger at `http://www.microsoft.com/downloads/details.aspx?familyid=2F465BE0-94FD-4569-B3C4-DFFDF19CCD99&displaylang=en`. The Microsoft Script Debugger is a debugging suite that allows you to set break points that stop the script execution until you tell it to go on. You can also use it to read the values of variables and change them while the script is running. All of this works outside the browser, which means you don't need to resort to the tricks mentioned earlier like `alert()`, own debugging consoles, or sequentially comment out of parts of code. An introduction to the Microsoft Script Debugger is available at `http://msdn.microsoft.com/library/default.asp?url=/library/en-us/sdbug/Html/sdbug_1.asp`.

Safari

Apple's flagship browser seemingly does not help you at all with JavaScript debugging. I said "seemingly" because there is a debugging menu in Safari that is very handy; the only problem is that it is hidden by default.

Enabling the debugging menu can be done in two ways: either via the command line or by installing the Safari enhancer. The command-line solution is pretty straightforward.

1. Close Safari.

2. Enter **% defaults write com.apple.Safari IncludeDebugMenu 1** in the Operating System console (Applications ➤ Utilities ➤ Console) and hit Enter.

3. Restart Safari.

You'll see that you have a new Debug menu option in the top menubar as shown in Figure A-5. Among many other useful features like a DOM tree viewer and the chance to simulate other browsers for web sites that block out Safari, you have the options either to log JavaScript errors to the OS console or to show errors in a JavaScript console window.

If you prefer a graphical user interface to change Safari, download the Safari enhancer shown in Figure A-6 at `http://www.versiontracker.com/dyn/moreinfo/macosx/17776` and tick the box that states Activate Debugging Menu before pressing the Apply All Settings button.

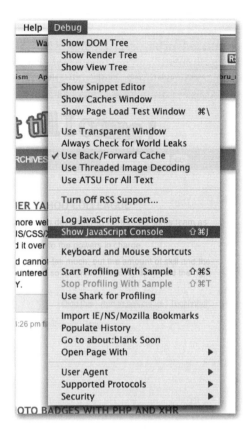

Figure A-5. *The debugging menu of Safari*

Figure A-6. *Enabling the debugging menu with Safari Enhancer*

Opera 8.5

Opera not only comes with options to quickly turn off all kinds of browser support (JavaScript, cookies, plug-ins, pop-ups) by pressing F12, which helps immensely to test whether your web page is dependent on JavaScript or not, it also has a built-in JavaScript console that gives very detailed error reports. You can turn on the console via Tools ➤ Advanced ➤ JavaScript console as shown in Figure A-7.

Figure A-7. *Showing the JavaScript console in Opera*

Firefox 1.5.0.3

Firefox stays silent and doesn't bother the visitor by reporting JavaScript errors. However, it comes with a very powerful JavaScript console, which you can show by selecting Tools ➤ JavaScript console on the main toolbar as shown in Figure A-8.

■**Note** Don't be confused if your Firefox browser doesn't have the same options as shown in Figure A-8; some of them are dependent on extensions I installed. However, you should have the JavaScript console.

Figure A-8. *Showing the JavaScript console in Firefox*

Once activated, the JavaScript console is visible in its own browser window, which lists the JavaScript errors that occur in any page you open in any of your Firefox windows or tabs. It is quite amazing to see how many errors accumulate when you surf the Web a bit with the console open. The error in `exampleMissingCurly.html` would display as shown in Figure A-9.

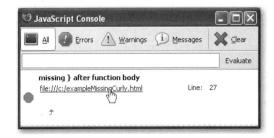

Figure A-9. *The Firefox JavaScript console showing an error*

You can either show errors, warnings, and messages, or filter the list for each of them. Clicking the Clear button will wipe the list clean. You can even evaluate any JavaScript by pasting it into the code box and clicking the Evaluate button.

By default, the JavaScript console will open in a new window, but there is a trick you can use to show it in the sidebar instead.

1. Make sure the bookmarks toolbar is visible by selecting View ➤ Toolbars ➤ Bookmarks Toolbar.

2. Right-click the toolbar and select New Bookmark.

3. Add the information shown in Figure A-10. The location must be `chrome://global/content/console.xul`, but you can name the bookmark anything you like.

4. Make sure the Load this bookmark in the sidebar option is activated.

This will add a new bookmark button to the toolbar that opens the JavaScript console in the sidebar when you click it.

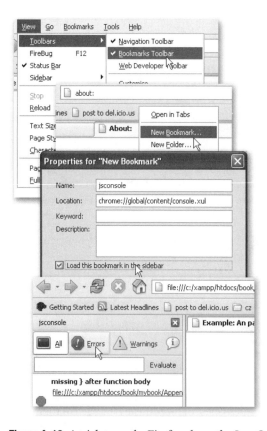

Figure A-10. *A trick to make Firefox show the JavaScript console in the sidebar*

This should get you started in spotting errors quickly in Firefox; however, it is only the tip of the iceberg when it comes to great helpers available for this browser. Mozilla and Firefox can be easily improved with extensions written in JavaScript and an XML-based language called XUL.

Developers keep churning out new extensions and putting them on the Web. Two of those are very handy for you as a JavaScript developer:

The Web Developer Extension

The Web Developer extension is a toolbar by Chris Pederick that is available at `http://www.chrispederick.com/work/webdeveloper/`. This toolbar allows you to quickly toggle Java-Script support (which you can do otherwise via Tools ➤ Options ➤ Content ➤ Enable JavaScript), show HTML generated by JavaScript in the Source Viewer, populate forms automatically with data, edit the page's style sheet on the fly, and choose from many more options. It is a "Swiss Army Knife" for web development.

FireBug

If you thought the JavaScript console of Opera, Safari, and Firefox was handy, get the FireBug extension by Joe Hewitt (who is also responsible for the DOM inspector that is part of the default Firefox installation) at `http://www.joehewitt.com/software/firebug/`. The FireBug extension is visible in the bottom right of the browser window and either shows a warning icon with the number of errors in the console or a green icon indicating that everything is OK. If there are errors, you can click the icon (or press F12) to open the FireBug console in the bottom half of the browser window as shown in Figure A-11.

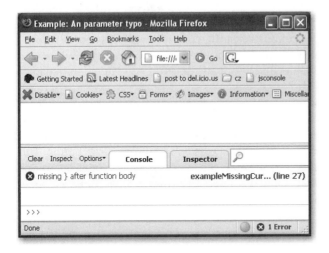

Figure A-11. *The FireBug extension with open console*

The features of FireBug are too many to mention here. Whatever is happening to the document, you can see it in the console. It shows the DOM structure, the applied CSS, the dimensions and properties of elements, events assigned to elements, the return values of Ajax requests, and much, much more. In the DOM inspector mode, you are even able to change the document on the fly to test changes quickly in a remote document. This is for testing purposes only—you cannot save the changes on the remote server, of course.

Venkman

Mozilla's answer to the Microsoft Script Debugger is called Venkman and is available at https:// addons.mozilla.org/firefox/216/. Venkman is a full debugging suite that allows you to watch variables, set debugging points, and really go down into the depths of JavaScript development. Explaining all the features of Venkman would fill its own chapter, and for day-to-day JavaScript tasks, it may be overkill to use. If you want to know all the features of Venkman and how to use it, check the walkthrough provided on the homepage at http://www.mozilla.org/projects/ venkman/venkman-walkthrough.html. Another good start is the introductory article "Learning Venkman" by Svend Tofte, available at http://www.svendtofte.com/code/learning_venkman/. The newest versions of the aforementioned FireBug extension also include a debugger like Venkman, which makes it obsolete in some way; however, it is worth mentioning as it is in use in some companies.

JSLint and JSUNIT

Some browser-independent tools are available that could also help you with JavaScript development. One is the online JavaScript verifier JSLint by Douglas Crockford, available at http:// www.jslint.com/lint.html. JSLint is a tool written in JavaScript that verifies scripts in terms of syntactical validity and tries to ensure good coding style. As "good coding style" is a subjective matter, you may want to take JSLint reports with a grain of salt. JavaScript development happens mostly in browser environments, and from time to time you need to bend the rules or cut corners to make a script work faster or work around browser issues. That being said, it is still a great tool to find ways to optimize your scripts in terms of cleanliness of code if you don't have to cut corners. The great thing about JSLint is that it gives you a full analysis of your script, including reports on global variables and how many times different functions have been called.

If you come from a back-end coding environment, you may have already used or at least heard about unit testing (http://en.wikipedia.org/wiki/Unit_testing). In a very small nutshell, unit testing means that you write test cases for all your methods and functions, and a "testing harness" allows you to run all these tests in succession when you press a button. This way you can ensure that your code works as you define the test cases it has to fulfill before you develop the code. For Java, there is JUnit; for PHP, there is PHPUnit; and yes, for JavaScript there is JSUnit, available at http://www.jsunit.net/.

Summary

All in all, debugging JavaScript is much easier these days than it was some years ago, and especially in the Firefox extension world it is very important to keep your eyes open, as new products that you may profit from are released almost weekly. The renaissance of JavaScript as part of the Ajax methodology has also made development IDE vendors a lot more aware of the need for good JavaScript debugging tools. Products that were traditionally meant exclusively for Java or .NET development are beginning to add support for JavaScript that goes beyond color-coding the sources.

Index

■Special Characters

#text nodes, 89

$1 variable, 362

$(document).ready ( ) method, 421

$.get( ) method, 425

% operator, 21

&& operator, 48

* operator, 21

*/ syntax, JavaScript, 8

/* syntax, JavaScript, 8

// syntax, JavaScript, 8

\\ escape sequence, 20

|| operator, 48

+ operator, 21, 23

++ operator, 21

!= operator, 46

== operator, 46

> operator, 46

>= operator, 46

\' escape sequence, 20

/ operator, 21

! operator, 49

■A

abort( ) method, 321, 445

accessibility, 69–71

accesskey attribute, 179

addEvent( ) method, 166, 190, 325, 330, 433

addEventListener( ) method, 156, 166

addListener( ) method, 441

addMap( ) function, 429

addOverlay( ) method, 432, 436

ADDRESS element, 125

advantages of JavaScript, 5–6

after( ) method, 425

Ajax, back-end interaction with

    and caching, 309

    connected select boxes, 323–331

    optional dynamic Ajax menus, 331–340

    overview, 299–309

    replacing XML with JSON, 314–316

    turning XML into HTML, 309–314

    using server-side scripts to reach third-party content, 316–320

    XHR on slow connections, 320–322

alert( ) method, 10, 90–95, 101, 121, 308, 452, 456, 458–459

Anim( ) method, 442–443

animate( ) method, 443

animation, 222–230

APIs (application programming interfaces), 4

appendChild( ) method, 312

application/x-www-form-urlencoded content type, 329

appName attribute, 65

appVersion attribute, 65

Array data type, 30

array_slice( ) method, 409

arrays

    Array object

        converting array to string and back, 43–44

        cutting slice of array, 42–43

        joining two arrays, 43

        overview, 42

        sorting array, 44–45

    overview, 39–42

asynchronously, 300

attachEvent( ) method, 166

attributes of elements

changing, 107–108

reading, 117

■B

\b escape sequence, 20

back( ) method, 230, 246

background image, 192

background-position property, 191

before( ) method, 422

behavior layer, JavaScript as

object detection vs. browser dependence, 65–68

overview, 63–65

progressive enhancement, 68–69

block property, 261

blocking software, 238

blur( ) method, 215, 219–220, 238, 276, 278

BODY element, 448

Boolean data type, 18, 45

border property, 185

 line breaks, 426

braces, closing, 454–456

brackets (<>), 86

branches, breaking out of, 52

break statement, 52, 58

browser cache settings, 212

browser window, navigation methods of

layer ads, 231–238

overview, 230–231

browsers

browser dependence vs. object detection, 65–68

error reporting in

Firefox, 466–470

Microsoft Internet Explorer, 6 (MSIE6), 463–464

Opera, 466

overview, 463

Safari, 464–465

vendors, 212

business logic layer, 63

button, 295

button attribute, event object, 157

buttons, radio buttons, 281–284

■C

caching, 309

camel notation, 24

camelCase, 72

Campbell, Chris, 364

cancelClick( ) method, 169, 211, 219, 228, 325, 329–330, 372, 393, 395, 404, 413–414

captions, displaying in thumbnail galleries, 396–401

Cascading Style Sheets (CSS), 61, 64

easing maintenance, 139–143

overview, 131

styling dynamic pages, 131–139

support problems

:hover pseudo-class, 148–152

multiple columns with same height, 143–148

overview, 143

thumbnail galleries, 388

case statements, 52

case-sensitivity issues, 451

catch( ) method, 459–462

CDATA commenting syntax, 7

ceil( ) function, Math object, 37

CGI (Common Gateway Interface), 3

chainable methods, 420

character encoding method, 20

charAt(n) method, 346

charCodeAt( ) method, 346, 349

check boxes, 279–281

checked attribute, 273, 279

checked property, 275, 279–281, 283–284, 294

childNodes property, 100

children, 99–100

Clark, Chris, 139

click( ) method, 276

click event, 163, 247, 249, 257, 259, 294

click event handler, 335

client-side validation, pros and cons of, 343–344

close( ) method, 215, 220

closestSibling( ) method, 120, 125, 178, 203, 294

closing braces, incorrect number of, 454–456

CMS (Content Management System), 139

CODE element, 420, 426

code execution, 9–11

code layout, 72–74

code library, 426

coding syntax, 24

cols attribute, 276

columns, multiple with same height, 143–148

commenting, 74–76

complete property, 185

composite data types, 30

concat( ) method, Array object, 43

concatenation, 27, 456–457

concatenation operator, 23

conditional statements, 17
    breaking out of branch or loop, 52
    overview, 49–52

confirm( ) method, 90–95, 215

console elements, tracing errors with, 458–459

constraintoviewport property, 447

Content-length, 329

continue keyword, 58

converting array to string and back, 43–44

converting different types of data, 26–30

Cross-Site Scripting (XSS), 213

CSS. *See* Cascading Style Sheets

CSS class, 248, 257, 398

cssjs method, 149

curly braces {} syntax, 8

custom attribute, 366–367

custom elements, 297

cutting slice of array, 42–43

■ **D**

data comparison, 45–48

data conversion, 26–30

data types, 17

Date object, 30, 355–356
    overview, 34
    using, 35–37

DDA (Digital Discrimination Act), 6, 62

Debug menu option, 464

debugging
    common mistakes
        assigning instead of testing value of variable, 458
        concatenation gone wrong, 456–457
        incorrect number of closing braces and parentheses, 454–456
        misspellings and case-sensitivity issues, 451
        overview, 451
        trying to access undefined variables, 452–454
    error handling with try and catch( ), 459–462
    error reporting in browsers
        Firefox, 466–470
        Microsoft Internet Explorer, 6 (MSIE6), 463–464
        Opera, 466
        overview, 463
        Safari, 464–465
    JSLint and JSUNIT, 470
    overview, 451

debugging *(continued)*

   sequential uncommenting, 462

   tracing errors with alert( ) and console elements, 458–459

decision making

   comparing data, 46–48

   conditional statements

     breaking out of branch or loop, 52

     overview, 49–52

   logical operators, 48

   loops

     continuing, 58–59

     for loop, 54–56

     overview, 54

     while loop, 56–58

   overview, 45

   switch statement, 52–54

   testing multiple values, 52–54

delimiters, 18

Developer Network, 438

DHTML, 5

Diaz, Dustin, 139

Digital Discrimination Act (DDA), 6, 62

dimensions of windows, 221

disabled attribute, 136, 285, 295

disabled property, 138

disadvantages of JavaScript, 5–6

display property, 125, 130

DOCTYPE element, 85–86

document object, 12, 15, 96, 184, 413

Document Object Model. *See* DOM

Document Type Definition (DTD), 86

document.createElement( ) method, 109, 117

document.createTextNode( ) method, 109, 117

documentElement.scrollTop property, 413

document.getElementById('id') element, 116

document.getElementsByTagName ('tagname') element, 116

document.write( ) method, 15, 41, 89, 96, 174

DOJO toolkit, 340

DOM (Document Object Model), 67, 85

   accessing document via, 96–99

   creating new nodes, 117

   methods, 277

   navigating between nodes, 117

   overview, 116

   reaching elements in document, 116

   reading element attributes, node values, and other node data, 117

   scripting, 63, 289

DOM-2 event handling, 183

DOMhelp library, 123, 190, 198, 419

do.while loop, 56, 59

drag-and-drop interface, 179

dyn class, 232

dynamic Ajax menus, 331–340

dynamic class, 127, 267

dynamic pages, styling, 131–139

dynamic slide shows, 207–211

dynamic technology syntax, 3

■E

each( ) method, 425

Easing utility, 442

Edward, Dean, 345

Eisenberg, David, 367

element node, 100

element.innerHTML node, 117

elements, 39, 297

   attributes of, changing, 107–108

   creating, removing, and replacing

     avoiding NOSCRIPT, 113–115

     DOM features, 116–117

     overview, 109–113

     shortening scripts via innerHTML, 115–116

     buttons, 284–286

     check boxes, 279–281

     overview, 275–276

radio buttons, 281–284

select boxes, 286–291

text fields, text areas, hidden and password fields, 278–279

using blur( ) and focus( ), 278

reading element attributes, node values, other node data, 117

elements collection, 276–277, 288

else condition, 281

else statement, 9, 15

<embed> tag, 153

embedded slide shows, 197–207

enctype attribute, 274

error handling, with try and catch( ), 459–462

error reporting, in browsers

Firefox, 466–470

Microsoft Internet Explorer, 463–464

Opera, 466

overview, 463

Safari, 464–465

escape sequence, 19

escape sequences, 19–20

eval( ) method, 188, 315–316

event bubbling, 158

event capturing, 156

event handling

changing document's behavior via

events in W3C-compliant world, 156–165

fixing events for non-W3C-compliant world, 165–172

overview, 153–156

reading and filtering keyboard entries, 174–179

ugly page load problem, 173–174

dangers of, 179–180

event listener, 156

event object, 157

event target, 156

Exception object, 460

exec( ) method, 357

explanatory comments, 75

F

\f escape sequence, 20

failed( ) method, 307–308, 313, 320, 330, 336

false keyword, 281

feedback

data validation

highlighting erroneous fields individually, 376–379

instant validation feedback, 379–380

overview, 369

replacing main form with clickable error message, 374–376

showing list of erroneous fields, 369–374

user feedback methods, 215

in web pages, 89–95

filtering keyboard entries, 174–179

FireBug, 469

Firefox, error reporting in

FireBug, 469

overview, 466–469

Venkman, 470

Web Developer extension, 469

firstChild property, 100

flash of unstyled content (FOUC), 173

Flash Satay, 153

Flickr, 417

Flickr badges, 406

floor( ) function, Math object, 37

focus( ) method, 215, 219, 238, 276, 278

focus event, 243

focus pseudo-selector, 152

for attribute, 365

for keyword, 54

for loop, 54–56, 59, 98

for.in loop, 55

FORM element, 274, 305

Form object, 274

form property, 275, 277

form validation techniques

CSS classes method, 366

custom attribute method, 366–367

designating mandatory fields, 364

failures of these methods, 367

hidden field method, 364–365

indicator element method, 365–366

overview, 364

sharing validation rules, 367–369

formmail.pl script, 364

forms, 297

collection, 275–277

custom elements, 297

elements

buttons, 284–286

check boxes, 279–281

globally supported properties, 277

HTML attributes not contained in elements collection, 276

overview, 275–276

radio buttons, 281–284

select boxes, 286–291

text fields, text areas, hidden and password fields, 278–279

using blur( ) and focus( ), 278

interactive, 291–297

methods, 274–275

overview, 272–274

properties, 274

forms object, 274

forward( ) method, 230, 246

FOUC (flash of unstyled content), 173

Friedl, Jeffrey, 363

function keyword, 77, 83

functions, 11, 76–80

calling, 11

creating own, 11

functionality, reusable code block wrappers, 11

sorting and reuse of, 80

variables and function scope, 80–81

G

GBrowserIsCompatible( ) function, 429

GET method, 305, 324

GET parameter, 319

getAttribute( ) method, 108, 126, 249, 367

getEl( ) method, 443

getElementById( ) method, 96, 98–99, 103, 184, 249, 251, 274, 448, 451

getElementById object, 68

getElementsByClassName( ) method, 96

getElementsByTagName( ) method, 96–99, 184, 274, 384, 448, 451

getTimezoneOffset( ) method, 37

GEvent.addListener( ) method, 432

GLatLng( ) method, 430

global reset, 209

global variable, 80

GMap2( ) method, 430, 435

GMapTypeControl( ) method, 431

GMarker( ) method, 432, 436

go(n) method, 246

Good, Nathan A., 363

Google AdSense, 416

Google Maps, 427–432, 434–437

Google Suggest, 381

GOverviewMapControl( ) method, 431

GScaleControl( ) method, 431

GSmallMapControl( ) method, 430

GUnload( ) function, 429

H

handleFailure( ) method, 447, 449

handleSuccess( ) method, 447–448

hasChildNodes( ) method, 100, 120

hash property, 245

HEAD element, 85

<head> tag, 85

height attribute, 186

height property, 185

hidden fields, 278–279, 364–365

hide( ) method, 422, 425

HIJAX, 323

history object, 246

home( ) method, 230

host property, 245

hostname property, 245

hover method, 165

:hover pseudo-class, 148–152

href attribute, 110, 137, 235, 246, 249–250, 252–253, 257, 262, 269–270, 320, 330, 335, 338, 393, 399, 404, 410, 413–414, 425, 447

href property, 245

hspace property, 185

HTML, 87

   accessing document via DOM, 96–99

   anatomy of HTML document, 85–89

   changing attributes of elements, 107–108

   children, 99–102

   creating, removing, and replacing elements

      avoiding NOSCRIPT, 113–115

      DOM features, 116–117

      DOMhelp, 118–122

      overview, 109–113

      shortening scripts via innerHTML, 115–116

   overview, 85

   parents, 99–103

   providing feedback in web pages, 89–95

   siblings, 99–100, 103–107

   turning XML into, 309–314

html( ) method, 422

HTML 4.01 STRICT, 87

HTML element, 85, 428

.html file extension, 9

I

id attribute, 89, 101, 246, 282

if( ) method, 456

if condition, 67, 79, 172

If keyword, 451

if statement, 9, 14, 49, 56

IFRAME elements, 237

images

   image scripting basics, 184–186

   overview, 183

   preloading, 186

   rollover effects

      dynamic slide shows, 207–211

      embedded slide shows, 197–207

      overview, 187

      on parent elements, 192–196

      slide shows, 196

      using several images, 187–191

      using single image, 191–192

images object, 67

IMG element, 409, 414

index numbers, 40, 274

index property, 194

indexKey, 56

indexOf( ) method, 32, 346, 348, 350

innerHeight property, 213

innerHTML, 261

innerHTML method, 308, 313–314

innerHTML property, 115–116, 394, 414, 422

innerWidth property, 213

in-page navigation, 246–255

input element, 54, 295–297

<input type="image">, 285

insertBefore( ) method, 267–268

instant validation feedback, 379–380

interactive forms, 291–297

IrfanView, 388
isCallInProgress( ) method, 445
isNaN( ) method, 49, 352
isNumber( ) method, 352
item( ) method, 100

■J

JavaScript object property syntax, 126
JavaScript overview, 1–4
  definition, 4
  functions, 11
  objects, 12–13
  problems and merits of, 5–6
  reasons for using despite reliability
    problems, 6–7
  running JavaScript, 9
  simple example, 13–15
  in web page and essential syntax
    code execution, 9–11
    functions, 11
    JavaScript syntax, 8–9
    overview, 7
  what it is, 4
JavaScript Triggers article, 366
join( ) method, 43, 288
joining two arrays, 43
jQuery, 419–427
.js file, 64, 80
JSLint, 470
JSON, replacing XML with, 314–316
JSUNIT, 470

■K

Keith, Jeremy, 323
Keyboard access, 243
keyboard entries, reading and filtering,
  174–179
keyboard event handling, 179
keyCode/data/charCode attribute, event
  object, 157
keydown handler, 175

keypress handler, 175
Koch, Peter-Paul, 160, 366

■L

label element, 108
lang attribute, 85
Langridge, Stuart, 62
lastIndexOf( ) method, 32, 346, 348, 350
layer ads, 231–238
Learning Venkman article, 470
Lemon, Gez, 247
length property, 31, 98, 203, 246, 274, 286, 290
line break (\n), 101
line-wrap option, 74
links, 110
literal values, 23
LiveScript, 4
load event, 156
load method, 404, 412–413
local variables, 23
location property, 245
logical operators, 45, 48
loops, 17
  breaking out of, 52
  continuing, 58–59
  for loop, 54–56
  overview, 54
  while loop, 56–58
lowsrc property, 185
Ludwin, Daniel, 139

■M

Macromedia Dreamweaver, 188
mandatory field, 364–365
map_overview, 432
mapContainer, 435
maps, adding to sites with Google Maps,
  427–432, 434–437
mashups, 437
Mastering Regular Expressions book, 363

match( ) method, 129, 347, 357

Math object, 30, 357

generating random number, 38

overview, 37

rounding numbers, 37–38

META element, 85

methods

of forms, 274–275

of String object, 32–34

of window object

animation with window intervals and timeouts, 222–230

changing position and dimensions of window, 221

navigation methods of browser window, 230–238

opening new windows, 215–221

overview, 215

user feedback methods, 215

microformat, 309

Microsoft Internet Explorer (MSIE), 5, 64, 463–464

Microsoft Script Debugger, 464

misspellings, 451

moofx, 341

mouseout event, 163

mouseover event, 159, 163, 243

mouseover handler, 252–253

moveBy(x,y) window, 221

multicolumn layout, 145

multiple attribute, 287

N

\n (line break), 101

name attribute, 187, 246, 274, 282, 284

name property, 185, 213, 274–275, 277

naming conventions, 71–72

navigation

browser navigation, 245–246

in-page navigation, 246–255

overview, 241–244

pagination, 263–271

site navigation, 255–263

navigator data, 416

navigator object, 65

nested loops, 173

Netscape Navigator (NN) browser, 4

new keyword, 32

nextSibling node, 118, 120

Nicholls, Stu, 152

node parameter, 120

node tree, 173

nodeName object, 100, 102, 277, 336, 393, 395

node.nextSibling node, 117

node.nodeName attribute, 117

node.nodeType attribute, 117

node.nodeValue attribute, 117

node.parentNode node, 117

node.previousSibling node, 117

nodes, 117

node.setAttribute('attribute', 'value') attribute, 117

nodeType node, 118

nodeType object, 100

nodeValue object, 100

Nolan, Daniel, 188

NOSCRIPT element, 113–115

<noscript> tag, 7, 113

Null data type, 18

number, 18

Number( ) method, 28, 36, 352

Number data type, 18, 23

numbers

random, generating, 38

rounding, 37–38

numeric validation methods, 352–357

O

obfuscating, 345

Object data type, 30

Find it faster at http://superindex.apress.com

object detection, vs. browser dependence, 65–68

object literal, 82

<object> tag, 153

object-oriented programming (OOP), 3

objects

Date object

overview, 34

using, 35–37

Math object

generating random number, 38

overview, 37

rounding numbers, 37–38

String object

creating, 31–32

methods of, 32–34

overview, 30

obj.removeChild(oldNode) method, 109

offsetHeight attribute, 147

offsetHeight property, 235, 441

onAvailable( ) method, 444

onchange event handlers, 70

onclick handler, 447

onCloseFn property, 434

onComplete event, 443

onComplete.subscribe( ) method, 443

one-size-fits-all validation myth, 345–346

onevent properties, 157

onevent syntax, 169

onload event, 97, 173

onload event handler, window object, 69

onmouseout event handler, 149

onmouseover event handler, 149

onreadystatechange event, 306, 321

openInfoWindow( ) method, 433

openInfoWindowHtml( ) method, 434, 436–437

opening new windows, 215–221

Opera, 66, 217, 466

operators, 21–23

optgroup, 295

Option constructor, 289

options arrays, 323, 374

options object, 286

options property, 276

outerHeight property, 213

outerWidth property, 213

■P

P element, 86

<p></p> tags, 3

pageXOffset property, 213

pageYOffset property, 213

pageYOffset window object, 413

pagination, 263–271

Panel( ) method, 448

panTo( ) method, 435, 437

parameters, 11, 77

parentheses, 22

grouping, 361–362

incorrect number of, 454–456

parentNode, 102, 131, 165, 267–268, 336

parents, 100–103

parseFloat( ) method, 28, 352

parseInt( ) function, 28, 37, 352

password fields, 278–279

password parameters, 305

pathname property, 245

period character (.), 358

php file extension, 338

PHP script, 405, 408

phpThumb( ) class, 388

Picasa, 388, 396

Podcast Networks, 417

pop-up windows, 444–449

port property, 245

POST method, 305, 324, 328

PRE element, 420, 422, 425

preloading images, 186

presentation layer, changing, 123–131. *See also* Cascading Style Sheets

preventDefault( ) method, 161, 164, 168, 404

previousSibling node, 120

previousSibling property, 103

primitive data types, 18

print( ) method, 230

problems with JavaScript, 5–6

progressive enhancement, 68–69

prompt( ) method, 24–25, 33, 90–95, 215

properties of forms, 274

properties string, 215

protocol property, 245

prototype, 340

proxy servers, 212

push buttons, 284

Q

quantifiers, 359

quotation marks, 18

R

\r escape sequence, 20

radio buttons, 281–284

random( ) method, Math object, 38

random number, generating, 38

readability/functionality, 25

reading keyboard entries, 174–179

ready( ) method, 424

readyState property, 306–307, 321

readystatechange event, 306

RegEx Advice, 363

RegExp constructor, 361

Regular Expression Library, 363

regular expressions
    constraining scope, 358–359
    methods using, 361
    overview, 357

parenthesis grouping, 361–362

resources, 363

restricting number of characters with quantifiers, 359–360

syntax and attributes, 357–358

whitespace, 360–361

wildcard searches, 358–359

word boundaries, 360–361

rel attribute, 137

reload( )method, 245

removeAttribute( ) method, 128

removeChild( ) method, 236, 410

render( ) method, 448

replace( ) method, 129, 204, 245–246, 249, 361

reset( ) method, 274, 278–279

reset buttons, 284

responseText method, 308, 313, 330

responseXML method, 308–309, 319

REST APIs, 417–419

return keyword, 77

reuse of functions, 80

reverse( ) method, 45

Rico, 341

rollover effects
    dynamic slide shows, 207–211
    embedded slide shows, 197–207
    overview, 187
    on parent elements, 192–196
    slide shows, 196
    using several images, 187–191
    using single image, 191–192

round( ) function, Math object, 37

rounding numbers, 37–38

rows attribute, 276

RSS feeds, 417–418

S

S@rdalya, 341

Safari browser, 168, 404, 464–465

Sarissa, 341

Scott, Leland, 340

screen object, 13, 15

screen readers, 69

script block, 9

SCRIPT element, 113, 429, 438, 462

<script> tags, 7, 9, 64, 438

script.aculo.us, 340

scrollbars, 216

search( ) method, 347, 357

search property, 245

select( ) method, 276, 279

select boxes, 242, 286–291, 323–331

SELECT element, 276, 297, 323, 366

selected attribute, 273

selected property, 286, 288

selectedIndex property, 286–287, 374

select-one type, 374

semicolon syntax, JavaScript, 8

send( ) method, 307, 309, 329, 365, 370, 375–377

sequential uncommenting, 462

server-side includes (SSIs), 230

server-side scripts, using to reach third-party content, 316–320

setAttribute( ) method, 108, 126

setBody( ) method, 449

setCenter( ) method, 430, 436

setDebug( ) method, 121, 458

setHeader( ) method, 449

setInterval( ) method, 222, 228, 239

setTimeout( ) method, 222, 239

setZoom( ) method, 434, 437

Sharing Validation Rules section, 346

short code via ternary operator, 79–80

shortcut notation, 82

shortening scripts via innerHTML, 115–116

siblings, 103–107

site navigation, 255–263

slice( ) method, 42, 346

slide shows
    dynamic, 207–211
    embedded, 197–207

slideDown( ) method, 422

slideUp( ) method, 422

Sluis, Bobby van der, 153

sorting array, 44–45

Sowden, Paul, 139

SPAN element, 202, 257, 267, 365, 367, 378–379, 382–384, 409

split( ) method, 44

src attribute, 64, 210, 235, 237, 414

src property, 185, 187–188, 190

SSIs (server-side includes), 230

static thumbnail galleries, 388–389

status property, 213, 307, 309

stop( ) method, 230

stopBubble( ) method, 168

stopDefault( ) method, 168

stopPropagation( ) method, 164, 168

str_replace( ) method, 409

String( ) constructor, 32

string data type
    escape sequences, 19–20
    overview, 18–19

String object, 47, 204, 245
    creating, 31–32
    methods of, 32–34
    overview, 30

string parameter, 394

string type, 394

string validation methods, 346–352

string.match(pattern), 361

String.replace( ) method, 308, 313, 361

STRONG element, 192–193, 257, 259, 262, 332–334, 336, 338

structure layer, 63

Stubblebine, Tony, 363

STYLE and LINK element, 130

style attribute, 123

style attributes, 127

style collection, 125

style switchers, 136

stylesheet attribute, 138

styling dynamic pages, 131–139

submit( ) method, 274

Submit button, 91, 110, 113, 178, 284, 370

submit handler, 243, 379

substr( ) method, 350

substring( ) method, 32, 42, 347–348, 350

subtraction operator, 27

switch statement, 52–54, 79

switch/case block, 173

switch/case line, 357

sync parameter, 305

syntax error, 19

■ T

\t escape sequence, 20

table node, 269

table value, 269

<table> parameter, 314

tags, 86

target attribute, 157, 217, 238

target property, 274

TBODY element, 266, 312

ternary operator, 79–80

test( ) method, 94, 357

text areas, 278–279

text browser users, 212

text fields, 278–279

text option, 287

text property, 286

TEXTAREA element, 279, 295, 297, 366, 373

text/javascript header, 369

Thatcher, Jim, 69

third-party content, using server-side scripts
    to reach, 316–320

third-party JavaScript

    adding maps to sites with Google Maps,
        427–432, 434–437

    code libraries, 419–427

    examples of REST APIs, 418–419

    jQuery, 419–427

    overview, 415–416

    RSS feeds and REST APIs, 417–418

    Yahoo User Interface (YUI)

        bouncy headlines using, 439–444

        replacing pop-up windows using YUI
            connection manager and container
            components, 444–449

this keyword, 138, 149, 155, 443

thumbnail galleries

    creating image badge from folder, 406–414

    displaying captions, 396–401

    dynamic, 401–405

    faking, 389–396

    overview, 387–388

    static, 388–389

title attribute, 138, 210, 396, 399

TITLE element, 85

toDateString( ) method, 37

Tofte, Svend, 470

toggle( ) method, 422, 441

toLowerCase( ) method, 47, 158

toolbar property, 213

toString( ) method, 37

toUpperCase( ) method, String object, 47

true keyword, 281, 284

try statement, 304, 460

try...catch construct, 459–462

type attribute, event object, 157

type element, 280

type property, 275, 277

typeof( ) operator, 27, 31

■U

UAs (user agents), 5, 62, 212

\uDDDD escape sequence, 20

UFO (Unobtrusive Flash Object), 153

UL element, 99, 101, 200, 257, 259–261, 320

uncommenting, 462

Undefined data type, 18

undefined variables, 452–454

Unobtrusive Flash Object (UFO), 153

unobtrusive JavaScript, 62, 153

Upcoming.org, 418

url parameter, 305

useCapture Boolean value, 156

user agents (UAs), 5, 62, 212

user feedback mechanism, 90

user feedback methods, 215

■V

validate( ) function, 82

validation techniques

client-side validation, pros and cons of, 343–344

feedback

highlighting erroneous fields individually, 376–379

instant validation feedback, 379–380

overview, 369

replacing main form with clickable error message, 374–376

showing list of erroneous fields, 369–374

form validation techniques

CSS classes method, 366

custom attribute method, 366–367

designating mandatory fields, 364

failures of these methods, 367

hidden field method, 364–365

indicator element method, 365–366

overview, 364

sharing validation rules, 367–369

numeric validation methods, 352–357

one-size-fits-all validation myth, 345–346

overview, 343

protecting content, 344–345

regular expressions

constraining scope, 358–359

methods using regular expressions, 361

overview, 357

power of parenthesis grouping, 361–362

resources, 363

restricting number of characters with quantifiers, 359–360

syntax and attributes, 357–358

whitespace, 360–361

wildcard searches, 358–359

word boundaries, 360–361

string validation methods, 346–352

validationRules object, 369, 373–374

value attribute, 373

value option, 287

value property, 275, 277–278, 286

valueOf( ) method, 48

var keyword, 24, 80, 201, 452

variables, 23–26

assigning instead of testing value of, 458

declaring, 24

and function scope, 80–81

initializing, 24

undefined, trying to access, 452–454

Venkman, 470

visibility property, 130

vspace property, 185

■W

WaSP DOM Scripting Task Force, 63

Web Developer extension, Firefox, 469

while loop, 56–59, 94, 102

whitespace, 120, 360–361

width attribute, 186

width property, 185

wildcard searches, 358–359

Willison, Simon, 155

window methods, 239

window object, 25, 90, 97, 165, 213, 215, 238, 245, 413

window parameters, 218

window property, 245

window.back( ) method, 245

window.history object, 246

window.history property, 245

window.location object, 244–245

window.location.href property, 244–245

window.open( ) method, 217, 219

window.opener property, 220

window.opener.close( ) method, 221

windows

    animation with window intervals and timeouts, 222–230

    changing position and dimensions of, 221

    navigation methods of browser window

        layer ads, 231–238

        overview, 230–231

    opening new windows, 215–221

    overview, 212–213

    properties, 213–214

    user feedback methods, 215

window.timeout( ) method, 320

word boundaries, 360–361

Wright, Matt, 364

X

XAMPP installs, 299

XHR, 310, 316, 319–323, 334, 382, 385, 396, 401–403

XHR object, 299, 302

XHTML, 7, 87

XML

    replacing with JSON, 314–316

    turning into HTML, 309–314

XMLHttpRequest object, 302, 304–305, 340

\xNN escape sequence, 20

XSS (Cross-Site Scripting), 213

Y

Yahoo User Interface (YUI)

    bouncy headlines using, 439–444

    replacing pop-up windows, 444–449

YAHOO.util.Anim( ) constructor, 443

YAHOO.util.Connect.abort( ) method, 445

YAHOO.util.Connect.asyncRequest( ) method, 444

YAHOO.util.Connect.isCallInProgress( ) method, 445

YAHOO.widget.Panel( ) constructor method, 447

YUI. *See* Yahoo User Interface

Z

zero-based array, 42

You Need the Companion eBook

Your purchase of this book entitles you to buy the companion PDF-version eBook for only $10. Take the weightless companion with you anywhere.

We believe this Apress title will prove so indispensable that you'll want to carry it with you everywhere, which is why we are offering the companion eBook (in PDF format) for $10 to customers who purchase this book now. Convenient and fully searchable, the PDF version of any content-rich, page-heavy Apress book makes a valuable addition to your programming library. You can easily find and copy code—or perform examples by quickly toggling between instructions and the application. Even simultaneously tackling a donut, diet soda, and complex code becomes simplified with hands-free eBooks!

Once you purchase your book, getting the $10 companion eBook is simple:

❶ Visit **www.apress.com/promo/tendollars/**.

❷ Complete a basic registration form to receive a randomly generated question about this title.

❸ Answer the question correctly in 60 seconds, and you will receive a promotional code to redeem for the $10.00 eBook.

2560 Ninth Street • Suite 219 • Berkeley, CA 94710

eBookshop

THE EXPERT'S VOICE™

Offer valid through 1/17/07.